CYNICS, PAUL AND THE PAULINE CHURCHES

CYNICS, PAUL AND THE PAULINE CHURCHES

Cynics and Christian Origins II

F. Gerald Downing

London and New York

First published 1988
by Routledge
11 New Fetter Lane, London EC4P 4EE

Simultaneously published in the USA and Canada
by Routledge
29 West 35th Street, New York, NY 10001

© 1998 F. Gerald Downing

The right of F. Gerald Downing to be identified as the Author of this
Work has been asserted by him in accordance with the Copyright,
Designs and Patents Act 1988

Printed and bound in Great Britain by
Redwood Books, Trowbridge, Wiltshire

British Library Cataloguing in Publication Data
A catalogue record for this book is available from the British Library

Library of Congress Cataloging in Publishing Data
A catalog record for this book has been requested

ISBN 0–415–17159–8

FOR DIANA

quid enim iucundius
quam uxori tam carum esse
ut propter hoc tibi carior fias?
(Senaca, *ep. mor*. civ)

And with thanks to members of the
Ehrhardt Biblical Studies Seminar in the University of
Manchester; and to John Rylands University of
Manchester Library and its patient, friendly and very
efficient staff

CONTENTS

PREFACE

There are a great many Pauls on the market, and by no means all of them have even walking-on parts in what follows.

The Paul on offer here is a Paul aware of the market around him: life-styles, images, ideas that went to make up the very varied world of which he was a part.

He seems to have had some measure of success in showing and articulating his new faith in terms that made some sense to those who met him.

F. Gerald Downing
on the eve of the Feast
of the Conversion of
St. Paul, 1998.

A CYNIC PREPARATION FOR PAUL'S GOSPEL FOR JEW AND GREEK, SLAVE AND FREE, MALE AND FEMALE [1]

(i) How may Paul have been heard and his behaviour perceived?

How well Paul was in fact understood by the people he persuaded to join the Christian movement it is hard for us to assess with any certainty. But it is clear that he persuaded some, among them some of those to whom his surviving letters were addressed. The problems he decides he has to sort out in these letters would suggest that communication had not been completely successful, either in quantity or quality. Yet people had been persuaded to join the movement, and so to share in common activities, deploying common phrases as part of their active belonging.

Paul himself tells us that he is fully aware of the importance of using language that people will understand (1 Cor 14.6–12), even attempting to be 'all things to all people' (1 Cor 9.22); as well as being aware of the danger involved in all this, the danger of the sophist's superficial

---

[1] For an earlier version of this chapter, *NTS* 42 (1996), 454–62; used here with permission.

persuasiveness (Gal 1.10; 2 Cor 5.11).[2] Paul's success or failure, as said, is hard to gauge. Still harder to assess is the extent of his own actual awareness of the match or mismatch between his proclamation and others' appropriation of it; though in noting that we need also to take account of the high standards of rapport between speaker and hearers expected in the culture of Paul's day. It remains the case that it is worth trying to discern and assess the contents of Paul's initial approaches to people in the Hellenistic towns he visited. These will have been gentiles in the main (Gal 2.9).[3] Many if not all Paul's gentile contacts seem to have been fully 'pagan' (1 Thess 1.9; Gal 4.8; 1 Cor 12.2), not 'God-fearers' in the sense indicated in Acts 16.14; 18.7, for instance: when first they encountered Paul they had not yet 'turned from idols'. Some, admittedly, could have had some contact with Jewish ideas, but not as a group that had already 'turned'.[4] This study attempts to discern something of what Paul may have felt - and found - such ordinary Hellenistic townspeople would without too much difficulty understand.

For the investigation to go ahead we have to make the minimum preliminary assumption that Paul was fairly confident (even if unreflectively) that he could make sense to these Hellenised gentiles whom he addressed; and for

---

[2] For the importance of rhetoric in Paul's world, even with disclaimers like Paul's at 1 Cor 1.17–20, see, e.g., S. M. Pogoloff (1992) and B. Winter (1997); on Paul's disclaimers, p. 136, below; and on Paul's self-presentation as speaker and teacher, in more detail, ch. 6, below.

[3] Gal 2.9 has, of course, to be taken along with 1 Cor 9.20 and 2 Cor. 11.24. These comments afford just one of many indications that Paul's addressees share a common late Hellenism; cf., e.g., T. Engberg-Pedersen (1995a), xv.

[4] On the Galatian Christians as gentiles, cf. J. Murphy-O'Connor (1996), 200 and n. 62; and further in what follows here.

that to be so, he must have felt reasonably at ease with some ranges of their existing vocabularies of ideas-in-words. We must also accept for the sake of the discussion the common conviction that in his letters Paul refers back to the practices and beliefs and specific verbal formulae[5] shared in those earliest stages of forming congregations in Galatia, in Macedonia and in Achaea, some years before writing the letters preserved for us.

Obviously most scholarly attention is directed – entirely properly – towards attempts to discern what is being said and perhaps heard in the extant letters in their 'Christian' context around the time of writing and first listening, so far as that can be reconstructed.[6] On the other hand, although detailed discussions of the likely intelligibility of the language of Paul's supposed prior proclamation to as yet uncommitted gentiles may be on the shelves, they have so far escaped the present writer. Thus, while it is noted, for instance, that 1 Thessalonians 1.9–10 ('You turned to God from idols, to serve a living and true God, and to wait for his Son from heaven, whom he raised from the dead, Jesus who delivers us from the wrath to come') may be a formulaic (even pre-Pauline) summary of early missionary success among gentiles; yet the 'unabridged', 'full-length' wording supposedly implied appears to be nowhere reconstructed. Assuming that what we have here is a summary, and that Paul would not have restricted

---

[5] Noting the proper caution entered by H. Koester, (1979), 41: the supposed 'formulae' are never repeated by Paul. As in much ancient communication, we must expect variations on formulated themes, rather than precise verbal reproduction as such.

[6] Thus, for instance, when J. P. Sampley (1991), 3–14, writes on 'From Text to Thought World', it is to *Paul*'s thought world that he moves without further explanation, not to the thought-world of Paul's hearers, let alone of his early hearers.

himself to so terse a formulation, we are still not told how this or any other themes of his preaching might have been fleshed out in speeches or conversations in terms likely to have been comprehensible and also persuasive. Available studies seem only to sketch-in the early stages of Paul's work with a very broad brush, and briefly.[7]

With no detailed lead available, at least to the present writer, we proceed to Paul's *inventio*, his εὕρεσις, his combined quest for what to say and how to say it when first making contact with 'idolatrous' gentiles.[8] What 'preparation for his gospel', what at all serviceable words and ideas-in-words may he have been able to discern and deploy? The most common inference (based primarily on

---

[7] Most studies on early Paul focus on his links with the Hellenistic synagogues and their supposed missionary propaganda (see below and the next two notes). On 1 Thess 1.9–10 compare the discussion in J. Munck (1962/63), 95–110, arguing that it is an *ad hoc* formulation; R. F. Collins (1984), 20–22, affording no sign of interest in the issue posed here; so too, K. P. Donfried (1990), 20–23 on 'The Early Paul'; C. A. Wanamaker (1990), 84–89. Wanamaker doubts whether this is either a 'formula' (or pre-Pauline), but also offers no indication of any attempt to 'unpack' what this 'summary' may be supposed to have 'summarised'; cf. also T. Holtz (1986), 54–64. Other recent studies whose titles might lead the reader to expect an attempt to reconstruct the content of Paul's initial approach to gentiles neither include nor refer to any such discussion; e.g., J. C. Beker (1980); G. Lüdemann (1984); C. Roetzel (1991); J. Becker (1993), cf. 86–87 and 118 (the section 130–40, 'First Thessalonians as Evidence of Antiochene Mission Theology' deals only with instruction for the young congregation); M. Goulder (1994); J. Murphy-O'Connor (1996). F. Bovon (1982), 'Pratiques Missionnaires', 369–81, touches on relevant issues ('contextualisation', 'accessibility') but with no detail nor further promising references. It is obviously difficult to establish even a carefully qualified negative generalisation such as the one entered here. The discussion that follows does attempt to engage positively with quite a wide range of nonetheless relevant studies.

[8] See, again, S. M. Pogoloff (1992), ch. 2, 'Form and Content in Classical Rhetoric', and there especially 44–48.

Acts) is that Paul had to hand and used the topics, language
and ethos of a long–established and relatively successful
'Jewish Hellenistic mission'. Whether there was any such
'Jewish Hellenistic mission' cannot be debated here.[9] But
it is argued by a number of authors that from some of the
Greek-speaking synagogues Paul would not only have
found many of its 'god-fearing' converts responsive to his
law-free messianic Judaism, while themselves still closely
in touch with the wider gentile world; but here would have
been available a ready-made and tested vocabulary of
Hellenistic Jewish ideas-in-words for Paul's own preaching.[10] So it is often, but far too readily, concluded.

For the people Paul addresses in his letters do *not*
seem to have been 'acculturated' to the thought-forms of
even the most free-thinking Greek-speaking synagogues.
Paul's arguments in what is taken to be his earliest letter,
1 Thessalonians, clearly presuppose little if any prior

---

[9] On the question of Hellenistic Jewish proselytising, 'missionary'
activity, see, e.g., A. L. Segal (1990), ch. 3, 'Conversion in Paul's
Society', 72–114. Though apologetic and polemic for internal con-
sumption are well evidenced, and gentiles were influenced, with some
making a full conversion, there is little to support a picture of any
widespread deliberate 'missionising' by Jewish groups; so, too, M.
Goodman (1989), 175–85 and (1994), 60–90; cf. J. Sievers (1995),
280. For a contrary assessment of the evidence, J. C. Paget (1996); but
Paget (102) wants to make the Thessalonians into 'God-fearers' even
before Paul encouraged them to 'turn from idols', which seems odd.
He really only succeeds in showing that gentiles might well have
received a welcome, aided by the apologetic and polemical materials of
which we are aware. He adduces no evidence for even a single
orthodox (non-Christian) Jewish figure analogous to Paul. Cf. also J.
M. G. Barclay (1996), 317–18 and n. 89, on 'attraction' rather than
'mission' as such, and 408 with n. 11.

[10] Cf. C. Bussmann (1971). The material collected is clearly apposite,
but the question of its impact on gentiles not yet drawn into the ambit
of the synagogues is not touched on; also J. Becker (1980), 43, 55–56;
C. A. Wanamaker (1990), 85; D. Seeley (1994a), 145-48.

awareness of, let alone authority accorded to Jewish scriptures.[11] Although the Corinthian congregation may well at the time of writing have included Jewish Christians (1 Cor 1.24; 9.20), Paul addresses these, too, in general terms as converts from paganism (12.2).[12] Galatian Christians were, it seemed to Paul, now beginning to take Jewish tradition seriously, and so here he could - or must - *now* argue from a Jewish scriptural basis.[13] But when he appeals to what *first* convinced them in their introduction to Christian commitment, there is no sign of their having been given much at all by way of biblical 'texts'. We may note for example Galatians 3.1–5, where Paul reminds his hearers of factors in their early believing with no reference to scripture (none to fulfilled prophecy, for instance), and contrast that with Acts 13.[14]

The Paul of the letters certainly displays amply his own Jewish roots and also evinces some acquaintance with the ideals and attitudes instanced elsewhere in Hellenistic Jewish sources, and we shall revert to this later in the present study. But, as J. M. G. Barclay has recently argued with great thoroughness, even writing to established congregations Paul does not use much of this latter, Hellenistic Jewish material. Its apologetic aim may well have been simply to gain respect or at least tolerance, but what is

---

[11] C. A. Wanamaker (1990), 7; for Galatians, cf. again J. Murphy-O'Connor (1996), 200 and n. 62.

[12] Cf. H. Conzelmann (1975), 205. C. Senft (1979), 22, concludes that in Corinth in particular Paul had to learn 'un langage nouveau' as he faced 'un pagano-christianisme tout neuf'.

[13] Even so, J. Murphy-O'Connor argues that Paul 'could not have expected [these] converts from paganism to grasp the force of arguments which depended on detailed knowledge of Jewish tradition' (1996), 200.

[14] See, e.g., J. M. G. Barclay (1988), 52.

actually urged is a total acceptance of the Jewish Torah and a full assimilation into the Jewish community. By contrast, 'Paul's tone is radically different from that total commitment to the law which we find in writers as diverse as Aristeas, Josephus, Philo and the author of 4 Maccabees.'[15] Barclay finds no sign of Paul having built on any of the more positive elements of this diverse Hellenistic Judaism, nor even of his having to distinguish his approach from it. All Paul seems to use, and that very occasionally, is a restricted range of Jewish anti-pagan polemic.[16]

Another avenue of approach Paul is thought by some to have adopted would have been the practice, language and ethos of Graeco-Roman cults, civic or more private, and gnostic, if such there were around in Paul's day. If we had more relevant and contemporary texts available, the case might of course be stronger.[17] But as things stand it certainly seems worth exploring further, and asking whether any other encompassing field of contemporary discourse available to us may have been popular enough and at least apparently appropriate enough for Paul to have adopted it in some measure, both to sort out what

---

[15] J. M. G. Barclay (1996), 387; M. Goodman (1994), 65–66, 78–90.

[16] J. M. G. Barclay (1996), 388. Barclay also argues (390–93) that Paul makes little independent use of any other elements of Hellenistic culture, either. What Barclay has ignored is the Cynic strand in particular, which is, as I hope to show, often just as critical of conventional Hellenistic belief and practice as is Paul – and often in very similar language, and enacted in a very similar praxis.

[17] On pagan cults, cf. A. J. M. Wedderburn (1987); J. M. G. Barclay (1996), 390; on gnosticism and Paul, E. Yamauchi (1973), 36-49; M. A. Plunkett (1988); P. Perkins (1993), 74–91: 'systematic formalization of gnostic theology does not appear to have existed in the first century' (91); and W. Deming (1995).

he wanted to say, and to say it, when first trying to make contact.

The title of this study indicates that the complex to which further attention is being invited is that of popular Cynicism. A number of writers over the years have noted occasional apparent echoes of Cynic terms and *topoi* in Paul (R. Bultmann – though I would discount the 'Cynic–Stoic diatribe'; H. Conzelmann, H. D. Betz, D. Georgi, V. C. Pfiztner, H. Funke, H. Koester, R. Hock, S. Vollenweider, M. Plunkett, M. Ebner, to mention but a few; but especially, of course, A. J. Malherbe).[18] Malherbe in particular expresses himself convinced that 'Paul himself was familiar with Cynic tradition.'[19] In the present writer's recent *Cynics and Christian Origins*, however, it was suggested that Cynic traces in Paul were interesting but scattered and occasional.[20] Further investigation now leads to the conclusion that for early Paul at least there is much more to be found.

Evidence is to be presented to substantiate the following five *theses* (which will be recalled at the end of each chapter): (*a*) That Paul would regularly have been heard and seen as some sort of Cynic. If that turns out to be at all persuasive, the exercise will have been worthwhile. Such a conclusion would be interesting enough an addition to our picture of Paul. The Cynic-sounding matter could then well provide some important indications of how Paul came to be understood (or, of course, misunderstood), and

---

[18] Most of these writers will be referred to in detail later; for now, see the Bibliography.

[19] A. J. Malherbe (1988), 573. In Malherbe (1989), 8, he concludes that 'Paul knew these [mainly Cynic] traditions first-hand, not through the mediation of other Jews before him who had come to terms with the Greek experience.'

[20] F. G. Downing (1992a), 61–63 and 153.

in what manner. But we shall then also argue further (*b*) that these similarities appear so often and in so many contexts that Paul cannot but have been aware of them. At the very least he must have been content with them, and found them no hindrance. That is the next step. However, these 'Cynic-seeming' elements in Paul are often so closely bound up with the rest of what he says and says he did, that we must further still consider that they are deliberate. Cynic discourse and praxis (*c*) may now seem to have been part of the total field of discourse and action available to Paul, and would have allowed him to articulate and enact important elements of the faith and life he was developing and attempting to share. Just how suggestive, how formative this or any other available field of discourse was for Paul is a further question that is very hard to answer with any certainty. But Paul does not seem to have been 'cherry-picking' adventitious quotes. The Cynic strands are understood and used as some Cynics themselves understood and used them, and are integral to what Paul is about.[21]

Since Samuel Sandmel invented the term, an investigation of this sort often attracts the charge of 'parallelomania'.[22] If we stopped with (*a*), verbal echoes and visual resemblances, while ignoring the clues they provide to common discourse in Paul's world, the charge might seem to stick. However, the more of such resemblances we find, and the more the actual inter-connected *use* of similar words, phrases, ideas, pictures and

---

[21] A. J. Malherbe (1989), 7, 'Paul was aware of the differences among Cynics, and deftly situated himself in the philosophical landscape'; and (1995), 255, 'not merely a pile of topoi or slogans from which he can draw'.

[22] S. Sandmel (1962).

praxis appears on deeper analysis to be 'the same' or very similar, the more significant the discoveries must be judged. 'Parallels' with a writer among materials at least potentially available to her or him do no more on their own than pose the questions, are these perhaps (part of) his or her socio-cultural context? and, are the resemblances anything more than superficial? Further analysis attempts to answer the questions. Part of that further analysis consists in (*d*) discerning how some of Paul's hearers seem to Paul to be accepting as such the Cynic strands in his message and example, if on occasion interpreting them more radically than Paul himself can accept. The final step in the argument as presented here is an attempt (*e*) to show that there would seem already to have been Cynic strands in early Christianity before Paul and around him: his Cynic interpetation (if so it be agreed to be) of Christian life and faith is not an imposition from outside. The Jewish–Christian life-style(s), attitudes and beliefs that Paul encountered, first as fierce opponent and then as 'convert' *already* invited an interpretation and then an expansion along Cynic lines. (However, this final step of the argument will not be discussed in any detail until chapter 10.)

Paul is not – is *not* – here being portrayed as 'a Cynic'.[23] But he and many other early Christians would seem to have engaged with, deployed, and assimilated, a number of strands of contemporary Cynicism, and to have integrated them, more or less well, more or less readily, with strands drawn from contemporary Judaism and, obviously, with strands quite particular to emerging (and diverse) early Christianity. Paul is a Christian Jew with some important Cynic traces in his discourse and life-style.

---

[23] Sharing this negative insistence with A. J. Malherbe (1989), 8.

It is time to examine an important sample, an item which Paul himself sees as having wide ramifications for the believing and living of 'his' gospel, and so a very useful instance with which to start the investigation and with which to indicate and illustrate the way the argument and the analysis will run.

(ii) For example: what Cynics and Paul and some early Christians said and did about Greeks and barbarians, bond and free, male and female.

Let us suppose, then, that Paul was already convinced or (more likely) was finding his way towards the express conviction that the death and resurrection of Jesus as Messiah, Son of God, entailed God's welcome to all comers into a community free from important clusters of Jewish *and* of other, 'pagan' Graeco-Roman conventions. In that case there would have been available to him a popular and widely disseminated tradition of articulating, enjoying and encouraging just such a critical response to accepted norms: the quite variegated tradition of popular Cynicism:[24] 'God has drawn us to reject hallowed communal codes of behaviour and ideas . . . this affords us the language in which we can talk of such issues.'[25]

When Paul wants to remind Christians in Galatia in a little detail of their original introduction to the new community, the baptism in which they became 'Sons of

---

[24] See, most recently, R. B. Branham and M.-O. Goulet-Cazé (1996), 16, 'unique among classical intellectual traditions in becoming something like a "mass movement"'; 25, 'the popular philosophy of antiquity'.

[25] See further below, n. 40, and in some detail, ch. 3.

God' and 'put on Christ', he cites (as most modern
commentators take it) a 'formula'[26] (again, widely thought
to be pre-Pauline) used either as part of the rite or (more
likely) in preparation for it. 'There is neither Jew nor
Greek, there is neither slave nor free, there is no male and
female, for you are all one in Christ Jesus' (Gal 3.28). This
is the first instance of possible Cynicism in Paul that we
shall consider, using a passage with very considerable
significance for our understanding of Paul's approach to
the non-Jews with whom in the early days he attempted to
share his gospel.

The possibility or otherwise of adumbrations for
such an approach to gentiles in Paul's pre-Christian
Judaism is not here at issue. It is simply in these terms that
Paul makes his point to gentiles, and no scriptural backing
for the slogan is offered.[27]

One of the drawbacks in much discussion of this
passage in Paul is the tendency to sunder the parts - and we
shall ourselves here leave vv. 26–27 and 29a, possibly also
part of Paul's 'quotation', for only a brief consideration
towards the end. Not even H. D. Betz, in the very useful
analysis in his *Galatians*, asks how these three pairs of
negations might have been 'heard' and their enactment
understood when strung together as they are here.[28] An

---

[26] Recalling the reservation, n. 5, above.

[27] The echo of Gen 1.27 ('no male *and* female', rather than 'nor')
hardly constitutes a scriptural warrant; nor is there any at 1 Cor 12.13,
nor at Col 3.11. Paul might well have been aware of the prophetic hope
that God would bring gentiles in when bringing everything to an end
(Rom 10.16–21); but, apart from a possible echo at 1 Thessalonians
1.8, he makes no such reference in his earlier writings.

[28] H. D. Betz (1979), 181–201. The likely social impact is summarised, 'Introduction', 3, but not the resonances of the three pairs taken
together.

analysis in detail is fine, and, of course, though we have near parallels to the pairs singly and in sets of two, and even in sets of more than three, we have no close parallel for this trio itself, not even in Paul (certainly not in so succinct a formula). It may well be, then, that each negation has a history of its own that is both interesting and relevant for our understanding here. But we really do need to consider how the passage as a whole would have sounded to people in Galatia taking up the invitation to baptism, and how observers would have reacted to its public enactment. We should reflect on the cumulative resonances Paul would at the very least have been made aware of, and here at least did nothing to guard against - resonances more likely deliberately intended.

(ii – α) Neither Jew nor Greek

In his very thorough discussion H. D. Betz commends the standard derivation of the first pair as arising from Hellenistic Judaism and the early Christian mission, where '"mission" and "Hellenization" must necessarily have become one and the same thing'.[29] But Paul's formula does not say 'x becomes y', 'Hellene becomes Jew' or 'Jew becomes Hellene'. It says neither x nor y. It thus *contrasts* with the note from Plutarch cited in illustration by Betz, Plutarch's account of the effects of Alexander's campaigns, where every man of excellence was to be seen as a Hellene, every corrupt man as a barbarian.[30] In Galatians we have instead, quite bluntly, 'neither'.

---

[29] H. D. Betz (1979), 190.

[30] Plutarch, *De Alex. Magni fort.* 329CD; only the earlier part of the passage is cited by Betz (1979), 190 n.71. J. L. Jaquette (1995), 164–

In fact it is among Cynics, claiming to be κοσμο-
πολῖται, citizens of the world,[31] that the similar frequently
opposed pairs, 'Hellenes and barbarians' or '. . . Persians',
'Scythians' and so on, are ruled irrelevant (rather than
honorary transfer being accorded). So Antisthenes rules
foreign or mixed origin irrelevant, as does Demonax.[32]
Pseudo-Anacharsis 2 insists that 'stupidity ... is the same
for barbarians as for Greeks'. In pseudo-Diogenes 7 only a
Cynic escapes the common slavishness of Greeks and
barbarians.[33] Dio's Diogenes excels Greeks and barbarians,
and contradicts precisely the kind of picture Plutarch
presents of Alexander's unifying Hellenisation, belittling
the contrasts Greek–Persian, slave–free (and, less '
explicitly) male–female (true 'manliness' is not male
superiority over women, but anyone's superiority over the
passions). Dio's Diogenes also insists, 'Bad people are
injurious to all who make use of them, whether Phrygian or
Athenian, bond or free' (ἐάν τε Φρύγες ὦσιν ἐάν τε
Ἀθηναῖοι, ἐάν τε ἐλεύθεροι ἐάν τε δοῦλοι.)[34]

This is often said to be a Stoic stance,[35] and,
admittedly, Zeno may have accepted something of
Diogenes' Cynic teaching on the point. But H. C. Baldry –
cited in support on this by Betz, among others – is surely

65, also misrepresents Paul by paraphrasing his slogan in terms of
'both . . . and', '*both* Jew and Greek' (his italics), although Jaquette
may be right that this is what Paul intends in Romans.

[31] Diogenes Laertius, *Lives of Eminent Philosophers* 6.63; Julius
Jüthner (1923), 54–55.

[32] Antisthenes in Diogenes Laertius, 6.1; Lucian, *Demonax* 34.

[33] Ps.-Anacharsis, ps.-Diogenes, etc., in A.J. Malherbe, ed. (1977).

[34] Dio Chrysostom (of Prusa), *Discourse* 9.1, and 4.4–6 and 73–74,
etc.; and the passage quoted, 10.4 (LCL).

[35] E.g., H. D. Betz (1979), 192; J. P. Sampley (1991), 154; cited by J.
L. Jaquette (1995), 154

right to insist there is actually scant evidence to warrant the conjecture.[36] We should note the high evaluation of good Greek and the disparaging of 'barbarism' ascribed to Zeno by Diogenes Laertius (7.59) and contrast the insistence that this 'essential' mark of Hellenism matters not at all, in pseudo-Anacharsis 1 and 2. Linguistic chauvinism is central to the distinction Hellene/non-Hellene – and Stoics maintained it while Cynics refused it.[37] We may further note Epictetus, with his very guarded and idealised Cynicism, as a Stoic firmly maintaining national–cultural distinctions: 'Why do you act the part of a Jew when you are a Greek?'[38] The Stoic position is in fact much the same as that noted in Plutarch - anyone can become a Hellene - even someone from Citium.[39] To say '*neither* Jew *nor* Hellene' *and to act upon it* is surely to appear to be Cynic.

Some of the enactment is made explicit, if briefly, in Galatians (4.8–11) and in the Corinthian and Thessalonian letters (1 Cor 12.2; 2 Cor 11.23–29; 1 Thess 1.9; 2 Thess 1.5). It had clearly involved the rejection of both Jewish and local civic cults and festivals, as noted, and the very important acceptance of open table-fellowship (Gal 2.11–14; 4.8–11). The socio-political impact of withdrawing from participation in the rituals of the civic or any other recognised local community must not be underestimated. We may gauge something of the impact from the comments of Cicero, Juvenal, and Tacitus, reacting

---

[36] H. C. Baldry (1965), 152.

[37] See the discussion of Col 3.11 in T. W. Martin (1995), 254.

[38] Epictetus 2.19.20–21 and 2.9.20–21 (LCL). *Contra* J. L. Jaquette (1995), 154–81, Paul clearly is not encouraging the Galatian Christians to accept a Stoic quietism, remain loyal Jews or observant 'Greeks', as though these were *adiaphora*, matters of indifference.

[39] Diogenes Laertius 7.12.

simply to Judaism (which could at least claim the advantage of antiquity). Tacitus comments, 'Among the Jews, everything that we hold sacred is considered profane, and everything permitted to them is abhorrent to us... [Proselytes] are the worst kind of people, abandoning their ancestral religion.'[40] Of Christians, Lucian could insist, 'they have transgressed totally (ἄπαξ) by denying the Greek Gods and by worshipping that crucified sophist and living under his laws.'[41]

The full extent of the divergence from hallowed custom can only be gauged from hints in Paul's letters. But the impact of what is related must have been considerable. Becoming 'neither Jew nor Greek' was a major step with massive implications for 'Greeks' (quite as significant as it was for Jews); and, of course, this distancing from both had continued to be at the core of Paul's mission.

(We shall consider this issue again shortly below, and in more detail in chapter 3. The relations of bond and free, and of male and female, are discussed in what follows, and also in more detail in chapter 4, where we

---

[40] Tacitus, *History* 5.4.1, 5.5.1; compare the passages collected in M. Whittaker (1984), and the discussion in J. M. G. Barclay (1996), 286-87: (Cicero, *Pro Flacco*) and 314-18 (Tacitus) and Juvenal (Satires 3, 6, and 14); noted also by D. A. deSilva (1996), 61, 'Participation showed one's support of the social body, one's desire for doing what was necessary to secure the welfare of the city.' Most scholars focus on Pauline Christians' attitudes to Jewish law and ignore the social consequences of the break with Hellenistic religion and culture; see ch. 3, below. Stoics and Epicureans might criticise civic religion for its theories and attitudes, but still tended to conform in practice (M.-O. Goulet-Cazé (1992a), 141–42 and (1996), 66; cf. Cicero, *De natura deorum* 1.45, 1.123; Diogenes Laertius 10.118; Epictetus 2.20.27; 3.7.12.

[41] Lucian, *Peregrinus* 1.13; cf. M. Whittaker (1984) again, ad loc.

shall further note apparently Cynic deductions about food laws among Corinthian Christians.)

(ii – β) Neither slave nor free.

For now we move on to 'neither slave nor free'. Here again, if commentators note the wider cultural world, it is usually to Stoics that they turn. For Stoics, freedom is internalised, so external slavery is irrelevant. It is all a question of your own self-awareness, self-assessment. Whether you are a slave or a consul, as a Stoic you act out the social role, while remaining free within.[42] For Cynics, freedom must be overt, active, socially effective. The stories of Diogenes kidnapped into slavery insist that he continues to *act* openly as a free man.[43] By contrast, when Epictetus repeats the story he immediately explains that Diogenes had gained a Stoic internalised freedom from his teacher Antisthenes.[44] Then again, in the first of Dio's *Discourses* on 'Slavery and Freedom', his slave speaks his mind freely and fearlessly in discussion with a free citizen, and Dio concludes, 'Now they'll have to wear different clothes for you to tell slave and free apart.' In the second,

---

[42] *Pace* D. B. Martin (1990), 88, but compare, e.g., Epictetus 3.7.26–27; 24.98–99. However, the Stoic–Cynic contrast must not be absolutised. Cynics also reflected, and Stoics also acted in character; and some individuals combined both ways, as already noted. On this distinction as it relates to Paul's Corinthian Christians, S. Vollenweider (1989), 226–30.

[43] Philo, *Quod omnis prober liber sit* 121–25; ps.-Crates 34; Diogenes Laertius 6.74–75. On Stoics and slavery, see further H. C. Baldry (1965), 113-203; on slavery as such, see D. B. Martin (1990), again; J. A. Harrill (1995).

[44] Epictetus 3.24.65–66; cf. 4.1.114–15.

Discourse 15, Dio insists that none of the distinctions 'γενναίους καὶ εὐγενεῖς', or 'ἐλευθέρους', over against 'ἀγεννεῖς καὶ ταπεινούς . . . δούλους', should be made among humans.[45] In his *Hermotimus* Lucian pictures an imagined Utopia, a city (based on Crates' Cynic Πολιτεία it would seem) peopled by aliens, barbarians, cripples... 'inferior, superior, noble or common, bond or free, simply did not exist in, and were not mentioned in that city'.[46]

That still leaves us, of course, needing to decide what sense or senses of freedom and slavery were apparent in the Galatians' original appropriation of this part of the formula within the whole. Many commentators have preferred the socially quietist and therefore Stoic-aligned interpretation.[47] That is freedom in hope, in awareness of one's new standing with God, at best made overt only when the congregation meets, nothing more.

But what Paul is obviously trying to recall to mind is the very real and open and disruptive breach with social custom and civic convention that the Galatian Christians' original conversion constituted.[48] They really had become 'neither Jew nor Hellene'; they really had broken publicly with the latter without identifying with the former. That was certainly very practical, as we have just argued. They had decided no longer to be bound by many of the laws and customs of either group, dispensing with many of the constraints of both (and subject only, as Paul goes on to

---

[45] Dio 14.24 and 15.32; cf. *Discourse* 10, again.

[46] Lucian, *Hermotimus* 24 (LCL); cf. Diogener Laertius 6.85.

[47] E.g., Averil Cameron (1980), 'Neither Male nor Female' (*sic*) 60–68, simply assumes that only 'spiritual equality' was offered (64).

[48] As forcefully argued by H. D. Betz (1979) 2–3, 29, and 189–90; cf. Lucian, *Peregrinus* 13, again: Christians had made a complete break by denying the Greek Gods.

make explicit, 'to the law of Christ'). Categorising written law and community custom as bondage, the critique which Paul is recalling in Galatians, is characteristically and distinctively Cynic.[49] And, like Cynics, Paul's Christians had come to exercise a freedom in which these labels, including 'slave' and 'free', were irrelevant. The commentators are right, of course, there is no pretence that the institution of slavery is or is to be abolished; what does seem to be intended is that slaves would no longer behave as custom dictated those in their position should conduct themselves - just as free citizens were no longer bound by civic rites and ceremonies (Gal 4.8–10). All three parts of the formula (and not just the 'neither Jew...' part which Paul needs now some years later for the argument of the letter) must in all probability originally have been *equally* practical and overt - articulating an open breach with a wide range of the laws and customs of established communities - and not only in the field we demarcate as 'religious'. Much more was involved than simply joining a new cult association and enjoying the temporary and occasional freedom of its meetings. Cult associations did not withdraw adherents from the rites and festivals of the wider community.[50]

---

[49] J. Jüthner (1923), 54-55; cf. M.-O. Goulet-Cazé (1986), 214-40, and *eadem*, (1990), 2746-63; and here, see chapter 3 below. Mme. Goulet-Cazé's response in correspondence to the article on which this chapter is based was encouraging: 'je suis tout à fait convaincue.'

[50] J. Kloppenborg (1996) suggests the Pauline churches were offering little if anything more than did various collegia or *thiasoi* (256-59), but ignores the fact that the latter did not take their members away from recognised civic cults. J. M. G. Barclay has rightly pointed out how 'anomalous' Paul and Paul's way appears, (1996), 381–95 (and note 392), but, regrettably, without allowing for the many similar 'anomalous' traits of contemporary Cynicism.

(ii – γ) No 'male and female'

The analogy of the first two phrases, with their very
practical import for which we have argued, must also affect
our understanding of the third. Significant aspects at least
of distinctive male and female roles had been abrogated
among these early Christians. Our most obvious comparison is afforded by the Cynics. In pseudo-Crates 29,
leading into the assertion that 'all are slaves, either by law
or through wickedness' (Cynics only excepted), we are
assured that women are in no way inferior to men: virtue,
excellence, is the same for both, and equally attainable by
both in practice, in the way they live. And much the same
opinion is attributed to Antisthenes and to Musonius.[51]
Later Christian writers regularly interpret the 'no male and
female' of Galatians 3.28 in terms of this Cynic *topos* of
'unisex virtue'.[52]

   The nearest parallels to the actual verbal pairings
(but not the negations!) occur, as R. M. Grant has recently
pointed out, in discussions of the *genus* 'human' - which,
it is widely agreed, includes Hellene and barbarian, male
and female, as 'species'.[53] Grant is able to cite Philo, *De
specialibus legibus* 1.211 (though Philo is not consistent),
and Sextus Empiricus from the second century, as well as
Aristotle much earlier, allowing that slaves can be classed
as human. But to draw very practical social consequences
from this theoretical stance would be Cynic. (Epicureans

---

[51] Antisthenes in Diogenes Laertius 6.12; Musonius, *Discourse* 3
(C Lutz (1947), 38–43 (Hense 8-13); cf. also ps.-Crates 28.
[52] Palladius, *Lausiac History* 49; Gregory Nazianzus, *Discourse* 18.7
(cf. 7.23); Gregory of Nyssa, *De virginitate* 20; John Chrysostom, *De
Sancti Ignatio* 1; *In Matthaeum* 73.3.
[53] R. M. Grant (1992) 5–14.

might in all likelihood be similarly free in private, while
their aim of living a quiet life meant agreeing to maintain
civic conventions in public).[54]

Actual appearance was also involved. In his
Runaways Lucian has his Cynic slaves run off to freedom
taking a married woman along with them, her hair cut
short, 'ἀρρενωπὴν καὶ κομιδῇ ἀνδρικήν', boyishly
masculine.[55] Identical dress for men and women is picked
out as a Cynic aberration (albeit stemming from Plato) by
Philodemus.[56]

The trouble Paul faced over women in Corinth not
long after he had first moved on from Galatia suggests that
somewhat revolutionary *practical* implications for women,
implications with clear Cynic resonances, had been part of
the original package he had offered there. Certainly Paul's
insistence now on distinctive hair-dressing in 1 Corinthians
11 (which many have linked with Gal 3.28) seems to
suggest there had emerged a 'unisex' approach actually put
into practice elsewhere only among Cynics.[57]   If it is
accepted that we are here concerned with a *common* early
baptismal formula (liturgical or catechetical), that would
have afforded still further encouragement to the women
Paul confronted. It is rightly pointed out, of course, that the
third couplet simply rides where it is quoted in Galatians,

---

[54] E.g., Epictetus 2.20.27, again; see further, below, ch. 3.

[55] Unisex dress had been urged by Plato, but seems only to have been
actually adopted among Cynics: Lucian, *Runaways* 27; ps.-Crates 29
urges Hipparchia to eschew what is 'effeminate'; cf. 32; and at
Diogenes Laertius 6.97, she refuses any expected 'womanly' response.
The standard adopted is, of course, that all should be 'male', but in a
Cynic way, as all can if they work at it.

[56] Philodemus in R. G. Andria (1980), 129–51.

[57] A. C. Wire (1990), too readily dismisses Cynic analogies, 122; on
which see M. Plunkett (1988), cited widely in chapter 4 below.

without being taken up in any way in the letter, and fails to reappear at all overtly at 1 Corinthians 12.13 or Colossians 3.11.[58] But it does not seem to disappear as an irrelevant formality; rather does it seem to have been dropped by Paul himself as an all too practical disturbing influence. (And, as has just been noted, the third couplet is by no means ignored in Christian 'Cynic' readings of Galatians in the succeeding centuries.)

Very briefly we consider the framing phrases, vv. 26–27 and 28b, allowing for the possibility that they are part of the original quotation. It would not be at all paradoxical for our three Cynic-sounding negations to be introduced by a claim to be sons of God.[59] 'Putting on' distinctive dress, often taken to lie behind the metaphor of 'putting on Christ' is also important to Cynics.[60] Unity, v. 28b, is the obvious goal of all three of the negative pairs; but one may compare the vision of unity in Crates' 'City of Pera'.[61]

(iii) Interim conclusions

This is not at all to suggest this formula would have seemed indistinguishably Cynic. It was to join a group centred on the crucified and risen Jew, Jesus, not a group focused on Diogenes, that Paul will have invited people in

---

[58] E. g., A. Cameron (1980), 64.

[59] See ps.-Diogenes 34.3; A. J. Malherbe (1978), 42–64; and, e.g., Epictetus' Cynic Odysseus, 3.24.16.

[60] Ps.-Crates 23, etc.; cf. M.-O. Goulet-Cazé, (1990) 2738–46, 'L'accoutrement'.

[61] Diogenes Laertius 6.85; cf. the passage from Lucian's *Hermotimus* 24, cited in n. 45, above.

Galatia. Nor are possible adumbrations of the formula in Jewish sources to be discounted; in particular the third pair, 'no male and female' (rather than 'neither...nor') may have been influenced by Genesis 1.27–28.[62] But the breach with social convention that becoming a member of the Christian movement entailed, a movement flaunting the slogan 'neither Jew nor Greek, neither bond nor free, no male and female', *and engaging in a public life-style to match* could only have appeared as some sort of Cynicism in the towns of first-century Galatia.

Reflecting on the elaboration so far of the five theses of this book, perhaps the reader will agree (*a*), that it is with Cynic resonances that the triple slogan (Gal 3.28) would most likely have been heard, and its public enaction viewed. Paul's Christian gospel will have seemed to ordinary 'Greeks' to offer a (disturbing) 'fulfilment' of important ideals already propagated in popular Cynicism.[63] It is hard (*b*) to imagine that Paul would not have realised this, or been made to realise it, hard therefore to imagine that the choice could have been other than deliberate. Then (*c*), we have argued that this Cynic-sounding formula must have summarised a great deal of what Paul and his associates and their first converts at that stage had wanted to have said – and enacted. It was by no means a casual aside, no mere provocative discussion-starter. The first

---

[62] A. C. Wire (1990),123–25. B. Witherington's collection of Rabbinic passages (1981), 593–604, are not provided with any anchorage in the first century; nor – as he himself notes, 593 – are they concerned at all directly with humans' relations to one another.

[63] A. J. Malherbe (1989), 8, again: 'Paul knew these [mainly Cynic] traditions first-hand, and not through the mediation of other Jews who before him had come to terms with the Greek experience . . . Paul himself used the philosophic traditions with at least as much originality as his contemporaries did.'

gospel at the time of writing, years later than when the Galatians had first learned it, as was the catchword 'freedom'; even if the third part was now somewhat unwelcome to Paul in the light of the response of people in Corinth. As to how formative for other early Christians and for Paul the Cynicism which seems to have provided the model both for the words and their enactment may have been, we have as yet found no indication.

We have also only so far touched lightly on step (*d*) of the argument of this book: people apparently displaying an acceptance of a Cynic sense to what Paul taught, most clearly when interpeting his teaching in a more radical Cynic sense than Paul himself was happy with. It is some of his Galatian friends in this instance who seem to be uneasy with their new 'freedom', involving a Cynic-like rejection of time-hallowed civic custom. Otherwise we have only referred to possible problems in Corinth, a topic that will occupy us in chapter 4. We shall, however, also find hints that Paul himself became a little unsure of the 'neither Jew nor Greek', for in Romans (where there is anyway very little perceivable debt to Cynicism) he seems to prefer 'both . . . and'.

And we have also up to now only noted in passing (*e*) the setting of the matter under discussion in the wider context of the early Christian churches, accepting that this Cynic-sounding element in Paul's original mission in Galatia appears to many to have been a summary Paul took over from young Christians before him, rather than it (and its Cynic link) being an introduction of his own. As announced, (*e*) will mostly be dealt with in chapter 10.

In the next chapter (2) we shall briefly review scholarly work on early Christians and Cynicism, and the major sources of evidence available to us. In the following chapters, sometimes with the help of other scholars, chapters, sometimes with the help of other scholars, sometimes as yet independently, we shall consider many more Cynic resonances in Paul, their place in his life and thought, and some of the reactions he seems to have discerned among his converts, before, finally, we also try to 'place' this Cynic-seeming material in the context of the traditions of other early Jewish–Christian groups.

2

SCHOLARLY PERCEPTIONS OF CYNICS, AND OF CYNICS AND EARLY CHRISTIANS; AND OUR SOURCES

We have just argued in the preceding chapter that Paul's converts in Galatia, and Paul himself, all seem to have been content to repeat and enact a Cynic-sounding trio of slogans to focus their Christian commitment, to express in deed as much as in word important aspects (at least) of their new self-understanding. It was further argued that in the Graeco-Roman urban culture of the day such public pronouncements and practice could hardly have been interpreted otherwise than as Cynic. Paul and his followers, it was urged, could but have been aware of this, and their persistence must indicate that they were content to be aligned with Cynicism at least this far.

We noted in passing that a number of historians of Christian origins have concluded that other, more or less important aspects of Paul's ideas, methods and life-style, may also have had links of one kind or another with Cynic tradition. In the first part of this chapter some of these recent discussions are briefly reviewed. Then we consider some of the ways in which Cynics are presented by writers this century; and next we offer a preliminary sketch of ways in which Cynics were perceived by writers (varied insiders and varied outsiders) around the time of Paul; and as a final preliminary to our main continuing investigation, we consider our sources for first century-Cynicism, and for Paul himself.

(i) Recent Studies of Cynic traces in Paul's writings.

Among studies linking Paul with Cynics, one often quoted is Rudolph Bultmann's monograph, from around the beginning of this present century, on the 'Cynic–Stoic Diatribe'.[1] In this it is argued that there was a style of public speaking marked by stretches of imagined dialogue between speaker and objector, deploying quite specific and characteristic rhetorical devices and structures: a manner of address deployed in particular by Cynics (and possibly by philosophers on the Cynic wing of Stoicism). Although primarily an oral form, it is then said to be found more widely than just in notes for or transcripts of speeches; and, it is further concluded, the form appears quite significantly in Paul's Romans in particular. So, at Romans 9.19 we find ἐρεῖς μοι οὖν, 'so you'll say to me . . .' (and see also Rom 11.19), as well as many other implicit allusions to what an audience or an individual in it is imagined to be thinking or wanting to say (Rom 2.1, 3; 6.3, 16; 7.1). There are similar devices, but less frequent, elsewhere (e.g., 1 Cor 15.35–36).

A refinement to this suggestion more recently argued by S. K. Stowers has won considerable support. Rather than 'the diatribe' being a style of public speaking, he argues that it was a form deployed in the classroom by such as the Stoic freed slave, Epictetus (a teacher for whom an idealised form of Cynicism was important).[2] More

---

[1] R. Bultmann (1910).
[2] S. K. Stowers (1981a).

recently still, however, P. P. Fuentes González has reviewed all the major discussions in search of evidence for any
awareness of any such form or *genre*, and has drawn a
complete blank.[3] He concludes that 'the diatribe' is a pure
construction of late nineteenth-century philologists. The
individual tricks of style are used, of course, but by a wide
range of writers, and in no particular conjunction. Here as
elsewhere Paul must be taken simply to have picked up
commonplace rhetorical devices, ways of attempting to
persuade, rather than some specifically Cynic form.[4]

   Much more cogent have been the discussions of
Paul's accounts of his life-style as a travelling missionary.
Paul from time to time uses the popular motif of the
'athlete' (e.g., 1 Cor 9. 24–27). Commonplace though it is,
the obvious starting point for any comparison with
contempory usage is with 'the Cynics, followed by the
Stoics', as V. C. Pfitzner noted.[5] (We shall discuss further
below the important distinction already made between
many Stoics and many Cynics; though various continuing
agreements - among some - are also significant.) Pfitzner
argued in the end that Paul's usage of 'the *agôn* motif'
was importantly distinctive (and we shall have to continue
to ask of this as of every apparent parallel, every supposed
similarity, how close it really is in context). In a later
study, however, H. Funke argued that in 1 Corinthians
9.24–27, 'they all run, but there's only one prize', Paul
seems to have been citing rather carelessly an argument
that only makes full sense precisely in a Cynic context:

---

[3] P. P. Fuentes González (1990).

[4] On Pauline rhetoric, see, for instance, H. D. Betz (1979); G. A.
Kennedy (1984); F. W. Hughes (1989); J.-N. Aletti (1990) and (1992);
M. M. Mitchell (1991).

[5] V. C. Pfitzner (1967).

here a Cynic motif comes so readily to Paul's mind that he doesn't even ensure it is complete.[6] In similar vein Paul likens himself to a besieging general (2 Cor 10. 3–6), and A. J. Malherbe has been able to demonstrate that passage's Cynic echoes.[7]

Closely allied with the metaphor or simile of the athlete is the listing of hardships, as for instance in 1 Corinthians 4.9–13 and in 2 Corinthians 6.3–10. R. Hoïstad argued that the latter was strikingly similar to one in a specifically Cynic text.[8] (D. Georgi later suggested the influence here of the (supposed) 'Cynic–Stoic diatribe'.)[9] J. T. Fitzgerald (following R. Hodgson)[10] then rightly insisted that relevant examples of such lists are to be found in various settings in a wide variety of authors; yet many of Fitzgerald's instances are nonetheless drawn from Cynic sources. However, in a more recent study, to which we shall of course return, M. Ebner has discerned elements in the Pauline passages which indicate specifically Cynic rather than merely general popular resonances.[11]

Particularly significant for our study is R. F. Hock's monograph, *The Social Context of Paul's Ministry*.[12] The most obvious model for Paul 'labouring night and day' (1 Thess 2.9; 2 Thess 3.8) is the legendary Cynic 'Simon the Shoemaker', a model followed by some (but by no means all) Cynic philosophers. For Paul an open shop-front would have afforded his main opportunity to make contact

---

6   H. Funke (1970).
7   A. J. Malherbe (1983a).
8   R. Hoïstad (1944).
9   D. Georgi [1964] (1986), 73, n.124.
10 R. Hodgson (1983); J. T. Fitzgerald (1988), 31.
11 M. Ebner (1991).
12 R.F. Hock (1980).

and proclaim his gospel, as well as maintain one form of independence.

To use such a setting is already to adopt in effect something of Socrates' example, and H. D. Betz argued some while ago that the self-portrait Paul offers in 2 Corinthians 10, of himself as 'meek', 'gentle', 'weak', stems from the Socratic tradition as developed especially among Cynics and about Cynics in discussions of authentic and pretend philosophers.[13] A. J. Malherbe has explored further Cynic motifs in Paul's discussion of his activity as teacher and pastor, 'gentle as a nurse', refusing flattery, eschewing covetousness (1 Thess 2. 6–7), and fighting like a Cynic Herakles against the beasts within (1 Cor 15.32).[14]

It is not only Paul among early Christians who deploys ideas and imagery from these circles. It has seemed to D. Georgi and to G. Theissen that Paul's opponents in 2 Corinthians 10–13 had adopted the stance of more radical Cynics, demanding support as a right.[15]

Paul argues forcefully that his Galatian converts should not surrender their new-found freedom (and we touched on part of that discussion in the previous chapter); in Corinth Paul seems to find Christian freedom too readily abused. The various positions taken have again seemed to some scholars most tellingly illustrated from Cynic writings.[16] Mark Plunkett in particular finds that the sexual freedoms claimed by some of the Christians in Corinth mirror most consistently the ideals of the more radical Cynics - ideals they seem to suppose Paul had been at least

---

[13] H. D. Betz (1972).

[14] A. J. Malherbe (1968), (1970), (1983), and many more studies.

[15] D. Georgi (1964/86); G. Theissen (1975/82).

[16] F. S. Jones (1981); W. L. Willis (1985); S. Vollenweider (1989).

implicitly inculcating.[17] A. J. Malherbe considers that in the Thessalonian correspondence new Christians are being urged to eschew some of the Cynic attitudes they seem to have supposed appropriate to their new allegiance.[18]

In the light of the foregoing it is unfortunate that in his recent very detailed survey of Jews in the Mediterranean Diaspora, J. M. G. Barclay so readily concludes that his 'anomalous' Jew, Paul, owes very little to anything in his Graeco-Roman context[19] when it should already be clear that much of Paul's refusal of 'cultural convergence' mirrors the stance of contemporary 'pagan' Cynics; but more of this in later chapters.

In my earlier *Cynics and Christian Origins* I concluded that Cynic traces among early Christians were mainly to be found in the synoptic tradition and in the later use of these strands. I supposed then that, although there were important echoes of Cynic thought and practice in Paul, providing evidence for the pervasiveness of a lively Cynicism in Galatia, Macedonia and Achaea, yet veins of Cynicism in his writings had been pretty well exhaustively quarried (by Abraham Malherbe in particular; I had not at that point read Ebner or Plunkett nor other studies that have since become available).[20] Further reading of others' investigations and my own researches convince me that there is much more of Cynicism to be shown, both in what Paul continued to avow and in what he came to find unpalatable, especially among his converts. (And, I would emphasise again, it is much more likely to have been

---

[17] M. Plunkett (1988).

[18] A. J. Malherbe (1987), 99-101, 107.

[19] J. M. G. Barclay (1996), 390-91.

[20] F. G. Downing (1992), 61-63, 142.

Cynicism than gnosticism – even 'incipient gnosticism' –
that was causing Paul trouble.)[21]

Cynicism, need it be repeated, is, on this thesis,
only a part of Paul's religio-cultural context and make-up,
albeit an integral part. Much of his initial formation comes
from the traditional Jewish strands in his Hellenistic Jewish
upbringing. That formation was fundamentally reshaped by
his conviction that he had been encountered by and enlisted
by the crucified Jesus, now raised to glory as Lord. Some
of his new or revised insights came from the shared faith of
other new Christian communities, some from his own
reflections and discussions in the groups he helped to form.
Paul's awareness of popular Cynic (and also occasionally
Stoic and very occasionally Epicurean) practice and ideas
also allowed him to do and say things that expressed some
important elements of his new convictions; and some of the
(provisional) conclusions he reached may well also have
been prompted in some measure by the Cynic strands that
were part of his intellectual and moral stock. It is the thesis
of this study, then, as already announced, not just (*a*) that
Paul will often have looked and sounded to many more
than a little like a Cynic, and (*b*) that he was content that it
should be so, but (*c*) that Cynicism also played an
important, albeit not dominant, role in Paul's life and
thought as a Christian (especially earlier on), as well as in
the thought and life (*d*) of his and (*e*) of other Christian
communities.

---

[21] See the rejection of the 'gnostic' interpretation in M. Plunkett
(1988), 114–17; 150; and cf. P. Perkins (1993), 76–92; W. Deming
(1995), 35–40 (on 1 Cor. 7).

(*ii*) *Cynics: The popular generalisations*

Cynics make a brief appearance in many more recent studies of early Christianity than those just noted, but are usually swiftly dismissed as being of only marginal importance. Twinned with the Stoics, they have, as noted, supposedly provided the 'diatribe' discounted above, and they might also seem to provide a possible model for ill-clad wandering preachers, affording some significant similarities at just this point with early missionaries like Paul. But quickly, we are assured, the Cynics were really quite distinctive, and their characteristic and distinctive and unvarying differences from every kind of Christian makes comparison of the two groups and their ideas mostly quite irrelevant.[22]

In effect, many writers who refer to Cynics in the context of a study of the early church rely on a stereotypical caricature, with scant reference or none at all to the actual Cynic sources, and with little or no account taken of the available scholarly discussions of those sources.

The impression is constantly given that the short, doubled and dirty cloak, the staff and the begging-bag, long hair and beard (and the forgoing of shoes) constituted a compulsory uniform for Cynics who are nonetheless

---

[22] The following summarises F. G. Downing (1992a), 26-56, but now with reference to Paul and his churches. For such very limited acknowledgment of (stereotyped) Cynics as possible models for aspects of Paul's thought and practice, see, e.g., D. Georgi [1964] (1986), 156–57, 160, esp. 188 n.111, 218 n.451, 220 n.469; G. Theissen (1975) 192–221; H. C. Kee (1980), 68–70; J. Stambaugh & D. Balch (1986), 45–46, 105, 143–45; C. A. Wanamaker (1990) 92–93, 101; C. Roetzel (1991), 40–41. Better, but in the end offering an over-simplified set of contrasts, W. Klassen (1996).

individualists without exception; so any Christian lacking
one or more of these marks would be seen to be different,
and deliberately different.[23] In fact, it is clear from the
sources that for any ill-clad figure to draw attention to him-
or herself in public would most likely be to present him- or
herself as and to be perceived as Cynic,[24] even though
explicitly self-styled Cynics varied widely in their
appearance. Lucian's Demonax rebuked other Cynics for
their ostentatious variations on the theme, while adopting a
form of Cynic appearance himself.[25] The cloak on its own
would seem to have been quite enough.[26] Diogenes
Laertius has Diogenes the Cynic mostly without a staff, as
does Dio (who seems to have forgone it himself on his
Cynic travels). Teles commends forgoing the begging-
bag.[27] This is not at all to deny that in many instances
cloak, staff and bag do all appear.[28] It is only to point out
that they are not *necessary* for someone to be identified as
a Cynic, and that much less than the full tally is
sufficient.[29]

---

[23] So G. Theissen (1973), 259, with reference to pre-Pauline missionaries as evidenced in the gospel 'mission charges'; cited by, among
others, R. A. Horsley (1987), C. Tuckett (1989).

[24] H. E. Butler, *Quintilian* (LCL, 1921), note p. 530 on 4.2.30,
referring to ps.-Quintilian, *Declamations* 28.3; cf. Epictetus 3.1.24;
3.22.10, 50; 4.8.11–12, 34 (Epictetus does not approve); and Dio
33.14, 72.2; and also L. Vaage (1994a) 24-30, and (1995b), 208–10.

[25] Lucian, *Demonax* 19, 48 and 5.

[26] Epictetus 3.22.47; 4.8.34; ps.-Crates 18; ps.-Diogenes 32.1; 34.1;
37.5; 44; *Socratic Epistle* 9.2.

[27] Diogenes Laertius 6.23; Dio 6.15, 60; Teles 44H.

[28] On this see especially M.-O. Goulet-Cazé (1990), 2738–46.

[29] Compare the 'standing Cynic' in the photograph included by
D. Clay (1996), 384, fig. 10.1. 'This Cynic does not carry a beggar's
cup [nor a bag] or a staff; he is wearing sandals and has a cloak – and
not a *tribôn* – wrapped round him' (385). We may compare this with a

In much the same way as we are often led to expect
a uniform appearance, so we are often led to expect a
standard set of keywords, 'slogans', marking out a Cynic's
public speech and conversation. Words such as ἀπάθεια,
ἄσκησις, αὐτάρκεια, ἐλευθερία, ἡδονή, κύων itself,
παρρησία, and πόνος are listed for us (and others, too,
but less frequently).[30] In fact, both in our present-day
writers and in our older sources, these are convenient terms
used mostly by outsiders in discussing and summarising
Cynic practice and views.[31] The term κύων, 'doggish',
'Cynic', itself, is the one that appears in most scholars'
lists; yet many documents widely acknowledged as Cynic
do not use it at all. In fact it is possible to write quite
obviously Cynic pieces, and pass on popular Cynic *chreiai*,
anecdotes, without using any of these (or other) supposed
Cynic slogans.[32] It is recurrent Cynic themes, and even
more the actions and life-styles which actualise them, that
are significant, whether caught by these catchwords or not:
not the catchwords themselves.[33] And then we have to note

---

quite naked 'Diogenes' with a cup, a staff and a dog (fig. 9), 381 and
383.

[30] 'Disregard for feeling'; 'hard training'; 'sufficiency' (often mis-
rendered as 'self-sufficiency'); 'public opinion' and/or 'fame';
'freedom'; 'dog' but thence 'doggish' Cynic; 'frankness' and/or
'boldness' and/or 'free-speech'; and 'painful hard work'.

[31] The largest tallies of catchwords that the present author has been
able to find are both in *non*-Cynics writing about them: Philo of
Alexandria, *Quod omnis probus liber sit*, and Lucian, *Philosophies for
Sale* 7-10; see F. G. Downing (1992) 49.

[32] See in more detail, F. G. Downing (1992a), 45–50, with references.

[33] L. Vaage (1994b) criticises F. G. Downing (1992a) for starting with
publicly observed characteristics of Cynics and then lapsing into such
generalities as 'themes', 'attitudes', 'commitments'. A little more
attention might have allowed Vaage to discern that these general terms
refer to quite specific intentional acts, including pronouncements, of

that even on their major themes, thematic forms of life, Cynics differ while remaining Cynics to themselves and to others (as do early Christians, remaining Christians to themselves and others, differing among themselves while still warranting the common appellation).[34]

We have already set aside the supposed Cynic or Cynic–Stoic diatribe. But a continuing problem is scholars' refusal to note the differences as well as the similarities between the stated views of various Cynics, Cynic-inclined Stoics, and Stoics largely free of their Cynic roots. We saw some of the contrasts in the first chapter, and they will concern us again in what follows.

It is worth picking out just one example at this point. Epictetus' *Dissertation* 3.22, on 'the true Cynic' is sometimes the main, even the only source quoted. It seems taken for granted that all Cynics other than those vilified as out-and-out charlatans shared the views there outlined by Epictetus. So it is very important to consider that much of this portrait may be both drastically 'idealised' and also 'Stoicised', and that popular Cynicism, relevant to this study, appears much more in the attitudes and practices Epictetus there repudiates as 'false' than in those he espouses and commends.[35]

---

the kinds which Vaage himself discerns; in fact he then immediately criticises Downing for not discerning 'shamelessness' as a continuing constant (see below).

[34] Compare R. B. Branham and M.-O. Goulet-Cazé (1996), 16, on the very varied 'reception' of Cynicism in our period and onwards: 'We should resist the temptation to reduce the very individual acts of reception to a single structure or pattern.'

[35] See in particular M. Billerbeck (1978) and (1993). Epictetus (and 3.22 in particular) seems to be the main source for Cynicism in D. Georgi [1964] (1986); G. Theissen [1975] (1982), 39; (1978), 15; even V. K. Robbins (1996). In some of my own earliest writing on

(iii) The Variegated Cynic 'Family' in the First Century: A preliminary Sketch.

Scholars have been aware for a very long time that much of our evidence for early Christianity suggests considerable diversity in life-style and in beliefs, in attitudes to Judaism, and in response to the power of Rome and the Empire's ideals. We have been used to employing, overtly or implicitly, a 'family resemblance' model.[36] It is much harder to persuade critics to deploy this working model for other contemporary groups, let alone to deal with the similarities *and* differences between, say, various Cynics and various Christian communities. Cynics differ, but may still be usefully compared *as well as contrasted*, because they share many *differing* sets of family resemblances.[37] (I have recently discussed elsewhere the problems of comparing sets of similarities and sets of differences. Scholars often see these as difficulties only in positions they themselves do not hold.)[38] Briefly stated, the overall argument of this present book is that there are sufficient resemblances between varied Cynics and varied Pauline Christians (Paul himself included) to constitute a family relationship, albeit one which (as in all families) allows for very real differences between members at many points.

Cynics I was not sufficiently aware of this important distinction. See further M.-O. Goulet-Cazé (1990) 2729–31.

[36] L. Wittgenstein (1953), §§ 66–67, 31–32; F. G. Downing (1972). On diversity among Christians, see most recently G. Lüdemann (1996).

[37] For a failure to register the evidence for this conclusion, see, e.g., H. Chadwick (1994), 209–10, reviewing F. G. Downing (1992a); B. Witherington (1994), 123–45 (with reference to F. G. Downing and others on Cynics); P. R. Eddy (1996).

[38] F. G. Downing (1994a).

In the sketch of variegated first-century popular Cynicism that follows I am again summarising what I have argued before at greater length,[39] but now with special reference to Paul and Paul's churches.

The social milieu is similar. Although both groups can point to a handful of members who had good education, social standing and influence, most adherents had not; and it was with the latter that the former were accepting identification. Pauline Christians, like most (but not all) Cynics for whom we have evidence, are towns-people (even if some of both do touch the countryside in their travels).[40] Many Cynics, the more prominent among them in particular, appear as assiduous travellers, and we find references to them moving through the countryside to and from many of the urban centres and provinces we associate with Paul.[41]

While the portrait of Paul's mission in Acts may well suggest the model of the 'school', the evidence in Paul's letters indicates something much less formal, much less prestigious. M.-O. Goulet-Cazé presents a similar picture of Cynics in the first century: there are many references to Cynics congregating together, but (with the

---

[39] F. G. Downing (1992a) chs. 1–3, 1–84. It was gratifying to find F. Williams (1994), 140, in a not uncritical review of F. G. Downing (1992), remark, 'he is well-informed on ancient Cynicism (for which his opening chapters provide what is in many ways the best introduction available in English)'. But for a survey now also see R. B. Branham and M.-O. Goulet-Cazé (1996) and A. A. Long (1996).

[40] M.-O. Goulet-Cazé (1990), 2734–36, 1 Cor 1.26–28; W. A. Meeks (1983), ch. 2, 51–73; F. G. Downing (1992a), 88–98. (For evidence, nonetheless, of Cynics and Christians in the countryside, see F. G. Downing (1992) 82-84.)

[41] M.-O. Goulet-Cazé (1990), 2731–34, Rome, Athens, Corinth in particular, Cilicia (and add Tarsus, Dio 34.2), Cyprus; as well as Gadara in the Decapolis, and other parts of Syria; see further, below.

possible exception of Agathobulus in Alexandria) no hint of formal philosophical 'schools'.[42] A 'shortcut to excellence' would neither demand nor warrant such formal organisation. On the other hand, A. J. Malherbe (followed by M.-O. Goulet-Cazé) argues for the importance of letter-writing as a means of disseminating popular Cynicism in our period, and keeping adherents in touch: 'Letters are worth a great deal, and are not inferior to conversation with people actually present', insists pseudo-Diogenes to Hipparchia.[43]

We ought also to note that other philosophical movements or 'schools' in our sense are at times proposed as affording more promising 'models' for the Pauline communities as such, as having a stronger organisation – Epicureans and Pythagoreans in particular. M.-O. Goulet-Cazé's attention to evidence for 'la faune cynique' is therefore especially important. The case being argued here does not in any way attempt to exclude the possible usefulness of other careful comparisons, although alleged similarities in ethos between Paul and Epicureans in particular are far fewer and much weaker, it will be argued below, than those between Paul and his early converts on the one hand, and many Cynics, on the other. Though Paul was not 'a Cynic', from his behaviour and dress and many of the things he said he might well have been mistaken for

---

[42] M.-O. Goulet-Cazé (1990), 2736–38; for Paul as a school-philosopher, E. A. Judge (1960), (1972) and L. Alexander (1995); and for the alternative view, R. F. Hock (1980), again.

[43] M.-O. Goulet-Cazé (1990), 2743–46, quoting A. J. Malherbe (1977), 2–3, and citing ps.-Diogenes 3. One may also note the later example of Peregrinus, though he might have been influenced by Paul's earlier example (Lucian, *Peregrinus* 41).

one; there would seem no real likelihood at all of his being taken for an Epicurean.[44]

There is one distinction among Cynics that has been quite widely recognised on the basis of work by A. J. Malherbe: that between a harsh and severe (and perhaps especially plebeian) Cynicism, and a more easy-going, even 'hedonist' variant.[45] So when Peregrinus (who ultimately 'gave his body to be burned', in imitation of Herakles) rebuked the gentle Demonax for being too light-hearted, not living a truly Cynic life: οὐ κυνᾷς, 'You're not living doggedly', Demonax riposted, 'And you're not living humanly.'[46]   Another example is pseudo-Crates, *Epistle* 19: 'Do not call Odysseus, who was the most effeminate of all his companions, and who put pleasure above all else, the father of Cynicism, because he once put on the garb of a Cynic; for the cloak does not make the Cynic, but the Cynic the cloak.' Epictetus would have agreed about the cloak, but not about Odysseus or about Diogenes.[47] (In the fourth century, the emperor Julian berated a Cynic who had criticised Diogenes himself, as not whole-hearted enough.)[48] As we have already noted, and will consider later in more detail, Malherbe brings this distinction into focus in his discussion of Paul, 'gentle as a nurse', in contrast with the more acerbic Cynics' pastoral

---

[44] W. Meeks (1983), 83–84 and notes; A. J. Malherbe (1982), (1987), 40–43, 84–87; C. E. Glad (1995) and (1996); M.-O. Goulet-Cazé (1990), 2743–46, as in the previous note.

[45] A. J. Malherbe (1970), 203–17; (1978), 48–49; (1982), 49–52; F. G. Downing (1992a), 27–28 and n. 6.

[46] Lucian, *Demonax*, 21.

[47] Epictetus 3.24.13–21 and 64; cf. Dio's Odysseus-style portrait of Diogenes, *Discourse* 9.9.

[48] Julian, *To the uneducated Cynics* 180D–181B.

ethos,[49] but it is also more widely relevant. Early Christianity (the Pauline churches included) exhibited similar divergencies over standards of asceticism.[50] And 'gentle, loving' Paul can himself offer the alternative of 'a rod' and 'severity'.[51] Paul's coarseness at times would have sounded typically Cynic (in particular, the reference to gelding (Gal 5.12) and to shit (Phil 3.8)); but even more than the crudeness or the tone, there is the constant readiness to scold.[52] These variations will concern us frequently in what follows, not least in necessary efforts to compare and contrast Stoics and Cynics and Cynicising Stoics (or Stoicising Cynics).[53]

---

[49] A. J. Malherbe (1970). L. Vaage (1995b), 204–205, finds too clear a division of Cynics into just two groups along these lines in A. J. Malherbe (1982), while noting much subtler variations analysed by Malherbe elsewhere. The latter is more characteristic of Malherbe's discussions of Cynicism.

[50] Luke 7.31–34; 1 Cor 7.8–9; Col 2.16–18; 1 Tim 4.1–5; Rev 2.20.

[51] Cf. ps.-Diogenes 7.1 (ῥάβδον) and 29.1; Paul in 1 Cor 4.21 and 2 Cor 13.10.

[52] M.-O. Goulet-Cazé (1990), 2746–47, citing, e.g., the approach of which Epictetus disapproved, 3.22.80. Writers such as L. Vaage (1994b) and D. Krueger (1996) have suggested that sexual and excretory shamelessness are necessary features of Cynicism (even while allowing that Cynics could be very different). In fact these particular kinds of shameless behaviour are not part of the reception of Cynicism by Demetrius, Dio, Demonax or ps.-Lucian's Cynic. They constitute one part of the Diogenes tradition, but are not necessary: there are many other forms of shamelessness – being poor, ill-clad, begging, eating in public, crude language, any one or any combination of which would suffice. See further, below, in this chapter; and ch. 4.

[53] C. E. Glad (1995), 89–98, seems to suppose that this debate about 'harshness' and 'gentleness' is proposed as itself a distinguishing feature of Cynics. It is not so proposed here; but neither, it would seem, is it by such as A. J. Malherbe. Glad argues that a more significant difference is whether people at large are seen as 'improvable',

Paul, like the Cynics (but unlike most other teachers) exhorted his hearers to refuse to conform to the ideal (and not just the actual) life-style of those around, not to maintain the common priorities and prejudices of their neighbours, but to adopt a quite new mind-set.[54] We have already noted important aspects of this radical (and Cynic-seeming) demand in the first chapter. Further particulars of the alternative way of living Paul seems to have proposed (or seems to have appeared to have been proposing) in his early contacts with his first converts, its similarities with and its occasional divergencies from that of varied Cynics, is what concerns us in detail in other chapters of this book; here we continue to offer a brief outline of some salient features.

Cynics, like Stoics, claimed to live 'according to nature', κατὰ φύσιν (Paul only occasionally appeals to 'nature', 1 Cor 11.14; Rom 2.14). What constitutes 'nature' is conveniently vague; who is the more 'natural', Demonax or Peregrinus? Are honeyed cakes 'natural' or is only the simplicity of an animal in the wild?[55] One important difference between many Cynics and all but the most Cynic-inclined Stoics lay in their attitude to the attainment of the τέλος of this 'natural' perfection. Stoicism advocated a slowly maturing intellectual inner discipline and enlightenment (albeit with some adopting a Cynic life-style as an optional extra, as we shall note), while Cynics

---

whatever the mode, with Cynics sceptical and Epicureans and Paul optimistic. We shall revert to this issue below.

[54] Paul at, e.g., Rom 12.2, μὴ συσχηματίζεσθε . . . ἀνακαινώσει τοῦ νοός, and the *Cynic Epistles,* passim; but cf., e.g, ps.-Crates 7 and 8; ps.-Diogenes 34 (for the alternative σχῆμα); and Diogenes Laertius 6.3 for the 'new mind' demanded; and cf. M.-O. Goulet-Cazé (1990), 2721–22 and 2751.

[55] Lucian, *Demonax* 52; Diogenes Laertius 6.56.

tended to claim the ability to climb straight into the 'natural' life-style, whether harsh or easy-going (or anywhere in between). Cynicism is essentially a practical 'way of life', rather than an intellectual disicipline. It takes a very practical 'shortcut', σύντομος ὁδός.[56]

The latter term does not reappear in Paul, but, it will be argued, the issues do. Paul, too, had invited people to step very quickly into a new life-style, one dominated neither by Hellenic nor barbarian (Jewish) law, written or customary. It would have been easy for these new converts to assume that they had 'already' reached their goal, were already in their kingdom (1 Cor 4.8), as those plebeian Cynics who displeased Epictetus claimed for themselves (4.8.34; but cf. 3.22.76), and to formulate their opposition to convention in some of the terms ready-made by the similarly unconventional Cynics. They were now 'free', as Paul stressed to the Galatians. In Corinth, freedom readily took a very Cynic turn in discussions of diet, cultus, and sexual relations, where the positions Paul opposes all seemed 'natural' to many, though not all, Cynics. The question of reliance on others' support was a live issue among Cynics in particular, and both in Corinth and in Thessalonica Paul discusses it in terms that clearly recall that Cynic debate. Cynics differing among themselves on the details of the life-style to be adopted and promoted provided much of the framework for the arguments among

---

[56] M.-O. Goulet-Cazé (1986), 22–28, (1990), 2759–63, 2806–12, especially the conclusion, 2812. It is true, as C. E. Glad points out (1995), 162, that it would seem that Philodemus' Epicureans, too, welcomed newcomers without prior 'screening'. But Paul seems to have expected the decision to join already to involve a significant psycho-social change, rather than welcoming newcomers to 'psychogogy' and Epicurean empiricist metaphysics; see further, below. The Epicurean analogy, such as it is, is very limited.

Pauline Christians sorting out in various ways their new discipleship.

Despite Paul's unease at or outright opposition to some of the more radical (and Cynic-looking) conclusions adopted by some of his converts, his own attitudes at many other points resemble Cynic, even distinctively Cynic stances (as, again, we shall consider in much more detail below). For instance, when challenged, he cites not only the hardships he has been able to accept, but those which he has deliberately chosen. Stoics hoped to accept the circumstances that befell them (and Paul can sometimes say much the same: Phil 4.11–13). Cynics were likely to invite trouble so as to be able to display the truth, the validity, of their claims: grappling with hunger and cold, withstanding thirst . . . hunger, exile, loss of reputation and the like have no terrors (Dio 8.16). Paul's 'success' in confronting troubles demonstrates the truth of his claims (albeit as to God's power, not Paul's own, 2 Cor 4.7–10). Others might find this kind of 'proof' unpersuasive, in fact ridiculous (Lucian, *Philosophies for Sale* 9-10); Paul, like many a Cynic, finds and expects others to find an argument from ascetic performance very cogent.[57]

The other side of this emphasis on *praxis* is a refusal to rely for persuasion on abstract intellectual argument and its rhetorical expression (a companion contrast with Cynicism's nearest relative, Stoicism in particular; but with other philosophies, too, of course). Some Cynics were cultured and highly literate (Diogenes and Crates in the tradition; Demetrius, Dio, Demonax and Oenomaus around our period); others (the writers of the

---

[57] On Cynic ἄσκησις, see again M.-O. Goulet-Cazé (1986), especially 66–71, 182–90; and R. B. Branham and M.-O. Goulet-Cazé (1996), 26; A. A. Long (1996), 42–43.

Cynic Epistles for instance) were not. Here again there was variety. Educated Cynics were quite willing to use their intellectual skills to 'deconstruct' others' wordy edifices, but all refused to substitute any rival metaphysical structures of their own. Other contemporaries, too, disclaimed any reliance on 'mere rhetoric'; but, as again A. J. Malherbe has shown, Paul's own disclaimers seem particularly to echo those of, for instance, Dio in Cynic mood distancing himself from harsher, plebeian Cynics.[58] Once more, a characteristic debate among divergent Cynics provides the terms for a discussion among the Pauline Christians.

As we have already noted, it is often allowed, at least initially, that Paul as an impoverished wandering preacher might well have seemed at this point to have had something in common with Cynics. But here again it is worth noting that Cynics themselves varied. Dio Chrysostom and Peregrinus and Lucian's plebeian Cynics seem to be wanderers; Dio supposes the townspeople he visits will be used to other Cynic visitors. Diogenes in some of the *Epistles*, and in Maximus of Tyre, is a wanderer;[59] but in other traditions he, like Crates (and, later, Musonius, Demetrius and Demonax) seem settled in one place. That not all Christian preachers were as mobile as Paul, Kephas and the Lord's brothers would not itself have dispelled the Cynic impression they all probably conveyed.

A major divergence between most Cynics and most Stoics was over providence. Cynic ascetic pragmatism

---

[58] A. J. Malherbe (1987), 3–4, citing Dio 32.11–12; cf. M.-O. Goulet-Cazé (1990), 2724.

[59] Ps.-Diogenes 30–40; Dio 1.50; 12.16; 13.9; Lucian, *Peregrinus* 15–16 and *Philosophies for Sale* 7–10, and *Runaways*; Maximus of Tyre, 36.5; Giannantoni (1990) V B 299; cf. M.-O. Goulet-Cazé (1990), 2733–34.

entailed a strong conviction that one could act to make a difference to the way things turned out, at least in one's own case. Events are not determined in advance by destiny, necessity, fortune. For Stoics there is only the choice whether providence takes you along willingly or unwillingly (like a dog tied to a cart).[60] Yet even here the divide is not clear. Seneca quotes his friend Demetrius as saying, 'Immortal Gods, I have this one complaint against you, that you did not earlier make your will known to me . . .', and Goulet-Cazé argues persuasively that Seneca is unlikely to have invented so strong an assertion for his friend.[61] Seneca himself, for all his Stoic leanings, could evince a markedly Cynic pragmatic attitude to ἄσκησις, as could Epictetus, too.[62] Paul displays a similar ambivalence: on the one hand we have, for instance, Romans 8.28–30 ('those God foreknew he predestined . . .') and 9.16–17 ('it does not depend on human will but on God'); on the other, there is Paul's apparently very physical self-discipline, 'lest he find himself rejected', in (among other passages) one whose Cynic echoes we have already heard, 1 Corinthians 9.23–27.[63] In the importance he accords 'the body', but without any conventional athletic leanings, here and elsewhere Paul is very close to Cynicism, as we shall argue later.

Much of Paul's 'determinism' could, however, be read primarily in terms of divine 'election', divine choice, as in both the passages from Romans cited. Cynics can often appear as sceptical or ᵪtheist, as do Diogenes in many

---

[60] Hippolytus, *Refutation* 1.18.

[61] Seneca, *De providentia* 5.5-6; M.-O. Goulet-Cazé (1990), 2772–76.

[62] M.-O. Goulet-Cazé (1986), 182–90, again.

[63] On this see A. J. Malherbe (1995), and especially 252–54; but also *idem* (1978), 56–58.

of the popular stories, Menippus as reproduced by Lucian, and Oenomaus in the lengthy extracts preserved by Eusebius of Caesara. Yet, here, too, there is no clear consistency. Some of the stories have Diogenes talk quite positively of the Gods; late tradition saw Antisthenes as a staunch monotheist; Musonius, Dio and Peregrinus all display 'a warm religious strain'. In particular do we find at times a strong sense of being 'called' by God or Gods, chosen and sent for service.[64] (All of these issues will be discussed in more detail in ensuing chapters.)

Perhaps the readiest contrast between Paul and his churches on the one hand, and Cynicism as often presented, on the other, would be on the issue of 'shamelessness', ἀναίδεια. In the tradition, Diogenes is not simply loudmouthed and even violent, but he offends public convention not only by eating in the market place, but farting, pissing, shitting and masturbating publicly; Crates and Hipparchia copulate in the temple porticos, just as dogs naturally do. Even when rebuking incest in Corinth (1 Cor 5), Paul never seems to have had this sort of behaviour to contend with. Yet here again, there does not seem to have been a standard practice among Cynic individualists: ἀναίδεια was not *de rigueur*. The most shocking tale Seneca can tell of Demetrius is the latter's likening the talk of ignorant fools to a belch or a fart.[65] Though Dio refers to Diogenes defecating in public, and masturbating in the wild, he never suggests he himself was bound or even tempted to emulate him; and when he complains of the

---

[64] Diogenes in Diogenes Laertius 6.20 (repeated by others); Dio 1.50 13.8–12; 32.12–14; as well as Epictetus' very Stoic ideal Cynic, 3.22.46, 56; M.-O. Goulet-Cazé (1990), 2781–88; J. H. Moles (1996), 113–14.

[65] Seneca, *Epistulae morales* 91.19.

plebeian radicals in Alexandria, it is only to their abrasive jokes that he takes exception.[66] Lucian does not raise the issue in his account of Demonax, nor even in his criticism of working-class Cynics in *The Runaways*; although there is some reference to such actions in *Philosophies for Sale* (10) and just one in his *Peregrinus* (17). There is nothing of the sort in pseudo-Lucian, *The Cynic*. It would not have been necessary for Paul to have behaved in so unseemly a manner, nor for his converts to have felt obliged or permitted to, for Paul's many close contacts with Cynicism to have been obvious, even very swiftly obvious.[67]

There does remain one major apparent difference which must exercise us in this discussion: that is, an item of concern to Cynics that does not seem to have exercised Paul greatly. It is the issue of wealth for Christians in general. There is already a striking difference on this (as on other points) between Paul and the Jesus tradition in Q[68] and in Mark (though many other 'family resemblances' remain); but also a contrast with Cynicism as a whole. Wealth for most Cynics is a threat, it enslaves.[69] The Paul of the undisputed letters never preaches against wealth as

---

[66] Dio 8.36; 6.17–20; 32.9.

[67] Such behaviour does seem part of any 'rounded' sketch of Diogenes, but not part of the essential reception of Cynicism in our period (see n. 52, above), and *contra* D. Krueger (1996). To repeat, to make specifically sexual provocative behaviour a 'necessary' feature of all Cynicism from which therefore all known Christian conduct can be distinguished (H. Chadwick (1994), L. Vaage (1994b)) is to fly quite perversely in the face of the known evidence.

[68] The present writer is convinced that the evidence for Luke and Matthew having had a common source, 'Q', not used by Mark, is overwhelming. For a recent account, F. G. Downing (1994a); for its Cynic content, F. G. Downing (1992a), 115–42.

[69] Ps.-Crates 8 and 9; ps.-Diogenes 37.6; Diogenes Laertius 6.50, 87; ps.-Lucian, *The Cynic*; Lucian, *Peregrinus* 15.

such (cf. 1 Cor 13.3). He accepts poverty for himself, as a personal discipline, but never urges it on others; not even when reminding the Corinthians of Jesus' 'poverty' does Paul ask them to do more than 'share their wealth' (1 Cor 8.8–15). And yet, even here we may find a similar difference of approach among the Cynics for whom we have evidence. Seneca's Cynic friend Demetrius clearly seems to have maintained his austere life-style, even in the home of his wealthy patron. But at no point does Seneca suggest he has had to respond to constant exhortations himself to accept dispossession. Nor, for that matter, does Lucian's Demonax seem to worry much about wealth. To see poverty as a personal rather than as general calling may have been one more variant opinion among Cynics. Or perhaps this is another point where Paul is closer to the Stoics.

The foregoing sketch has attempted to display something of the varied concerns and practices of first-century popular Cynicism, and at the same time to show some more of the ways in which many Cynics differed from most Stoics, but also differed among themselves. It has also been suggested in brief that many of the concerns, and the varied responses to them, can also be found expressed in Paul, often in very similar ways. But this is only a sketch, a sketch-map perhaps, of the ground that remains to be covered in much more detail. At best the reader may have been persuaded that the journey is reasonably promising, and that we may properly operate with a model of 'family resemblances', not only within Cynicism and within early Christianity and Paul's own churches, but also as a valid *question* about the relationship between Paul and varied Cynicism. It is presented as a question worth asking; there is no pretence that the evidence so far offered is sufficient to warrant the conclusion to which the book as a whole argues.

(iv) Sources for Cynics and for Paul

Most of our major sources for variegated first century Cynicism have already been mentioned in passing. Popular, more or less 'plebeian' Cynicism is best repre- sented in the *Cynic Epistles*. Many of these letters seem to have been composed in the first century CE, with older ones still in circulation.[70] Produced much later, but widely used in studies of Cynicism, is book 6 of Diogenes Laertius' *Lives of Eminent Philosophers*. His frequent claim to be quoting older sources, themselves in circulation in our first century, is well supported by other data available to us. Many of the brief *chreiai* he included can be paralleled in Epictetus, Dio, Plutarch and Philo, among other first-century writers. Dio in particular notes 'the mass of ordinary people retain a clear memory of the sayings ascribed to Diogenes.'[71]

It is assumed that many of the works of Menippus of Gadara in the Decapolis were widely available in Paul's day, for they influenced Roman writers such as Varro (first century BCE) and Seneca, Paul's near–contemporary, while their most extensive remains are in the re-worked versions produced in the next century by Lucian of Samosata. Seneca has preserved for us only a handful of

---

[70] On the Cynic sources as a whole, M.-O. Goulet-Cazé (1990), 2800– 2806; for the *Cynic Epistles*, A. J. Malherbe (1977); F. G. Downing (1992a), ch. 3, 'Sorting and Dating the Cynic Evidence', 55–84.

[71] Dio 72.11; Diogenes Laertius is readily available (if somewhat bowdlerised by R. D. Hicks (1925)) in LCL; most of the other Cynic sources listed here also appear in LCL.

scattered fragments of the Cynic philosophy of his friend, Demetrius, and much may have been reinterpreted in Stoic vein, but some is arguably authentic Cynicism.[72] There are other references, too, to Cynic themes, in Seneca's writings. Epictetus, as we have noted, is to be taken as primarily a Stoic (and that includes his portrait of the ideal Cynic, 3.22). But some items, perhaps especially his rebukes to Cynic 'pretenders' of whom he disapproved, are unquestionably relevant.[73]

Philo of Alexandria preserved some stories of Diogenes, in his *Quod omnis probus liber sit*; but also Cynic arguments against pleasure, in *De legum allegoria* 2 and 3 in particular. The Diogenes Papyrus from Alexandria and Dio's later references to plebeian Cynics in the city would support the impression Philo himself gives that he is responding to a live tradition.[74]

Our next major source is Dio (Chrysostom) of Prusa himself, born in the first century CE, writing mostly after the turn of the next. His *Discourses* 4, 6, 8, 9 and 10 are widely accepted as significantly Cynic, stemming from the time he was wandering in exile; but also relevant are his other passing references to Cynics (including those of whom he quite strongly disapproved).

And then from Syria in the next century, we have Oenomaus of Gadara and Lucian of Samosata (especially his admired *Demonax* and his despised *Peregrinus* and *The Runaways*).

---

[72] M. Billerbeck (1979), finds little; but cf. M.-O. Goulet-Cazé (1986), 182–85 and (1990), 2768–73.ʼ

[73] M. Billerbeck (1978); cf. M.-O. Goulet-Cazé (1986) 189–90.

[74] The Vienna Diogenes Papyrus, C. Wessely [1902] (1979); Philo, *De plantatione* 151; Dio 32.9.

I have argued elsewhere for a cautiously parsimon-
ious rule of thumb: to wit, that cultural sources in the
ancient world may readily be accepted as relevant if dated
within two generations of the generation being studied, a
'moving bracket' of around a century from the mid-point
of the current focus of attention. Matter from earlier or
later may also be adduced, but only to support matter from
within the bracket.[75] This rule is arbitrary it is more
generous than some would allow, but is also much stricter
than the scope most permit themselves. By this rule of
thumb we have a considerable amount of material with
which we may compare the 'genuine' letters of Paul.

On the face of it, our sources for Paul comprise a
large part of the New Testament collection: thirteen letters
(fourteen with Hebrews, but that does not claim to be by
Paul), and a large part of The Acts of the Apostles.
However, as most readers will be well aware, it has long
been obvious to scholars that the convictions, style and
language of many of the letters differ extensively. If we
take as a starting point Romans, 1 and 2 Corinthians and
Galatians, then 1 and 2 Timothy and Titus seem to be by
someone else; and Colossians and Ephesians seem each to
be by different writers again. It is widely accepted that
Jewish writers had made ready use of pseudonyms, 'pen-
names', over the previous centuries; schoolchildren were
set the task of writing in the character of some famous
person; and, of course, our *Cynic Epistles* are all pseud-
onymous.[76] On the other hand, Philemon, Philippians and

---

[75] F. G. Downing (1988a), 214–15.

[76] Cf. the useful survey in M. Kitchen (1994), 22–28. D. J. Doughty
(1994) has recently urged a 'systematic scepticism' in the face of the
'normative paradigm' deployed by most students of Paul (whom he
sees as also over-dependent on Acts). Doughty then insists that 'the
balance of proof' (*sic*) lies with those who accept the paradigm;

1 Thessalonians appear to most who engage in this dissection as genuinely Paul's own; leaving 2 Thessalonians as something of a puzzle. It seems to be addressing a very similar situation to that envisaged in 1 Thessalonians, yet taking a distinctive stance in Paul's name: not the most likely context for the use of a pseudonym (let alone for a claim to be using Paul's signature). However, it is not necesssary to argue, let alone resolve these issues here. The letters which seem most clearly to reflect what Paul first tried to share (and in some measure must be taken to have succeeded in sharing) with Greek-speaking gentiles are Galatians, 1 Thessalonians (supplemented by 2 Thessalonians), and 1 Corinthians (supplemented by 2 Corinthians). There is little relevant to the present discussion of Paul's initial approaches and explorations in Philippians or Philemon; and Paul was, of course, aware that the intended listeners to Romans had been introduced to Christian discipleship by others.[77] It will in fact be argued that Paul became quite rapidly disenchanted with many of the Cynic strands and motifs in his initial Christian thinking (if not his life-style); by the time he wrote Philippians and

---

apparently unaware that a systematic scepticism is unanswerably beyond proof or disproof (and, so, meaningless). Of course, alternative paradigms may well be deployed, and assessed as presented, by the extent of the evidence they adduce and the coherence of their ordering of it; on which see F. G. Downing (1968), (1987a) and (1994a). The number of possible scenarios is theoretically infinite. Sceptics are under an obligation to propose some other comprehensive reconstruction for colleagues to examine as sceptically.

[77] On these issues see the introductions to recent commentaries; on sorting the evidence so as to construct a portrait of Paul, the works that have most influenced the present writer include the following: J. Knox (1950); M. Dibelius [1947] (1953); G. Bornkamm [1969] (1971); S. Sandmel [1958] (1979); R. Jewett (1979); E. P. Sanders (1977) and (1983); G. Lüdemann [1980] (1984); G. Lyons (1985); A. J. Malherbe (1987); A. F. Segal (1990); see further the Bibliography to this volume.

Romans the more Stoic tendencies in his thought and attitudes had come to the fore.

The Acts of the Apostles seems to have little if anything of Paul's own language in it: Luke, like other historical writers of the day, composed its speeches with a view to the movement of the narrative and the situation of his own intended audience.[78] (Luke would also seem to have tried to make it clear that the radical and Cynic-sounding Jesus tradition belonged in the past, and were not expected to reappear in the post-resurrection Christian communities.)[79]

We continue with our exploration of Paul's initial approach to Greek-speaking gentiles who had little or no prior involvement with Jewish communities or Jewish ideas, asking whose language and whose models for living he would have needed to use or might have seemed to be using as he tried to share by example and in conversation his own faith and discipleship which were themselves all the while being worked out in these encounters.

---

[78] Cf. the discussion in F. G. Downing (1981) and (1982), and bibliography there.

[79] Luke 22.35–36; cf. F. G. Downing (1992a), 12 and (1995d), 101–102.

3

WHY THEN THE LAW?

(i) Recent debate

Paul's arguments about 'the law' (in Galatians and in Romans in particular) have been much assessed and re-assessed over recent years. The view had long been dominant in western scholarly discussion, that Paul had been making a 'Lutheran' contrast between the achieving of merit and the receiving in faith of divine grace. 'Law', and first-century Judaism's response to its *Torah*, so it was said, either encouraged attempts to earn divine favour by meticulous observance, or led to despairing failure in the face of impossible demands. Through the risen Christ's encounter with him, Paul had been released from the attempt to attain a perfect compliance as well as the temptation to boast of perceived success. Now, instead, Paul could trust God in Christ, and on the basis of that faith could enjoy the pure gift of an acquittal by God, and so, a right relationship with God. And the negative contrast with the unattainable goal of a perfection to be earned in detail importantly defined the gratuitous new status or relation-ship Paul was said to have believed was his and so urged others to accept.[1]

---

[1] For this characterisation of the Judaism against which Paul is thought to be reacting, see E. P. Sanders (1977), 2–6, and (1985), 23–58; for

An alternative view has been argued in a number of works by E. P. Sanders, with variants suggested by others largely in sympathy. Sanders himself argues that Paul is concerned with 'getting in and staying in', not with resisting forms of Jewish legalism imagined by the heirs of the Protestant Reformation. For Paul's Jewish contemporaries you were a Jew by birth or by male circumcision, and you stayed in God's covenantal people by responding positively to the opportunities as well as the demands of the *Torah*, its procedures for atoning for failures as much as its positive requirements. 'Being in' God's people was a gift; staying in, retaining the gift, was a matter of choice actively carried through, but still not a matter of earning your passage. Paul's system as a Christian was structurally no different; but for Paul, 'getting in', God's gift of inclusion, was now given solely in and through the risen Jesus. The Jewish way was therefore simply irrelevant (though a potentially dangerous distraction).[2]

J. D. G. Dunn has suggested a particular interpretation of 'doing the works of the law', also arguing that Paul is not objecting to any stress on 'doing', but rather to any emphasis on items that separated Jews from gentiles in the eyes of both: circumcision and food-purity laws in particular.[3] Heikki Räisänen also expresses frequent agreements with Sander's arguments, while stressing much more than does the latter the very different – even contradictory

---

arguments against Sanders and others taking a similar stance, see, e.g., H. Hübner (1980), 445–73 and [1978] (1984); R. N. Longenecker (1990), 85–87, though sympathetic to some of Sanders' points, still refers to 'winning God's favour by merit-amassing observance of Torah'. Cf. also C. E. B. Cranfield (1991), 89–101; I. H. Marshall (1996).

[2] E. P. Sanders (1983), especially 4–10.

[3] J. D. G. Dunn (1990), 183–241; (1991), ch. 7; and (1992), 99–117.

– attitudes Paul seems to him to express towards 'the law'.[4]

However we decide the theological interpretation, it is clear that at the time of writing Galatians (and, later, Romans), Paul is concerned with arguments about *Torah*, about Jewish law as it appeared in the Penteteuch, and as it was interpreted and applied in his own day; and, as just noted, Paul's attention seems now concentrated on the 'identity markers' that the *Torah* afforded: circumcision and food laws (and, to a lesser extent, Sabbath and calendar). It is obviously understandable that scholarly discussion of 'law' in Paul also centres on just these issues, on the 'Judaising' debate as it developed a few years on in the early Christian communities.

However, there is no sign at all that such arguments about Jewish sacred tradition accompanied Paul's first approach to these 'pagans' in Galatia (or to other such people, later, in Macedonia and Achaea: Gal 1.6–10; 1 Thess 1.9–10; 1 Cor 2.2).[5] So it is clearly inappropriate that none of the writers cited above pays any but the most passing attention (and mostly not even that) to pagan Greek discussions of traditional and ancestral 'law' even when they agree (as most do) that the people to whom Paul, in Galatians at least, is writing have never been Jewish.[6] For

---

[4] H. Räisänen [1983] 1986.

[5] Paul shows no obvious sign of having himself worked out his position on the Law in terms taken from Scripture at this early stage. Galatians and then Romans indicate a quite new and developing Scriptural argument to which opponents at this later stage had drawn him. As J. M. G. Barclay (1996) shows, there is no preparation for Paul's stance, not even among the 'allegorisers' to whom Philo refers (*De migratione* 89–93; Barclay 176–78).

[6] J. D. G. Dunn (1993), 6; E. P. Sanders (1983), 18; H.Räisänen (1983), 20. Räisänen systematically looks for 'analogies' to Paul in

these pagan Galatians, for most of their lives, 'law' had comprised just these local and Hellenised customs and codes. These and these only were the customs and codes in question when Paul first invited them to the new Christian way of life. Yet there is a long tradition in the Hellenistic world of critical debate over questions of such laws and codes, written and customary, covering all areas of life, cultus, purity, diet, festivals, as well as marriage and inheritance, property, town-planning and (restricted) civic rights. There are widely publicised arguments in favour and arguments against statutes and customs, in particular and in general.

It is, then, worth noting that Galatians seems to many to show clear signs of its author's awareness of contemporary conventions for public address (even if the letter does not fit neatly any one of the three theoretical divisions, 'forensic', 'epideictic' or 'deliberative').[7] Paul seems to assume that his hearers share the common oral culture of their cities. On that assumption they will inevitably have been exposed from time to time to discussions of law – laws and customs – in most or all the

---

other Christian and in Jewish (including Greek Jewish) sources; but never in the wider contemporary debate. A. Segal (1995), 22, notes as do many the somewhat distant analogy of the 'allegorisers' of the law mentioned by Philo (*De migratione* 89–90 [given as 87–88 by Segal]), but not the wider Hellenistic context of their concerns (see further, below). It is perhaps also worth noting that recent discussions of 'law' in Luke–Acts have been similarly myopic; see F. G. Downing (1988b).

[7] H. D. Betz (1975) and (1979), 14–25 argues that it is an 'apologetic letter' heavily influenced by the rhetorical structure of the forensic speech, the address for the defence in court. R. N. Longenecker (1990), cix–cxix and 184–86, responding to Betz and subsequent discussions, concludes that we have a mixture of *genres* in the letter. He is followed in this by J. D. G. Dunn (1993), 20; cf. A. E. Harvey (1996), 14–15; J. Murphy-O'Connor (1996), 50–51.

standard settings, of courts, assemblies, theatres and the like.[8]

As we saw in the first chapter, and have just recalled, Paul's Christian converts had been invited from the very start to break with the religio-civic laws and customs of their Greek cities, at least in some measure: crucially, where these laid down the roles expected of slave and free, male and female. They had broken in some significant ways with the codes and ethos expected of good Greeks - without adopting the *Torah* of Judaism (or the code and practice of any other recognised ἔθνος, any other people, either), as John Barclay has also recently pointed out so clearly.[9] These new Christians had already at their 'conversion' been forced to consider issues of attitudes to accepted custom and code, and their practical responses – no light matter, as Barclay stresses[10] – well before trouble-some Jewish Christians (or others) forced Paul now to discuss such issues in relation to alien Jewish laws and life-styles. The urgency of the question of the *Torah* and of its identity markers in the situation out of which Galatians was written has perhaps blinded scholars to the likelihood – indeed, the near certainty – that this was not the first time questions of 'law' had had to be faced by the Galatian congregations. They had confronted the issues of social conformity in relation to their own law when first they accepted baptism, and they will have had available the

---

[8] See, further, F. G. Downing (1988a), especially 223–26; J. M. G. Barclay (1996), 383 and n. 8.

[9] J. M. G. Barclay (1996), 329. Paul initiated a break with local Hellenised culture without substituting any acculturation to Jewish law and custom (or, apparently, even raising the question). There is to be no conformity to *any* ancient code as currently understood and practised. Paul's approach is entirely 'anomalous'.

[10] J. M. G. Barclay (1996), 277, 287, 314–18.

current popular debates; now they were having to face issues of custom and code yet again, but in this instance, and for the first time, in relation to Jewish torah, or elements of it.

So when Paul asks, τί οὖν ὁ νόμος; 'What then is the law?' there is at least a very good chance that he will be understood in terms of these standard Hellenistic discussions, a very good chance, too, that he will have some awareness of the vocabulary of ideas-in-words already current with which he might hope to make his case in relation to further legal controversy.[11] The issue of the *Torah* was new when Paul wrote Galatians; the issue of 'law' as such could hardly have been so; it had been at stake from the beginning, as reiterated, in the break with local civic cults, festivals, statutes and conventions.

(ii) 'Law' in Graeco-Roman debate

It is worthwhile, then, to summarise something of that wider debate about law and custom in the Graeco-Roman world. Issues of law, codified or uncodified (custom) had been argued over by the sophists, pointing sceptically to the variety that obtained from place to place. But this scepticism, it was said, sharpened people's appreciation of order, its value and its fragility. It was important to find how one could achieve a viable lasting and coherent order 'in matters divine and human' that would be acknowledged

---

[11] H. D. Betz (1979), 161–180, 'a topic common for the philosophers and theologians of the Greco-Roman world' (162); however, it will be argued that Betz has importantly misconstrued some of the relevant data. On what follows, also see especially H. W. Hollander and J. Holleman (1993), kindly drawn to my attention but then overlooked by me in the following discussion.

on all sides, rather than a diversity allowing or even
encouraging conflict. Initially, in *The Republic*, Plato
unfolded his conviction that there just 'is' an ideal order
which the truly wise man, the philosopher-king, will be
aware of and will be able to impose on each and every
occasion on all others, overriding any other form of law.
This contrasts with his own later admission, in *The Laws*,
that only a second-best state is actually feasible, one in
which authority (executive power) is itself subject to law.
For Aristotle, in *The Politics*, the collective wisdom of 'the
people' (albeit very narrowly defined) may well be wiser
than that of any expert; and this entails according a very
high value to popular habit, to custom commonly observed,
whether codified or not, and however much it differed
between one community and the next. Thus tradition,
ensuring the antiquity of customs and laws, was of great
importance. If Egyptian or Jewish practices seemed
bizarre, at least they were old.[12]

The Stoics, convinced that all have some access to
the order inherent in things as they are, also took custom
and enacted law very seriously, especially where common
strands could be discerned: this must represent the 'law of
nature'. Cynics tended to maintain the scepticism of the
sophists, but also to insist on taking that scepticism to its
logical conclusions in practice. The enacted laws and
customs of civic societies were corrupt, artificial, false,
inauthentic: opposed to nature, not its expression. The
divergence is important for what follows; and again, H. D.
Betz, for instance, blurs the Stoic–Cynic distinction, misled
in particular by a passage in Diogenes Laertius which runs,
'As to Law, there can be no civic society without it, and
there is no benefit from refined culture apart from civic

---

[12] F. G. Downing (1988b), 152–53; Tacitus, *Hist*. 5.1–13.

society . . .'. But this eulogy of law-based civic culture has been shown by M.-O. Goulet-Cazé to be a Stoicising addition by Laertius, intent on displaying a tidy succession from Cynicism to the Stoics. Cynics, as we shall see in more detail shortly, had in fact little if anything good to say about civic culture, let alone its laws. [13]

Much of this general debate can then also be found reproduced in Hellenistic Jewish writers such as Philo and Josephus.[14] However, though Paul could have been introduced to these debates by fellow Jews, it is much more likely that he would have encountered them more immediately; and certainly his converts would have.[15] In particular, we have no Jewish thinkers making anything like the disparaging comments on 'the law' that we find in Galatians. Philo, as noted, is often cited in this connection for his reference to 'some who take the positive laws as pointers to intellectual realities. They are unduly precise in their interpetations of these latter, while quite casually belittling the laws as stated.'[16] But these 'allegorisers' do not, by Philo's account, argue that observance is actually counter-productive, destructive of any good human relationship with Israel's God; they simply find practical observance unnecessary. Josephus' Zambrias (on whom more below) comes closest to Paul's response, in his

---

[13] Diogenes Laertius 6.72; and M.-O. Goulet-Cazé (1982) and (1986), 33.

[14] For a fuller discussion, F. G. Downing (1988b), 150–52, citing F. Schulz (1946), G. H. Sabine (1952); J. W. Jones (1956); and A. A. Schiller (1978); and cf., also, H. D. Betz (1979), 161–80.

[15] Cf. A. J. Malherbe (1989), 10, again: '[Paul] knew these traditions first hand and not through the mediation of other Jews who before him had come to terms with the Greek experience.'

[16] Philo, *De migratione* 89; cf. the discussion in J. M. G. Barclay (1996), 177–78, noted above.

designation of the Mosaic legislation as tyrannously enslaving; but Zambrias does not object to traditional rules as such, only to being forbidden to make his own choice of which nation's laws he is to follow. [17]

Some additional illustrations from the wider Hellenistic world seem appropriate. First we note some further – and commonplace – high evaluations of 'law' as such (in addition to the one just cited from Diogenes Laertius). Dio Chrysostom composed a sophist's pair of pieces, one praising written law, its companion praising unwritten custom in contrast with enacted law. Dio begins the former discourse thus:

> The Law is a guide for life (τοῦ βίου... ἡγεμών [cf. κατὰ τὸν νόμον ζῶντες, below]), an arbiter cities have agreed in common, a straight-edge that remains true (δίκαιος) throughout our affairs, one each of us must use to rule our own line through life – or else we'll go wickedly (πονηρός) astray. So those who keep (φυλάττοντες) the law have gained salvation (σωτηρία, security, well-being). But those who transgress (παραβαίνοντες) begin by destroying (ἀπολλύουσιν) themselves and then destroy other people, offering them example and encitement to anarchic violence (75.1).

No one has ever repented of recourse to the Law (2); it gives impartial advice in difficult situations (3), clearer than any oracle, and itself working by persuasion, not force (4); it defends piety (5); it secures justice (δικαιοσύνη) more effectively than does family feeling (6); and it rewards those who do good (7); it really is son of Zeus (ὁ τοῦ διὸς ὄντως υἱός) (8); succour in old age, school-teacher (διδάσκαλος) in youth (9). 'A city cannot possibly

---

[17] Josephus, *Ant.* 4.145–49; cf. the discussion in P. Borgen (1995), 33–39.

be saved if the law has been destroyed . . . banish the law from your life, it's as though you've lost your mind, you're landed in chaos and insanity' (10). The wide dissemination of views of this kind can be readily illustrated.[18] And these terms were readily taken up by Hellenistic Jewish writers in commending the *Torah*, from *The Letter of Aristeas* to Philo and Josephus.[19]

Paul's urban world was basically orderly and law-abiding, both in attitude and behaviour. Of course there were disturbances: Paul himself notes 'danger in towns' (2 Cor 11.26) and Acts takes occasional mob violence for granted.[20] But much more telling are the confident appeals to due legal process narrated by Luke (Acts 16.21, 37–38; 17.8–9; 18.12–13; and 19.38–40; cf. Rom 13.1–7, further discussed in chapter 8). It was a world where the maintenance of traditional – at best, ancestral – law and custom in all areas of life – temple, market place, home – engaged widespread popular consent. Many provinces had no troops stationed in them, and there was no other 'law-enforcement agency' than the leading citizens and their loyal slaves; yet goods were produced and marketed, taxes collected and delivered, roads, aqueducts, drains, baths and theatres were erected and maintained; and law-courts kept busy.[21]

When Paul arrived in a town in Galatia (or in any other province) he would need to have had some very telling arguments with which to counter the prevailing

---

[18] For further examples of this sort of eulogy for Law, see H. D. Betz (1979), 162–65.

[19] See, further, F. G. Downing (1985), 114–15, where a selection of the evidence is set out in tabular form; and J. M. G. Barclay (1996), passim.

[20] R. MacMullen (1966) and (1974), 66 and 171, n. 30.

[21] R. L. Fox (1986), 48–63; but see also Epictetus 3.13.9; Dio 40.8, 43.11–12.

ethos, arguments honed to cut through the standard defences of the kind Dio the sophist would trot out. As we shall see, it would seem that only from among the Cynics could Paul have been able to find the countervailing words and ideas that people were likely to understand and respond to. But the readiness with which some of Paul's converts were now responding to *Torah*-observant Jewish Christians seeking to recall them to the realisation of what they had lost in deserting their own ancestral codes without transferring to a new framework of law, would seem to show just how powerful the old ethos remained.

On reflection it appears fairly likely that those Paul now opposes in Galatia had indeed been emphasising the importance of 'the law' in much the sort of vein displayed in Dio's encomium. It was, they seem to have been insisting, 'the law' that stood against παραβάσεις, transgressions, and afforded true piety; it was law that gave life, that ensured δικαιοσύνη, justice, that was the teacher directing us to our ultimate well-being (compare Gal 3.19–25). In place of Paul's Cynic-like anarchism his Galatian converts were now being offered the Jewish–Christian *Torah*, law which would afford as much as and more than had been assured in the abandoned laws of their traditional civic communities.

The companion piece by Dio, *Discourse* 76, then in turn commends custom (ἔθος) and criticises codified law. For our immediate purposes this sophistic contrasting of the two is not important. In many other instances the two are seen as complementary,[22] and in what follows we shall note that both may be rejected together. But some of a sophist's disparagement of enacted law is itself worth noting. Law works by compulsion, force, tyrannously (1–2;

---

[22] See, again, F. G. Downing (1988b), 150–52.

compare Paul's 'confined', 'under restraint', Gal 3.23). It is a human invention (1; compare Paul's 'by angels through an intermediary' – not directly from God – 3.19–20). 'Laws create a community of slaves' (4) 'no better than a slave', says Paul (4.1, 3). Laws can always be changed, their power is evanescent (3); the period of the law's sway is over, insists Paul (4.4). 'The law is for the wicked' (4); 'for the sake of transgressions', says Paul, even more strikingly (3.19). (The availability of Dio's common vocabulary of terms and ideas to Paul elsewhere is further shown in 2 Corinthians 3.3 and 3.7: 'the dispensation of death . . .' '. . . not on tablets of stone, but on tablets of human hearts'; 'laws', says Dio, 'inflict punishments on our bodies . . . laws are preserved on tablets of wood or stone, customs are guarded in our souls' (76.3–4)). Some of Paul's critique is common currency.

We appreciate that criticism of laws and of customs (unwritten laws) was not unusual. Epictetus could write dismissively of 'these miserable laws of ours, laws of the dead, not laws of the Gods' (1.13.5). But Stoics still seem to have looked expectantly to the laws of states, especially to their common features, expecting some genuine reflection of 'the law of nature' (Musonius 15). And in practice, the Stoic position was to obey, anyway. As noted already, the claim that 'society cannot exist without law' in Diogenes Laertius 6.72 is a Stoic dogma.[23] State law only dealt with externals, irrelevancies (Epictetus 1.29.9–10). A Stoic obeys the law of nature in what really matters, his inner consent or refusal; for the rest, as Epictetus insists, whether the order came from Caesar or a governor or from the city council, 'I must always obey the state law in every detail'; and 'good citizens submit to the law of the state.'

---

[23] See n. 12 above.

Might a Stoic's reserve make him despise the laws? he is asked, and replies, what could make one readier to obey?[24]

Epicureans could also criticise customary law codes, where they did not lead to their ideal for community (Diogenes Laertius 10.152–53); but nonetheless themselves tended to conform, for prudential reasons (Diogenes Laertius 10.118; Epictetus 2.20.27; 3.7.12; cf. Cicero, *De natura deorum* 1.45, 123).[25]

(iii) Cynic disparagement of laws and customs

The main overt, principled *and practical* critique of both the laws and customs of their civic societies came, as has already been indicated, from the Cynics. They were disparaging in practice, not just in theory, of most or all traditional and positive law, and particularly those relating to family, property, status and authority as well as to dietary, excretory and sexual customs and tabus, and to prescribed purificatory rites.

Thus Antisthenes in the tradition found laws irrelevant. Diogenes rejects νόμος in favour of φύσις, law in favour of nature. For Diogenes, in effect, all belongs to the Gods, who of course share all with their friends: everything is common property for common use by those who live 'naturally', as divinely intended;[26] and this is

---

[24] Epictetus 1.12.7, 3.24.107 and 4.7.33; cf. S. Vollenweider (1989), 82–96.

[25] On the conformist tendencies of both Stoics and Epicureans as contrasted with Cynics, M.-O. Goulet-Cazé (1993), 141–42 (= (1996), 66–67).

[26] Diogenes Laertius 6.11 (Antisthenes); and 6.38, 6.72–73 for Diogenes. How the apparent appeal to 'the Gods' may have been intended it is impossible to tell; M.-O. Goulet-Cazé (1993), 157, argues

worked out in terms of sexual relations (any consenting woman with any man), in terms of food (any living thing could be food for any other) and in terms of 'dedicated' items. We consider these particular themes in more detail in the next chapter, in the light of Paul's presentation of his and others' attitudes to them in Corinth; but, to anticipate the conclusions reached there, it will be argued that those Paul criticises seem (or appear to have seemed to him, at least) to have been adopting a consistently and characteristically Cynic freedom in the face of the rules and conventions that for Paul as much as for most pagan contemporaries governed these issues. And many of the anecdotes in Diogenes Laertius show Diogenes and others not just enunciating but enacting these convictions, deliberately flouting convention, whether encoded or not.[27] This is to 'falsify the currency', conceding nothing to 'law'.[28]

So, closer to Paul's time, Demonax dismisses the laws as useless. Plutarch's Cynic Onesecritus is told by the Indian Calanus that Socrates and Pythagoras had too much regard for the laws.[29] Pseudo-Diogenes rejects the laws the Greeks have contrived for themselves as delusive and corrupt; 'bad laws for bad people', concludes Dio.[30] And

---

for agnosticism. J. L. Moles (1993), 270-71, argues for a more positive sense of belonging in a total 'cosmos' including the Gods. Cynics in our period seem to have varied; some (and especially Stoics with Cynic leanings) appear to display 'a warm religious strain' as we noted in the previous chapter, p. 47 and n. 64.

[27] E. g., Diogenes Laertius 6.29, 32, 34–36, 38, 46, 48, 61, 62, 64, 69; 82, 87–89, 94, 96–97; ps.-Lucian, *The Cynic* 10; cf. R. B. Branham (1993), (1994) and (1996).

[28] Diogenes Laertius 6.56 and 71.

[29] Lucian, *Demonax* 59; Plutarch, *Alexander* 65.3.

[30] Ps.-Diogenes 28.1; Dio 80.4; cf. H. W. Hollander and J. Holleman (1993), again, 286–89.

later, Maximus of Tyre chides Socrates for being a slave, obeying the law, in contrast to Diogenes, who is free.[31]

The Cynic reclaims the Golden Age before men's evil deeds led to laws being imposed which curtailed their freedom and institutionalised their wickedness. The point is made overtly by Seneca, relying initially on the Stoic Posidonius: when wickedess intruded on the Golden Age, laws became necessary; but Seneca then prefers the Cynic insistence that the life-style of the Golden Age, Diogenes with his cupped hands, is still practicable and preferable.[32] For a still more consistently Cynic position, one may compare pseudo-Anacharsis 9, and also Maximus of Tyre 36.4.[33] Cynics expected to live here and now, and well, a life independent of the laws and customs of cities and peoples.

Again we need to take note of Dio. We have seen him praising 'law', and then lauding custom in preference. Elsewhere he compares existing laws very unfavourably with divine law, and he agrees with Demonax that laws are ineffective: humans are so wicked, and so corrupted by social pressures, there is no possibility that laws will make them live properly.[34] But elsewhere, in *Discourse* 80, he

---

[31] Maximus of Tyre 36.6; G. Giannantoni (1990), V B 299.54–55; H. D. Betz (1979), 166, n. 37, quotes also from Philo, *De ebrietate* 198, on 'slavery to customs and laws' (non-Jewish ones, that is); and Josephus' Zambrias, critical of 'the tyranny of Moses' laws (*Ant.* 4.145–49), as noted above. This critique was clearly available to other Hellenistic Jewish writers. One or two Cynic writings, on the other hand, allow grudgingly a positive function for law: ps.-Crates 5 (but philosophy is much more effective), and ps.-Heraclitus 7.10 (laws may influence behaviour, but not character).

[32] Seneca, *Epistulae morales* 90.5–6; cf. 7–14.

[33] Cf. A. O. Lovejoy and G. Boas (1935), 117–52; and F. S. Jones (1987), 93 and 206–207, n. 154.

[34] Dio 36.23; 69.8.

introduces himself as a wandering philosopher who has abandoned all thought of wealth, fame and pleasure, behaving much as he has elsewhere pictured Diogenes (but also Odysseus). As a Cynic, then, he is a free man among slaves. Others quarrel over the rival codes of Solon and Draco, Numa and Zaleucus; but their own authors admitted theirs were imperfect, bad laws to suit bad people, imposing slavery on themselves and then building city walls to protect their servitude.[35] Dio continues:

> It's not just people in the past who said they would suffer all sorts of hardships in defence of their laws. Even people nowadays say that's where justice is, in whatever laws the poor unfortunates write out for themselves or inherit from others no better than themselves. But the law that is true and authoritative and clear they do not consider, still less take as their guide for life . . . . With the law of nature abandoned, totally eclipsed, and bedevilled as you are, you keep tight hold on your tablets and scrolls and stone slabs with their pointless squiggles. You transgressed the commands of Zeus long ago, yet are vigilant to ensure no one transgresses laws given by some fellow human or other (80.5).

The law of Zeus is the only one worth preserving and keeping (80.6). Then the thought of most people's slavery to law leads Dio into a standard Cynic meditation on the plethora of related fetters people create for themselves in the culture of the day, chained by gluttony, lust, greed and fame (80.7–14).

---

[35] Dio 80.1–4, in precise disagreement with the Stoic Posidonius (Seneca, *Epistulae morales* 90.6–7).

(iv) Paul the mould-breaker

Paul seems to have first made contact with the townspeople
of Galatia (north or south)[36] as a Jew who did not merely
criticise but in practice himself renounced 'the traditions of
his fathers' (Gal 1.14; cf. Phil 3.5–8). But much more than
that, he had encouraged those he met to do the same with
their own ancestral, civic laws and customs (Gal 4.8–10),
in the name of some new freedom. Paul, some years later,
at the time of writing, links 'pagan' Greek and Jewish law
so closely, switching so readily (or confusingly) between
them (Gal 3.19–4.10)[37] that we seem to have to accept that
for him, 'phenomenologically', they were, at least in this
context, aspects of the same alienating structures. To be
sure, Paul does not seem to have proposed any 'law of
nature' instead, but perhaps had already urged 'the law of
Christ', which it would be possible both to keep and be
free (Gal 5.1, 14; 6.2). Paul's 'pagan' Galatian converts
were encouraged to abandon all their more obvious social
markers - festivals, dietary and other purity rules, all codes
regulating social rank, race and gender, rules that
structured civic life. These were to be seen not as enabling,
but enslaving; renounce them for Christ, and you would
enjoy a real freedom. (It seems not a little unfortunate that
John Barclay, despite having seen how firmly Paul opposes

---

[36] See the commentaries. A decision between north and south
'Galatia' is not important for the present discussion: Paul is, as we
noted in chapter 1, addressing acculturated Hellenes whether northern
or southern; cf. J. Murphy-O'Connor (1996), 24–31, 159–62.

[37] H. Räisänen [1983] (1986), 18–23.

the laws of both cultures, Jewish and non-Jewish, nonetheless fails to note the Cynic analogy.)[38]

It is hard to imagine how Paul could have been seen
as anything other than a renegade Cynic Jew. Cynics were
the only other people around who reached these very
negative conclusions, acted on them themselves, and urged
others to emulate them. And if Paul had wanted to
articulate a programme along these lines, it would have
been from an awareness of Cynic discourse very much
more than in any other source that he would initially, and
for pagans, have found clusters of words, of ideas-in-
words, suited to such an aim. It was the only currently
available field of discourse in which such a stance could
have come to expression. This is still not to determine that
in Paul's case Cynicism was the major spur; yet neither
(agreeing with Malherbe again), is it to suggest that he had
to go looking around to find this vocabulary.[39] But it is to
say that Cynic discourse would have been the obvious
language in which he might hope at all readily to articulate
his position in conversation with others and in reflection on
his own as he came to form it and make it understood.
There would have been no need, no spur to produce such
language *de novo* when so much that was apposite was
currently available.

As a Hellenistic Pharisee (Phil 3.5) Paul would
almost certainly have been aware of Stoicism and its

---

[38] J. M. G. Barclay (1996), 381–95. Of course, J. T. Sanders (1997) is
right to advise us that Paul then introduces his own boundary
definitions, as any leader of a new group would. Cynics and
Epicureans and others all had their own. The point is that Paul's
distinguish Pauline Christians from all their wider civic communities,
as well as from established outsider groups, such as local Jews in
particular, in ways most closely matched by the Cynics.

[39] Cf. A. J. Malherbe (1989), 8.

discussion of 'the law' (as were the author of 4 Maccabees, and Josephus, and Philo; and if Luke is right in placing Paul's origin in Tarsus, that had a strong Stoic tradition). Paul would then have been aware of Cynicism as the original nurse and continuing sparring-partner of Stoicism. But he is much more likely to have been aware of Cynicism in its own right; as Dio notes, the Tarsians were also familiar with Cynic philosophers.[40]

Later, when Galatian Christians are now being urged by others to adopt Jewish law (or elements at least of the *Torah*), Paul has, of course, to adduce arguments from (carefully re-interpreted) Jewish Scripture, from Abraham and Moses (Gal 3). Yet even now, as we have already seen in the previous section *(iii)*, many of the key terms he takes it are being used in favour of 'law' are similar to those of Dio's sophistic law-and-order piece, and much of the logic of the counter-argument, many of the issues touched on, are in fact very similar to those of Dio in Cynic mood. Though his illustrations are from the *Torah* (Abraham and Moses), it is Cynic-like language that Paul still deploys, the language we may best imagine he had used when first he made contact in the Galatian towns. In Dio's case, this is what someone who knows the arguments in favour of settled law and custom also knows must be said to counter them. If Paul were now to counter the law-and-order propaganda of the 'Judaisers', it would almost inevitably have been with the logic of the Cynic anarchistic counter-propaganda with which he had in all likelihood at first come to 'think-and-express' his arguments: law in enacted codes has no direct divine origin, law enslaves, law is ineffective, law makes no one righteous, law merely condemns, law encourages wickedness, or is at best a harsh

---

[40] Dio 33.13; 34.2.

discipline to be abandoned as soon as possible . . . . (On these last two themes, see below).

Of course Paul was not a replica run-of-the-tub Cynic (allowing, too, as we have noted, that Cynics were never uniform: one very 'common' strand was in fact their individualism). But no designated Cynic of the first century that we know of proclaimed a crucified Galilaean Jew as the focus of his challenge to all inherited custom and law. Yet when Paul writes to new Christians in Galatia who are being lured back into a high regard for 'the law' in Jewish guise he does little or nothing to hide all these Cynic resonances.

With the Corinthians Paul has to be more circum-spect, and (as we shall argue) along with others, seems at times to be moving towards a rather more Stoic position. Stoic strands are still clearer in Philippians. Then writing to Rome Paul urges yet more respect for those in authority than does even his contemporary, the Stoic Epictetus (Rom 13.1–7).[41] But at this juncture, addressing the Galatians, Paul retains much more of his early radicalism. What he had orginally said against the laws and customs of their civic communities he maintains as firmly when the laws and customs of his own people are now proposed to replace them. Nothing in the field of right, righteousness, justice, is gained by the kinds of law-observant behaviour proposed (Gal 2.16; 3.11).[42] Admirers of the law (like Dio

---

[41] See T. Engberg-Pedersen (1995b) on Paul's very Stoic understanding of community in Philippians; and also the very useful study by H. Moxnes (1995). He concludes (for Rom 12.17–21 and 13.1–7) 'We do not [I would add 'now'] meet with the Cynic aspects found in Dio's radical criticism [sc. of the ethos of civic life], but rather Stoic ideals of harmony and concord' (230).

[42] We have already noted J. D. G. Dunn's argument (1990), (1991) and (1992), as in n. 3 above, that it is food, purity, circumcision, Sabbath

in *Discourse* 75) might claim that we can rely on the law to foster peace, justice, temperance, faithfulness (πίστις); it prevents violence, and exalts virtue, excellence (ἀρετή) in general. Paul, by contrast, insists it is only by renouncing any such reliance that we can allow the Spirit to bring love, joy, peace, patience, kindness, goodness, faithfulness, gentleness and self-control to fruition (Gal 5.22).

(v) For the sake of transgressions; and the pedagogue

Paul's own first response to his question, 'Why then the law?' is to say it was τῶν παραβάσεων χάριν προσετέθη: it was added for the sake of transgressions (Gal 3.19). The standard interpretation is in terms of v. 22 and then Romans 4.15 and 5.13: law has the positive function of making wickedness deliberate and culpable and so, punishable.[43] Certainly Stoics could argue that laws were brought in, 'added' (προσετέθη), to cope with human decline,[44] and it could be that the image of the παιδαγωγός (to which we turn in a moment) might reinforce this interpretation. But, as we have just seen, Paul in Galatians allows no other positive results from law in

---

perhaps, public 'identity markers', that are at issue, not the thorough, total observance (Gal 2.14) which Paul here insists, as do both Stoics and Pharisees, is the only way to take law seriously, if you are going down that path at all (Cicero, *De paradoxa Stoicorum* 25–26; A. Segal (1990), 120 and n. 7.

[43] Cf. H. Hübner [1978] (1984), 26; H. D. Betz (1979), 165–67, again; R. N. Longenecker (1990), 138–39, prefers to leave it vague. J. D. G. Dunn (1993), 188–90, argues for 'in order to provide some sort of remedy for transgressions (cf. the value placed on law in Hellenistic society . . .' [citing Betz, 164]). But nothing else in Galatians suggests this.

[44] Seneca, *Epistulae morales* 90.5–14, again.

any sense, there are no positive effects of law observance; there is no reassurance at all in this letter that the law is '*not* sin', but 'holy and just and good' (Rom 7.7, 12). It seems we should accept that here in Galatians Paul is advancing a consistently negative criticism of law (or 'the law').[45] It was indeed added to produce transgressions. And if this is what Paul meant, then the closest analogy is in some of our Cynic sources.

Thus, as we have seen, Dio has Solon promulgate 'bad laws . . . laws to suit bad people' (πονηροὺς ἔγραψε νόμους . . . τοὺς ἀρέσοντας πονηροῖς ἔγραψεν).[46] This would seem to entail not simply that the laws are seen as ineffective (as in pseudo-Heraclitus 7);[47] here they actually suit wickedness, codify it, encourage it. People are enslaved by these laws: not just bound by rules, but bound to live counter to 'the commands of Zeus', under a curse (ἀρά; cf. κατάρα, Gal 3.10) – until some wandering Cynic arrives to display the only genuine freedom.

So, too, pseudo-Diogenes tells 'the Hellenes', 'In devising laws for yourselves you assigned yourselves the greatest, the most extensive delusion. All they afford is a witness to your ingrained wickedness.'[48] The invective that follows is much as in Dio: the society these laws reflect and structure is corrupt throughout; gluttonous, drink-

---

[45] So H. Hübner ([1978] (1984), 26–30; H. D. Betz (1979), 164–67.

[46] Dio 80.4–6; cf. J. H. Hollander and J. Holleman (1993), 283.

[47] Ps.-Heraclitus 9 is as dismissive of public life as currently regulated and administered as are Dio 80 and ps.-Diogenes 28; but ps.-Heraclitus 9 is more optimistic in theory about the likely effectiveness of 'good' laws which mirror 'the law of nature' (9.1, 7); cf. ps.-Heraclitus 7.10. Here as elsewhere Cynics differ – as, to some readers, Paul himself seems to in his evaluations of the law, in Romans. Comparison of similarities and differences remains worth the effort.

[48] Ps.-Diogenes 28.1.

sodden, envious, violent. Such a society affords no peace, joy, justice, self-control; (compare all of pseudo-Diogenes 28 with Gal 5.19–23).

Cynics have, of course, no monopoly on vice-lists. Their significance here, however, is to show that customary laws are seen as an important part of the problem of human societal wickedness, and no part of the solution. As we have seen, this is far from any other conventional view of law (or law and custom). Not even all Cynics went as far in their criticisms.[49] If Paul had been as forthright as that in his first approach to people in Galatia, the similarity on this issue between his message and that of the more radical Cynics would have been hard to ignore; and here he is (presumably) reaffirming this unsettling stance.

This is not to propose that the argument is identical in both, but it is to note that the attitudes to 'the law' articulated in Galatians, in Dio 80 and in pseudo-Diogenes 28 have much that is significant and that would have been seen as significant, in common.

Perhaps the model of the law as child-minder, παιδαγωγός, suggests a more positive stance, even enough to modify the very negative conclusions suggested so far? Much has been written on the word as it appears here in Galatians 3.24. D. J. Lull has assembled a wide range of sources from which to draw out what the image might convey.[50] Accounts of actual child-minders range from the sadistic disciplinarian to the admired and valued childhood friend. Without further guidance from the context, the word would probably convey a sense of an

---

[49] See n. 47 above.

[50] For what follows see especially D. J. Lull (1986); N. H. Young (1987); and H. Betz (1979), 177.

uncomfortable but still positive παιδεία, upbringing; yet, clearly, one an adult should no longer need.

Though Lull does include Cynic and near-Cynic sources in his discussion, he underestimates the relevance of their distinctive use of the model. A Cynic παιδ-αγωγός brings his young or adult pupil through harsh treatment, specifically from a slavish discipline to freedom, the transition Paul indicates here. In the *chreia* tradition Diogenes offers himself as a slave-master, δεσπότης, for Xeniades, his potential buyer; and is accepted as such. The Cynic's calling is 'to rule men' (ἄρχειν).[51] The anecdote reappears in Plutarch and in Philo.[52] Epictetus' idealised Cynic is a παιδαγωγός who must first demonstrate in practice his own freedom, before he can supervise (ἐπιστατεῖν) others.[53] Lucian's Cynic for sale claims to be a liberator of his fellow humans – but only by subjecting them to hardship.[54] But the most significant instances come in the *Cynic Epistles*. In yet another account of Diogenes sold by pirates, he promises his fellow captives that their enslavement will end in a more real freedom, freedom from luxury; and then, again, himself promises to be the master of any purchaser who is himself similarly enslaved to pleasure and lethargy. Pseudo-Diogenes promises Dionysius 'an Athenian παιδαγωγός . . . keen sighted, swift and precise, bearing a very painful whip'. This Cynic will, by strict discipline, 'save' the tyrant from

---

[51] Diogenes Laertius 6.74; cf. 6.29, 31. It was intriguing to find J. Klausner ([1943] 1944) refer to Talmud *Kidd.* 20a, *'Arakhin* 30b, *Siphra* 7.3 - 'Whoever buys a Hebrew slave is like one buying a master for himself.'

[52] Plutarch, *An vitiositas* 499B; Philo, *Quod omnis probus liber sit* 123; cf. Teles 24H.

[53] Epictetus 3.22.16–18; cf. 3.19.5–6.

[54] Lucian, *Philosophies for Sale* 8–9.

his present slavish condition; only with a whip and a master can he be saved from the way of life of his forefathers (29.1–2, 4). The model of the child-minder deployed by Paul in Galatians 3.24 is that of the harsh Cynic disciplinarian whose charge ultimately comes through to freedom.[55]

None of these examples suggests 'the law' as the παιδαγωγός. (Dio's encomium for the law sees the law as a διδάσκαλος for the young, but very much one that is kindly, and rules by persuasion.)[56] It is appropriate, however, to turn to Philo for further insight into the way the model of the child-minder can be deployed. Betz and Lull both remind us that Philo takes up with some enthusiasm the (Cynic) stress on our human need for stern discipline, while only rarely including laws and customs as that discipline's agents: 'trained by parents, child-minders, teachers, and, much more important, by the sacred laws and unwritten customs'.[57] In fact, Philo shies away from a purely Cynic emphasis on physical ἄσκησις and renunciation.[58] Nonetheless, given this reserve, he does seem to reproduce on one occasion the Cynic insistence on a period of harsh πόνος as an initial subjection to a kind of slavery,

---

[55] C. E. Glad (1995), 89–98, shows clearly that Epicureans, too, could exercise a harsh psychogogy; it was not a Cynic monopoly, though the theme is found 'in greater clarity' in Cynic sources (89, 97). There is no reference in our Epicurean texts to law as pedagogue.

[56] Dio 70.9 with 4–5. This passage nonetheless has some bearing on our discussion. The distinction between teacher, trainer and child-minder is not absolute, as the passages in the *Cynic Epistles* show; and cf., again, Epictetus 3.22.16–18, where παιδαγωγός and παιδευτής are used as synonyms for the function of the ideal (Stoic) Cynic philosopher.

[57] Philo, *De legatione* 115–16; cf. *De migratione* 115–16, 'child-minders, teachers, parents . . . laws'.

[58] Cf. *De fuga* 33–36; *De congressu* 25–28.

where in fact a Cynic withstanding of 'hunger and thirst, cold and heat, and all that enslaves most other people' is part of the training. The law is given in a place that means 'bitterness'; God 'afflicts' in the sense of 'disciplines, admonishes, chastens'; and this affliction is a form of slavery. One becomes 'a subject, a slave, obeying orders'. Then, quoting Proverbs 3.11–12 ('whom the Lord loves he rebukes, and chastises every son he acknowledges'), Philo in fact promises that the end of the law's bitter slave treatment is one's acknowledgment by God as a son: again, much as in Galatians 4.1–7.[59] Although here the word παιδαγωγός does not itself occur, yet most of its associations are present, along with the harsh Cynic insistence on slavish toil.

Whatever the source or sources of Paul's child-minder model, he employs a Cynic form of it as part of his very Cynic downgrading of 'the law'; even though we have no note of any named Cynic using the image in quite this manner, Paul must be accorded as much right as any other language user to deploy common images in a fresh way in common contexts. The word παιδαγωγός, used in a very Cynic disparagement of law, conveys a harshness that in no way softens or makes more positive what Paul is here saying.

(vi) Further thoughts on law

Paul's radical challenge to accepted laws and custom, and so to 'the law' as such, was by no means restricted to Galatia, even though there is no such discussion of law in

---

[59] Philo, *De congressu* 163, 165, 172, 175, 177 (and 179, it is the power of the law that enforces this chastening affliction).

the Thessalonian and Corinthian letters as we find in Galatians and later in Romans. As was pointed out above, new Christians in Macedonia and in Achaea, just as much as those in Galatia, had been drawn to break with the codes and conventions of their ancestors and of the towns where they lived as citizens, as resident aliens or as slaves (1 Thess 1.9; 1 Cor 12.2). Presumably this relative silence is to be explained by assuming that at the time of writing no one had arrived to urge the adoption of the Jewish law - or aspects of it - to replace those inherited systems not long abandoned. Significantly, the Corinthians could be expected to make sense of Paul's brief but very negative aside, 'the power of sin is the law' (1 Cor 15.56), whose echoes of a Cynic-sounding critique of Law have been pointed out by Hollander and Holleman. [60]

To replace a new convert's inherited custom there is now most importantly the example of the teacher and of other followers: not a uniquely Cynic alternative, but certainly a prominent feature of Cynicism, to which we shall return later. As A. J. Malherbe explains, most non-Cynic philosophers 'were hesitant to call others to follow their own examples . . . Paul in contrast, asserts that others had already become imitators of him and his associates and the Lord.' [61]

---

[60] For a Cynic reading, H. W. Hollander and J. Holleman (1993).

[61] 1 Thess 1.6, 2.14; 2 Thess 3.7, 9; 1 Cor 4.16, 11.1; in Cynic sources, it is the narrating of the example of Diogenes and others that counts, the encouragement to imitate is implicit; but cf. ps.-Crates 20; ps.-Diogenes 14, (37.6? 38.4?); ps.-Heraclitus 5.1; 6.4 (imitating God); Lucian, *Demonax* 2; *Philosophies for Sale* 8; ps.-Lucian, *The Cynic* 14. Cynics are, as noted, not the only moralists who included teaching by example (cf. R. A. Burridge (1992), 186); but with other approaches eschewed, example becomes the main persuasive tool: A. J. Malherbe (1989), 57–58; A. A. Long (1996), 31.

However much we may discern the continuing positive influence on Paul of his past formation by Jewish law and custom, nowhere in the Thessalonian letters does he base his appeal on the authority of Jewish (or of 'pagan') codes or conventions.

As time goes by, however, there are changes. Some aspects of the Cynic devaluation of codes and customs remain, but much is softened; and, as already noted, analogies with Stoicism become much more significant. There is every sign that in his first approaches in Corinth Paul had been as radical as in Galatia. We have noted something of this already, and will consider the Corinthian letters in some little detail in what follows. But by the time that he writes the letters to Corinth, as others have discerned and as we shall in due course argue, Paul is much more cautious about preaching overt freedom of action, and rather happier to urge an inner, more Stoic-seeming autonomy (1 Cor 6.12).[62] So, despite his rejection of 'worldly wisdom' in 1 Corinthians 1–3, despite his refusal to be bound by the clear implication of a command of Jesus (9.14–15), and despite his insistence that he is 'not under law' (9.20), Paul in fact makes a number of overt appeals to convention (3.16–17; 4.2; 5.1; 7.20–24; 9.7–12). 11.1–16, on women's hair-styles, is just the most blatant.

In 2 Corinthians we have already noticed the similar disparagement of codes on tablets with their penal clauses, in 3.6–7 as in Dio 76.3–4, as well as in Dio 80; and we shall note in more detail Paul relying heavily on the impression made by the example of his own poverty and austere life-style.

---

[62] S. Vollenweider (1988), 24–5; for the divergent approaches of Paul, J. W. Drane (1975), 2–3, summarising the book's argument (but too easily convinced that the freedom party in Corinth were gnostic).

Counting 'righteousness under law' as so much dung (Phil 3.6–8) retains strong Cynic resonances. But Philippians as a whole displays Stoic rather than Cynic traits.[63] As just one example, Paul's self-sufficiency, coping with plenty as well as with want (Phil 4.11), is Stoic; Cynics claim to be more consistently austere.

Although the repudiation of homosexual practice in Romans 1.26–27 may be more in line with Cynicism, at least as it evolved, than with Stoic sexual ethics,[64] the 'natural theology' of Romans 1.19–21 is more Stoic than Cynic, and so is the 'natural law' argument of 2.13–15 (and v. 27). It is Stoic rather than Cynic to expect 'natural morality' to coincide with what 'the law' requires; Cynics would expect 'the law of nature' to induce a very different behaviour than that inculcated by any code. And here 'the law' is very clearly the Jewish *Torah* throughout (3.2; 7.7; 9.4), without the ambiguity we found in Galatians, where νόμος seemed at times to embrace 'law' as such. In particular is 13.1–7 very close to the stance of Epictetus, and very unlike the traditional refusal of respect for authority evinced in the Cynic tradition.[65] Traces of the old radicalism remain. It is the law, 'the old written code' that arouses our passions (7.5). But it is 'sin' now that enslaves, rather than the law, it is really sin using the commandment that incites transgression, while 'the law is holy, and the commandment is holy and just and good' (7.12, 16; cf. 8.3–4). Paul to the Romans is Stoically undisturbing, firmly on the side of order and law.

---

[63] T. Engberg-Pedersen (1995).

[64] References, F. G. Downing (1992), 52 and n.97.

[65] For Epictetus, see above. Most of the items in the foregoing will be dealt with in more detail in succeeding chapters; Paul and Stoicism mostly in chapter 9.

(vii) *Conclusion*

In Galatians Paul says negative things about 'law' that look very like attitudes characteristically - and often distinctively - enunciated and put into practice by Cynics: law in enacted codes has no direct divine origin, law enslaves, law is ineffective, law makes no one righteous, law merely condemns, law encourages wickedness, or is at best a harsh discipline to be abandoned as soon as possible. It would seem very likely that he would have had to deploy such talk from the very start, when he encouraged the abandonment of inherited codes without even substituting some other ancient tradition. To return, then, to our five interlinked theses: still at the time of writing, Paul would (*a*) have sounded and seemed very much like a Cynic; so much so that (*b*) he could hardly not have realised it and intended it. But, again (*c*), these Cynic opinions are integral to his message and life-style, from the start, and in his argument in the letter, right at the heart of what he was about, far from any superficial window-dressing.

We have only touched on the issue (*d*) of others showing they understood Paul this way by pressing a Cynic stance more radically than Paul himself (we shall note more of this in the next chapter), and we have also only noted in passing Paul himself finally losing most of his apparent early enthusiasm for a Cynic interpretation of the gospel in favour of a Stoic conformist quietism. (The approaches (*e*) of other early Christian communities to 'law' we shall touch on in chapter 10.)

4

ALREADY THE SCEPTRE AND THE KINGDOM

(i) Taking Cynic freedom too far

Paul had encouraged people in Galatia to break free from the inherited codes and conventions of their civic communities, or at least, from many important elements in them. And when more recently they were now being urged to abandon this Cynic-looking antinomianism, and to adopt instead some important strands in an alternative ancient code, that of Paul's own Jewish people, Paul, as we have just reminded ourselves, reasserted his opposition to such pointless servitude. It would seem at least *prima facie* likely that when Paul encouraged people in Corinth to 'abandon their dumb idols' (1 Cor 12.2), it entailed much the same wide-ranging break with customary norms and traditions as is indicated in Galatians, the socio-cultural apostasy so excoriated by our Graeco-Roman writers. [1]

However, there would seem to have been some in the young Christian community in Corinth who were now pressing the logic of Paul's Christian–Cynic antinomianism much further than he himself could accept. Paul's is mostly a gentle, even genteel Cynicism (like that of a Dio or a Demonax), 'gentle as a nurse',[2] gentle with others

---

[1] See above, ch. 1, 15–16, and n. 40.

[2] 1 Thess. 2.7; cf. A. J. Malherbe (1970).

(mostly) though severe with himself (1 Cor 9.27). But once custom and convention are questioned, one persons's instinctive, 'natural', sense of right and wrong, of 'helpful' and 'unhelpful', will not always be everyone else's. At least, so it seems in this instance. The philosophical conclusion that now 'all things are lawful' (πάντα . . . ἔξεστιν, 1 Cor 6.12) is being taken far too far. 'Neither Jew nor Greek' could still be recalled without any unwelcome interpretation, as could 'neither slave nor free' (1 Cor 12.13), though it was perhaps safer to have ἔιτε . . . ἔιτε, 'whether Jew or Greek, whether slave or free'. But 'no male and female' seems now to be far too disruptive a slogan to be recalled explicitly; at most there may be apologetic echoes, as in the assertion of limited common rights for man and woman in marriage (1 Cor 7.5); and, more generally, 'neither the man without (or 'different from') the woman nor the woman . . . the man' (1 Cor 11.11–12).[3] This present chapter is particularly concerned with element (*d*) of the argument of the study as a whole: others interpreting their Christian faith in Cynic terms too radical for Paul, even though he himself may initially have prompted such a reading, by his own words and life-style.

Some people were indeed reaching conclusions Paul could not countenance at all, and, still worse, they were acting on them, in a wide range of relationships. There was incest (1 Cor 5.1–2), there was talk at least of resort to prostitutes (1 Cor 6.12–20) and objections were being raised against formal marriage (1 Cor 7.1). Some unavoidably charismatic women were rejecting traditional gender-marking by hair-style (1 Cor 11.1–16), and many were (it seems) refusing the gender role of silent docility when teaching and discussion were under way (1 Cor 14.

---

[3] Cf. E. Schlüssler-Fiorenza (1983), 219 and 229–30.

34–36). People were taking quarrels to civic courts (1 Cor 6.1–8). Meat offered to idols was being eaten, even in temple dining rooms (1 Cor 8.1–13; 10.14–30); at the Lord's supper some were eating just as they pleased, and did not so much as 'discern the body' (1 Cor 11.17–22 and 29). And these were not the only problems Paul discerned. He was convinced that there was far too much emphasis on rhetorical prowess (and perhaps on particular rhetors, 1 Cor 1.10–4.7); as well as too much attention paid to ecstatic speech (1 Cor 12–14). There was also disbelief in a future resurrection of dead Christians (1 Cor 15).

It is by no means clear in all this how well informed Paul in fact was.[4] It is not even clear to what extent he thought the same individuals or one particular group responsible for the convictions and practices (and perhaps still only potential dangers) he opposed, or whether he saw these as the several aberrations of distinct groups or of separate individuals. Some interpreters have wanted to apportion the issues among the claimed party leaders of 1 Corinthians 1.12: Paul, Apollos, Kephas (and possibly Christ).[5] Others have sought to find a single unifying motif underlying all the main issues raised, perhaps 'gnosticism',[6] perhaps charismatic fervour (maybe among some of the women),[7] perhaps argumentative dissension as such,[8] perhaps wealth and concomitant social distinctions and pressures,[9] perhaps 'honour and prestige'.[10]

---

4   M. M. Mitchell (1991), 301–303.
5   L. L. Wellborn (1987); M. M. Mitchell (1991), 67–68 and notes.
6   W. Schmithals (1971).
7   T. Söding, (1994), 69–92; A. C. Wire (1990).
8   M. M. Mitchell (`1991).
9   G. Theissen (1982).
10 S. M. Pogoloff (1992); A. D. Clarke (1993).

It will be urged here that what contemporary hearers would most likely have picked out as dominant would have been a strong Cynic flavour to many of these 'libertine' attitudes and actions as discerned and opposed, not least because that is how Paul himself seems to be characterising them and attempting to counter them, at times himself deploying further strands of Cynic-seeming tradition on his side of the argument.

(ii) Already?

'Already you are filled! Already you have become rich. Without us you have become kings!' (ἤδη κεκορεσμένοι, ἤδη ἐπλουτήσατε· χωρὶς ἡμῶν ἐβασιλεύσατε, 1 Cor 4.8). Commentators tend to discern here Stoic and Cynic τόποι indifferently.[11] For Stoics only the wise man 'is rich', 'is king'. But the 'is' for Stoics repres-ents an all but impossible ideal. Because all faults are equal the tiniest defect in someone's character or action tells that this is not really a 'wise man' at all.[12] Real people, as Cicero explains, are at best 'good', on the long journey to absolute perfection.[13] Cynics, on the other hand, as we have already noted, professeded to have a shortcut to virtue, the σύντομος ὁδός. 'We are indeed already (ἤδη) free,' says pseudo-Crates.[14] Cynics can claim they already enjoy the

---

[11] E. g., H. Conzelmann [1969] (1975), 87.

[12] Cicero, *De finibus* 1.61; 3.75–76; 4.7, 21–22; *De officiis* 3.12–17; *Paradoxa Stoicorum* 5, 33–52; Diogenes Laertius 7.121–29; Lucian, *Hermotimus* 1–8, 76–77 (cf. Giannantoni (1990), V B 302: Cynics claim just that). See also A. J. Malherbe (1976), 201–203.

[13] Cicero, *De officiis* 3.16.

[14] Ps.-Crates 8.

kingdom of Kronos.[15] 'Immediately they have their sceptre, their kingdom', scoffs Epictetus of the Cynics who shun the Stoic long haul. All that has really happened 'already', Epictetus counters, is that their premature shoots have got frost-bitten.[16] 'Oh, so you've arrived, have you?' is what critics say ironically to self-confident Cynics. No one with pretensions to Stoic philosophy would dream of inviting such a riposte.

In the light of these passages it seems most likely that Paul is mocking people for claims that sound Cynic to him, claims that in fact he seems to be taking as overtly Cynic. If he were taking them to be making the quite improbable claim to have reached a Stoic absolute perfection, the standard and obvious rejoinder would have been to point at once to some admitted failing of theirs, however minimal. 'Have you ever met a Stoic, one who's reached the top . . . perfectly happy?' asks Lucian's Lycinus, and Hermotimus confesses he has not.[17] 'Show me a Stoic!' begs Epictetus, only to admit, 'You can't find a true specimen at all . . .'. He laments, he's not even seen someone on the way to that perfection, not one who even wholeheartedly desires it.[18] Paul offers no such reference to any failing, be it never so minor, no such blemish that

---

[15] Lucian, *Runaways* 17; for the 'short cut', ps.-Crates 16; Diogenes Laertius 6.104; Lucian, *Sale* 11; M.-O. Goulet-Cazé (1986), 22–31.

[16] Epictetus 4.8.34–43; and for that 'royal rule', cf. Lucian, *Runaways* 12 (τυραννίδα); Diogenes Laertius 6.30, 36, 74; ps.-Crates 34; ps.-Diogenes 29; ps.-Heraclitus 8.2; Lucian, *Sale*, 10 (ἀρχή); Maximus of Tyre 36.6 (Giannantoni (1990) V B 299).

[17] Lucian, *Hermotimus* 76–77, again.

[18] Epictetus 2.19.24–25; cf. 3.7.17: no true Stoic disciple would claim perfection. For sure, Stoics, too, could deploy the Cynic short-cut; but the difference lay in the τέλος, the goal of absolute perfection which alone constituted wisdom and happiness, Diogenes Laertius 7.121.

would invalidate a Stoic claim to have reached perfection, to be rich, to be royal. Instead he reminds his hearers through his own example of the harsh ἄσκησις by which alone, as they should know, the *Cynic* goal may be swiftly and authentically reached (1 Cor 4.9–13).[19] If he had seen their stance as Stoic, or were trying to mock it as implying a Stoic claim, the response of the following lines would have been quite irrelevant.

It is not being suggested that this on its own decides the question of the pervasive stance of those being addressed here and in what follows, even in Paul's interpretation; but it does make it most likely that Paul thought he was confronting people making either overtly Cynic claims, or claims very like those characteristically and distinctively made by Cynics. We now consider to what extent the discussions and arguments which follow are consistent with this already strong indication.

(iii) Free for anything

'I am free to do anything', Paul goes on to say (1 Cor 6.11), 'everything is legitimately in my power' (πάντα μοι ἔξεστιν), quoting or imagining yet another claim made by some in Corinth. 'The language points to a previous history in Stoicism', asserts Conzelmann. 'Only the Stoics and Cynics provide material for comparison.'[20] The early Stoics retained much from their Cynic origins, including,

---

[19] The specifically Cynic character of Paul's voluntary hardships will be argued at length later; but cf. in particular M. Ebner (1991).

[20] H. Conzelmann ([1969] 1975), 108. W. Deming (1996), arguing against any 'libertine' interpretation of 1 Corinthians 5–6, completely ignores the Cynic evidence and its many echoes here, and makes no reference to Mark Plunkett's important study (1988).

so it seems, the conviction that cannibalism and incest
might be 'natural' and therefore right.[21] But later Stoics
carefully distanced themselves from such Cynic
radicalism.[22] In our period it was only the Cynics who
retained a reputation for repudiating dietary and sexual
tabus.

In his doxography for Diogenes, Diogenes Laertius
tells that the Cynic 'advocated community of women,
recognising no other marriage than the union of the man
inviting and the woman who consents'. With no further
restriction specified, incest would clearly not be excluded;
and then only a little later Diogenes is credited with a
version of Oedipus.[23] Dio has Diogenes explicitly discuss
the acceptability of incest in connection with the Oedipus
story, mocking the latter for bewailing his past actions,
when 'domestic fowls make no fuss about such unions,
nor do dogs, nor donkeys; nor the Persians, counted as the
best people in Asia.'[24] The Cynic founder also 'saw no
impropriety in stealing from a temple or eating the flesh of
any living thing whatsoever' (cannibalism included).[25]
Writing in the first century BCE Philodemus of Gadara
tells us that such were the views put forward in Diogenes'
Πολιτεία, and that this specifically implied that the
pairing of men with their sisters and with their mothers was
permissible.[26]

---

[21] Diogenes Laertius 7.121 (cannibalism), 131 (wives in common; on
this as legitimising incest, see below); the charge is made explicitly by
Philodemus: R. G. Andria (1980); cf. also Giannantoni (1990), V A
141. For what follows see F. G. Downing (1993a).

[22] Cicero, *De officiis* 1.128, 148.

[23] Diogenes Laertius 6.72; 6.80.

[24] Dio 10.29-30; cf. Giannantoni (1990), V A 141, Antisthenes.

[25] Diogenes Laertius 6.73.

[26] Philodemus, *On the Stoics* VII-IX, in R. G. Andria (1980), 131–32.

It is only here among Cynics in the cultural context of the Graeco-Roman world of the day that we find articulated views at all close to those discerned by Paul in Corinth. So Paul writes, 'It is actually reported that there's sexual misconduct among you of a kind you don't find even among other peoples - someone is cohabiting with his father's wife. And you are proud of it!' (1 Cor 5.1–2); 'such boasting' (5.6). Conzelmann notes that such a union seems to have been forbidden in Roman law,[27] and of course, most renderings of the Oedipus story take the enormity of incest for granted. It is quite clear that in Paul's view this Jewish, Greek (and Roman) convention has binding force. To be able to engage in and affirm such actions with self-congratulation, to insist on their legitimacy, actually to boast about them, demands either the creation of a discourse *de novo*, and then its acceptance, or the availability of an existing field of language allowing such forbidden intentional actions to be performed and recounted with pride.[28] The only local cultural context of which we know where people might be encouraged, even be offered the option to take pride in just such a breach of convention, this freedom from artificial restraint, would be in the Cynic tradition.

The continuing argument here, then, is that in 1 Corinthians it is Cynic (and Cynic rather than Stoic) usage that informs the views and behaviour Paul discerns and criticises. Admittedly, many scholars would still prefer to imagine a first-century pervasive but otherwise unevidenced Gnosticism, assembled by means of a simple – and

---

[27] H. Conzelmann [1969] (1975), 96, quoting both Gaius' *Institutes* and Cicero.

[28] See the discussion of intentional acts in F. G. Downing (1995a); and, e.g., D. Davidson (1980) and J. R. Searle (1983).

forced – 'mirror reading' of Paul.[29] But when we already have in Cynicism a quite richly evidenced and contemporary cultural context that makes good sense of what Paul reports, it seems quite arbitrary and unhelpful to import hypothetical projections (such as gnosticism) *praeter necessitatem.*[30]

No sweeping claim for Cynic influence is being made. As we insisted earlier, Paul's own religio-socio-cultural world is a rich one. So some of what we find in the Corinthian correspondence most obviously stems primarily from Paul's Hellenistic Jewish context. Handing over to the Jewish celestial prosecutor, Satan (1 Cor 5.5), is a quite distinctively Jewish motif (although we do also find Cynic notions of human prosecutors involved in divine judgment and punishment (cf. 1 Cor 6.2), and these will be discussed later). Further major clearly Jewish strands include 1 Corinthians 10.1–13 and much of chapter 15. Other items again come from Paul's new Christian faith (1 Cor 11.17–34; 15.1–9). But alongside these, a number of specific elements, it is here suggested, are distinctively Cynic. Some others, again, are simply compatible with Cynic influence, characteristic but not distinctive: on their own they would not demand such a reading; combined with what does seem distinctively Cynic, they do, however, enhance the plausibility of this interpretation.

---

[29] On 'mirror reading', G. Lyons (1985), 75–121; for a cautious defence of the procedure, J. M. G. Barclay (1987).

[30] On gnosticism, see ch. 1, n. 17. T. W. Martin (1996) argues a similar case to that sketched here, when seeking a context for Colossians, but then spoils his account in detail, creating his own ideal Cynic to match the issues in the epistle.

(iv) Paul rules

It is, then, perhaps significant that in his response to the case of incest Paul does not do as modern commentators do: he does not cite Leviticus 18.7–8 here. Instead he appeals to the consensus 'among the nations'. Cynics traditionally paid particular attention to 'barbarian' ways. Some nations (Persians in particular) might countenance incest; but the fact that Greeks, Romans and others eschewed it could afford for Paul a strong counter-indication of what is 'natural' among humans.[31] And then, with any appeal to actual law codes (Greek, Roman or Jewish) ruled out as inconsistent with his foundational preaching (in Corinth as in Galatia), and anyway fruitless when addressing people with the convictions he discerns here, the only further move available to Paul is for him to assert his own authority ('I have already pronounced judgment'), based on his own insight into the purity necessary for the integrity of the community (5.3 and 6–7).[32] Cynics expected a teacher to be able to 'rule' his fellows.[33] Some kinds of sexual (mis-)conduct are in fact included in the behaviour rebuked by Cynic masters, and even issues of purity can sometimes be taken seriously.[34] And so Paul simply issues his ruling.

---

[31] F. G. Downing (1992a), 82; compare also C. P. Jones (1993) and C. Muckensturm (1993).

[32] M. M. Mitchell (1991), 112–16 and 228–30; cf. J. T. Sanders (1997).

[33] Diogenes Laertius 6.29–30, 74; ps.-Crates 34.4–5; cf. ps.-Diogenes 29 and 40; ps.-Heraclitus 5.2; Epictetus 3.22.10, comparing his own past practice, 2.12.17–25; Dio 9.8.

[34] See ps.-Diogenes 28, ps.-Heraclitus 4. For Diogenes' practice in the tradition, Diogenes Laertius 6.28, 39, 41, 42 (including the crude joke

In a previous letter Paul had told the Corinthian Christians not to associate with people of whose sexual conduct he disapproved. Now Paul agrees that those he addresses could not be expected to isolate themselves from outsiders, any of whom may well behave badly on any of a number of counts. But his hearers are to refuse close association, including table-fellowship, to any claiming membership who do conduct themselves in ways Paul finds disgraceful (5.9–11; 6.9–11). We shall consider vice-lists in a little more detail in chapter 7; but it is worth noting here that Crates' imagined Cynic 'City of Pera' allows in 'no fool, parasite, glutton, or sexual deviant (πόρνης) . . . nor anyone who fights for money or for fame'.[35] In the wider Graeco-Roman world Cynic tradition was by and large quite distinctive in its opposition to homosexual activity (or some forms of it).[36] Paul's repudiation of such practices (6.9, albeit in keeping with Jewish morality) would have seemed to non-Jewish Corinthians quite in keeping with the other Cynic strands in his teaching and conduct.

However, if the Corinthian Christians' contrary tolerant mixing with miscreants was deliberate and consci-

---

about being 'hated by the Gods'), 49, 59–60. For issues of purity, cf. Diogenes Laertius 6.37, 64; *per contra*, 6.42.

[35] Diogenes Laertius 6.85; does πόρνης . . . πυγῆσιν mean sodomite? A. A. Long (1996), 43, renders it 'a lecher who delights in a whore's backside'. Cynics were very ready to repel any who refused to adopt their harsh regimen; even Demonax, who 'forgave sinners while assailing their sins' (Lucian, *Demonax* 7) could still be very cutting.

[36] Diogenes Laertius 6.46, 53, 65, 66; Epictetus 1.16.9–14, 3.1.24–35 (citing the Diogenes tradition), and 3.22.10; Lucian, *Demonax* 15, 16, 18, 50; ps.-Crates 29; ps.-Lucian, *The Cynic* 15–17; a possible contrary example, ps.-Diogenes 35.2. (It is a pity that J. T. Sanders (1997), 70–72, ignores this Cynic evidence in his generalisations about Paul's supposedly distinctive sexual morality.)

entious, that, too would have had clear precedent in other Cynic tradition - and at one of the points where the latter coincided with the Jesus tradition as well. 'On one occasion Antisthenes was criticised for mixing with ne'er-do-wells. "Physicians", he said, "can attend the sick without catching the fever."' [37] 'Someone rebuked Diogenes for visiting some unsavoury places. "Well," said he, "the sun visits dung-heaps without getting dirty."' [38] The tolerance (in this context) among the 'strong' Corinthians could well have been based on some such Cynic ideal and conviction.

Looked at in more general terms, of course, Paul's own way with his converts even at this point of disagreement is still closer to Cynicism than it is to other contemporary models. Rather than inviting to a long intellectual apprenticeship (as did Stoics, Epicureans and others), Paul (like the Cynics with their 'shortcut') has offered instant entry in the expectation of a swift (though not immediate) progress (1 Cor 6.9–11; Rom 6.17–18, etc.). Paul has clearly looked like a teacher of wisdom (1 Cor 1–3); the only other teachers of wisdom to evince this kind of expectation of quick results, on the basis of their own ascetic example (1 Cor 4.11–13, etc.), were the Cynics. The importance of such a 'structural', phenomenological similarity for informing people's interpretation of what Paul was up to should in no way be underestimated.[39]

---

[37] Diogenes Laertius 6.6.

[38] Diogenes Laertius 6.63; the 'physician (for sinners)' *topos* (Mk 2.16–17) appears at Diogenes Laertius 6.36; ps.-Diogenes 40.1; Epictetus 3.22.72 (cf. 4.8.28–29); Dio 8.7-8 (cf. 9.2, 4); Lucian, *Demonax* 7 (cf. 10), and *The Downward Journey* 7.

[39] If we accept, with L. Alexander (1995), that Paul's Christian groups would have seemed most like a philosophical (or even medical) 'school', it would only be Cynics who did not insist on a long 'apprenticeship' (compare, e.g., Lucian, *Hermotimus*; or Justin Martyr,

Paul is constantly attempting to modify his converts' perceptions of what he is about; but such seem to be the perceptions they had, perceptions looking very like and so in all probability informed by Cynic tradition. Indeed, as we have already seen, and will note again, Paul's attempted modifications in the early letters often appear to be aimed simply towards instilling a gentler and less disruptive Cynicism, 'gentle as a nurse' (gentle with others, severe with oneself) rather than expunging Christian Cynicism altogether.

The 'judgment' Paul has announced (harsh enough in this instance), and its focus on 'insiders' now prompts him to deal with the judgments he gathers some of the Corinthian congregation have been seeking from 'outsiders' in the local courts (1 Cor 5.12–6.8), before he then continues with the theme of πορνεία (6.9–20). In a very litigious culture, where trials were a source of popular entertainment, there would be nothing odd about meeting Cynic-minded contentious Christians in court. In fact our sources suggest that some Cynics may have found the courts as good an arena for exposing and possibly curing human folly as any other, and were willing at times to join in the proceedings, Musonius and Demetrius among them.[40] However, for litigants claiming Cynic 'wealth', Paul suggests that at issue is an inconsistent possessiveness (1 Cor 4.8 with 6.7–8). We might compare Lucian's criticism of Peregrinus' alleged un-Cynic attempt to regain the patrimony he had bequeathed to his native city.[41]

Trypho, 2); and note also the discussion with C. Glad (1995), above, ch. 2, n. 56; and cf. M. Griffin (1996), 198.

[40] F. G. Downing (1992a), 104; and ps.-Diogenes 50.

[41] Lucian, *Peregrinus* 16; cf. Diogenes Laertius 6.28; F. G. Downing (1988c), 25–26.

Conzelmann and others are likely right that Paul's preferred in-group arbitration is based on Jewish models; but Demonax also included conciliation among his activities, as did Epictetus' idealised Cynic.[42]

(v) I can do what I want

πάντα μοι ἔξεστιν, says Paul, twice, returning now to the theme of sexual relations. He is apparently quoting what he takes to be a slogan important among those he is addressing. πάντα μοι ἔξεστιν, ἀλλ᾽ οὐ πάντα συμφέρει. πάντα μοι ἔξεστιν, ἀλλ᾽ οὐκ ἐγὼ ἐξουσιασθήσομαι ὑπό τινος: 'All things are legitimately in my power ('all things are lawful for me'), but not all things are profitable. All things are legitimately in my power, but I'll not be overpowered by anything' (1 Cor 6.12).

Mark A. Plunkett's 1988 Princeton dissertation, *Sexual Ethics and the Christian Life: A Study of 1 Corinthians 6:12–7:7* affords a thorough and illuminating discussion of the issues involved.[43] Plunkett points out that previous commentators have been content to suggest the origins of πάντα μοι ἔξεστιν in philosophical discussions indiscriminately categorised as 'Stoic and Cynic', but have done so without adducing any instances of πάντα ἔξεστιν

---

[42] H. Conzelmann [1969] (1975), 104; Lucian, *Demonax* 9 and 16; and Epictetus 3.22.72; and Dio, too, but after his Cynic period, and on the level of inter-city relations, 38, 39, 40, 41.

[43] One pity is that Plunkett's chosen portion of Paul's text excludes any detailed discussion of 1 Cor 5.1–5, and so misses the matter of incest, which would have further supported the strong case he makes for Cynic influence in the Corinthian church.

as such.[44] Plunkett is able to demonstrate quite clearly that its home is in discussions of political kingship. The king is the one for whom (so it is claimed) 'all is legitimate', πάντα ἔξεστιν.[45] There is, Plunkett explains, a flexibility in the usage of ἔξεστιν which allows it to indicate the opportunity, freedom, lack of hindrance to do something: it may be that there is no moral or legal hindrance, it may be that there is no physical or other technical hindrance; there may be neither.[46] We might compare the vernacular use of 'can' in English, 'I can legitimately, easily (or both) do anything' (where purists would prefer 'may' to convey the distinct sense of 'am permitted'). In early Pythagorean discussion, with the breakdown of the Greek democracies, the king, Plunkett shows, is presented as a living law, the embodiment of justice, with the expectation that all the monarch decides and does will be right. But it is easy for the king and his sycophants to interpret this as categorising whatever he pleases as in itself right, so that by definition there is no moral hindrance to what is otherwise in his power; and Plunkett quotes Plutarch's anecdote of the philosopher Anaxarchus, who on this basis urged Alexander to forgo the scruples of an ordinary man.[47]

Πάντα μοι ἔξεστιν, then, is an integral part of talk of kingship, and so of Cynic or of Stoic discussions of the wise man as king. Like a true king, a Stoic wise man may do anything he will, because he only wills what is

---

[44] M. Plunkett (1988), 167, citing J. Dupont (1949), and also H. Conzelmann [1969] (1975) among others.

[45] Plunkett (1988), 174, cites Dio 3.10 and 62.2–4, but also Demosthenes *Or.* 23.140; and Plutarch, *Agiselaus* 4.2

[46] M. Plunkett (1988), 171, citing W. Foerster, *TDNT*, 'ἔξεστιν κτλ' (1964), 560–63.

[47] M. Plunkett (1988), 175–78, citing E. R. Goodenough (1928) and G. F. Chesnutt (1978); and Plutarch, *Alexander* 52.5–6.

legitimate, what is not shameful or unhelpful (ἀσύμ-
φερον).⁴⁸ His wisdom includes the knowledge of 'what is
legitimate and what is not'.⁴⁹ The law of nature has been
internalised by the Stoic wise man, who can obey it with an
inner freedom. He can in accord with nature make use of
everything that happens, as Epictetus says, 'ἔξεστιν οὖν
σοι παντὶ τῷ ἀποβάντι χρῆσθαι κατὰ φύσιν. No one
can forbid that.'⁵⁰

　　In 1 Corinthians 6.12 Paul himself is clearly also
pressing a more Stoic sort of line. Only what is helpful,
συμφέρει, can/may be done; otherwise you lose your inner
freedom to do what you know is right. 'All things are
legitimately in my power, but I'll not be overpowered by
anything.'⁵¹ Food itself is, as Paul allows here (and in more
detail later), a matter of indifference. But the question of
how things in themselves indifferent are to be regarded and
used, for Paul, as for Stoics, does matter (for individuals,
here in chapter 6; for the community, 8-10).⁵² Paul is not,
though, consistent. Some 'externals' (getting circumcised,
eating in temples) go on being important in themselves.⁵³

---

⁴⁸ M. Plunkett (1988), 169, citing Dio 14.17, 'the wise may do
whatever they want to do'; but also (172) citing Epictetus 2.1.23, etc.

⁴⁹ Epictetus 1.1.21 (cited as 1.1.26 by Plunkett (1988), 168–70); he
also cites Dio 14.17 and Philo, *Quod omnis probus liber sit* 59; and
J. Dupont (1949), 298–301.

⁵⁰ Epictetus 4.10.8, cited by Plunkett (1988), 169, n. 124.

⁵¹ M. Plunkett (1988), 243, citing H. Conzelmann ([1969] 1975), 109,
and S. K. Stowers (1981), 67–68.

⁵² J. L. Jaquette (1995), 65, 89, with reference to Epictetus 2.6.1.

⁵³ In Galatians, Paul is similarly able to say, 'neither circumcision nor
uncircumcision matters, but new creation' (Gal 5.6; 6.15; cf. 1 Cor
7.19). Just as Paul could be a Jew to Jews (1 Cor 9.20), perhaps he
could have allowed Peter to be (Gal 2.12), and so, too, the Galatians
who wanted to be circumcised – as long as they accorded such matters
no real importance. Yet Paul himself makes getting circumcised a

Those he is criticising are obviously (to Paul) claiming not to be subject to any such (Stoic) internalised sense of what is helpful. The wisdom, the knowledge, they claim can be expressed in similar language, but is very different in what is denoted and in its outcome. As those who 'have already . . . become kings' (1 Cor 4.8), they are claiming a royal prerogative without any conventional limits, clearly aligned with the more radical Cynics. We noted in the previous chapter Diogenes' and other Cynics' refusal of inherited codes and conventions in general, and we have noted at the start of this one a common Cynic willingness to countenance incest. Some Christians in Corinth are also asserting, at least in theory, that their legitimate freedom extends to coitus with prostitutes. (As Plunkett notes, it seems at this stage in fact to be a theoretical issue: Paul's tone now is much milder than in 5.1–13, no one here is threatened with explusion.)[54]

However, it is important at this juncture to recall what was said in chapter 2, about varieties within Cynicism, a theme also emphasised by Plunkett.[55] There is a radical and ascetic strand which would refuse all sexual intercourse, whoever the partner, as a curtailment of freedom. A man's awkward tumescence can be relieved quite naturally by masturbation: 'Diogenes found Aphrodite everywhere, without expense.'[56] Female prostitutes (the partners discussed in 1 Cor 6.12–20) are

---

matter of extreme (negative) importance (Gal 5.2); similarly, meals in temples in Corinth. J. L. Jaquette (1995), 160–65 notes something of this tension, but perhaps resolves it in Paul's favour too readily.

[54] M. Plunkett (1988), 105–106.

[55] M. Plunkett (1988), 181–216; referring also to S. K. Stowers (1981) and A. J. Malherbe (1970) and (1982).

[56] Dio 6.17–20; ps.-Diogenes 35.2; 42; 44; Diogenes Laertius 6.69; cf. 6.51.

singled out for opprobrium in some of the *chreiai* in Diogenes Laertius.[57] This then contrasts with the approval announced elsewhere in the Cynic tradition for a sexual liaison or partnership freely entered into.[58] So Plunkett reminds us of the sharp distinction in the tradition between the rigorous asceticism of much of the Diogenes tradition, and a more hedonist strand which can accept Odysseus as its hero, and is perhaps typified by Bion of Borysthenes, at one time Cynic, at another Cyrenaic, and which can imagine Diogenes in the arms of the prostitute he is elsewhere said to have criticised.[59] It is hard at this distance to distinguish between simple charges of hypocrisy on the one hand (as in Lucian, excoriating the greedy self-proclaimed ascetic), and a sincere difference of views among Cynics on the other, over whether 'sweet cakes' are 'natural'.[60] Other living things engage in promiscuous coitus; if it is natural for them, it is natural for humans, and perhaps not a debilitating or enslaving pleasure (for the strong).[61]

But better still than allowing for two fairly distinct 'wings' of Cynicism (and issues of sincerity apart) we should instead, as argued in chapter 2, allow for a spectrum or an even more complex diagram to express Cynic tradition.[62] There are ascetics and there are hedonists (for

---

[57] Diogenes Laertius 6.60, 61, 62, 63, 66, 85, 89–90; other references, M. Plunkett (1988), 194, n. 85.

[58] Diogenes Laertius 6.11, 72 and especially 96–98 (Hipparchia).

[59] Laïs, as noted by M. Plunkett (1988), 195 n. 190; 197 and n. 197.

[60] Diogenes Laertius 6.56; Lucian, *Demonax* 52; Giannantoni (1990), V B 189, 190; M. Plunkett (1988), 197 and n. 200.

[61] M. Plunkett (1988), 200–208.

[62] Regrettably, Plunkett (1988), 232, then minimises the Cynic character of the strong Corinthians, by noting that there is no sign of their having worn the supposed 'uniform' (of folded cloak, bag, staff

whom some pleasures are natural, and not enslaving), there are those who are harsh with others, and there are the gentle. But Demonax who is gentle (and allows himself sweet cakes) may rebuke Peregrinus for being barely human; yet neither countenance marriage for themselves, it would seem.[63] On the other hand again, some who appear as predominantly Stoic and much more conformist in their philosophising can commend a very rigorous Cynic *askêsis*.[64] There is a wide range of 'family resemblances', as already argued. So Paul, for instance, can continue to deploy quite positively a number of Cynic strands (including his own harsh personal *askêsis*, 1 Cor 4.10–13, etc.), while at other times (as here) he can adopt a more Stoic approach (and apparently expect it to carry some weight).

We should conclude, then, that some in Corinth seem to Paul to have adopted, at least in theory, their own variety of hedonist Cynic stance. All things, 'natural' pleasures included, are legitimate for these philosopher-kings, strong as they are, strong enough to enter a sexual liaison without being enslaved by it.[65] They can – and may – take it or leave it, take it and leave it.

---

and beard). He also concludes that it is they who have imposed a 'hedonistic Cynic' interpretation on Paul's message, rather than Paul himself having used coherent elements of this obvious field of discourse in working out and communicating his message. But Plunkett has, of course, concentrated on one important stretch of 1 Corinthians, without the opportunity to survey the wider evidence here and in the other letters.

[63] Lucian, *Demonax* 52; cf. 21, 55; and Lucian, *Peregrinus* (no mention).

[64] M.-O. Goulet-Cazé (1986), 182–91.

[65] M. Plunkett (1988), 196–216, especially 200–201, citing Teles 6.24–27 (53H). When Paul deals with sexual passion at 1 Thess 4.3–6 he makes no mention of any philosophical justification (dualist or

As we have already noted, there are two prime examples of freedom from inherited codes in the Cynic tradition. One is the refusal of sexual convention, the other is a rejection of food tabus. The two strands are as closely linked here (1 Cor 6.12–13) as they are in Diogenes Laertius 6.72–73, with Paul's subsequent lengthy discussion of dedicated meat focusing again on the same slogan at 10.23, 'everything is legitimately available', πάντα ἔξεστιν. Sexual desire is as natural as hunger, and both may be as readily satisfied without regard for any artificially imposed restrictions.[66]

(vi) Embodied freedom

Plunkett acknowledges that his interpretation of 1 Corinthians 6.13 along the lines summarised above is not among the commonly accepted readings. Many commentators have assumed that Paul is here dealing with a dualistic libertinism (probably 'gnostic'), in which what involves the physical body is irrelevant. Yet the Nag Hammadi texts support an ascetic rather than a libertinist interpretation of gnosticism; the texts later cited by such as Irenaeus could as readily be interpreted in a matching ascetic sense; and Irenaeus' and others' accusations of (hypocritical) immorality among opponents are a common-

---

other) being offered; but in the light of other Cynic motifs in the Thessalonian correspondence (still to be discussed), and especially the deliberate abandonment of work to rely on others, a similar 'naturalism' may well have been operative.

[66] 'The belly' is the seat of pleasure, food and sexual lust are as closely linked by Dio (8.14, 22; 4.103); cf. ps.-Diogenes 28.5, and 42; Diogenes Laertius 6.46 (stomach and penis distinguished but paired).

place of ancient polemic.[67] More than this, there is nothing in what Paul writes that actually tells us he is countering some form of metaphysical or anthropological dualism, not even a Stoic one, let alone a Platonic, Orphic, Pythagorean (or gnostic) one. It has, obviously, been possible so to interpret the talk of πνεῦμα and πνευματικός in 1 Corinthians 2, but none of the conventional dualist vocabulary is deployed there. Without any *clear* indications to the contrary, the discussion so far would almost inevitably be understood along the lines of the Cynic tradition adduced by Plunkett and here summarised. Paul is addressing people for whom this physical life is the only one (1 Cor 15.19), there is no other to come, whether by resurrection or by immortality (15.12); but neither is the true life of these wise Corinthians now essentially a matter of inner choice and serenity (of soul, mind, spirit or whatever). For sure, Epictetus' very Stoic idealised Cynic agrees that *nothing* which concerns the body, σῶμα, is free, that only with the exercise of inner assent and choice in whatever circumstances can any real freedom naturally be found: ἔστι τι ἐν ὑμῖν ἐλεύθερον φύσει. But Paul is sure that those he is addressing stand rather with such as the very un-Stoic Cynic then rebuked by Epictetus, the Cynic for whom freedom is entirely, it would seem, a matter of overt behaviour (including 'eating everything you give him').[68]

---

[67] M. Plunkett (1988), 165, n. 117 and 168, n. 121, quoting F. Wisse (1975); cf. W. Deming (1995), 36–37; P. Perkins (1993); on polemic, L. T. Johnson (1989); C. J. Schlueter (1994).

[68] Epictetus 3.22.36–50. I part company here from Plunkett (1988) in some measure: e.g., 249, where he discerns in the Corinthians 'a contempt for the body' as a lower, less worthy part of oneself. I would put much more weight on the implicit 'monism' he also attributes to them. It is Epictetus who talks disparagingly of his σωμάτιον (e.g.,

One further influential interpretation is also effectively countered by Plunkett. Rudolph Bultmann, followed by others, interpreted σῶμα, 'body', as the existential 'self', which could then be distinguished from 'the belly', and so forth. Thus Paul would be agreeing that 'the belly' is to perish (1 Cor 6.13), while insisting that the (body–)self is to be raised to new life (v. 14). But if that were what he was saying, it would certainly be a very weak argument, inviting the riposte, 'but the genitals, too, will perish'.[69] Epictetus' Stoic freedom is threatened by 'a girl, a boy, a sweet-meat'.[70] These Cynic-seeming Christians of Paul's seem to find their freedom precisely in being open to such very physical choices.

Yet in refusing the hedonist path Paul significantly still shares with those he addresses an implicit physical 'monism',[71] while quoting in support his Jewish tradition (Gen 2.24), perhaps aware that it was also linked with the teaching of Jesus he is going to cite a little later (1 Cor 7.10–11, Mk 10.8). For Paul, coitus constitutes a relationship which (most) eating does not; Plunkett urges the term 'participatory'. Whether Paul was aware of it or not, this then would align him with much of the more severe Cynic tradition, which, as we noted, rejected recourse to

---

3.22.33). These strong Corinthians can simply cope with any 'natural' physical situation, 'bodily': compare Dio's Herakles, 8.26–36, but especially 32, where he 'comes together with', 'but is in no way overpowered by', the Amazon.

[69] M. Plunkett (1988), 112–14, citing R. Bultmann (1951), 192–203; and in support of his own case, R. Gundry (1975), 52–56. Anyway, 'belly' can stand for sexual lust as well as gluttony.

[70] Epictetus 3.22.13.

[71] M. Plunkett (1988), 294; compare the discussion in V. K. Robbins (1996), 89–91, at this point concluding that Paul's discourse 'evokes a deeply embodied aesthetic' (91).

prostitutes as a surrender of autonomy to that person. The (male) hedonist tradition insists that coitus is no more involving (for a man) than is staying in a house or travelling in a ship. 'I have Laïs, not she me', insists Aristippus.[72] Paul, by contrast, says a little later of the married sexual relationship, that each party has legitimate power, ἐξουσιάζει, over the other (1 Cor 7.4), precisely the sort of subjection to another, participation in another, he here deplores, and assumes the 'strong' would not really welcome (6.12).[73]

(vii) Free from family ties

The austere Cynic tradition would then also and obviously tally with Paul's own preference for celibacy (1 Cor 7.7). Again, there are, of course, Jewish precedents, in the Therapeutae as reported by Philo, and the Essenes as reported by him and by Josephus.[74] But if, as is here being argued, Paul had from the start been deploying a wide range of very Cynic motifs as the most appropriate language in which to work out, articulate and communicate important strands in what he felt he had to say, his hearers would almost certainly have heard the Cynic rather than distant and esoteric Essene or other Jewish overtones; and Paul must have been aware or soon made aware of that. (Epicureans were also at least in theory opposed to

---

[72] Aristippus (the Cyrenaic) in Diogenes Laertius 2.74–75; but cf Dio's Cynic Herakles, 8.32 (n. 56, above).

[73] Plunkett comes to substantially this interpretation of Paul's position, without noting that it, too, has in some measure, Cynic antecedents; M. Plunkett (1988), 266–71, on Paul's asceticism.

[74] Philo, *De vita contemplativa* 13–20; 68; *Hypothetica* 11.14; Josephus, *War* 2.120.

marriage and the rearing of a family, as a threat to equanimity; while allowing that practice might well be more conformist.)[75]

However, Will Deming is clearly correct in insisting that our chapter 7 of 1 Corinthians is primarily concerned with marriage as a social institution, the foundation of civic society in the rearing of new citizens and heirs, safeguarding the possession and transfer of wealth.[76] Paul has completed his main discussion of aspects of sexual relations taken as an end in themselves, and is here concerned mainly with societal relationships, so that 'fornication' and 'burning passion' (1 Cor 7.2 and 9) are now in the background. It is with 'marriage and family', 'marriage and children' that most Cynic tradition takes issue, and precisely because this was so essential to the civic society the Cynics disparaged.

Thus, apart from Crates and Hipparchia, a saying of Antisthenes, and possibly the conclusions of Musonius,[77] the Cynic tradition has, it seems, no instances of marriage being approved of. Diogenes advises strongly against it. For a young man the best time is not yet, for an old man, never; for marriage is an alliance with an evil foe. The only acceptable union is by occasional consent, quite other than the conventional contract.[78] The true Cynic declines marriage and has no desire to raise children.[79] Demonax

---

[75] Diogenes Laertius 10.119, 133; cf. W. Deming (1995), 67 and n. 49, and Epictetus 1.23.7; 2.20.20; 3.7.19.

[76] W. Deming (1995), ch. 2, and especially 52.

[77] Diogenes Laertius 6.88, 96–97, and 11; ps.-Crates 28–33; Epictetus 3.22.76; and Musonius 14: but despite the Cynic influence Musonius accepts elsewhere, this is more likely Stoic.

[78] Diogenes Laertius 6.29, 54, 50, 72.

[79] Ps.-Diogenes 44, 47; Maximus of Tyre, *Dissertation* 36.6 (Giannantoni (1990) V B 299).

laughs at marriage (and at Epictetus' Stoic suggestion that he should undertake it.)[80]

Stoics by contrast, as Deming explains (and as we have noted), saw civil society as an important if imperfect expression and part of the divine order of things. It was therefore to be engaged in supportively. In most circumstances a man should marry and rear children. Deming also draws attention to a mid-way position: it might be necessary for a Stoic philosopher (but for him only) to avoid marriage, to allow him the freedom for even more important divine service. An obvious example would be Epictetus himself.[81] The second-century Stoic writer Hierocles in his *On Marriage* allows that other fraught circumstances, too, may legitimately free one from fulfilling family responsibilities.[82]

So Paul agrees, celibacy ('not to touch a woman') 'is good for a man (καλόν ἀνθρώπῳ)', morally good (1 Cor 7.1, 8, 26, etc.).[83] Paul would wish that all were as he (1 Cor 7.7), not free from all cares, but free to care for 'the things of the Lord' (7.32–35), as Epictetus' ideal Cynic philosopher is to be free for his God-given tasks.[84] It is not just the one person singled out and sent, 'apostled'

---

[80] Lucian, *Demonax* 55. Epictetus' own ideal Cynic teacher will not marry, either (though others should): 3.22.67–76.

[81] Epictetus 3.22.67–82; for those he teaches, marriage and children are obligatory, 3.7.19–28. W. Deming (1995), 50–89, very usefully and thoroughly discusses much further relevant material.

[82] W. Deming (1995), 81–83; Hierocles in von Arnim (1903).

[83] M. Plunkett (1988), 313–17 and W. Deming (1995), 110–14; both arriving at similar conclusions, apparently independently.

[84] M. Plunkett (1988), 313–17, again. In fact the analogy with the Stoic texts Plunkett discusses with D. Balch (1983) and with O. L. Yarbrough (1985) is closer at this point than Plunkett allows: Epictetus' Cynic is expected to be 'wholly devoted to the service of God', 3.22.69, and the whole section 3.22.67–82.

by God for whom celibacy is 'good' without qualification; Paul would have all celibate, if only they had the gift. With so many Cynic-sounding themes already having appeared in the letter, the insistence that celibacy is good in itself, good for all, at least in theory (and not just less troublesome), would have further confirmed for a gentile audience the impression that here was some kind of personally austere Cynicism, with its deliberate refusal of any compromise with society through marital, family ties.

Paul is concerned nonetheless to deal gently with those who have not received his gift of continence, a marriage-guidance counsellor like an Epictetus or a Demonax.[85] The married are certainly not to seek permanent separation, divorce. Temporary separation, abstention from (nightly) coitus for prayer, however, is allowed (1 Cor 7.5). While Deming appositely cites in illustration *The Testament of Naphtali*, he perhaps too readily dismisses the relevance of the Stoic or Cynic matter he himself notes.[86] Paul's own impulse may well come from his native Jewish tradition; but he is here dealing with those for whom marriage represents restriction (note the idea of being under the power of the other, 1 Cor 7.4, enslaved, 7.15), and offers a concession to their Christian–Cynic desire to be freer to follow their own path.

It is perhaps worth noting that Paul's emphasis on the consent of *both* partners to abstention from coitus as well as to remaining in a 'mixed' union (1 Cor 7.5 and 12–13) finds its closest analogy in the Diogenes doxography to which we have more than once drawn attention.[87] It is among Cynics (as we saw in our first chapter) that women

---

[85] Epictetus 3.22.72; Lucian, *Demonax* 9.
[86] *The Testament of Naphtali* 8.1, 7–10; W. Deming (1995), 123–25.
[87] Diogenes Laertius 6.71.

and men are most often accorded equal moral status.[88] That sexual desire is powerful and 'given' (by nature/God) is at home in Stoic and Cynic discourse; Deming notes that it is in this light that Epictetus presents Crates and Hipparchia, and that to the former is ascribed elsewhere the conclusion that sexual passion is a flame hard to quench (φλόξ, cf. πυροῦσθαι, 1 Cor 7.9).[89] Crates and Hipparchia could survive together, they were two of a kind, as the *Cynic Epistles* portray them, and as Epictetus also records.[90] Some at least of Paul's Corinthians seem to have felt that without such a shared discipleship they should separate from their non-Christian spouses. Paul gives his decision.

Marriage, we have noted, can be seen as restrictive, a kind of slavery, you are in the power of another: the thought leads Paul into further reflections on other restrictions, as Jew or not-Jew, slave or free (thus echoing, many suppose, the two other themes of Gal 3.28). Paul's response here sounds to Deming 'highly Stoicized'.[91] Some of the analogous sentiments Deming adduces are certainly telling. For Stoics, your socially recognised status is to be a matter of indifference, not important enough for you to give your attention to changing it. Taking it that the main issue continues to be the question of initiating a change in one's marital status, Paul is saying, one should no more do that than one should initiate a change in one's status as circumcised or as not circumcised. Paul, however,

---

[88] W. Deming (1995), 116–17, finds the closest linguistic analogies to the 'likewise', ὁμοίως δὲ καί, in Stoic texts, and also the idea of commonality he discerns here; but the insistence on consent makes this more Cynic.

[89] W. Deming (1995), 130–31; Epictetus 3.22.76; *Anth. Graec.* 9.497; cf. also Diogenes Laertius 6.96 (Hipparchia).

[90] Ps.Crates 28–33; Epictetus 3.22.76; W. Deming (1995), 147.

[91] W. Deming (1995), 157–73 ('highly Stoicised', 159).

does not frame his next illustration consistently, he does not say, 'slavery is nothing and freedom is nothing.' Deming supposes Paul refrains because it would make no sense to say, 'if free, don't become a slave.' But in fact people might choose to do just that for all sorts of reasons, including improving their own financial prospects; and later Christians did so in order to give the purchase price away).[92] It is more likely that Paul's Christian–Cynic libertarian leanings are still too strong to allow him to class changing from slavery or from freedom as being matters of indifference simply on a par with changing one's marital status. So he makes the more moderate Stoic point, that manumission (though not to be sought) can be chosen if offered, as being open to good use. Deming appositely quotes Epictetus' *Encheiridion*:

> Remember that you must behave yourself as you should at a party. A dish is passed round, and comes to you. Reach out politely and take some. It's passed on? don't grab it back! It's not got to you yet – well, don't set your heart on this distant dish, but stay put till it reaches you! And act just the same way towards children and wife, towards public office and wealth. Then some day you'll be fit to party with the gods.[93]

And, of course, when manumission was offered, Epictetus took and used it; or so tradition indicates.

Immediately before this in the *Encheiridion*, Epictetus is recorded as saying, 'Master over each is whoever has power (ἐξουσία) over what he wishes to have or avoid. So whoever wants to be free should not desire to

---

[92] D. B. Martin (1990), 36–42 and notes; S. S. Bartchy (1973) 46–48 and notes; and 1 Clement 50.2–3; *per contra*, J. A. Harrill (1995), 31.

[93] Epictetus, *Encheiridion* 15; cited by W. Deming (1995), 164, but my translation.

gain or lose anything; otherwise a slave he must be.'[94] So Paul also warns against wanting to change one's status and so becoming 'slave to fellow humans' (1 Cor 7.23). We may agree with Deming and others that there remains a perceptible difference between Paul's sense of being freed by God through the death of Jesus (1 Cor 7.23-24) and Epictetus' conviction of freedom granted by Zeus.[95] There are differences as well as similarities, of course (there are between Epictetus and other Stoics, Paul and other Christians). The similarities remain significant for any attempt to understand Paul. And so, however much his own Christian–Cynic sympathies initially show through, in this discussion of marriage and related issues, the more radical and Cynic-sounding positions adopted by others obviously draw Paul to a stance whose distinctly Stoic resonances are very strong and clear.[96]

A full and fruitful discussion of further Stoic echoes in the remainder of 1 Corinthians 7 is provided by Deming. In particular I would point to his very proper reminder that if Paul is thought to have urged ἀταραξία, and so 'freedom in the midst of involvement', so too did Epictetus. Stoics by no means counselled a simple retirement into the inner peace and freedom that they so earnestly sought to cultivate.[97]

---

[94] Epictetus, *Encheiridion* 14 (my translation, again).

[95] W. Deming (1995), 165, citing Epictetus 1.19.9.

[96] Resonances with Epictetus are noted by V. K. Robbins (1996), 182–84, who rightly points to the 'contra-cultural' conformity of this stance; however, that is Stoic in ethos, not the position of most Cynics (only of Epictetus' idealised and Stoicised Cynic); and, as we shall see, early Paul in particular is often more clearly Cynic and thus also less conformist, 'counter-cultural' rather than 'contra-cultural'.

[97] W. Deming (1995), 194–95. Deming, 206, also notes, intriguingly, Paul's denial that he is imposing 'a noose', βρόχος, on the unwed

(viii) I can eat anything, anywhere – I know

We now move on to the companion theme of food (1 Cor
8–10, including the 'excursus' on freedom). 'On the topic
of food Musonius used to speak often and emphatic-ally, as
a matter by no means indifferent.' 'What you can get hold
of easily is better than what's hard to come by.'[98] Food as
such figures largely among the Cynic *chreiai* and
dependent traditions. Managing with a simple diet is an
important part of the Cynic *askêsis*. Sometimes this may
mean vegetarianism.[99] But dogs and other animals are
'naturally' carnivores, and Diogenes' death from eating
raw squid can be presented as an affirmation of this
conviction (as well as critics taking it as an instance of
hypocritical gluttony).[100] 'Everything belongs to the
Gods', says Diogenes; 'The Gods are friends to the wise,
and friends have all in common. So everything belongs to
the wise'. Laertius adds, 'He saw nothing improper in
taking food from a temple, or in eating the flesh of any
living thing. Even human flesh was not to be ruled out, as
is obvious from the practice of other peoples.'[101] In

(1 Cor 7.35); Crates uses the same term in discussing the resolution of
sexual urges (*Anth. Graec.* 9.479).

[98] Musonius Rufus 18A and 18B (C. Lutz, ed. (1947), 112, 4–5 and
120, 7–8; O. Hense (1905), 95–105.

[99] Cf. Rom 14.2; Diogenes Laertius 6.34, 35, 37, 44, 47, 48, 49, 55,
57, 90, 104; ps.-Crates 7; ps.-Diogenes 13; 37.4–5; and 44 (where the
link with easy sexual 'relief' is also made); Dio 6.12–13; etc; cf. the
discussion in R. Stoneman (1994), 506–10.

[100] Diogenes Laertius 6.76; Julian, *To the Uneducated Cynics* 191C;
Lucian, *Philosophies for Sale* 10.

[101] Diogenes Laertius 6.71 (cf. 37), 72; cf Giannantoni (1990), V B
353. Laertius deduces a metaphysical basis for this, of a Stoic kind; but

Lucian's *Dialogues of the Dead* Diogenes introduces himself as 'having come with my satchel stuffed with lots of lupins and any food I've found dedicated to Hecate at the cross-roads, eggs for purificatory rites, anything like that'. In *The Downward Journey* it's the raw squid that figures in place of the lupins, along with the food dedicated to Hecate, and the eggs. [102]

Simply to eat in public itself shocks convention: 'Reprimanded for eating in the market place, Diogenes riposted, "That's where I felt hungry".' 'Bystanders gathered round to watch him having breakfast in the market place. "Dog", they jeered. "You're the dogs, standing round watching my breakfast."' [103] A Cynic modelling him- or herself on this Diogenes will not only eat anything, she or he will eat anywhere – and do anything else 'natural' anywhere, too. [104]

In Galatia Paul (along with Peter and Barnabas and the whole Christian community initially) was determined to eat anywhere they thought fit with anyone they acknowledged (and presumably, to eat anything that was contributed). The strong Corinthian Christians, similarly, seem convinced it is right to eat anything they wish, anywhere, however shocked others may be (1 Cor 8 and 10), even if Paul in Corinth now cannot bring himself to enjoy quite this freedom (1 Cor 9 with 10.29). For these 'wise' and strong Christians, as for the Cynic (or Stoic) wise man, 'all things are theirs' (3.18 and 21), all things

---

it is more likely an entailment of unelaborated Cynic monism (M.-O. Goulet-Cazé (1982); ps.-Lucian, *The Cynic* 5, 'anything you find'.

[102] Lucian, *Dialogues of the Dead* 1 (331); cf. 2 (425); *The Downward Journey* 7.

[103] Diogenes Laertius 6.58, 61, 69; cf. 34, 35, 48, 57.

[104] Cf. Diogenes Laertius 6.46, 69 and 97 (Crates and Hipparchia, public coitus); Dio 8.36; Lucian, *Philosophies for Sale* 10.

are legitimately theirs, πάντα ἔξεστιν (10.23, echoing 6.12).[105] But for the Stoic, as we have noted, all belongs to the wise man, in the sense that he is always free to decide his inner response to what comes to him from outside. For these strong Corinthians, as for Cynics, everything is theirs precisely to choose to *do* what they want with it. The significance of the issue can be further illustrated by a comparison of Mark 7.19b ('he made all food clean') and Acts 10.9–16, on the one hand, and with Revelation 2.14–15 and 20 ('food sacrificed to idols and immorality') and Lucian's Peregrinus the Cynic (excommunicated by his Christian community for eating forbidden food), on the other. To feel free to eat as commonplace food others hold consecrated would look to most ostentatiously Cynic.

The strong Corinthians 'know' that no idol represents anything real in the universe, for there is no God but one (1 Cor 8.4–6). Theological scepticism was by no means restricted to Cynics, but it is worth noting that when the unity of God and the irrelevance of idols are at issue, it Antisthenes in particular who is quoted.[106] Later, when Clement of Alexandria looked for Greek antecedents for

---

[105] Plunkett argues, as does Conzelmann, that both phrases with πάντα almost certainly echo the Cynic and Stoic 'all things belong to the wise'; M. Plunkett (1988), 179; cf. 108; H. Conzelmann [1969] (1975), 80; as well as the passages cited above, cf. Lucian, *Peregrinus* 16; ps.-Crates 26 and 27, ps.-Diogenes 10, where it is money (for food) that the Cynic claims belongs to him on this argument.

[106] Philodemus, *De pietate* 7a, 3–8 (G. Giannantoni (1990), V A 179); Cicero, *De natura deorum* 1.13, 32; Diogenes Laertius 6.51 (Diogenes); cf. ps.-Heraclitus 4 in particular, and H. W. Attridge (1976), M.-O. Goulet-Cazé (1996), 68–69. In popular opinion Epicureans are total atheists; but in fact they firmly insist that the Gods are 'real', just totally uninvolved with us even when in dreams and visions we are made aware of them: Diogenes Laertius 10.123; Cicero, *De natura deorum* 1.46–49.

Christian monotheism and its opposition to idolatry, it was Antisthenes and other Cynics that he instanced. [107]

The strong Corinthians assert that their actions are based on 'knowledge', γνῶσις, and this has been one of the bases for discerning 'gnostic' influence among them. Claims to knowledge, implicit or explicit, are in fact too commonplace to build much on them at all; but it is perhaps worth noting that among the philosophical schools it was Cynics who tended to be particularly dogmatic in their claims (they eschewed elaborate metaphysical arguments). So, for instance, the Cynic pseudo-Heraclitus says, 'I alone know God' and makes other claims to distinctive knowledge, while insisting others are ignorant. [108] Galen found it noteworthy that Christians and Cynics in particular shared a refusal to offer demonstrative argument or deploy logical theory. [109] So Antisthenes insists that virtue is a matter of deeds, it does not need lots of words and study; you just need to 'know' good is right and wickedness is wrong, and have the strength of a Socrates or a Herakles to express that awareness in action. [110]

Most who 'knew' the claims of popular Graeco-Roman religion were false preferred nonetheless to affirm

---

[107] Clement of Alexandria, *Protreptikos* 2 [22.1, 24.1, 24.5] and 4 [50.4], 6 [71.2] and 7 [75.3], and *Stromata* 5.14 [108.4], referring to Anacharsis, Antisthenes and Heraclitus (by now taken over as a Cynic; see the *Cynic Epistles*); and Minucius Felix, Lactantius and Theodoret (G. Giannantoni (1990), V A 180–83); also F. S. Jones (1987), 57–67; see further, below, ch. 7.

[108] Ps.-Heraclitus 4.5; 5.1; 6.1, 3; cf. ps.-Diogenes 28.8.

[109] Galen, in R. Walzer (1949), 15; and *De cuiusque animi peccatorum dignotione* 3.12 (D. C. G. Kühn (1823), 71).

[110] Diogenes Laertius 6.11, 12; cf. the discusssion in M.-O. Goulet-Cazé (1986), 144–45.

good social order and to keep up appearances by maintaining the practice with an inner detachment.[111] It was Cynics who courted disapproval by refusing outward compliance.[112] Eating in a temple, Diogenes treats the food as he would any other.[113] Just so could the strong Corinthians insist they were free, they had the ἐξουσία (8.9) to treat dedicated food as common sustenance, even in a temple setting (8.10). And to Paul they seemed to be treating the body-and-blood, bread-and-wine of the Lord's Supper in much the same way (1 Cor 11. 27–29).

(ix) The strong and the weak and freedom to adapt

The repeated ἐξουσία (1 Cor 8.9; 9.4, 5, 6, 12, 18) and ἐλεύθερος, ἐλευθερία (9.1, 19; 10.29) bind the discussions of food and of financial support together; with ἐξουσία also picking up the ἔξεστιν of 6.12, then resumed at 10.23.[114] The wise and strong among the Corinthians know what they can and may freely do, with the know-ledge and the freedom as much arising out of the action as enabling it. (This is not to deny that issues of wealth and status may also be involved, as has been widely argued of late;[115] it is to point out that the direct evidence we have is the

---

[111] E.g., Cicero's Epicurean, Stoic and Academic protagonists, *De natura deorum* 1.45, 123; 2.2; 3.5-6; M.-O. Goulet-Cazé (1996), 66-67.

[112] Diogenes Laertius 6.4, 39, 42, 59; Lucian, *Demonax* 11, 27.

[113] Diogenes Laertius 6.64; he throws temple bread away because it is physically messy; cf. 6.72, again.

[114] For what follows see the very helpful discussion in A. J. Malherbe (1995).

[115] E.g., by G. Theissen (1982); W. A. Meeks (1983); W. L. Willis (1985); P. Marshall (1987); D. B. Martin (1990).

language used, and it seems to be the language of Cynic freedom, which could be used by people in and from quite varied social settings.)

In his recent discussion of this section of 1 Corinthians, A. J. Malherbe argues that 'the meat-eaters' have been quoting Stoic slogans (and in a Stoic, not Cynic sense) to Paul, who answers them in thought-forms taken from both Cynic and Stoic tradition. The meat-eaters are accusing the more sensitive of the sort of intellectual 'weakness' that Stoics analysed, making the wrong judgments about external things. However, in the light of the arguments of the preceding pages it continues to seem much more likely that the 'strong' Corinthians were taking fairly consistently a pragmatic and Cynic-like, rather than an intellectualist and Stoic-like line. Had they been informed by central Stoic convictions they would surely not have needed Paul to indicate that 'eating and drinking . . . should be regarded as ἀδιάφορα'.[116] For these 'strong' Christians, it is precisely their actions that constitute their freedom, not internal judgments about giving or withholding assent. Rather is it Paul who is arguing like a Stoic, against making an indiscriminate diet a matter of urgent principle. Food in itself is a matter of indifference (1 Cor 8.8); how its use affects the community is a matter of proper concern. For Cynic Christians in Corinth, by contrast, breaching tabus seems to be an essential enactment of their freedom; purity laws may not be maintained as ἀδιάφορα.[117]

Those who claim to be 'strong' (ἰσχυροί, 1 Cor 4.10; cf. 10.22) are most likely so in the Diogenean sense suggested by M.-O. Goulet-Cazé, 'Alors qu'Antisthène

---

[116] A. J. Malherbe (1995), 237.
[117] So, too, J. L. Jaquette (1995), 143–46.

exigeait l'*ischus* pour rendre efficace la vertu, Diogène a fait de cette force l'essence même de la vertu.' This is the Diogenes who refused to take things easy when he grew old.[118] 'Diogenes was going into a theatre, against the stream of people coming out. Asked why, he said, "This is what I am spending my life practising."'[119] Epictetus' idealised Cynic, too, will be physically resilient, 'the quality of his body matters' (if only to persuade ordinary people).[120] However, for Epictetus, of course, one must first learn where to give and where to withhold assent, and the ascetic 'short cut' is useless on its own. Without proper Stoic intellectual and moral formation ('a winter's training') an ordinary Cynic's display of his strength and good health will be no help at all to the perplexed and the sickly, and only manifest his own (inner) weakness.[121] The 'strong' in Corinth are behaving and talking like the Cynics Epictetus criticises, and Paul perceives them in a very similar light.

---

[118] M.-O. Goulet-Cazé (1986), 154, and 151, citing Diogenes Laertius 6.34.

[119] Diogenes Laertius 6.64. For other examples of 'strength' in terms of decisive physical action, cf. Dio 6.22 (animals as good example); 8.17; 8.24 (most powerful); cf. 9.12 ('power of soul' - but not mind, intellect); ps.-Diogenes 31; Maximus of Tyre 36.6; and the theme of the contrast with athletes, passim.

[120] Epictetus 3.22.86–88; cf. 51.

[121] Epictetus 4.8.27–43. There is an informative discussion of other senses of 'weakness' and 'strength' in ancient philosophical pedagogy in C. E. Glad (1995), 78–82; but the Epicurean distinction between 'the weak and submissive' (who are hurt by harshness), and 'the strong' (who need harsh treatment) does not seem to be at all the distinction being made here by Paul, between 'the strong' who can act on convictions Paul actually shares, and 'the weak' who cannot. Paul's willingness to be weak with the weak (1 Cor 9.20) may well parallel Epicurean psychogogy, but Glad shows that adaptability in this sense is not distinctively Epicurean.

There is actually one Cynic passage which at first glance looks very apposite: 'God is like our good host, setting out all sorts of varied dishes, some for the healthy, some for the sickly, some for the strong (ἰσχυροῖς), others for the weak (ἀσθενοῦσιν), not for us all to use all of them, but only what each one needs.'[122] The word-picture is aimed in fact against the rich who grab everything; but it is easy to see how such language could be interpreted by the strong and free Corinthians who knew that all kinds of food were legitimately theirs to choose from.

For the response Paul himself makes to the meat-eaters and their slogans we may happily stay fairly close to Malherbe, only taking it that the 'cognitive' sense of the 'weakness' under discussion is to be understood as Paul's, not that of the strong Corinthians. They talk of the others as 'weak', just that. It is Paul who qualifies their design-ation by insisting it is their conscience (συνείδησις, aware-ness of things), that is weak: Paul is here again responding to Cynic attitudes in a more Stoic-like way. For people with such *intellectual* weakness, the display of strength by the meat-eaters is even less helpful than Epictetus thought the boasted strength of ordinary Cynics; it is actually counter-productive.[123]

(In Romans, where Paul is discussing some Christians' positive attitudes to special foods and special days – and not negative worries about pagan cult meals – his position sounds yet more clearly Stoic: the decision now depends entirely on inner conviction, on what is believed (Rom 14.5–6, 23). Paul still thinks those making a fuss mistaken, they are 'weak in faith'; but if such is their conviction, they must retain their dietary rules and their

---

[122] Ps.-Lucian, *The Cynic* 7.
[123] Epictetus 4.8.27–30, again.

calendars. Just so could Epictetus allow that an entirely valid sense for the holy could be expressed in terms of various and conflicting dietary codes.[124] In Galatians, by contrast, Paul had offered no hint of compromise on food, and had insisted that observing days and seasons was a return to slavery (Gal 2.11–12, 4.9–11).)

Paul's main argument in 1 Corinthians 9, in the middle of his discussion of dietary issues, is to present an alternative example of practical freedom, his own exercise of his apostolic commission and his decision not to accept any payment that would or might for any reason hinder his preaching.[125] The details of the discussion (working for his living, like some Cynic philosophers) are important, and we shall return to them in chapter 6. Here we need only note, again agreeing with Malherbe, that in 1 Corinthians 9.16–22 Paul goes into a deep discussion of freedom in relation to (divine) necessity, using terms with clear Stoic resonances to express convictions he can elsewhere couch in more biblical language (e.g., Gal. 1.15–16).[126] The Christian way of life which the Corinthians had adopted from him was not one of simple pragmatic (Cynic-style) autonomy. Yet if Paul accepts the divine necessity (ἀνάγκη) willingly (ἑκών) rather than unwillingly (ἄκων) he is then also able to choose *in practice* to forgo the payment for preaching he had a right to, and so to preach unhindered. He can be as pragmatically adaptable to other people as was the 'mild' Cynic Odysseus, and so be

---

[124] Epictetus 1.22.1–14.

[125] Arguing strongly for our chapter 9's integral place in the flow of Paul's argument, A. J. Malherbe (1995); J. L. Jaquette (1995), 146.

[126] Malherbe (1995), 245, notes among other passages Philo, *Quod omnis probus liber sit* 60–61; Seneca, *Epistulae morales* 54.7 and 61.3. We may also note the Stoic sound of Paul's 'Does God care for animals?' (1 Cor 9.9).

able to win them;[127] but able, too, himself to maintain a harsh *askêsis* (1 Cor 9.24–27) which, again (compare 1 Cor 4.9–13), should impress anyone with genuine Cynic leanings. Paul is as free to act as he deems appropriate as any Cynic might be; not his the mere inner accord of a Stoic 'freely' accepting what has to be. It was out of this entirely practical, overt free choice of Paul's, this use of his ἐξουσία, that the Christian good news reached the meat-eaters, and they should respond appropriately, with a similar free and pragmatic self-restraint for the sake of others.

As already mentioned, some further strands in 1 Corinthians will concern us in more detail later. But we recall that while Paul here again reacts against some kinds of Cynic-like behaviour, and at times sounds (in broad terms) somewhat Stoic, yet his claimed severity with himself combined with gentleness towards others also has clear and detailed Cynic parallels which Malherbe and others have effectively substantiated. Even in controversy over those Cynic traits he repudiates Paul retains yet other Cynic-sounding convictions which still make good sense to him. [128]

---

[127] Cf. D. B. Martin (1990), 86–116 and 117–49; however, I here follow A. J. Malherbe (1995), 245–51, on Paul's willingness and unwillingness, rather than Martin, 76 and 133; see further, ch. 5, below.

[128] 'Paul's use of Cynic tradition shows where he wants to place the emphasis – on the side of freedom. Unlike the Stoics . . . Paul places a premium on action, unconventional and contemptible, as a means of benefitting his hearers', A. J. Malherbe (1995), 254. The reader is again reminded that while this interpretation of Paul is here welcomed, the 'meat-eaters' have been interpreted in the foregoing as also 'Cynic' in outlook (albeit differently Cynic), rather than Stoic, as Malherbe concludes, and Cynic very much on the basis of their 'premium on action'.

(x) In conclusion

We have in this chapter been concerned chiefly with the twinned (and intertwined) issues of food and genital activity. Having presented a different and very cogent alternative model of freedom (1 Cor 9) Paul returns to these linked topics (1 Cor 10). He can assume now that the Jewish scriptural tradition carries weight among the Corinthians, and warns by way of scriptural examples against an over-confident sense of belonging. It is intriguing, at least, that when Josephus recounts the episode alluded to at 1 Corinthians 10.8 (Num 25.1–18) he includes a discussion of many of the same issues. Zambrias (Zimri) and the other rebels are sexually seduced into sacrificing to other Gods and eating 'strange food'. Zambrias says to Moses, 'You will not get me to follow your tyrannical orders . . . with all this talk of "laws" and "God", subjecting us to slavery, depriving us of our pleasures and all the autonomy (αὐτεξούσιον) which is ours as free men who own no master'; compare 'why should my liberty be subject to anyone else's view of things?' (1 Cor 10.29b).[129] Perhaps Paul the zealous Pharisee had once seen the Christian movement as just such an antinomian threat to 'the traditions of his forefathers' (Gal 1.14), in the name of a Cynic-like autonomy? and now the freedom for which Christ had set

---

[129] Josephus, *Ant* 4.146, noted in the previous chapter. Zambrias in fact announces that he does sacrifice to 'the Gods to whom he holds sacrifice is due', but on the basis of deciding for himself the truth on this issue, too, 149. Cf. S. Vollenweider (1989), 134–35; P. Borgen (1995), 33–39.

him and others free was being threatened by a hedonist rather than a personally austere ἄσκησις. This interpretation of Numbers 25 certainly seemed obvious to another, slightly later Pharisee of sorts, Josephus.[130]

Just a very few matters, mainly of dedicated food, remain for a brief comment. We noted earlier Mark Plunkett's emphasis on the 'participatory' motif in Paul,[131] and it becomes explicit in the κοινωνία of 1 Corinthians 10.14–22. Paul seems to assume that those he addresses take this seriously. Might it have linked up with the slogan in the syllogism we noted earlier, to the effect that 'friends have all things in common' (κοινὰ τὰ τῶν φίλων)? Diogenes Laertius' metaphysical explanation of Diogenes the Cynic's attitude to food may owe more to Stoicism than to Diogenes the Cynic. But in a less sophisticated way, a pious Cynic (we have noted there were such) might well have had a strong sense of sharing in the life of God or Gods.[132] This way of looking at food could then have transferred without too much difficulty into Christian eucharistic piety.[133] However, while the sense of participation might be very real, a Cynic-like lack of scruples about food might also involve the risk that the 'the body' might not be acknowledged (1 Cor 11.29; as already

---

[130] Phineas, who thrusts his spear through the bellies of both (κοιλία, Num, not Josephus) is, of course, the prototype Jewish zealot, whose act was 'counted to him for righteousness' (Ps. 106.30).

[131] M. Plunkett (1988), 255–59.

[132] Diogenes Laertius 6.72–73; cf. J. H. Moles (1993), 269–71, on the participatory implications of this slogan.

[133] Though Paul's Jewish heritage would allow him to assert (in common with some Cynics, as we have seen) that there exist no Gods to be represented by idols, for there is only one God, yet his past will not allow him to say the idols represent nothing at all real in the universe. Dio 4.83–end clearly only imagines daimons.

noted). Furthermore, the idea of eating human flesh, drinking human blood, would have been as shocking to most pagans as it was to Jews; later scandal and persecution bears this out. Initially at least the idea could only have indicated yet another Cynic-like disregard for convention among the young Christian communities. [134]

We have been mainly concerned in this chapter with strand (*d*) of the argument of the book. Paul seems quite clearly to suppose he is addressing people who look to him to be adopting and enacting Cynic ideas and behaviour. They are 'kings' already, with royal rights – and the strength – to do as they will, in sexual and in dietary matters. In terms of the known cultural movements of his day, this is where much of what Paul opposes seems to fit. Nonetheless he can himself still (*a*) deploy yet other Cynic ideas and practices on his own side of the argument. His *askêsis* is Cynic (we examine this in more detail in the next chapter), his decision to work 'slavishly' for his living, all things to all people, is Cynic (see further, chapter 6), his pragmatic freedom is defined as a Cynic's would be, over against a Stoic analysis. Engaged in such arguments, (*b*) Paul can hardly have been unaware of how Cynic he himself would inevitably appear. The choice can only (*c*) have been deliberate. For this must have been how he had first approached people in Corinth, with an invitation that involved a Cynic-like breach with traditional codes and conventions; clearly this is how he and his message had then and since been perceived. Some were indeed taking the Cynic line too far; but the Cynic components were still too integral to Paul's own understanding of Christian discipleship for him to relinquish the many Cynic elements that had become part of his living, thinking, praying.

---

[134] See F. G. Downing (1993a).

It is perhaps worth noting that at no point does Paul imagine that those he supposes are fans of Kephas or of Apollos will find this discussion of important elements of Christian faith and life in Cynic-sounding terms itself at all questionable. As such it needs no apology, only careful qualification. Presumably, then, Cynic strands in early Christianity are not a Pauline novelty, they are at this point (*e*) an accepted part of the wider Christian scene. It was only later, in Galatia, that Cynic antinomianism was to be challenged. Later still, however (and as we shall see), Paul himself seems to become disenchanted. Perhaps his disenchantment with a Cynic strand in the new life began with this dispute with the Corinthian radicals.

There are very obviously many diverse strands in Paul's writing: varieties of Judaism and early Christianity, elements of variegated Cynicism, and some elements which seem strongly to echo Stoic discussions, perhaps even traces of an Epicurean ethos. But the most important common field of discourse, informing both those he addresses and Paul himself, throughout this long series of arguments about freedom as it relates to dedicated food and to genital sexual activity (and, for illustration, Paul's own ministry), would seem to have been afforded by elements of variegated Cynicism. Variegated Cynicism seems to have offered Paul, in the earliest preaching of the gospel for which we have evidence, the obvious terminology and thought-forms with which to work out and articulate large and important areas of what he wanted to say and exemplify and share – and himself believed.

5

TROUBLES INVITED, TROUBLES WITHSTOOD

(i) Distinctively Cynic physical self-discipline

The metaphors of 'soldier' and of 'athlete' are as commonplace in Paul as they are among the general run of moralists in the ancient world.[1] Life is presented as an *agôn*, a struggle. One best prepares for the struggle by appropriate *askêsis*, training, which will allow one to endure troubles that arrive uninvited. But preparatory training in effect amounts to engaging in hardships voluntarily, and so a very important spectrum emerges between (at the hedonistic end of the scale) preparing to cope with difficulties that are absolutely unavoidable, and (at the other end) positively inviting trouble so as to be able to face and to overcome it as well as each and every challenge that may arrive unbidden.

This distinction – albeit along a continuum – is important for this section of the present study. Recent scholars who have very properly called our attention to the wide dispersion of the motif of 'struggle' in ancient Mediterranean literature but have also noted its particular prevalence among 'Stoics and Cynics', have nevertheless

---

[1] See especially V. C. Pfitzner (1967); and cf. 1 Tim 6.12; Heb 10.32; 12.1.

tended to leave the matter there.[2] It is there, however, as we have already noted in passing, that an important difference lies: between many if not all Stoics on the one hand, and most if not all Cynics on the other.

For most who used the trope, as Marie-Odile Goulet-Cazé has pointed out, the 'athlete' metaphor is only a metaphor. 'For the Cynic philosopher it is quite different. Far from mere metaphor, his *askêsis* . . . is entirely concrete, even though it has its own methods . . . it remains physical, bodily.'[3] This stress on the sage's physical self-discipline is uniquely Cynic.[4] 'By physical training (γυμνασία) we arrrive at excellence (ἀρετή - "virtue").'[5] This would seem to provide the most significant mark of the thorough-going Cynic, not only in terms of self-definition,[6] but (as importantly) in the eyes of spectators. The Stoic way (as the most significant comparison) was to bring the soul into conformity with the universal Logos, it was a matter of interior spirituality, intellectualist in the Socratic tradition. You had to learn and to understand. The end result should be an increasingly disciplined life 'according to nature', as your intellectual conversion took hold, and your body obediently responded to the progress of your rational soul. The (hypothetical) truly wise man

---

[2] For a recent example, A. E. Harvey (1996), 16, 'Stoic'; 56, 'Stoic and Cynic philosophers', indiscriminately.

[3] M.-O. Goulet-Cazé (1986), 53, my translation ('Pour le philosophe cynique il en va tout autrement. Loin d'être une métaphore . . . une ascèse bien concrète qui, même si dans ses modalités elle diffère . . . reste avant tout de nature corporelle' (see the whole section 53–76); and *eadem* (1990), 2738–52; also R. B. Branham and M.-O. Goulet-Cazé (1996), 26; and A. A. Long (1996), 40–43.

[4] T. W. Martin (1996), 62; and the whole section 58–78.

[5] Diogenes Laertius 6.70.

[6] A. J. Malherbe (1982), 49–52, on 'Cynic self-definition'.

would necessarily be an ascetic - asceticism was not ultimately an optional extra. But physically ascetic practices and life-style in themselves were no guaranteed or necessary way to strength of soul and inner αὐτάρκεια.

A Cynic, by contrast, was determinedly pragmatic. Virtue, excellence, could be acquired by any human, and perfection reached (and held) by physical self-discipline. A Stoic could opt to include the Cynic 'shortcut' as part of the lengthy programme of adaptation, with intellectual formation still the goal. Chosen hardships could also test a would-be Stoic's progress, could provide matter for reflection. So there could be some overlap of Stoic and Cynic practice (as in Musonius and others). Philo, for instance, advances this option through his figure of Jacob, the ἀσκητής. Jacob achieves intellectual virtue, albeit very gradually, and by strenuous and quite physical effort.[7] But the real concern, the τέλος, is the inward disposition. All external matters (including the body) are ἀδιάφορα, matters of no significance in themselves. So Epictetus insists, 'First of all you must purify your governing [rational] faculty, and adopt this unswerving principle: "Now the matter I have to work on is my mind . . . My little body is nothing."' [8] For the Cynic, on the other hand, the ascetic life-style - the poor clothing, the meagre diet, the lack of shelter, the physical effort - was of the essence.[9]

---

[7] See M.-O.Goulet-Cazé (1986), 182–9; Philo, *De migratione* 214; *De mutatione* 83-87; *De somniis* 1 120-25, for a Cynic style regimen.

[8] Epictetus 3.22.19–21.

[9] See in particular, M.-O. Goulet-Cazé (1986), 22–29, 53–55, 158–91; A. J. Malherbe (1978), 55–59; E. Bréhier (1950), 263–71, on this Cynic theme in Philo; F. G. Downing (1992a), 36–37. Note in particular Diogenes Laertius 6.104; 7.121; Epictetus 3.22.9–13, 50–51; 4.8.34–43; ps.-Diogenes 30; ps.-Crates 6; Lucian, *Hermotimus*; Julian, *To the Uneducated Cynics* 194D–195A, 197A; *To the Cynic*

In particular, for a Stoic, poverty was a matter of indifference: a Stoic could cope with wealth or its absence.[10] For a Cynic (shams aside), poverty was a necessary part of well-being.[11]

When Paul talks of troubles he has coped with we must ask where along the continuum just sketched does what he claims seem to fit. We shall depend quite extensively on others' recent researches; but it will be argued (against a widespread failure to note or effectively to deploy the distinctions just drawn) that both the details of the life-style Paul outlines and his emphasis on activities he has undertaken (rather than on any mental attitude, inner calm in particular), mean that often (and especially earlier) he stands at the Cynic end of the spectrum, even though occasionally (and especially later) he may sound more Stoic. If and when Paul paraded himself, drew attention to himself by public speaking in whatever contexts, while obviously and persistently poor, hungry, scarred by beatings, (half-)naked (rather than merely 'ill-clad'; see further, below), he would inescapably appear (*a*) to be some sort of Cynic teacher. Of course many other people were poor, hungry, and half-naked; but not as teachers making converts to a non-conformist life-style opposed to important civic conventions. What we shall further find is that when Paul talks about his harsh self-discipline, it is in terms that are themselves distinctively Cynic, and integral to some of the arguments he has with fellow Christians. Paul's Cynic-looking and Cynic-*sounding askêsis* is (*b*) overt and (*c*) deliberate. And it seems quite clear that Paul

---

Herakleios 225C, 235C. It is this distinction that A. E. Harvey, cited above, signally misses (1996), 56.

[10] Diogenes Laertius 7.105.

[11] Ps.-Crates 8; ps.-Diogenes 26; 37.6; etc.

expects his *askêsis* to carry weight, to be acknowledged as unquestionably significant, even by those fellow Christians with whom he is in dispute. It is not simply a peculiarity of his, it is (*e*) part of the wider early Christian scene.

There is a further distinction, also already noted above, that will concern us again here, that between the more severe and the more easy going of Cynics. It has been argued above that there are still more variations to be discerned than will fall tidily into these two groups, but here we shall note the willingness of gentler Cynics to accept Odysseus as a model (perhaps influenced by surviving work of Antisthenes, with the latter seen – albeit mistakenly – as the founder of Cynicism), over against the outright refusal of others to countenance Odysseus' softness and readiness to adapt as in any way a pattern for Cynics to follow.[12] But one could be severe with oneself while gentle with others, as Crates is sometimes portrayed, and as Paul presents himself.

And so to Paul in more detail. At 1 Corinthians 9.24–27 Paul deploys an extended athletic metaphor:

> (α) You know, don't you, that all the runners in the stadium run, *with just one winning the prize.* (β) *Run in such a way that you* (plural) *will win.* Everyone entering the contest (ἀγωνιζόμενος) is self-controlled (ἐγκρατεύεται) in every way. (γ) Runners behave like this to gain a wreath that withers. We exercise self-control to gain one that never withers. (δ) I don't run purposelessly, my boxing (πυκτεύω) isn't punching the air. (ε) I beat my own body and subdue it, lest after preaching to others I find myself disqualified.

---

[12] On this see above, ch. 2; and A. J. Malherbe (1982); and, e.g., Dio 9.9 (Diogenes is an Odysseus-like figure) against ps.-Crates 19. For Antisthenes, G. Giannantoni (1990), V A 54.

We register the puzzling discrepancy between Paul's comment that only one gets a prize in the races, and his insistence that *all* his Corinthian friends are to 'run' for an 'imperishable crown'.[13]

Hermann Funke in his 'Antisthenes bei Paulus' notes that commentators have seemed satisfied to see a nondescript Stoic–Cynic background to Paul's imagery here, happy to quote from Lucian's *Anacharsis*, 'Do all the contestants get prizes?' with Solon's reply, 'No, only one, the overall winner.'[14] But Anacharsis' question is of course ironic, in line with the standard Cynic disparagement of actual athletes and their pointless contests.[15]

There is, however, a much closer parallel with the passage from Paul, in Dio, *Discourse* 8, often thought in turn to depend on Antisthenes, but here focusing on Diogenes.[16] Just as Paul explains (α) that he (and the Corinthians) are here to 'run', so Diogenes says he's not come to the Isthmian Games as a spectator, but to take part (ἀλλ' ἀγωνιούμενος) (8.11). Both then (β) demand total concentration: the ideal contestant proposed by Dio's 'Diogenes' engages in the struggle night and day, it's a full-time occupation (8.15). (γ) Both next disparage the athletic prizes, preferring their own. So 'Diogenes' does not strive for a bit of parsley, as goats might, nor wild olive, or pine, but for well-being and for excellence throughout his life (8.15, again). (δ) Both then pick up the

---

[13] Cf. H. Conzelmann (1969/1976), 162, 'the moral that Paul derives from it – namely that only one receives the prize – appears out of place'.

[14] H. Funke (1970), 460–71; Lucian, *Anacharsis* 13; cf. H. Conzelmann, (1969/1976), 162, n. 34. It is strange that A. Papathomas (1997), ignores Funke's article and the parallel motif in Dio.

[15] Cf. Dio 9; ps.-Diogenes 31; Diogenes Laertius 6.49, 62.

[16] H. Funke (1970), 468–71.

theme of boxing, hitting and not hitting, with 'Diogenes' choosing those who know how to box (οἱ πυκτεύειν εἰδότες), anticipating their opponents, avoiding being hit and often coming off victorious (8.18). (ε) Both adduce their own example offered to others, 'Diogenes' telling us, 'This is the struggle I risk keeping on with, while worthless wretches pay no attention' (8.26). (Dio then moves on to consider Herakles, performing his wretched, slavish tasks, subject to Eurystheus (8.26–36) which may be echoed in Paul's δουλαγωγῶ, 'I bring my body into subjection.')[17]

Dio's disquisition is obviously much longer than Paul's; but the two include many of the same motifs. And, most significantly, Dio's version clarifies the contradiction we noted in Paul. Dio's Cynic is engaged in a contest where there *is* a prize for every entrant: the victory over hunger, thirst and cold, and over pleasure and public opinion. This contest is much more worthwhile than any in which only a single showy crown is at stake. So we may conclude with Funke, a complex of Cynic 'athletic' motifs comes readily to Paul's lips – so readily that he alludes explicitly to the complex, but fails to integrate his theme – all can win prizes – a motif which is clearly there in Dio's version.

But even more important than the similarities in the rhetoric is the actual distinctive thrust of Paul's words which this comparison brings into focus. In context Paul can only be referring to a very physical (and so, Cynic) *askêsis*, although in the light of Dio 8 and Paul's own reference to self-control, his talk of 'beating his own body to subdue it' has to be taken as metaphor rather than

---

[17] H. Funke (1970), 467–68; cf. 1 Cor 9.19, Paul as slave to all; and see next note. (Funke offers many further detailed comparisons and supporting arguments.)

indicating self-inflicted injury. Dio says as much of himself, as an Odysseus figure, 'subduing his own body with severe blows'; so, too, did Maximus of Tyre, of Diogenes.[18] Paul is reminding his Corinthian friends of his own life-style, and encouraging them to emulate it. His words sound Cynic; yet, still more significant, the habitual discipline he sought to share would in practice look Cynic. There was no other comparable movement around according such prominence to such practice in such terms, as the major means to achieve its chosen end.[19] We have to give full weight to the fact that this physical *askêsis* is present-ed as a powerful argument in its own right; its validity as an argument in Paul's circle can simply be assumed. And this can only make sense in a context where a broadly Cynic ethos obtains.

We must, however, also note a contrast with the later Paul of Philippians 3.12–14; there a more Stoic-sounding progress to an as yet unattained goal of under-standing is at issue;[20] here, earlier, Paul talks rather of maintaining the 'fitness' he has achieved.

---

[18] Dio 33.14; cf. Maximus of Tyre 15.9, as in Giannantoni (1990) V B 265.

[19] For sure, Paul's 'prize' is to be raised incorruptible, to be for ever with the Lord. That is what he presumably means here by an 'incorruptible crown'. Most (but by no means all) Cynics were sceptical as to life of any kind after physical death. Yet, distinctive though Paul's final aim must therefore seem to us, he does not appear to have got this distinctive goal over to all his converts in Corinth (1 Cor 15.12, 19). His very physical and so 'this-worldly' seeming asceticism would doubtless have been from the start a very important indicator that here was some sort of Cynic teacher of this-worldly well-being, *eudaimonia* (on which see M.-O. Goulet-Cazé (1986), 71–76.

[20] G. F. Hawthorne (1983), 152; cf. Phil 3.8 and 10, and the emphasis here on attitudes and awareness.

A few years earlier than H. Funke's article, V. C. Pfitzner published a study entitled *Paul and the Agôn Motif*. He allowed that in many instances in Paul, as elsewhere, the athletic metaphor was simply a colloquial idiom, as at Galatians 5.7. However, in the passage we have been considering, and at Galatians 2.2 and Philippians 2.16, he judged that the language had more force, even evoking an awareness of the original context of the imagery.[21] Unfortunately Pfitzner glossed over any possible difference between Cynic and Stoic use of the motif, citing mostly Epictetus' idealised and very Stoic Cynicism, then concentrating on Stoics as such. It is, then, however, of considerable interest to find him insisting that in Paul, over against the Stoics, the motif is not at all concerned with an inner moral struggle: that would be to miss the real point of what Paul says.[22] In effect, what Pfiztner sees as distinguishing Paul's use of the *agôn* motif from its Stoic use is also precisely what distinguishes a Cynic understanding of their *agôn* from a Stoic stance. Paul's *agôn* is Cynic.

We would of course have to agree that Paul does not present the aim of his struggle as simply the avoidance of defeat by fame, pleasure or riches. His struggle, as Pfitzner rightly insists, is for the sake of spreading the Gospel.[23] However, neither does this afford a clear contrast with the Cynic *agôn*, as we have already seen. Cynics claim to engage in their struggle for the sake of influencing others, even if those others take no notice, as well as for

---

[21] V. C. Pfitzner (1967), 127.
[22] V. C. Pfitzner (1967), 80–81, 111–12.
[23] V. C. Pfitzner (1967), 93–94.

their own sakes; and just so does Paul 'run' to share the Gospel *and* to maintain his own share in it (1 Cor 9.23).[24]

(ii) Weapons for the fight

At 2 Corinthians 10.3–6 Paul seems to be deploying ideas reminiscent of the figure of Odysseus, as originally analysed by Antisthenes; so Abraham J. Malherbe has cogently argued. Malherbe quotes Moffatt's translation:

> I do live in the flesh, but I do not make war as the flesh does; the weapons of my warfare are not weapons of the flesh, but divinely strong to demolish fortresses - I demolish theories [better, reasoning powers, λογισμούς; so Malherbe, later] and any rampart thrown up to resist the knowledge of God. I take every project prisoner to make it obey Christ. I am prepared to court-martial anyone who remains insubordinate, once your submission is complete.

There is similar imagery in the Greek Bible (Proverbs 21.22), but with much less detail. There are passages in Philo that have more details in common with Paul here, but with the difference Malherbe notes that Paul is attacking defences set up against 'the knowledge of God', while Philo is concerned with intellectual defence against sophistic attack.[25]

A major impetus behind such elaborate use of such military language seems, from available fragments, to have been provided by Antisthenes, himself perhaps influenced

---

[24] Even the severe Cynic of ps.-Crates 19 talks of Diogenes 'delivering many from evil to excellence'; but cf. also the frequent 'physician' image: F. G. Downing (1988c), 122–23.

[25] A. J. Malherbe (1983a), 143–47 = (1989), 91–95; citing Philo *De confusione* 128–31.

by the example of Sparta's virile defences. A city can be betrayed from within, Antisthenes is quoted as saying, but each individual human can build walls which may be neither shaken nor toppled.[26] Elsewhere Antisthenes designates virtue, excellence, as a weapon that cannot be taken from you, and you need to be allied with others so armed. But also, 'Prudence (φρόνησις) affords an unshakeable defensive wall, never crumbling away, never betrayed. Such defensive walls must be constructed from indestructible reasoning powers (ἀναλώτοις λογισμοῖς).'[27] Malherbe concludes, 'Here for the first time we have Paul's imagery in which the reasoning faculties . . . function in the inner fortification of a person.'[28]

Stoics such as Epictetus took up the imagery of the wise man's inner defences.[29] The opposition Paul faces is pictured as building just such a self-assured (Stoic-like) intellectualist stronghold which Paul is armed to overcome. He has 'weapons with divine power', ὅπλα . . . δυνατὰ τῷ θεῷ, just as the more severe Cynics have the 'weapons of the Gods'.[30] Paul is here using Cynic talk against a Stoic-sounding opposition.

The metaphor of 'weaponry' also appears in the surviving fragments of Antisthenes' apology for Odysseus

---

[26] A. J. Malherbe (1983a), 148–50 = (1989), 95–98; the quotation is from Epiphanius, *Panarion* 3.26 (Giannantoni (1990), V A 107).

[27] Diogenes Laertius 6.12, 13.

[28] A. J. Malherbe (1983a), 150–51 = (1989), 97–98.

[29] Epictetus 4.6.14 (body armour); 4.8.33 (his self-respect is walls, doors, door-keepers); cf. 3.22.13; as cited by A. J. Malherbe (1983a), 154–55 = (1989), 102.

[30] Cf. Diogenes Laertius 6.13–14. Cynics deploy the metaphor of divine offensive weapons with reference to their gear (most often, but not always, the folded cloak, satchel and staff); ps.-Crates 16, 23; ps.-Diogenes 34.1.

as a proper model for true excellence, virtue, set in an unfavourable comparison with Ajax. 'Odysseus is unarmed. He does not rush the enemies' walls but enters their city stealthily and overpowers them from within with their own weapons.' And Odysseus acts this way to 'save' others, it is his kind of 'daring', even though his weapons are servile, just the rags he wears in disguise. This Odysseus adapts to circumstance (as of course Paul claims he does, 1 Corinthians 9.19–23; see chapter 6, below).[31] Similarly Paul is (or senses he is) accused of being humble (ταπεινός) when present, bold (θαρρῶ) when absent (2 Cor 10.1, cf. 9; and, earlier, 1 Cor 2.4), inconsistent and servile. And this, again, is how Odysseus the (over-) adaptable is adversely characterised (by, among others, the harsher Cynics).[32] But this humble, servile role is what Paul himself chose, working for his keep (2 Cor 11.7), just as Dio had chosen 'humble garb' (στολήν ταπεινὴν) in emulation of Odysseus, and had also worked for his keep.[33] Paul is as confident (2 Cor 10.2) in his unimpressive campaign as Antisthenes' philosophical Odysseus appears in the fragment referred to.

Malherbe concludes, 'Paul is like the Cynics in describing his manner of life, which for them was symbolised by their garb, as weapons, and by relating them to

---

[31] A. J. Malherbe (1983a), 151–53 = (1989), 99–101; for the passages cited, Giannantoni (1990) V A 53 and 54; and cf. D. B. Martin (1990), chs 3 and 4.

[32] Cf. ps.-Crates 19 in particular; A. J. Malherbe (1983a), 163–67 = (1989), 110–15. Malherbe argues that the Antisthenic background is more apposite than that adduced by H. D. Betz, from arguments between philosophers and sophists in general: H. D. Betz (1972), 44–68.

[33] Dio 13.10, and Philostratus, *Lives of the Sophists* 488; A. J. Malherbe (1983a), 161 = (1989), 108.

God. He differs radically from them, however, in that his confidence is not in himself, but in God's power.'[34] Whatever the contrasts in 'theology' (which we shall reassess in due course), it is again significant to find Paul deploying such motifs, Cynic as distinct from Stoic, and in gentler as opposed to harsher Cynic mode. Paul is in effect importantly defining his apostolic mission and methods in metaphors that seem to have been carefully selected on the basis of an awareness of their resonances – and in the expectation that these would be recognised. Paul knows that he behaves and appears like a quite specific kind of Cynic; and, although he has not a few 'un-Cynic' things to say, yet for many important purposes he is quite content to continue to conduct himself and to present himself in this light. Obviously, there seems to have been much more to be gained by using this language than might be lost even were the 'wrong' Cynic (or Stoic) resonances to be picked up. Paul knows his way round this field of contemporary discourse, he is 'at home' in it, and deploys it with confidence. He is not looking for illustrations in someone else's anthology. This language affords him the most 'natural and telling way to display and convey what he intends to share'.[35]

There is one further relevant reference in Paul to a kind of warfare, his 'fight with wild beasts in Ephesus' (1 Cor 15.32). Again we are indebted to Abraham Malherbe's

---

[34] A. J. Malherbe (1983a), 171 = (1989), 117. The issue of Paul's seemingly distinctive (over against any ordinary Cynic's) reliance on God will be discussed later. There are closer Cynic analogies to Paul's conviction than Malherbe here allows.

[35] A. J. Malherbe (1995), 255, 'The philosophic traditions are for him not merely a pile of topoi or slogans from which he can draw . . . [they] do not constitute a "background" . . . [but] a milieu in which issues that engaged him and his converts were already widely discussed.'

researches. Malherbe has shown with ample documentation that this sort of language would have been taken to refer to the conquest of the passions, especially when contrasted with the (imputedly Epicurean) hedonism of the second half of the verse, and was most at home in Cynic discourse: for instance, in Dio's *Discourses* 5 (on Herakles) and 8 and 9 (on Diogenes).[36]

(iii) Troubles taken on

More significant still, and not simply more frequent than athletic or military metaphors, are the lists of hardships which Paul includes from time to time: 1 Corinthians 4.9–13; 2 Corinthians 4.8–9, 6.4–5, 11.23–29, 12.10; Philippians 4.12; and Romans 8.35. Part of the first of these runs as follows:

> Continuously, up to the present day, we go hungry and thirsty and (half-)naked (γυμνιτεύομεν), we're beaten up, we wander around homeless. We take on hard manual labour. We're jeered at – and return a blessing, we're persecuted – and we still persist. We're slandered – and we reply kindly. We're treated as everyone's dirt, the refuse from everywhere (1 Cor 4.11–13).

Here again we benefit from a number of recent studies which survey the ground and provide the usual brief history of research. Various distinctions are drawn as to the style of each list. Some, it is noted, contrast 'antithetically' Paul's distress with others' well-being, or his sense of well-being in the midst of distress; while others catalogue hardships in terms ranging from the very general to the

---

[36] A. J. Malherbe [1968] (1989); the references here are to Dio 5.23–24; and 8.2–29; and 9.12.

quite specific.[37] More importantly for our present purposes, while earlier studies tried to place the Pauline lists
either purely in the Jewish apocalyptic tradition or in
Stoicism, Robert Hodgson showed very clearly if quite
briefly that such lists are found in many more contexts
around the first century CE.[38] Longer studies appearing
subsequently acknowledge Hodgson's conclusions. Jewish
sources remain significant, but they are of course part of
their own wider Hellenistic culture. It then emerges from
John T. Fitzgerald's more elaborate study that it is the
'pagan' Hellenistic discussions of the tribulations of the
wise man that offer the most fruitful cultural context for
Paul's inventories of troubles, (harsh) circumstances,
περιστάσεις.[39] However, despite Fitzgerald's wide-
ranging survey of the 'the hardships of the sage', noting
some differences between and among Stoics and Cynics in
particular, most of his illustrations when he reaches the
Corinthian epistles are drawn indiscriminately from mainly
Stoic sources. And although Martin Ebner's more recent
study also ranges widely and brings very cogently to our
attention a number of Cynic specifics in the Pauline lists,
he also ignores the important underlying difference
between Cynic and Stoic attitudes to harsh circumstances.[40] It is, then, necessary to recall and further
emphasise the distinction sketched just above.

---

[37] R. Hodgson (1983), 63.

[38] R. Hodgson (1983), 60, arguing against W. Schrage (1974) and
R. Bultmann (1910).

[39] J. T. Fitzgerald (1988), 30–31; cf. C. G. Montefiore (1914), 203.

[40] M. Ebner (1991); see further, below. M. S. Ferrari (1991) affords a
useful supplement to Ebner's study, including some helpful tables,
comprising very full lists of comparable passages in various ancient
east Mediterranean sources. He also makes some cogent comments on
method. Unfortunately, his own study turns out to be very formal,

Stoics and Cynics both expect to encounter harsh circumstances, and hope to cope with them. Their anticipated and past 'external' trials and troubles as such do not seem to differ much in themselves; their respective lists can properly be used to illustrate one another's approaches to life. But there is a significant difference. A Stoic will expect troubles to confront him; a Cynic will initiate such confrontations. A Stoic may take on some hardship as part of his education, or to test out the progress of his inner resolve.[41]. A Cynic is essentially pragmatic, and enacts his or her commitment openly by openly looking for trouble all the while (at least in theory).

Thus Epictetus castigates his would-be Cynic, who to his rough cloak and hard bed is going to add wallet and staff and the habit of going round begging from and abusing those he meets, while reprimanding any appearance of soft self-indulgence in others.[42] Epictetus confesses that such was his own practice at one time, but not now.[43] His present, clearly Stoic, practice is *not* to invite people to accept reprimand; and if someone does find his philosophic analysis grating, then he will simply excuse

---

based largely on the very small number of passages in Epictetus which deploy a similar vocabulary. The contrasts with Epictetus which Ferrari then notes might well have led him to pay attention to very similar contrasts with Epictetus' Stoicism to be found in Paul's tribulation lists. S. B. Andrews (1995) locates 2 Cor 11.23–33, as we shall note below, in the area of Antisthenes–Odysseus that we have just considered, but without reference to the crucial Cynic motif here distinguished.

[41] J. T. Fitzgerald (1988), 78–79, quoting extensively from Seneca; one might compare, e.g., Epictetus 3.22.56–57 (Zeus exercises the sage this way); see also M. Griffin (1996), 198–200.

[42] Epictetus 3.22.10–11; cf. 4.8.34.

[43] Epictetus 2.12.17–25.

himself.[44] By contrast, of course, the Diogenes of the *chreiai* abuses all and sundry,[45] as does Lucian's auctioned Cynic, 'impudent and bold, abusing each and everyone', and as do his plebeian Cynics when they leave their workshops.[46] Even Lucian's gentle Demonax fell foul of the Athenian crowd, took the initiative in criticising hordes of people around him, and stood up for a fellow Cynic in trouble for the customary mockery of hairless legs, but aimed rather riskily at a proconsul.[47]

Perhaps most tellingly, Epictetus advises, 'If you want to be crucified, just wait. The cross will come. If it seems reasonable to comply, and the circumstances are right, then it's to be carried through, and your integrity maintained.'[48] If maintaining his integrity demands accepting hardship and pain, then he will. But he will not seek it. His calling is to wait for what happens, as ordained by God who exercises him. It is God who decides whether Epictetus' Stoic 'Cynic' becomes great, or receives a beating. Perhaps a beating 'must' happen (δεῖ), and then the ideal Stoic Cynic will exercise his inner restraint and brotherly love for all.[49] But he does nothing to bring it on himself.

The Diogenes of the tradition, on the other hand, challenges Fate and Fortune, always striving to maintain

---

[44] Epictetus 3.23.27–29; cf. 1.12.21.

[45] Diogenes Laertius 6.26–29, 32–33, 38, 44, 56, etc.

[46] Lucian, *Philosophies for Sale 10; The Runaways* 12–19.

[47] Lucian, *Demonax* 11 (he risks being stoned (despite 7)), and 50, in particular, but many anecdotes in between where Demonax' criticisms are constantly unsolicited.

[48] Epictetus 2.2.20.

[49] Epictetus 3.22.53–55.

the initiative.[50] A Cynic makes trouble for himself (and in fulfilment of his mission). So pseudo-Crates urges, 'Whether toil (trouble, hardship, πόνος) is something to be chosen or to be avoided, toil on so toil won't trouble you. You won't get away from toublesome toil by giving up toiling, you're only in for more trouble (εἴθ᾽ αἱρετὸν πόνος, εἴτε φευκτόν, πόνει, ἵνα μὴ πονῇς).'[51] Pseudo-Crates thus dismisses a Stoic distinction between what might be preferred and chosen, or might be refused, and instead urges harsh and incessant toil, come what may. 'Toils' are to be sought. The Cynic can be defined as the one who toils: 'ὁ δὲ κύων . . . ὁ πονῶν, in the philosophy of Diogenes'.[52]

So it is significant that the Stoic περιστάσεις lists cited by Fitzgerald (and by Ebner) have the sage always reactive, responding to the promptings of divine providence or fate, never himself taking the initiative:

> Would you have me bear poverty?
>> Bring it on and you shall see what poverty is
>> when it finds a good actor to play the part.
> Would you have me hold office?
>> Bring it on.
> Would you have me suffer deprivation of office?
>> Bring it on.
> Well, and would you have me bear troubles (πόνους)?
>> Bring them on, too.
> Well, and exile?...[53]

---

[50] Ps.-Dio 64.18; ps.-Crates 19; Diogenes Laertius 6.105.

[51] Ps.-Crates 4.

[52] Ps.-Crates 15 and 16; cf. also 20, 33, and 34.4; and ps.-Diogenes 14.

[53] Epictetus 4.7.13, cited by J. T. Fitzgerald (1988), 72-73, with further lines (LCL); there are intriguing echoes of this in the Methodist Covenant Service, 'Put me to what thou wilt . . .'.

Thus, when Epictetus' ideal Cynic notes what he does without, 'having nothing, naked, without house or home, unkempt, without slave or city', this has to be taken in context as the situation he deals with (and chooses to affirm), not one he has selected among other possibilities.[54]

So, too, Fitzgerald cites Seneca,

Let us think of everything that can happen as something
  that will happen.
I may become a poor man;
I shall then be one among many.
I may be exiled;
I shall regard myself as [having been] born in the place to
  which I shall be sent.
They may put me in chains . . . .[55]

And we may compare the Stoic paradoxes from Plutarch, quoted by both Fitzgerald and Ebner:

The sage of the Stoics is unimpeded when confined, uncompelled when thrown down a precipice, untormented when racked, uninjured when mutilated, unbeaten when he's suffered a fall in the ring, unblockaded when besieged, remains uncaptured when sold by his enemies.[56]

Each circumstance is given in a passive participle, save 'suffered a fall' (which is presumably not deliberate!); in passives, too, are the notes of the sage's inner condition. The Stoic wise man is primarily reactive, with a stress on his inner response. He is not solely reactive, nor entirely inactive: as we have noted already, he may adopt a

---

[54] Epictetus 3.22.47, cited by M. Ebner (1991), 28.

[55] Seneca, *Epistulae morales* 24.17 (LCL), part of quotation by J. T. Fitzgerald (1988), 93.

[56] Plutarch, *Comp. arg. Stoicos* 1057DE, cited by J. T. Fitzgerald (1988), 100, M. Ebner (1991), 216.

personal physical ἄσκησις as rigorous as any Cynic's.[57] But reactive he is in the main, so far as the wider world is concerned. 'We ought not to lead events, but to follow them', insists Epictetus.[58]

Very different is the active initiative taken by Dio's Diogenes, in his distinctively Cynic *Discourse* 8. Diogenes 'comes to take part in the contest'. He chooses 'to compete with the toughest of antagonists, real hardships, τοὺς πόνους'. He asks for none other, but deliberately 'challenges them all in turn (προκαλούμενον ἐφεξῆς ἄπαντας), grappling with hunger and cold, engaging with thirst. He remains steadfast if he has to take a flogging, shows no weakness if he's cut about or burned. Hunger, exile, loss of reputation count for nothing.' The Cynic chooses to fight, and what or who to fight, and does not wait for contests to be forced on him (though, of course, many may).[59]

We find the same emphasis in pseudo-Lucian, *The Cynic*. His interrogator demands, 'Why do you have that beard and long hair, but no tunic, half-naked and barefoot, choosing (ἐπιλεξάμενος) this inhuman and beastly nomadic existence?' His interlocutor, ripostes Cyniscus, is

---

[57] See n. 3, above.

[58] Epictetus 3.10.19; cf. 1.12.15, learning to will each thing the way it happens.

[59] Dio 8.12, 15–16 (cf.9.11–12) cited by J. T. Fitzgerald (1988), 99; and the former passage by M. Ebner (1991), 29; compare also Dio 6.8–34, where, again, Diogenes' deliberate choice is emphasised; and Seneca, *De providentia* 2.9: issuing a challenge is more noble than accepting one, of Cato (seen by Seneca as a Cynic kind of hero). Cf. F. G. Downing (1992a), 39–42 on Cynics provoking Fate or Fortune. Neither Fitzgerald nor Ebner (nor K. Berger (1984a), 225–28) seems to have noted the very different underlying tone of the Cynic over against the Stoic attitude to troublesome circumstances.

like someone on a runaway horse; by contrast, the Cynic does what he decides (ὅ τι βούλομαι) and keeps the company of his own choice.[60] Lucian himself makes fun of precisely this attitude in his *Philosophies for Sale*. This Cynic is 'no conscript, but a volunteer'. Anyone else who chooses to accept his or her course of training will be liberated from her or his existing place in society (quite clearly so; there is no question of being fitted to cope better with it).[61] Of course, the models for this deliberate abandonment of a given social role are Crates and then Hipparchia, even more than Diogenes forced into exile. Crates voluntarily dispossesses himself of inherited wealth (one way or another), and adopts the Cynic life-style. This was to set himself free.[62] Hipparchia chooses Crates and his way of life.[63] A Cynic, then, chooses 'poverty . . . hunger, cold, contempt', 'poverty, disrepute, lowly status, exile', rather than simply learning to cope with them if he or she has to, or to make use of them as part of some further mental discipline.[64]

This is not to ignore the possibility that some Cynics may have thought of themselves as responding in their choice to some sort of call from God or a God;[65] but

---

[60] Ps.-Lucian, *The Cynic* 1 and 18–19.

[61] Lucian, *Philosophies for Sale* 8–9; cf. *The Runaways* 17; and *Peregrinus* 14–20.

[62] Diogenes Laertius 6.87; ps.-Diogenes 9, 26, 38.

[63] Diogenes Laertius 6.96–98; ps.-Crates 28; ps.-Diogenes 3.

[64] Ps.-Diogenes 36.4; 31.4 (with δυσγενεία as 'low status' in this context, rather than 'lowly birth' as such); and cf. 30.3. (To deploy a misshapen neologism, a Cynic is 'proactive', not (as the Stoics) reactive.)

[65] Diogenes himself, in some traditions: cf. Diogenes Laertius 6.20, Julian, *To the Uneducated Cynics* 188AB; but especially Dio 13.9: 'The deity ordered me to keep on with the good and useful activity

that is still very different from the sense of divine appoint-
ment to maintain your integrity (and possibly so help
others to maintain theirs) in whatever circumstances befall
you, which we find in Epictetus.[66] A Cynic, then, who
talks in terms of a divine commissioning is articulating a
perceived invitation to choose to adopt a whole new social
role and pattern of behaviour, to opt for fresh initiatives,
deliberately to engage in a harsh life-style.

Martin Ebner is able to point to significant details
in Paul's tribulation lists that in fact tally with the Cynic
side of this division, as we shall now see. But it remains
important, along the lines just sketched above, to note in
this how often Paul talks about his own actions, the
ventures he undertakes (albeit in response to a strong sense
of divine call and divine initiative), rather than his simply
reacting to what befalls him.[67]

In what follows, 1 Corinthians 4.9–13 provides the
main framework. Paul opens the first of the lists with the
image of being put on show (to which we shall return
later), and follows it with 'three sarcastic antitheses: "We
are fools for Christ's sake, but you are wise in Christ. We

I was already enthusiastically engaged in, "till you reach the very ends
of the earth"'; cf. 34.4, 12.20 (but also 32.12, 'not my own choice');
and see further, below, ch.6.

[66] E.g., Epictetus 1.29.44–49: 'God says, "Go and bear witness for me,
for you are well suited to be produced by me as a witness. Is any of
those things that lie outside the range of your inner moral choice
(προαίρεσις) either good or bad?"' 'A (true) Cynic must know that he
has been sent by Zeus to men to show them that they've gone astray
over what's good and bad' (3.22.23; cf. 3.22.69).

[67] More like the Stoic 'passive' lists is 2 Cor 4.8–9, where the
emphasis is on divine support, rather than on Paul's activity; but this is
still in the context of Paul's execution of his mission (4.1–2). Paul does
not affect a Stoic inner impassivity as his goal; rather are his troubles
appropriate aids in the work of evangelising; see further, below.

are weak, but you are strong. You are held in honour, but
we are in disrepute"' (1 Cor 4.9–10),[68] taking us back to
the other strong Cynic claims that Paul has already alluded
to: 'already filled, already rich, already reigning – without
us!' (v.8). Paul, like a true Cynic, and by contrast with
others' pseudo-Cynic boasts, courts dishonour, perhaps
even glories in it (as we shall note again in a little more
detail below), for public repute is less than worthless;[69] and
a Cynic will appear as a fool to others.[70]

(iii) Troubles taken on – (α) Hunger, thirst and cold

Paul then lists the particular hardships he undertakes
(rather than endures uninvited). For 'we hunger and we
thirst' and 'I have been in hunger and in thirst, and
frequent fasts' (1 Cor 4.11; 2 Cor 6.5, 11.27) there are of
course parallels in Cynic minded Stoics. For instance,
Musonius says, 'We train both body and soul, accustoming
ourselves to cold and heat, to thirst and hunger, on a
meagre diet.'[71] Paul, however, is not here talking of
training 'body and soul' for the further end of his and
others' souls' improvement (as is Musonius), but of
activities that seem to have and be expected to show their
own validity, a 'spectacle' that makes its own point (1 Cor
4.9). Particularly intriguing is a passage from Epictetus.

---

[68] R. Hodgson (1983), 65.

[69] Ps.-Crates 8, 13, 16, 29; ps.-Diogenes 7, 9, 10, 34; *Socratic Epistle*
6.3; Dio 4.4, 8.16; Giannantoni (1990), V B 20 (Plutarch, *Moralia*
632E).

[70] Diogenes Laertius 6.53; *Socratic Epistles* 6.1, 9.3; 12; 13 (Simon);
Dio 34.4; 72.15–16. (For 'weak' and 'strong' see ch. 4, above.)

[71] Musonius 6 (Lutz (1947), 54, ll.12–13 (O. Hense (1905), 125, 4–9);
cf. Philo, *De somniis* 1.124–25, cited above.

His sage must already and always have all that he wishes, he must seem fulfilled (πεπληρωμένος); neither hunger nor thirst can reach him.[72] Paul makes no such Stoic claim. Again, elsewhere, Epictetus lists going hungry and thirsty along with 'fever' as circumstances that arrive;[73] Paul's 'fasting' is deliberate. Like any Cynic, he chooses 'poverty . . . hunger, cold, contempt';[74] 'grappling with hunger and cold, engaging with the thirst he has challenged'.[75]

(iii) Troubles taken on (β) Half-naked, dispossessed, homeless

And very much like a Cynic, Paul 'goes naked' (γυμνιτεύ- ομεν, 1 Cor 4.11; cf. 2 Cor 11.27; Rom 8.35). Martin Ebner cogently argues that Paul's claim will have had this Cynic significance, with the meaning, clearly, 'scantily clad', 'half-naked' (not totally bare).[76] He compares Paul here with Dio's use of the same word (*Discourse* 25.3), of the 'lightly clad' Spartans (who are, of course, as we have already seen, models for Cynics, especially in the Antisthenic tradition). Antisthenes, it was widely claimed, pioneered the doubled cloak as his only garment.[77] In Epictetus 'naked' (γυμνός), 'with one cloak', and 'without a tunic' seem all to be equivalents, though he himself does not approve of those un-Stoic Cynics who make a display

---

[72] Epictetus 3.24.17; cf. 4.6.23.

[73] Epictetus 3.10.8–9; compare 3.26.5, 'if it so happen'.

[74] Cf. ps.-Diogenes 36.4, again; *Socratic Epistle* 12; Dio 6.12.

[75] Dio 8.16, again.

[76] M. Ebner (1991), 39–42; but cf. the statue of a naked Diogenes, D. Clay (1996), 381, fig. 9.

[77] Diogenes Laertius 6.7–8, 13.

of their bare flesh: 'you show off your fine shoulder'.[78] Yet
it is a mark of a Cynic in particular, both in itself and also
as a symbol of his or her dispossession: 'How much more
naked could I be than now?' asks Dio's Diogenes.[79] 'To go
naked is better than wear any scarlet robe', claims
Epictetus' Diogenes.[80] 'It makes a difference', says
Seneca, 'to the way I listen to our (Cynic) Demetrius when
I've seen him lying down without even a cloak to cover
him.'[81] A Cynic goes round like Herakles, 'naked, wearing
only a skin'.[82] Quintilian cites as an example a father
'indicting his son turned Cynic, accusing him before the
censors of indecent behaviour', and pseudo-Quintilian,
Declamations, indicates that it is simply a matter of
disreputable dress.[83] A Paul who went round ill-clad
enough to make and to warrant the claim γυμνιτεύομεν
and drew attention to himself so (un)dressed by accosting
strangers in any context with a socially disruptive message
could only have been interpreted as some kind of Cynic in

---

[78] Epictetus 3.22.45–47; 4.8.31 (Ebner (1991), 41, n.104, cites R. F.
Hock (1980), 84, n.94); cf. 3.22.51, 4.8.34. Compare the photograph of
the Christian Cynic philosopher as the frontispiece of F G Downing
(1992a), chosen from one of many such images on third- and fourth-
century sarcophagi; and most of the (pagan) Cynics pictured in D. Clay
(1996). On Jewish attitudes to nakedness, cf. S. L. Satlow (1997).

[79] Dio 6.62, cf. 72.2, but also 34.3, 35.3; cf. Hipparchia, Diogenes
Laertius 6.97; and Lucian, *Peregrinus* 17. Ebner (1991), 41–42, notes
that along with the Spartans, Herakles provides a further model of the
ill-clad fighter for excellence; so also, of course, do the 'naked
philosophers' of both India and Egypt; cf. C. Muckensturm (1993);
R. Stoneman (1995).

[80] Epictetus 1.24.7.

[81] Seneca, *Epistulae morales* 20.9.

[82] Ps.-Lucian, *The Cynic*, 13; cf. 1 and 20; and Lucian, *Symposion* 14.

[83] Quintilian, *Institutes* 4.2.30; ps.-Quintilian, *Declamations* 283; in
H. Butler (1921), 530, s.v. 'Cynicus' (LCL).

the Hellenistic towns he visited. Had Paul not wanted to make this impression, he could have accepted a few more clothes from friends, and worn them; and, at least, not drawn attention to his shameless appearance (with the shameful scars from his frequent beatings!) so crudely. We are obliged to assume he meant to be (or was at least content to be) perceived as some sort of Cynic.

A prime and distinctive feature of the Cynic rejection of all but the minimum property is voluntary homelessness (1 Cor 4.11) as a part of the chosen itinerant life-style (cf. 2 Cor 11.25–26). So Lycinus charges Cyniscus with behaving 'unlike most people', choosing to sleep just anywhere on the hard ground.[84] Psuedo-Anacharsis has the whole earth for his bed, pseudo-Crates reminds 'Hipparchia' that she has commited herself to lodging in porticos; pseudo-Diogenes has these and his jar.[85] The tradition has Diogenes apply to himself the lines:

No city, no house (ἄοικος), no fatherland,

a wandering beggar, living a day at a time.[86]

And this is the example Dio emulated, 'I have travelled around for so long, without hearth or home, without even a single attendant to accompany me.'[87] Epictetus, too, cites this aspect of the Cynic's life, 'without home (ἄοικος) or hearth, no slave, no city'.[88] But in general Epictetus' attitude to home-ownership is Stoic: you retain your home without being attached to it (just as you retain your body without attachment); you surrender any external but useful

---

[84] Ps.-Lucian, *The Cynic* 1, 15; ps.-Diogenes 37.5.

[85] Ps.-Anacharsis 5; ps.-Crates 28; ps.-Diogenes 16, cf. 37.6; Dio 4.12; 6.8–10; 8.30, Herakles as a Cynic model, again.

[86] Diogenes Laertius 6.38; cf. 22 (porticos), 23 (jar).

[87] Dio 40.2.

[88] Epictetus 3.22.45, 47; 4.8.31.

thing only if someone with the power or the authority demands it or seizes it.[89] Like any true Cynic, Paul insists for himself on being homeless.

Paul further emphasises his own poverty (2 Cor 6.10). It might be held to be significant that he uses the word πτωχός, rather than πένης, πενία which we find for the most part in our Cynic sources. The terms are sometimes distinguished as between 'beggar' and 'in straitened circumstances'; thus Paul might be thought to be committed to a still more drastic poverty than Cynics conventionally were. However, it is clear from a number of writers that the Cynic πενία amounted in others' eyes to πτωχεία, and Cynics did not disagree.[90] Because of their acceptance of πενία, most (not all) themselves of course relied on begging (αἰτεῖν), anyway. And just as pseudo-Crates says having nothing amounts to possessing everything (ἔχοντες μηδὲν, πάντ' ἔχομεν),[91] so does Paul (μηδὲν ἔχοντες, πάντα κατέχοντες).

At this point, however, Paul's own behaviour is closer to that of Epictetus' idealised Cynic, and Seneca's Cynic friend, Demetrius: Paul accepts poverty, dispossession, homelessness for himself, but does not demand it, or even urge it, of others, at least not overtly (as already noted earlier: cf. 1 Cor 13.3, again; 2 Cor 8.13–15; 9.8).[92] Somewhat later, at Philippians 4.11–12 Paul's talk about coping

---

[89] Epictetus 3.6.5–7; 3.24.67–69; 4.1.100–102.

[90] πτωχός, πτωχεία, Dio 9.8-9 (Diogenes–Odysseus); of Dio himself, 13.11; ps.-Diogenes 28.5; ps.-Lucian, *The Cynic* 2, 5; Diogenes Laertius 6.56; Plutarch, *Quaest. conviv vi, Moralia* 632E, again; for Paul, cf. 1 Cor 13.3.

[91] Ps.-Crates 7.

[92] Cf. M. Griffin (1996), 204.

'in want and in plenty' is almost explicitly Stoic (even if the language is by now commonplace).[93] For Cynics, of course (again, as registered above), poverty was of the essence for any and all who would aim for Cynic well-being and happiness.[94]

(iii) Trouble taken on (γ) Ill-treated

In the list with which we began Paul reminds his hearers of the rough treatment he is used to risking, receiving, even inviting; and this theme is expanded in subsequent lists (1 Cor 4.11; 2 Cor 6.9, 11.23–25, 12.10; Rom 8.35). Being 'buffetted' is a characteristic (though, of course, not a distinctive feature) of Cynics. Going out of one's way to invite this kind of retaliation or magisterial punishment is more specifically Cynic.[95] By way of contrast there is Epictetus' Stoic advice which we noted above, that, while punishment would come if it were ordained, there is no call to induce it.

The catalogue in 2 Corinthians 11 as a whole stresses Paul's active involvement in events. He is not a captive, not in any legal sense a slave, not being carried around as a passive object by any human agency, but is actively travelling and talking with people, fulfilling his apostolic mission, and doing these things freely, willingly

---

[93] M. Ebner (1991), 338–45; J. L. Jaquette (1995), 100–108; with the proper caution entered by T. Engeberg-Pedersen (1995), 263.

[94] Ps.-Crates 8; ps.-Diogenes 9, 26, 33.2–3, 36.4; Lucian, *Philosophies for Sale* 9; Dio 4.6, 10; the point is pressed emphatically by M. Ebner (1991), 341–43.

[95] Lucian, *Philosophies for Sale* 9–10; *Peregrinus* 12, 18; *Demonax* 11, 50; ps.-Diogenes 20 with Diogenes Laertius 6.33; cf. *idem*, 6.42, 44, 48; ps.-Crates 34.2–3; Dio 4.11–19; 8.16; 9.10–11.

(as at 1 Cor 9).[96] 'Troubles and dangers' are a conventional pair constituting laudable personal achievements.[97] But in the list of punishments and lynchings at 2 Corinthians 11.23–25, the synagogue beatings if no others must surely have been deliberately drawn down on himself by Paul: '(at least in the diaspora) the jurisdiction of a Jewish court extended only so far as it was willingly accepted.'[98] Yet not only in the occasional synagogue, but also in every other sector he frequented of the towns he visited, Paul presumably learned from experience to gauge the kind of response that was building up to his preaching and presence – and still deliberately courted the human violence he here lists.

(iii) Trouble taken on (δ) Like Herakles or Odysseus

In an excursus to his *Leidenlisten und Apostelbrief*, Martin Ebner notes the underlying influence on lists of this kind of the labours and travails of Herakles (and sometimes of Odysseus).[99] Other people than Cynics (and Stoics)

---

[96] Compare again A. J. Malherbe (1995). M. Ebner (1991), 118–22 appositely cites here Alexander's list of troubles he involved himself in, as his personal achievements, not Fortune's; citing Plutarch, *De Alexandri Magni fortuna*, 326E–327B; and Arrian, *Anabasis* 7.9.8–10.3; on the sense of κόπος assumed here, see Ebner, 134, and 162–65. With all that Paul *does* here, we may perhaps contrast Phil 1.12–14, where he talks instead of what has been happening to him; Philippians, as we shall argue, displays a much more Stoic Paul.

[97] M. Ebner (1991), 153–55, citing Plutarch, Arrian, Cicero, Sallust, Ovid and Quintilian.

[98] On the synagogue beatings, A. E. Harvey (1985), here, 80.

[99] M. Ebner (1991), 161–72. It would have been a nice touch if Paul had kindly used πόνος (the usual term for Herakles' labours) instead

admired Herakles, but with Ebner it is worth citing parts of Dio's sketch of Herakles as emulated by Diogenes:

> People pitied him as he toiled and struggled, and called him the most wretchedly troubled of men, and termed his troublesome labours 'wretched', too . . . He journeyed all over Europe and Asia . . . [needing little sleep] . . . caring nothing for cold or heat, having no need of bed, blanket or rug, wearing only a dirty skin, looking hungry, as he helped the good and punished the wicked.[100]

Dio presents his own wearisome journeys, divinely commissioned, in much the same way, (exile, threats to safety, danger, prolonged wanderings with neither hearth nor home . . .) but prefers on the whole to compare his mission with that of the exiled and wandering Odysseus.[101] We noted earlier that harsher Cynics would repudiate any such model, while the gentler (such as Dio) found it congenial. Scott B. Andrews has recently argued that underlying 2 Corinthians 11 is indeed the image of the philosopher as an Odyssean figure of the kind portrayed by Antisthenes: Paul, like Odysseus, is 'weak', behaves slavishly, is beaten.[102] More may be added. As Odysseus failed to scale the walls of Troy, but crept in,[103] so Paul was even more ignominiously let down from the walls of

---

of or as well as κόπος and μόχθος; but Ebner shows that πόνος and κόπος are often interchangeable (see further, below).

[100] Dio 8.28–30; M. Ebner (1991), 168 (quoting more than he does), and the detailed comparison with Paul, 170–72. Paul's self-ascribed περικάθαρμα is a probably a stronger form of Dio's ἀθλιώτατος for Herakles; cf. B. H. McLean (1996), 98, n. 109 and 99, n. 114.

[101] Dio 40.2; cf. 13.9 and 9.9; cf. Epictetus 3.24.13.

[102] S. B. Andrews (1995): Paul is the over-adaptable demagogue (cf. 1 Cor 9; a theme we shall return to yet again in the next chapter). For Antisthenes, Giannantoni (1990), V A 54.

[103] Giannantoni (1990), V A 54.8.

Damascus. When Dio pictures Diogenes as an Odysseus, it is because he is thought mad, despised as a beggar, worthless; yet really a lord, a king, coping easily with the situation.[104] And Paul, too, acts the fool, knows he is behaving like someone of low status, knows he will be despised – but also knows he is effective (2 Cor 12.10–12).[105] Epictetus, also, admired Odysseus, but (as a Stoic) could not imagine the hero would ever have let external circumstances get to him, would ever have longed for what he hadn't got, would ever have wept.[106] Paul admits readily that he is weighed down by worries about the churches. He is strong and effective in a very 'un-virile' way (2 Cor 12.10–12, again; cf. 6.10, 'grieving'); very much an Odysseus-style figure in the hardships he takes on.[107]

Paul uses the the word κόπος rather than the πόνος which we have noted frequently in the foregoing. The two are used as synonyms in the Septuagint. Martin Ebner suggests that Paul's choice may well have been deliberate. 2 Corinthians 11.23–29 in particular echoes so much of the popular Herakles tradition; Paul must have been aware of the resonances others would hear, so he selects the word which for him focuses attention on his purposeful missionary service, rather than the one that emphasises the laborious trouble as such.[108]

---

[104] Dio 9.9.

[105] Cf. 1 Cor 4.10 and 2 Cor 5.13; and above, 149–50.

[106] Epictetus 3.24.13–21.

[107] Cf. also 1 Cor 2.1–5; 4.10; and 2 Cor 1–2 (afflicted); ps.-Crates 19; Dio 9.9; 77/78.40; and ch.6, below.

[108] M. Ebner (1991), 170–72, and n. 98, above; for κόπος in Paul, see, e.g., 1 Cor 3.8; 2 Cor 10.15; 1 Thess 3.5; κοπιάω, 1 Cor 15.10; Gal 4.11.

In Paul's mind his work to earn his keep is an integral part of this purposeful struggle: 'We toil (κοπι- ῶμεν), working with our own hands' (1 Cor 4.12 and all of chapter 9, but especially vv. 12 and 19; 2 Cor 11.27; 1 Thess 2.9). We shall discuss this option of Paul's in a little detail later; here we may simply note that in the wider Greek speaking world such a choice is elsewhere mainly found in the Cynic tradition (with the ideal figure of Simon the shoemaker, Dio, and Musonius as a very Cynic Stoic).[109] The ability to do without sleep (2 Cor. 6.5; 11.27) is also an aim among Cynics.[110]

(iii) Trouble taken on (ε) Contrary kindness

Paul then adds three further antitheses (1 Cor 4.12–13, picking up v. 8):[111]

when reviled	we bless
λοιδρούμενοι	εὐλογοῦμεν
persecuted	we endure
διωκόμενοι	ἀνεχόμεθα,
defamed	we conciliate
δυσημούμενοι	παρακαλοῦμεν.

With this Ebner compares Epictetus:

λοιδρούμενος	ἀνέχεσθαι,
ἀτιμεσθεὶς	μὴ ἀχθεσθῆναι,

'train . . . when reviled to endure, when insulted to put up with it . . .', which is followed by, 'And even if someone strikes you, you'll say to yourself "Imagine you've

---

[109] R. F. Hock (1980), 37–42; M. Ebner (1991), 69–75.

[110] Dio 6.11, 8.30 (quoted above); ps.-Crates 19.

[111] See above, 149–50.

embraced a statue.'"[112] For his part Epictetus is emphasising simply a Stoic's inner invulnerability, as in the much
quoted 'love those who are beating you', where 'love'
(φιλεῖν) in Epictetus seems always to mean an inner
reaction.[113] Paul, on the other hand, starts and finishes with
an overt positive response to the miscreant ('we bless . . .
we conciliate'). In fact we can find Epictetus elsewhere
also urging an outgoing positive reaction to mistreatment,
in his admiration for Lycurgus' 'making a good man' of
the youth who had blinded him in one eye.[114] So Seneca,
too, can advise, 'When someone gets angry with you,
challenge him with kindness.'[115]

The motif of conciliation is by no means
distinctively Cynic. Some of the Diogenes *chreiai* display
him as viciously vindictive. However, it should be noted
that Seneca in this context refers to Sextius, in whose
thought Cynic strands have also been discerned.[116] In fact
it is clear that a positive response to verbal or other
mistreatment is urged with greater consistency by some of
those with a strong gentle-Cynic ethos.[117] So, after arguing

---

[112] Epictetus 3.12.10; M. Ebner (1991), 80, citing just the two
antitheses. He points out how frequently the pair λοιδρούμενος
ἀνέχεσθαι occurs in Epictetus (e.g., 2.12.14; 3.4.11, 21.5; 4.1.18. We
must not forget, of course, the extent to which philosophers insulted
one another as a matter of course (L. T. Johnson (1989)); but here we
are concerned with attitudes to insult and ill-repute.

[113] Epictetus 3.22.54.

[114] Epictetus, fragment 5.

[115] Seneca, *De ira* 2.34.5.

[116] A. Oltramare (1926), 226–51 and 252–93; M.-O. Goulet-Cazé
(1990), 2728; cf. *eadem* (1986), 184, n. 119; M. Billerbeck (1979),
5–13, takes issue with Oltramare, but still allows some links between
the Sextian family and Cynicism.

[117] For the 'refuse', 'scum' (περικαθάρματα, περίψημα) of 1 Cor.
4.13, see J. T. Fitzgerald (1988), 142–43, n. 86. 'Κάθαρμα' in partic-

that insults can be ignored, and offenders should certainly
not be taken to court, Musonius urges,

> Well, if a philosopher cannot despise a slap or abuse, what
> use is he? . . . . People offend (sin) against you. You take it
> without going wild, without harming the offender. Instead
> you give them hope of better things (ἀλλ' αἴτιον εἶναι
> αὐτοῖς ἐλπίδος χρηστῆς). That's what it takes to be
> civilised and humane.[118]

'"How shall I defend myself against my enemy? By being
good and kind towards him", replied Diogenes', in another
element from the popular tradition.[119] It is probably in this
sense that we should take the *chreia*, 'Someone told
Diogenes that his friends were conspiring against him.
Diogenes replied, "Well now, what's to be done, if you
have to treat friends and foes the same?"'[120] Plutarch tells
of Crates' encounter with the ex-tyrant, Demetrius of
Phalerum, who 'was not pleased to see Crates approaching,
and expected some harsh Cynical plain speaking. But
Crates met him with gentleness (πράως) . . . encouraging
him (παρακαλοῦντος) . . .'.[121] As Ebner points out, Dio
considers 'admonishing' (νουθετεῖν - which Paul goes on
to use as 1 Cor 4.14) and 'entreating' (παρακαλεῖν) as the
prime functions of a philosopher of his conciliatory kind
(though Dio allows that his work may also involve him in

---

ular is a very general term of abuse. The two words sum up the verbal
and other ill-treatment Paul and other apostles receive. But see also
B. H. McLean (1996), n. 100, above.

[118] Musonius 10, Lutz (1947), 76, ll. 22–24; 78, ll. 31–33; O. Hense
(1905) 53, 1–2 and 56, 6–8; noted also by M. Ebner (1991), 80 and
notes.

[119] In Plutarch, *De capienda ex inimicis, Moralia* 88B; *Gnomologion
Vaticanum* 187; Giannantoni (1990), V B 421.

[120] Diogenes Laertius 6.68.

[121] Plutarch, *Quomodo adulator, Moralia* 69 CD.

abusing and reproaching).[122] So, for example, Dio urges, 'If the citizens of Mallus have behaved stupidly - and they have! - it's up to you (citizens of Tarsus) to put anger aside and forgive them the punitive revenge you thought you had a right to; and, instead, work for a solution to this dispute over boundaries';[123] and one may compare much of *Discourses* 38–41, on (re-)conciliation. Reconciliation and peace-making between individuals were Demonax' fraught vocation, according to Lucian.[124]

Adducing this evidence is not at all to preclude the likely impact on Paul of Jewish wisdom teaching[125] and of the tradition of Jesus' injunction to love one's enemies (Luke 6.27–35, etc.; itself arguably influenced by Cynicism); especially in the light of Romans 12.17–21. But it is to say that what we find here would be entirely in keeping with the other gentler-Cynic resonances in Paul's lists of the troubles he provokes by the tasks he undertakes.

(iii) Trouble taken on (ζ) An active, costly success

One of Paul's lists, 2 Corinthians 4.7–11, however, is (at first sight at least) rather different. Here, as we noted

---

[122] Dio 77/78.38; M. Ebner (1991), 80–87; cf. also Dio 72.2, and 8–10: the insulted philosopher still does his best to improve those who deride and insult him, in the tradition of Socrates and Diogenes (13–16). As Ebner notes, the philosopher is thus acting 'as a father or brother or friend' (Dio 77/78.42; cf. again Epictetus 3.22.54); so Paul goes on to claim a fatherly relationship with the Corinthians (1 Cor 4.14–15).

[123] Dio 34.43.

[124] Lucian, *Demonax* 6–9, 11, 16.

[125] Rightly noted, amid the clear Cynic resonances, by A. E. Harvey (1996), 74–75.

earlier, he deploys a series of antithetic passive participles, 'pressed in on every side yet not confined, confused but not concussed, hunted but not hunted down, struck down but not dispatched', very much in the manner of the one Plutarch adduces to demonstrate the emptiness of Stoic 'paradoxical' claims, 'unimpeded when confined, uncompelled when thrown down a precipice . . .' (cited above). There is a very similar use of close synonyms (especially note Paul's ἀπορούμενοι - οὐκ ἐξαπορούμενοι, here rendered 'confused – not concussed').[126] Ebner also quotes a list from Epictetus, though it is not quite so similar in form, 'Show me someone who is sick and happy, in danger and happy, dying and happy, exiled and happy, dishonoured and happy.' But here, as Ebner emphasises, Epictetus is also sure that such a true, perfect Stoic sage is nowhere to be found; indeed, he despairs of ever finding anyone even showing progress towards that goal.[127] Certainly a Stoic would not do what Paul does here, make such a claim for himself. That would amount to a Cynic arrogance.[128]

---

[126] Plutarch, *Comp. arg. Stoicos* 1057DE (n. 49).

[127] Epictetus 2.19.24–25; M. Ebner (1991), 216–18; cf. Seneca, *De constantia* 3, and his attempt in what follows to argue that 'external' injuries do not reach into the true wise man. For Ebner (219–21), the most noteworthy difference between Paul and the Stoics lies in their respective anthropologies. We have already argued that neither Paul nor the Cynics (by common contrast with the Stoics) take refuge in some human individual's 'inner' impregnable reality. Thus Ebner rightly insists that Paul's 'inner man' refers to the 'new creation', the whole person being renewed, not to a naturally given element in each person (230–32).

[128] Epictetus 4.8.26–30. M. S. Ferrari (1991), 134–35, 140, notes the difference between Paul's first-person claims and their avoidance by Epictetus, but fails to pursue the point. As is Paul, Cynics are much readier to announce their success – to Epictetus' disgust.

At 1 Corinthians 4.8 Paul had criticised some of the congregation for making bold Cynic claims for themselves. Already they had achieved their goals ('already rich . . . filled . . . reigning'!). Yet now Paul seems to be doing the same as they: as a (Jewish–Christian) Cynic he boasts he is effecting in practice what Stoics only dreamt of achieving. Even so, his claims in fact still remain distinct from those he previously criticised. As he did then, now, here too, Paul stresses again the hardship, the cost this Christian–Cynic achievement of his necessarily involves; and despite the apparent Stoic form of the antitheses, Paul is not calling attention to his equanimity, his interior calm: he is talking about the activities he continues to be effectively engaged in.[129]

(We also find here that Paul emphasises not only the divine initiative but now also the divine empowerment in response to which he executes his mission in the midst of such harsh circumstances. We attend to this strand shortly.)

We encounter a further set of paradoxical antitheses at 2 Corinthians 6.8–10. The content of some of the negative elements we have already noted, together with their Cynic echoes (dishonour, disrepute, punished, beggars, destitute). Here again Paul could seem to be making Cynic boasts to have realised the Stoic day-dream, boasts even closer to those he mocked at 1 Corinthians 4.8: now he tells us he it is who can offer riches to others, he it is who owns all things (v. 10). But again he insists that this is only achieved in the midst of 'distress, hardships, dire straits, flogging, imprisonment, lynching, overwork, sleeplessness, fasting' (vv. 4–5), troubles we have already consid-

---

[129] See above, notes 107 and 127; and further, below.

ered above. His is not the fake-Cynic facile 'shortcut' he had previously imputed to some of his hearers.[130]

It is not so easy to find ready parallels in the wider Graeco-Roman literature to this last set of antitheses as a whole, 'honour as well as dishonour, good repute and ill-repute'. Martin Ebner notes that contrasts between true and false fame (2 Cor 6.8–9) are fairly commonplace, and appositely cites an example from Philo where the latter reflects on true and false (popular) reputation, real goodness or wickedness, happiness and cheerfulness.[131] More helpful to this book's thesis is Ebner's discussion of a passage in one of Dio's treatments of these themes, where Dio seems clearly to be sketching his own Cynic unconcern for the fickleness of the reputation public opinion accords, at the mercy of those who wish to give you grief (βουλομένοις λυπεῖν), have you happy and cheerful or sad and dejected at the whim of others (cf. Paul's 'sorrowful . . . rejoicing'), who'll call you layabout if you're around in public ('well-known'), ignoramus if you maintain your privacy ('unknown'), and so on. Early on in the discourse Dio also ridicules any would-be Cynic following Crates' example in the hope of such notoriety. Far better to have a consistent Cynic disregard for the opinion of others, and only so pursue your ill-clad course, risking persecution, as Socrates did.[132]

---

[130] See, again, above, ch. 4, § *(ii), 'Already'*, 88–90.

[131] Philo, *De migratione* 86–88; M. Ebner (1991), 311, without calling attention to the 'joy', 88; cf. Dio 4.128–31; and cf. M. S. Ferrari (1991), 147.

[132] Dio 66.24, 12, 2, 25–26; M. Ebner (1991) 305–308. I take it that the overall theme of despising reputation and any pain or grief which others' opinion may threaten, together with the Socratic reference, support Ebner's contention. The end of paragraph 6 suggests a date

In fact the more rigorous Cynics whose πόνοι we are arguing Paul insists he consistently invites and engages in could also on occasion make the positive claims Paul here advances, or at least they could be accorded them by others: 'honour, good repute; true, acknowledged, joyful, enriching others, owning everything.' Thus Diogenes, for instance, is honoured in Athens, and widely known thoughout the Greek (and Roman) world. [133] Not just people at large, but such sticklers for propriety as Cicero, Plutarch and Philo among others could quote the sayings of Diogenes or Crates as obviously valid. Pseudo-Diogenes finds it easier to be cheerful than to be made to grieve (εὐφραίνεσθαι - λυπεῖσθαι). [134] The Socratic letters talk of the Cynic philosopher as rich and able to enrich others. [135] And, of course, alongside pseudo-Crates' contention that he has everything while possessing nothing there is the repeated Cynic claim to own everything, as friend of the Gods to whom all belongs and with whom therefore all is shared. [136]

But the most significant issue is not whether or not one can in these Cynic as opposed to Stoic texts find verbal parallels to Paul's paradoxical antitheses (important as these are as initial pointers). Clearly the most striking available examples of word-for-word similarity that we have considered *are* from among Stoics, and Epictetus in particular. Much more important, however, is the way in

---

towards the end of Domitian's reign, with Dio still pursuing his Cynic course.

[133] Diogenes Laertius 6.43, 78; Dio 72.11; Lucian, *Dialogues of the Dead*, etc.; cf. the *progymnasmata*, passim, e.g., in R. F. Hock and E. N. O'Neill (1986).

[134] Ps.-Diogenes 28.7.

[135] *Socratic Epistles* 27.5; 6.8; ps.-Diogenes 10.1.

[136] Diogenes Laertius 6.37, 72; ps.-Crates 7; 26; 27, etc.

which Paul deploys his antitheses. As we have seen, time and again, Paul does not use them to display any equanimity, inner mental calm and reserve of his in the face of whatever divine providence brings him to. Unlike Epictetus, he makes no reference to being 'undisturbed': ἀταραξία, so important to Epictetus, has no place in Paul's surviving vocabulary.[137] Rather does he point to his physical ability to keep going, keep travelling, fulfil his divinely appointed mission. As Martin Ebner insists, these are not contrasts between outer and inner, but between what one might expect to occur in Paul's situation, and what in fact is done. They are paradoxical activities, not (as in the Stoic parallels) antithetical contrasts between external circumstances and interior responses. (This is so even at Romans 8.35, where Paul is clearly listing things that may 'happen to' any Christian. Whereas an Epictetus as Stoic would be expected to express concern for his true self in dire circumstances, Paul makes no reference to inner disposition at all.)[138]

And so, clearly, the paradoxes will have sounded Cynic rather than Stoic. One further illustration must suffice: Diogenes can tell Xeniades, 'You must obey me, even though I am a slave.' A Stoic claims an inner freedom although 'externally' a slave; the Cynic acts externally as a free man, even if a slave. Paul chooses freely to act as a slave, although a free man, to win others' obedience to the

---

[137] Epictetus 3.11.2; cf. 1.24.8; 2.1.21, 24; 2.2; 3.13.13; 3.15.12; 3.18; 3.21.9; 3.22.61; *Encheiridion* 2.6. M. S. Ferrari (1991) seems to note terms (138–46) that appear in Paul and in his other sources (Epictetus in particular), but not significant *absences* from Paul, in this instance, ἀταραξία. Thus a main Stoic aim among troubles is of no importance to Paul, who (like the Cynics) is pragmatic rather than introspective.

[138] M. Ebner (1991), 376, contrasting the 'innerweltlich Sieg' in Epictetus, 1.17.23–28, etc.

gospel. It is a paradoxical activity, not an inner–outer antithesis; and so throughout the troubles he engages and invites. [139]

(iv) Divinely called – empowered – displayed

Admittedly, Paul's insistence not just on the divine call to which he responds, but on a divine empowering (2 Cor 4.7; 6.6; 12.9) might well have made him sound more Stoic than Cynic. The best 'pagan' illustration Fitzgerald can find for this important aspect of Paul is a passage from Seneca, 'a divine power has descended upon that man'.[140] Even so, we would instead have expected most Stoics to agree with Epictetus' insistence that in things that really matter (our inner attitudes, judgments, decisions) 'God has put the whole thing in our hands . . . without reserving for himself any power to prevent or hinder.'[141] The closest we come to any idea of divine enabling in Cynic writing on the other hand is the (presumably metaphorical) hope of pseudo-Diogenes that the φρόνημα, 'the mind-set' of Herakles 'might stir' in Crates.[142] We shall consider this issue again (in chapters 6 and 7). Here, to repeat, there are,

---

[139] Cf. Diogenes Laertius 6.30 and 74–5; Epictetus 3.24.65–67, and 4.1.114–15, noted above, ch. 1, n. 44; and 1 Cor 9 and 10, with special reference to 9.1 and 19. For further paradoxical *activities* , cf. Diogenes Laertius 6. 26 (end); 27 (whistling and then reprimanding); 32 (spitting and calling for 'men'); 34 (ungrateful host); 35–36; 49; and R. B. Branham (1993) and (1994). This is *'para-doxa'* in a literal sense, practice in conflict with popular opinion. Cf. also Dio 8.36; Lucian, *Philosophies for Sale* 10; Philo, *Quod omnis probus liber sit* 121–25; ps.-Diogenes 34.

[140] Seneca, *Epistulae morales* 41.4; J. T. Fitzgerald (1988), 171.

[141] Epictetus 1.6.40.

[142] Ps.-Diogenes 26.

of course, important points of difference between Paul's recorded praxis and expressed thought, and those of any known Cynics so designated by themselves or others (just as there are important divergencies between Paul and other known early Christians). In both cases, there seem also to be some significant similarities.

As part of his very thorough survey Martin Ebner considers in some detail possible Jewish parallels for the lists of troubles, and especially for the antitheses Paul produces. Of course, even if matter from Jewish sources turned out to be very similar, it would have little direct bearing on the argument here being pursued: Jewish models would not have provided the introduction to or context for any response to Paul's letters for most if any of his Corinthian converts, nor could Paul have relied on such preparation for his deployment of them. Ebner in fact notes that the longest example he adduces, from *Testament of Joseph* 1.4–7, displays a rather different formal structure:'I was in bonds and [God] loosed me', involving a temporal progression. Both terms of each of the Stoic and Cynic and Pauline antitheses remain contemporaneous. It is while Paul is weak that he is strong; he is not weak and then strengthened.[143] We must also note that when Paul launches his longest tribulation list against 'super apostles' claiming a Jewish heritage (2 Cor 11.22–33) the only scriptural reference is to the forty stripes of Deuteronomy 25.3. As with all the others, this list finds its closest analogies in 'pagan' sources.[144]

---

[143] M. Ebner (1991), 221–24, 227. Ebner finds in fact very few Jewish examples; as he notes, 4 Macc 11.26 is already itself heavily Hellenised.

[144] D. Georgi [1964] (1987), 99–100, and G. Theissen (1975), 47 both see these opponents of Paul as themselves akin to Cynics in their confident expectation of support.

The idea of a divine bidding obeyed is very readily paralleled in many ancient sources; and quite clearly Paul is strongly influenced here by his Jewish inheritance (e.g., Gal 1.15). It is only necessary for the present thesis to indicate that such language would by no means sound strange to those who were picking up the many possibly Stoic but more likely Cynic resonances in what Paul was choosing to say. So Epictetus can announce, 'You're a witness summoned by God. He says, "Go and bear witness for me, you're well fitted to give your testimony on my behalf"'; and 'a true Cynic will not rest satisfied with having been well trained himself; must realise he has been sent as God's messenger to his fellow human beings . . .'.[145] Still more apposite, as we have already noted, is Dio's conviction of being sent to travel laboriously, like Odysseus: 'The Deity ordered me to keep on with the good work I was already enthusiastically engaged in "till you reach the very ends of the earth".'[146] The travelling messenger is Cynic, while the Stoic shares his message wherever he happens to be placed. And long before Dio, a divine commission involving travel is part of the foundation legend for Diogenes.[147]

One important reason for all these labours and troubles being undertaken and sustained is that they should be seen, and provide object lessons for others. God displays the apostles as a spectacle (θέατρον) for a hostile world to see (1 Cor 4.9). The image is found in Stoic and

---

[145] Epictetus 1.29.47; 3.22.23.

[146] Dio 13.9; cf. 12.20; 32.12; 34.4; cf. F. G . Downing (1988c), 46.

[147] Diogenes Laertius 6.20–21. For itinerant Cynics see F. G. Downing (1992a), 33–34; note also ps.-Diogenes 30–40; Lucian's *Peregrinus* and *Runaways*; Maximus of Tyre 36.5 (Giannantoni (1990) V B 299); and the discussion in M.-O. Goulet-Cazé (1990), 2733–34.

Cynic sources (and elsewhere; and it appears in another Jewish writing probably contemporary with Paul's, 4 Maccabees 15.20; 17.14).[148] In particular Epictetus is often cited in this connection: his ideal (Stoicised) Cynic is called to 'show' people the truth, 'to mount the tragic stage' – even though, as we have noted, the longed-for spectacle (θέαμα) of a true Stoic (or even one progressing towards true wisdom) is in all probability nowhere going to be seen.[149] Certainly Epictetus, as we may recall, would not have ventured to offer himself as an example.[150] When he includes a tale about Diogenes which contrasts the sight the latter afforded as he fought a fever, 'exhibiting his excellence', with the 'contest of worthless athletes', Epictetus consistently selects an instance of an unprovoked challenge.[151] In the more clearly Cynic accounts of Diogenes, the Cynic himself contrasts the spectacle he affords with the pointless displays of athletes, putting the emphasis, as we observed above, on his own very deliberate 'grappling with hunger, coping with going thirsty'.[152] Diogenes (even in Epictetus' anecdote) knows he is already a spectacle worth emulating. And we saw that Paul, too, stresses the hardships he chooses to accept, and is also clear that he is already an example to be followed. Well short of perfection though he is (1 Cor 9.27), Paul's

---

[148] J. T. Fitzgerald (1988), 140–42 and notes.

[149] Epictetus 3.22.23–26; 3.24.113; 2.19.25. It has to be admitted that the passages cited by J. T. Fitzgerald (1988), 140–42 in this connection do not all seem particularly apposite. Seneca, *Epistulae morales* 64.6 has Seneca as *spectator* of wisdom, only; in *De providentia* 2.9, the suffering sage is a spectacle for God; cf. the references in H. Conzelmann [1969] (1975), 88–89.

[150] Cf. A. J. Malherbe [1983b] (1989), 246; A. A. Long (1996), 31.

[151] Epictetus 3.22.58–59; Jerome, *Ad Iovinianum* 2.14; ps.-Crates 1.

[152] Dio 8.16, again (see above, n. 59); cf. Dio 9; and ps.-Diogenes 31.

confidence in presenting himself and his progress as already a worthwhile model would have reinforced the impression of a brash ascetic Cynicism, rather than any reticent Stoic perfectionism.

A. E. Harvey has recently claimed that 'an unmerited illness' contradicted 'Stoic, and, still more, Cynic . . . pretensions', and so was 'banished from serious philosophical discussion'. Paul's own response to a near-death experience referred to (so Harvey argues) at 2 Corinthians 1.8 (where Paul 'despaired of life') shows that he is quite distinctive, 'a world away', 'without precedent', albeit with a spirituality of weakness rooted in his Jewish heritage. It is clear, however, from the incident of the fever related by Epictetus, and even more in the version recorded by Jerome from Satyrus, that Harvey is simply mistaken. The struggle between a man and a life-threatening fever was of deep philosophical signficance.[153] By relying on Fitzgerald alone and not consulting more recent studies, Harvey has neglected a whole range of Cynic appraisals of 'strength in weakness'.[154] Paul, weak in Galatia (Gal 4.13–14), 'despairing of life' in Asia (2 Cor 1.8), with an unrelieved 'thorn in the flesh' (2 Cor 12.7–10) still has clear Cynic precedent for seeing such a contest as part of a divine mission.

The Cynic insistence on teaching by example and by practice which we have been considering here is, as we noted earlier, the positive side of the Cynics' disparagement of speculation and abstract philosophising.[155] In our

---

[153] Epictetus 3.22.58–59, again, with Jerome, *Ad Iovinianum* 2.14 and ps.-Crates 1.

[154] A. E. Harvey (1996), 24, 125, 127.

[155] Ch. 2, 44, above; cf., e.g., ps.-Diogenes 37.5–6; 38.3; 50; F. G. Downing (1992a), 34–39.

next chapter we consider further strands of Paul's teaching style: the way it appears, the ways he himself discusses it, and the ways it might have been perceived by the Hellenistic townspeople he encountered. But it should already be clear (*a*) that the way Paul chose to live would have looked Cynic, and the way he talked about it would most often have sounded Cynic; and (*b*) his insistence on parading it as itself significant would have clinched the issue. So much, so emphasised, could hardly have been other than deliberate. His tribulation lists are no mere ornaments to his writings to Corinth, they (*c*) appear frequently, integrally and importantly within his ongoing arguments. Although we do not find him chiding others for taking their asceticism too far, we did (*d*) note earlier his rebuke to those who claimed to have entered trouble-free into their kingdom. It also must seem significant that when Paul deploys his longest list of troubles against opponents claiming a Jewish heritage, not only is there no obvious reliance on distinctively Jewish tribulation lists, but Paul can take it for granted that trial by Cynic ordeal will be a powerfully relevant argument. A Cynic-looking and Cynic-sounding *askêsis* is no Pauline idiosyncrasy; it is (*e*) common ground for Paul and Paul's 'own' converts, and for some at least of his most explicitly Jewish Christian opponents.

6

PAUL THE TEACHER AND PASTOR

(i) The True Cynic Philosopher

He appears in the towns of Galatia, Macedonia, Achaea, urging people from all walks of life to adopt a new and socially disruptive life-style while exploring disturbing ideas about Gods and humans. He appears ill-clad and clearly impoverished, but obviously a philosopher, for reflections on 'Gods and men' are by definition 'philosophical' topics (Acts 17.18). The first impression could only be, 'Here's another Cynic.' If he'd thought the Cynic impression made by his appearance misleading, he had only to accept a decent tunic and cloak and wear them, behave like a respectable teacher, accept a patron or at least charge fees, and then leave people to practise their traditional civic way of life, enjoyably passing the time in discussions of deep and abstract ideas. Though on further acquaintance you would find he had lots of Jewish convictions, and focused a great deal of attention on his cult of a dead and resurrected Jew, most Cynics had their idiosyncrasies, and this Paul does little if anything to dispel the initial impression that he is nonetheless some sort of Cynic.

'In the first half of the chapter [chapter 2 of 1 Thessalonians] Paul uses Cynic traditions about the ideal philosopher to describe his early ministry in Thessalonica,' concludes A. J. Malherbe.[1] Malherbe has devoted a great deal of careful attention to Paul's unacknowledged (and likely unexplicit) debt to the popular philosophers of his day, and has also repeatedly insisted, as I have here, that this is not to be taken as the whole story. Paul's Jewish and early Christian heritage may well have been at least as formative, often more so (see chapters 8 and 10, below). And among non-Jewish sources Malherbe has also spread his net well beyond the Cynics and Stoics.[2] Nonetheless, as the opening quotation indicates, it is again frequently our Cynic remains that provide the most significant comparative matter to illuminate Paul's discussion of his manner and methods as a teacher and pastor. What follows in this and the next chapter will be in the main a discussion with Malherbe, suggesting that some at least of the differences he finds between Paul and various Cynics, while mostly still important for a proper understanding of both, are perhaps in significant instances less clear (and less distancing) than he concludes. In particular, Paul's reliance on divine power and also his eschatological convictions would perhaps have seemed less distinctive to an audience used to popular and especially Cynic preachers than Malherbe seems to allow.

But first a study which seems very cogent. In 1 Thessalonians 2.1–7, referred to above, Paul writes:

> You yourselves, my brothers and sisters, know that our arrival among you was not without results. Even though we had suffered severe ill-treatment at Philippi, we boldly (ἐπαρρησιασάμεθα), by God's power, declared God's gospel to you. We outfaced considerable opposition (ἐν

---

[1] A. J. Malherbe [1983b], 248, referring to *idem*, (1970), 203–17.

[2] See for instance his survey article: A. J. Malherbe [1986] (1989), 67–77; and *idem*, [1982] (1989), 11–24.

πολλῷ ἀγῶνι), for the appeal we make is never based in
error or impurity (ἐξ ἀκαθαρσίας) or deceit (ἐν δολῷ).
Rather, as God has thought us fit to be entrusted with the
Gospel, we speak as we do. It is not our fellow human
beings whom we are trying to please, but God who tests
our minds and wills. We never open our mouths for
flattery (κολακείας), as you know, nor as a cloak for
greed, as God is our witness. We have never looked for
prestige (δόξαν) from humans, from you or anyone else,
though as Christ's emissaries we could have placed
burdens on you. Rather were we gentle with you, like a
nurse taking care of her children.

A little later Paul changes the image, and reminds the
Thessalonian Christians, 'As you well know, we exhorted
you (παρακαλοῦντες) one by one, as a father does his
own children, and encouraged you' (1 Thess 2.11–12).
Malherbe appositely aligns this with various passages in
which Dio compares his own idealised and gentle Cynic
approach with that of harsher Cynics and others who are
brusque, coarse – and untrustworthy. In particular he cites
Dio in Alexandria, dismissing the plebeian Cynics he
found there, 'people whose ideas are genuine and noble
enough . . . but whose rough jokes . . . do no good at all,
but rather the maximum damage'.[3] Dio then goes on to
characterise his own approach:

> But it is not easy to find someone who will speak purely
> (καθαρῶς), without deceit (ἀδόλως) and yet boldly
> (παρρησιαζόμενον), and do that neither for prestige
> (δόξης) nor for money, but out of good will and a real
> concern for others; someone who is ready, if needs be, to
> face ridicule from a disorderly and rowdy mob. It is not

---

[3] On this rendering of the passage see, e.g., R. Höistad (1948), 163.

easy to find someone like this, though a city may be so very fortunate. There is a great dearth of really noble and free-minded individuals, but plenty of flatterers (κολάκων) . . . (32.11).[4]

The tally of similar sets of contrasting ideas, with significant key terms in common, is striking (and Paul himself also says much the same elsewhere: compare 1 Cor 4.14–16; 2 Cor 3.12; Gal 1.10).

Malherbe then concludes that Dio is still here specifically contrasting himself with the plebeian Cynics he has criticised. It would in fact seem more likely that Dio has finished with this named group (τῶν δὲ κυνικῶν λεγομένων) and now is considering other more educated would-be philosophers in general, those 'who declaim speeches intended for display'.[5] Whatever our decision on this, Malherbe is certainly able to show that the ideal Dio sets out is itself that of the Cynic, 'the morally free man [who] conceived it his right and duty to speak with *parrhêsia* and to act as an example. He did so because of his *philanthrôpia*.' But Dio could also be 'harsh when occasion demanded', adapting his message to his hearers' needs. [6]

---

[4] Dio 32.9, 11; cf. also Philo, *De Iosepho* 58–75, especially from 67 on.

[5] A. J. Malherbe (1970), 206–207; Dio 32.9–10, again.

[6] A. J. Malherbe (1970), 208. C. E. Glad (1995), 92–93 rightly reminds us that others besides Cynics claimed to exercise *parrhêsia* ('Philodemus, Plutarch, Sextus Empiricus, Maximus of Tyre, Clement of Alexandria'). An important difference would remain, that while Cynics claimed the right and duty to criticise frankly all and sundry, in public (Epictetus 2.12.17–35; 3.22.50), others saw such frankness as only appropriate among close friends. Paul exercises *parrhêsia* widely: Gal 3.1; 2 Cor 3.12; 4.2–5; 7.4; 10.9–10; Phil 1.14–20; 1 Thess 2.2; Philem 8–9. Cf. D. E. Fredrickson (1996), 172–73.

Dio reflects on the theme elsewhere, and Malherbe cites the discourse *On Envy* (77/78). Here Dio again contrasts his own ideal with other 'so-called philosophers'. 'The whole world', Dio announces, 'is full of flatterers.' But his ideal philosopher is 'genuinely virile and high-minded . . . he would never surrender his freedom and *parrhêsia* for any disgraceful reward in terms either of power or wealth.' He will maintain his own integrity, never desert his post, but

> will honour and promote excellence and restraint, leading all men in that direction. He will sometimes work by persuasion and exhortation (πείθων καὶ παρακαλῶν), at other times by abuse and reproach (λοιδορούμενος καὶ ὀνειδίζων), [hoping] he may rescue some from folly . . . taking them on one side on their own but also admonishing (νουθετῶν) them together, whenever the opportunity arises,

"with gentle words at times, at others harsh". [7]

Such a philosopher 'trains his body, accustoming it with all his strength to hard labour', even though people around will think him mad for refusing wealth, honour and pleasure. Yet he will not be enraged or annoyed; 'on the contrary, I guess, he'll be kinder to each one than are a father or brothers or friends'.[8] And in one of his most clearly Cynic pieces Dio has his Diogenes promise to

---

[7] Dio 77/78.35–38. Here Dio does in passing liken his 'so-called philosophers' to skulking dogs (34–35), and may have 'false Cynics' particularly in mind; but since those whom he criticises are willing to surrender the outward signs, the dress and long hair (37), they are certainly not the harshly radical Cynics with whom Dio clearly does also contrast himself.

[8] Dio 77/78.41–42, as drawn to our attention by A. J. Malherbe (1970), 209, but citing more than he does. For the 'father' image, see above, ch. 5, n. 122.

elaborate a myth for his much rebuked Alexander, 'just as nurses, after whipping the children, tell them a story to comfort and please them', a similar image to the one Paul uses in his self-description.[9]

If we can agree with Malherbe that here and in similar passages[10] Dio is outlining a clearly recognisable Cynic ideal which he sought to follow during his exile, and which he still considered relevant even when his Cynic wanderings were over, then we must also agree that it is very significant that 'Paul's description of his Thessalonian ministry in 1 Thessalonians 2 is strikingly similar to the picture sketched by Dio, both in what is said and in the way in which it is formulated.'[11] Both are shaped by Cynic discussions of the calling of a philosophical teacher.

(ii) God's agent

Malherbe then takes us back through a detailed comparison to which any concerned reader is referred. Among the considerations to which our attention is recalled is 'Dio claims that he was divinely directed to speak. So does

---

[9] The image of a nurse's gentleness occurs at Dio 4.74 (cf. 5.16). Malherbe is able to cite Maximus of Tyre, *Discourse* 4.3, contrasting the greater effectiveness of the nurse's gentle manner over against a harsh *parrhêsia*; A. J. Malherbe, (1970), 212; with some support from Julian, *To the Cynic Herkeleios*, 204A, rejecting such an approach from Cynics; and, more generally, a passage in Plutarch.

[10] Malherbe refers us in addition to the *proemia* to Dio's *Discourses* 12, 33, and 35; A. J. Malherbe, (1970), 205. We may also compare ps.-Diogenes 50; *Socratic Epistle* 14. 4 and 6; Diogenes Laertius 6.30–31, 51, 68 and 71; Lucian, *Philosophies for Sale*, 8; F. G. Downing (1992a), 34–37.

[11] A. J. Malherbe, (1970), 216. Other models may of course also be relevant (e.g., sophist, but much overpressed by B. W. Winter (1997)).

Paul.'[12] In a later article Malherbe chooses rather to offer a contrast: 'Philosophers would have drawn attention to their own words and deeds; Paul draws attention to the gospel and the divine role in their [the Thessalonians'] conversion. It is only as a divine power is exhibited in Paul's ministry that he becomes an example that is to be followed.'[13] (Elsewhere, however, Malherbe has noted that Cynics were unusual in doing what Paul nonetheless also does, offering themselves as examples.) [14]

Paul certainly and quite obviously places a much heavier stress on divine involvement in his mission than does Dio (as our main example). But Paul would nonetheless in all likelihood still have seemed at this point also to be working on much the same lines as Cynics of Dio's preferred kind. As we shall see, at least some such Cynics also contrasted conventional wisdom and techniques of persuasion with an announced conviction that their message was divinely inspired and enabled (as well as, of course, continuing to use the techniques they affected to disparage, just as Paul does).

In the passage from 1 Thessalonians given above, Paul includes the insistence, 'It is not our fellow human beings whom we are trying to please, but God who tests our minds and wills (1 Thessalonians 2.4).' And Paul says much the same to the Galatians:

> Am I now trying to persuade fellow humans - or am I appealing to God? If I were seeking to please fellow humans, I'd be no slave of Christ. For I tell you most

---

[12] A. J. Malherbe, (1970), 216, again.

[13] A. J. Malherbe [1986] (1989), 70; cf. *idem* (1983b), 249: 'Paul's dependence on God for [his] speech is completely non-Cynic'; and *idem* (1987), 22–23, where this is said to be a Stoic trait.

[14] A. J. Malherbe [1983b], 246–47; see further, below, 194–99.

emphatically, the good news broadcast by me is no human contrivance, and I received it from no human source, no human taught it me. I received it, I was taught it, through a revelation of Jesus Christ. [15]

On v. 10 commentators refer us to standard disparagements of rhetoric, 'the art of persuasion', from Plato onwards. Most of thr commentators (and the translators) then make a break at the end of the verse, separating the disparagement of rhetoric from the insistence on the divine source of Paul's conviction; and that despite Paul's conjunction, γὰρ, joining the two sentences, and despite the analogy of the similar discussion in 1 Thessalonians 2 (and briefer but kindred passages expressing the same paired convictions found elsewhere in Paul). [16]

Cynics in general, of course, were among the most vehemently opposed to rhetorical art, consisting as it must in an appeal to δόξα, corrupt public opinion. 'It is eunuchs, rather than philosophers, who please the masses', says pseudo-Diogenes. So, too, Demonax 'ran counter to public opinion', for all his gentleness.[17] If one takes very seriously the Diogenes of many of the *chreiai*, that might

---

[15] Gal 1.10–11. Commentators find puzzling the laconic ἢ τὸν θεόν; in ἄρτι γὰρ ἀνθρώπους πείθω ἢ τὸν θεόν; The sequence seems to demand two senses for πείθω (cf. Arndt & Gingrich (1979), 639, πείθω 1.β), though 'appeal to' might work for both phrases.

[16] G. N. Longenecker (1990), 20; J. D. G. Dunn (1993), 51; H. D. Betz (1979), 54–56, terms 10–11 a 'transition', but still makes v. 11 'open up a new section'. For further insistence that persuasion (πείθω) must come from God, cf. 1 Thess 2.13; 2 Cor 1.9; 5.11; Gal 5.7; Phil 1.25; 2 Thess 3.4. Could Paul still have been seen primarily as a sophist (B. W. Winter (1997))? *Per contra*, F. G. Downing (1998c).

[17] Ps.-Diogenes 11; Lucian, *Demonax* 11; cf. *idem, Philosophies for Sale* 10–11; *Socratic Epistles* 1.12; 6.3; Dio 4.10, 15, 124; 8.36; 9.6–7; Julian, *Herakleios* 207–208; M.-O. Goulet-Cazé (1986), 17–22; *eadem* (1990), 2746–52.

then be the end of the matter. All that a consistent Cynic might be able to do would be to present his or her own life and conduct as an example and make fun of received opinion and practice. R. Bracht Branham makes just such a point, citing as one illustration Diogenes trying to enter a theatre just as everyone else was leaving, and explaining 'This is what I practise doing all my life.'[18] But even this Diogenes claims to be living according to nature, sharing everything with the Gods, and thus sharing their life-style. And quite strikingly, John Moles can offer a 'pious' reading of Diogenes on the basis mainly of Diogenes Laertius 6, and which runs as follows: The Gods are our benefactors (6.44); a pattern for Cynic independence (6.51, 104); the Cynic's friends (6.37, 72); the Cynic is the agent of God (6.102).[19] This latter strand in particular we noted in passing in the previous chapter. With no general human warrant offered or acceptable, the only recourse left (beside the Cynic's own conviction and example) is to backing from [a] God, divine commissioning and empowering. (For a Stoic like Epictetus, by contrast – and as we saw in the previous chapter – though his essential mission was God-given, it was 'entirely in his own hands', deliberately free from any divine interference.)[20]

And so we find pseudo-Diogenes 'living in a style that is not determined by public opinion, but according to nature, free under Zeus, crediting the good to him and not to my neighbour . . .' equipped by the Gods, and under

---

[18] R. B. Branham (1993), the entire essay; but note pp. 451, 471; the *chreia* is from Diogenes Laertius 6.64.

[19] According to nature, Diogenes Laertius 6.71; J. H. Moles (1996), 113–14. He would also insist that Diogenes' 'cosmopolitanism' must be taken to include the entire cosmos of heaven as well as earth. He adds further supporting references, some of which are included here.

[20] Epictetus 1.6.40, again.

their protection.[21] Unlike Bellerophon, dominated by hostile public opinion, pseudo-Socrates maintains his *parrhêsia*, and so pleases God, who is his counsellor and guardian. It is God who appointed him to the task.[22] When Dio addresses the Alexandrians and talks of a message that does not aim to please, he does more than claim divine direction to speak: 'I have accepted the role, not of my own choice, but as willed by some divine power. For the Gods in their providence provide (παρασκευάζουσι) not only willing counsellors, but words that are appropriate and profitable . . . like a physician who arrives in time to save his patient . . . a helper come from God . . . So, too, if we hear words of wisdom, we must believe they have been sent by God.'[23] Again, in Tarsus, Dio claims that his kind of explicitly Cynic message has come to his hearers by divine guidance.[24]

As already insisted, this is not to suggest that Paul meant the same as, or no more than Dio did. It is not at this juncture even to raise imponderable questions of authorial intention. It is simply to demonstrate that a Paul who claimed the ethos of a gentler sort of Cynic would not at all disturb the impression this would create by also claiming divine commissioning and enabling. However he might subsequently choose to explain his meaning, the claim would seem entirely in place. If you were in Cynic vein resisting the lure of rhetorical persuasion, you would very

---

[21] Ps.-Diogenes 7.1–2; cf. 22; 34, and ch. 5, above, 137–41, on the Cynic's divinely provided weaponry.

[22] Ps.-Socrates 1.7, 12; cf. 6.3–4, again: the opinion of the masses is immediately contrasted with the example of the divine way of life.

[23] Dio 32.12–14.

[24] Dio 34.1, 4. We may compare also Epictetus 3.22.23; Julian, *Herakleios*, 225D.

likely be expected to claim instead a divine empowering, just as Paul does.

Paul discusses divine and human wisdom more elaborately in 1 Corinthians 1–4. The final step in the contrast is Paul's comparison of his own tribulations with the over-ready claim of others to have attained the Cynic goal of true riches and regal authority (as we saw in chapter 4). Much if not all of the preceding argument in Paul would have sounded just as Cynic to 'pagan' hearers, however indebted it may in fact have been to Paul's Jewish antecedents and to other early Christians. On the one hand stand the values Cynics disparaged: conventional wisdom, civic power and gentle birth (1 Cor 1.20, 22, 26). Against them is ranged the figure of a man crucified, the complete antithesis of socially accepted values (1 Cor 1.23). Someone so daft, so foolish as to offer initiation into a life-style so focused could only be some kind of crazy Cynic, as 'foolish' as Paul here openly proclaims.[25]

---

[25] On 'wisdom', 'power', 'birth' as values Cynics despised (or affected to) see, e.g., Diogenes Laertius 6.1, 24, 32; 38, 43, 58–60, 72; ps.-Crates 13; *Socratic Epistle* 14; 15; Dio 4.2; 9.8; Lucian, *Dialogues of the Dead*, passim; on 'wisdom' in particular, the references above. On the foolishness of a suffering example, Lucian, *Philosophies for Sale* 9–11; Dio 8.36; 9.9; 77/8.33–34; Diogenes Laertius 6.54; *Socratic Epistle* 6.1. Cynics, of course, claimed their own kind of wisdom: ps.-Crates 31; ps.-Diogenes 20; 34; Diogenes Laertius 6.11, 12. On the Cynic sound of this disjunction between the 'folly' of God and the 'wisdom' of man, D. Kinney (1996), 314. Dio's Diogenes uses the metaphor of 'initiation' (4.31–32); cf. ps.-Diogenes 25. On crucifixion as a sort of limit-concept, cf. Epictetus' very Stoic advice, with reference to the example of Socrates, 'if you wish to be crucified, wait, and the cross will come' (2.2.20); clearly it would be Cynic to invite it (as we noted in the previous chapter). Lucian's character Cyniscus had been threatened with crucifixion: *Downward Journey* 13.

(iii) Paul as Odysseus, again

Yet despite his rejection of any reliance on human persuasiveness in Galatia and in Thessalonica, and despite the similar refusal stated more elaborately at the start of 1 Corinthians, Paul knows he has laid himself open to the accusation of trimming his message to suit his audience, and is very sensitive on the point. It is impossible to tell for sure whether he was already answering others' overt complaints on this score in the earlier letters. Only when we reach 2 Corinthians 10–13 is Paul indisputably answering explicit charges; it is at least as plausible that in the earlier letters he is doing no more than defending himself in advance against a standard popular criticism of the sort of approach he adopts.[26] However we decide this question, it is quite clear from 1 Corinthians 9 that Paul has consciously determined to be adaptable, 'all things to all people' (v. 22; cf. 10.33); even though from another standpoint he may as a result simply appear as an unprincipled, shifty, ingratiating, weak and servile character – like the Odysseus we have already considered.

Odysseus as model (and Cyrus, too) for a gentler, philanthropic Cynicism is discussed in detail by a number of recent writers. Very influential has been the contribution of Ragnar Hoïstad, with further important contributions from A. J. Malherbe and Dale B. Martin in particular.[27]

---

[26] See, e.g., the whole discussion in G. Lyons (1985), but also D. B. Martin (1990), 83.

[27] R. Hoïstad (1948); A. J. Malherbe [1983a] (1989), and also (1995), referring to W. B. Stanford, *The Ulysses Theme* (Ann Arbor, Michigan, 1976); D. B. Martin (1990); see also S. B. Andrews (1995). It is because V. K. Robbins (1996), 133–37 restricts himself to Epictetus' idealised and Stoic Cynic that he can find no Graeco-Roman

Hoïstad picks out a number of features in Antisthenes' 'defence' of Odysseus as especially significant. He notes (α) Odysseus works to 'save' others (σῴζω; compare 'to save some', 1 Cor 9.22). (β) He makes his own decisions, does not adopt a conventional approach, but adapts to circumstances (ἐγὼ δὲ; cf. 1 Cor 9.15). (γ) He abases himself, appears as a slave, 'slavishly' accepts rough treatment (compare 1 Cor 9.19 and 2.3), in order to gain his goal (κερδαίνειν; cf. 1 Cor 9.22).[28] Yet those who accepted Odysseus as a model were sure that it was he who was truly free (cf. 1 Cor 9.1), as Dio insists of his Diogenes, 'a king and master in the guise of a beggar'.[29] For the gentler Cynics Odysseus is there to be emulated by all, but particularly by the philosopher–teacher who attempts to deal with all kinds of fellow human beings (cf. 1 Cor 9.22).[30] And as just one further example we may recall the second-century Cynic Peregrinus, who, according to Lucian, chose a name with similar implications, 'Proteus', the infinitely adaptable (but, in Lucian's view, simply a con-man); Dale Martin notes that Maximus of Tyre takes Proteus as his model of the adaptable philosopher.[31]

'intertexture' for freely choosing to act the slave for the sake of others. This Stoic comparison also allows Robbins to suggest, 183, that Paul merely 'spiritualises' the prevailing patronal culture, rather than subverting it. Our Cynic comparison indicates a different conclusion.

[28] R. Hoïstad (1948), 97–98 (my lettering, α, β, γ); for Antisthenes' text, G. Giannantoni (1990), V A 54.

[29] Dio 9.9. It is worth noting again (with A. J. Malherbe (1995), 253) that Paul's 'I buffet my body', 1 Cor 9.27, is very close to the Homeric line on Odysseus (4.244–46) which Dio applies to himself as a vagrant Cynic, 33.15.

[30] Dio 71.3.

[31] Lucian, *Peregrinus* 1; D. B. Martin (1990), 94–95, citing Maximus, *That the Discourse of the Philosopher is adapted to every Subject.*

As already observed, Odysseus and those who followed his example could also be heavily criticised. The severe, 'strong' Cynics disparaged and dismissed him: 'Do not call Odysseus the father of Cynicism . . . he never did anything apart from God and fortune. He begged from everyone . . . Rather, Diogenes . . . who trusted in reason, not guile.'[32] Indeed, anyone who attempted to communicate with the public at large was likely to be accused of being the people's slave, of being insincere, of speaking to please rather than inform and improve (cf. 2 Cor 1–3).

Yet Dale Martin has shown that there was also a widespread approval of the adaptable communicator who accepted the risks involved; it clearly emerges from his survey that this was not simply an internal Cynic debate. Particularly striking is Philo's at times sympathetic portrayals of Joseph as the accommodating politician, 'who must needs be of many sides and many forms'. The philosopher, too, must adapt his words to his audience. 'The wise man requires a versatile art . . . from which he may profit in imitating those mockers who say one thing and do another, in order to save whom they can.'[33]

In the end, however, Philo comes down heavily against Joseph's willingness to be the slave of many masters, prey to empty ambition, vainglory.[34] Summarising later discussions in Maximus of Tyre, Martin concludes, 'When a speaker wished to stress the need for flexibility, he admitted it as necessary, philosophical

---

[32] Ps.-Crates 19; others of the Cynic letters are more positive or at least not dismissive: ps.-Diogenes 7.2; 34.2–3; 36.6.

[33] D. B. Martin (1990), 93–94, citing Philo, *De Iosepho* 32, 34; and then *Questions on Genesis* 4.69.

[34] D. B. Martin (1990), 113–14, citing *De Iosepho* 35; cf. Julian, *To Herakleios* 207–208.

accommodation. On the other hand, when people wished to castigate the same behaviour, they portrayed it as demagogic flattery.'[35]

It is hard to imagine in the light of the foregoing that when Paul used so much of the language of this contemporary debate, he did so with no awareness of its normal context. And we must then also give due weight to the fact that what he writes so clearly mirrors one of the preferred Cynic models, Odysseus. Consistently Paul chooses the kind of approach approved and defended by gentler 'Odyssean' Cynics, especially over and against the harsher and more radical followers of Diogenes. We may usefully recall again Plutarch's anecdote:

> Demetrius of Phaleron was not pleased to see Crates approaching. He expected some harsh words, uttered with the usual Cynic frankness. But Crates spoke gently with him, talking about his exile, arguing there was no real evil involved . . . encouraging and consoling him in his present situation.[36]

However, by the time that he writes 2 Corinthians 10–13 Paul knows for sure that he has to defend his gentle adaptability (as he sees it) against those who despise it and can only respect a strong-minded Christian–Cynic toughness. To the strong Paul appears abject, ταπεινός, quite lacking in confidence when he's with them, yet inconsistently bold (θαρρῶ) when away and writing (2 Cor 10.1). As Malherbe shows, these, too, are terms from the debate about Odysseus. In his Odyssean wanderings Dio accepted a beggar's dress as 'abject garb' (στολὴν ταπεινὴν), not as a defiant gesture. The tougher Cynic, explicitly refusing the Odyssean model, will have nothing to do with any who

---

[35] D. B. Martin (1990), 94–95.

[36] Plutarch, *Quo modo adulator*, *Moralia* 69CD.

are abject, ταπεινοί, while he himself displays self-confidence (ἐφ' ἑαυτῷ θαρροῦντα) consistently.[37] We saw in the previous chapter how Paul then goes on to deploy the motifs of weapons and defences that seem to stem at least ultimately from Antisthenes' defence of Odysseus, and which continue to be seen as characteristic for discussions of the ethos of the Cynic sage.[38] Paul is sure that with divinely strong weapons he can be effectively bold and daring in the face of entrenched opposition to his mission (2 Cor 10.3–6: as productively bold as Antisthenes' Odysseus had claimed to be). Just so had he earlier threatened those in the Corinthian congregation making strong Cynic claims that he could himself appear like an aggressive Cynic, 'with a staff', ἐν ῥάβδῳ, rather than meekly (1 Cor 4.2; we may compare pseudo-Diogenes 29.1).[39] But Paul states his clear preference that others should be as accommodating as he tries to be in not tripping or trapping 'the weak', the issue that prompted the discussion in 1 Corinthians 9 (reviewed above, chapter 4).

(iv) Working for a living

Paul explained to the congregation in Corinth that an important part of his approach to those he hoped to gain was his choosing to work for his living rather than accepting pay for sharing the gospel. In the argument in

---

[37] A. J. Malherbe [1983a], 168–69, citing Dio 13.10, and ps.-Crates 19 once more.

[38] These motifs reappear in summary in Diogenes Laertius' sketch of Antisthenes' teaching ('virtue is a weapon . . . fighting against all evils . . . wisdom is a sure stronghold'), 6.12–13.

[39] Ps.-Diogenes 7 uses ῥάβδος for the Cynic's staff; but see also ps.-Diogenes 30.4, etc.

1 Corinthians 8–10 this is simply but importantly a further example of the kind of renunciation of rights which Paul insists is proper among Christians; we considered aspects of his exposition in some little detail in chapter 4. It is, however, obvious that for people of any wealth manual labour, craft work, was socially (and intellectually) demeaning. Cicero is often quoted: 'Unbecoming to a gentleman, and vulgar, is the work of all hired men whom we pay for mere manual labour . . . the standard wage they receive is a measure of their slavery.'[40] But one can find very similar attitudes expressed by such as Epictetus (though he is prepared for a student of philosophy to work for his keep) and Lucian (though he had himself originally been apprenticed as a sculptor), and many more.[41] We shall consider Paul's possible motives further below. But first we note (with the help of R. F. Hock in particular) that Paul's decision to engage in teaching activity while supporting himself by the kind of artisan activity that had him sweating away by night and day (1 Cor 4.12; 2 Cor 11.27; 1 Thess 2.9 (and 2 Thess 3.7–8)) would still further reinforce the impression that here was some kind of Cynic philosopher.

Paul himself does not tell us precisely what work it was that he engaged in. Most commentators are happy enough to accept at this point the aside at Acts 18.3, explaining that he was a leather-worker;[42] especially since Luke makes nothing more of this detail, and (with leather

---

[40] Cicero, *De officiis* 1.150 (LCL).

[41] Epictetus 2.14.4–6 (though see below); Lucian, *Runaways*, 12, 17; R. F. Hock (1980), 35–37; R. MacMullen (1974), 114–15.

[42] R. F. Hock (1980), 20–21. Long hours and small returns are certainly the lot of Lucian's Micyllus, ibidem, 34, quoting *Gallus* (*the Cock*) and *Cataplus* (*Downward Journey*).

working one of the more despised crafts) this item runs somewhat contrary to the general impression that Acts seems to intend to convey, to wit, that Paul found his support from wealthy and socially acceptable patrons.[43] On the basis of much later rabbinic tradition it has often been argued that learning a trade of this sort would have been part of Paul's Pharisaic upbringing. Ronald Hock has argued cogently against this conclusion; but that issue is not important for the argument proceeding here, which concerns the impression Paul would have made (probably aware, probably intentionally) in the Greek and Graeco-Roman cities he visited.

Following Hock still, we are invited to picture Paul working hard to scrape a living in an open-fronted shop where customers could lounge and converse and read aloud (and even sit on benches).[44] The most obvious analogy would be Simon the shoemaker, who figures in accounts of Socrates,[45] but who also appears as a clearly Cynic figure in the *Socratic Epistles*. Teles reports Zeno recalling seeing Crates reading from Aristotle in Simon's shop, and the *Socratic Epistles* place Antisthenes there.[46] And, as Hock notes, Lucian suggests many of his (despised) Cynics were former artisans, suggesting that Cynic philosophers and artisans were in frequent contact, presumably in the artisans' places of work and trade.[47]

---

[43] E. A. Judge (1960) and (1972), who, however, accepts the validity of this picture in Acts; cf. R. F. Hock (1980), 65.

[44] R. F. Hock (1980), 33; cf. also M. Ebner (1991), 69–75.

[45] Xenophon, *Memorabilia* 4.2.1; Diogenes Laertius 2.122; R. F. Hock (1980), 38.

[46] Teles IVB, (46H); *Socratic Epistle* 9.4 and 13.1; R. F. Hock (1980), 38.

[47] R. F. Hock (1980), 38, referring again to Lucian, *Runaways* 12 and 17.

Lucian claimed bitterly that his artisans adopted Cynic philosophy as a complete and welcome change from hard labour. However, there is evidence that some later philosophers themselves also worked for their living. The Stoic Cleanthes is noted as one such.[48] The way Simon is portrayed in the *Socratic Epistles* suggests this continued to be a model, and specifically as a way of maintaining a prized (Cynic) independence, battling with hunger and thirst (just as Paul describes his life-style, 1 Cor 4.11–12).[49] Emulating this model we find named Cynics in and around the first century. Hock lists three: Demetrius of Sunium, a Cynic who (according to Lucian) worked for a time as a docker;[50] Musonius, who preferred farming or herding (and whose chosen life-style can count as Cynic, even while he maintained Stoic intellectual convictions); and Dio of Prusa. In fact Musonius does not tell us that he acted on his own good advice, but his disquisition sounds autobiographical.[51] Dio is said by Philostratus to have done various jobs – digging, planting, drawing water – for his living during his exile; and Dio himself indicates as much.[52]

As Hock and then Ebner point out, there were four ways for a philosopher without private means to gain a living. He (much more likely than she) could charge, could

---

[48] Diogenes Laertius 7.168–69; Epictetus 3.26.23.

[49] R. F. Hock (1980), 39, referring to *Socratic Epistle* 8 and 12; cf. Lucian, *Timon* (before Timon regained his wealth); *Nigrinus* 25; *Philosophies for Sale* 11.

[50] Lucian, *Toxaris* 31; probably not Seneca's friend Demetrius.

[51] Musonius Rufus 11, in C. Lutz (1947) or O. Hense (1905). On Musonius' Cynic character, see above, and F. G. Downing (1992a), 69. But note also Epictetus 3.26.7, and 23–24, again.

[52] Philostratus, *Lives of the Sophists* 488; Dio himself, 1.9 and his ideal Herakles, 60.8; but cf. 80.1 (he can change his opinion).

find a patron, could beg – or could work.[53] Each had their
drawbacks for anyone seeking to have (and display) a
genuine independence. Making articles and selling them
might well seem the most promising option, as the *Socratic
Epistles* argue, with implicit or explicit reference to
Simon.[54] We can nonetheless find instances of a Cynic
with a patron, certainly Cynics begging, and possibly,
Cynics accepting 'gifts in exchange' (payment by another
name).[55] However, the fourth option, working for a living,
is only ever proposed as a philosophical ideal by some
Cynics; and only among Cynics in the first century do we
hear of philosophers putting this ideal into practice.

Paul says working for his living affords him the
freedom and the independence he needs for his mission; it
is enough his own decision for him to make it a plausible
matter of boasting. And (as Hock and Martin and others
have pointed out), it will have put him alongside most
ordinary townspeople, where he might have opportunity to
'gain' some.[56] We have just noted the Cynic resonances of
the former aim; but the latter is a Cynic goal, too – to be
where most people are (whether or not they are respons-

---

[53] R. F. Hock (1980), 52–59; M. Ebner (1991), 71–73.

[54] *Socratic Epistles* 8; 9.4; 12, again.

[55] Seneca was patron to Demetrius; Cynics begging, e.g., Diogenes
Laertius 6.59; ps.-Crates 17; it is a fair exchange, ps.-Crates 2;
ps.-Diogenes 10.

[56] It should be noted that in chapter 4 it was argued that 'the strong'
from whom Paul distances himself are the self-styled strong-minded
Cynic Christians, and the 'weak' are any unaligned with them; these
are not then in themselves indicators of social rank, as that is argued
briefly by R. F. Hock (1980), 60, and by D. B. Martin (1990), 123.
However, the different attitudes to work of the wealthy leisured and of
the craftsmen which Martin distinguishes do need to be borne in mind.
Paul, here, seems to focus on work as demeaning, not something the
craftsman would be proud of.

ive).[57] Working this way, and explaining it as he does, Paul could only look and sound Cynic.

It ought also probably to be taken as significant that Paul in 1 Corinthians 9 seems to most scholars to be responding (albeit with declared freedom) to the way in which 'all the apostles' are interpreting in practice something very like the synoptic mission charge.[58] This is one of the strands of the Jesus tradition where Cynic analogies are most clearly discerned, even by those who then discount them.[59] Whatever the adversely critical responses from people in Corinth Paul is aware of or anticipates, he does not seem to expect anyone to tell him that his response runs in any way importantly counter to the sense of this (Cynic-seeming) teaching and example of Jesus.

(v) My own example

In 1 Corinthians 9.1–12 Paul evinces no qualms in principle about payment for apostles, and even seems to recommend it for others (Gal 6.6). He may possibly have chosen to refuse payment to avoid any suspicion that he was preaching in part or in whole for the money (1 Thess 2.5), but he does not stress this aim. As we recalled a little while back, Paul actually introduces the topic at 1 Corinthians 9 to provide an example of self-restraint for the benefit of others. In 2 Thessalonians Paul (or a disciple)

---

[57] Ps.-Crates 21; ps.-Diogenes 6; Dio 32.9; Lucian, *Philosophies for Sale* 10; F. G. Downing (1988c), 2.

[58] For the evidence, D. Wenham (1995), 190–98.

[59] Cf. F. G. Downing (1992a), 10–12, 133–34; and L. Vaage (1994a) 17–39; V. K. Robbins (1996), 137–41.

explains that a quite precise imitation of this working for one's living was his intention: 'It was not because we lacked the right, but to offer our conduct as a model for you to copy' (2 Thess 3.7–9).[60] Paul is in fact very ready to offer his own conduct as an example for his converts to follow, for (as we may recall) he and his fellow apostles are a spectacle provided by God (1 Cor 4.9).[61] And, as noted at the end of the previous chapter, to be willing to offer yourself (rather than some idealised figure in the past) as an example would align you with the Cynics.

So A. J. Malherbe writes, 'While the philosophers did use the imitation motif, they were hesitant to call others to follow their own examples . . . this diffidence is clearest among the Stoics.' Paul, by contrast, tells us that his hearers were already 'imitators of him and his associates and the Lord . . .'. Malherbe then allows that contemporary Cynics made similar claims. Elsewhere Malherbe quotes Seneca:

> Of course, a living voice and a common life will help you more than a sermon (*oratio*). You need to be where the action is. In the first place that's because people trust their eyes more than their ears. But secondly, it's because the route by way of precepts is lengthy, while example provides an effective shortcut.[62]

(The 'shortcut' image is, as we have seen, importantly Cynic.)[63]

---

[60] On using 2 Thessalonians along with 1 Thessalonians as evidence for Paul, see chapter 2, above.

[61] Cf. also 1 Cor 4.6; 11.1; 1 Thess 1.6; 2.14; Phil 3.17.

[62] Seneca, *Epistulae morales* 6.5, cited at greater length by A. J. Malherbe (1987), 52–53, using the LCL translation; that above is my own; Seneca refers to past great Stoics, and to Epicurus.

[63] Ch. 2 and n. 47, above.

Malherbe notes Seneca's further elaboration of the theme of imitation, Seneca this time himself quoting Epicurus:

> 'We should take to our hearts some noble character, and imagine that person always in view, living as though they were always watching us, behaving as though in their sight.' . . . .It's great when someone can improve us not just when they're present in person, but when they're simply present in our thoughts.[64]

As Seneca's citation from Epicurus indicates, along with the conclusions quoted from Malherbe, the 'imitation' theme is itself a philosophical commonplace.[65] Imitation of the present speaker, however, figures (as we have intimated) particularly importantly among Cynics, eschewing as they did the long intellectual training insisted on by all the other schools including the Stoics, rejecting even systematic ethical reflection. A free and sovereign wise perfection could be quickly reached by copying the simple life-style of those who were already practising it.

Thus it is Epictetus' heavily criticised brash populist Cynic who says simply:

> 'I'm free from any pain or disturbance. You must recognise, my friends, that while you're in a noisy crowd jostling round worthless fripperies, I alone stand unperturbed.' Are you really not satisfied with having no aches and pains, but must go on and advertise? 'Come and see me, anyone whose head is aching, who's got a fever, or who's lame or blind, and see how healthy I am, nothing

---

[64] Seneca, *Epistulae morales* 11.8–9; cited at greater length by A. J. Malherbe (1987), 53, LCL; here my own translation.

[65] Elsewhere Malherbe notes ps.-Isocrates, *To Demonicus* 11.36; Lucian, *Nigrinus* 26; Pliny the Younger. *Epistle* 8.13; ps.-Libanius, *Epistolary Styles* 52; A. J. Malherbe [1983b] (1989), 248 (with some difference in the final reference); cf. also *idem* (1978), 55.

wrong with me at all!' That's a useless and insensitive thing to do - unless, of course, you are someone like Asclepius, and can show them there and then how they can be restored there and then to good health, and you're only pointing to your good health with theirs in mind. [66]

By contrast, although Epictetus' own and ideal Cynic would also display his serenity for all to see, it would only be to draw attention to the remedies that cured him: and those remedies will have been a 'winter's training', the long hidden (Stoic) progress to wisdom, quite explicitly not the Cynic shortcut. Epictetus concludes emphatically, he himself is not yet ready to be put on display. [67] Paul, as we saw at the end of the previous chapter (1 Cor 4.9, 16 etc.), is quite content to be on show, and that even when he is far short of perfection (1 Cor 9.27 and Phil 3.12).

So Antisthenes (in later Cynic tradition) learned the Cynic life-style from copying Socrates. [68] Diogenes himself is taught simplicity by a mouse and then by a young boy's example. [69] In turn, he teaches others to imitate him as their model, especially in competition with worthless athletes. [70] It is a Cynic's deeds (rather than logical or rhetorical persuasion) that justifies the little that he does say. [71] And so Diogenes, as quoted above, displayed his fight to the death with a fever as the most important spectacle on view; and it would have been important, so 'Crates' insisted, for Hipparchia to return quickly to Diogenes' death-bed to see

---

[66] Epictetus 4.8.28–29.

[67] Epictetus 4.8.30–31, 34–39, and then 43.

[68] Diogenes Laertius 6.2.

[69] Diogenes Laertius 6.22, 37; ps.-Diogenes 6.1; and 11.

[70] Ps.-Diogenes 14; 31; Dio 8 and 9.

[71] Ps.-Crates 20; 21; ps.-Diogenes 15; 27; 28; 29; cf. A. J. Malherbe [1983b], 247.

philosophy in action.[72] 'Our actions teach endurance much faster than words do', says pseudo-Crates, claiming to speak from experience.[73] Seneca says he is sure that providence provides his Cynic friend Demetrius 'so that our age may not lack an example to challenge it'; and since Demetrius intended to be a man of few words, we may assume this was also his own intention.[74] So, too, Demonax 'gave himself whole-heartedly to freedom and frank-speaking, persevered in a living a life straightforward, sound, and irreproachable, providing an example to all who saw and heard him'.[75] And Peregrinus went to the pyre 'to teach people how to face death and master their fears'.[76]

On occasion Paul says more. 'Be imitators of me as I am of Christ', he urges (1 Cor 11.1). 'You became imitators of us and of the Lord' (1 Thess 1.6).[77] If anything, some Cynics were even readier still to base the example they offered on a divine or semi-divine or classic heroic example. We have already noted Odysseus, and then Herakles in particular (and we shall consider talk of God and God-like beings in the next chapter). Pseudo-Heraclitus claims to imitate God.[78] Diogenes in the trad-

---

[72] Epictetus 3.22.58–59 (and Jerome, *Ad Iovinianum* 2.14); ps.-Crates 1.

[73] Ps.-Crates 20; cf. ps.-Diogenes 2; 9.

[74] Seneca, *De beneficiis* 7.8.3; 7.1.3–4. In his 13th *Discourse* Dio presents himself as one who quickly adapted to an Odysseus-style of life, and is therefore now able to teach others a Cynic lesson from Socrates that's not hard to learn (13.1–12 and 34–37).

[75] Lucian, *Demonax* 3.

[76] Lucian, *Peregrinus* 23 (Lucian mocks the idea, 9).

[77] Cf. also 2 Cor 8.9; Phil 2.5–11; Rom 15.3; 7–8; see further, below, ch.7.

[78] Ps.-Heraclitus 4.2–3; 5.1.

ition claimed good men were images of the Gods.[79] Dio
said Diogenes himself 'imitated the life of the Gods'.[80] By
emulating the Gods who have no needs, the Cynic becomes
like them.[81] To urge the imitation of a divine figure, a
God-like man who took his opposition to 'the rulers of this
world' as far as accepting crucifixion, would be entirely in
keeping with the many other Cynic-seeming elements we
have found in Paul.

(vi) In conclusion

We sum up the contribution of this chapter to our five
theses. Several leading elements of Paul's self-presentation
as a teacher are thus clearly very similar to characteristic
and distinctive features of the image of themselves offered
by Cynic philosophers. His dress and his behaviour,
appearing in public half-naked and scarred, drawing
attention to the example he afforded, could, at the outset at
least, only appear as Cynic (*a*), especially combined with
the precise manner in which he uses his athletic and
military metaphors, and even more significantly with the
details and manner of presentation of the frequent lists of
troubles he has invited and accepted, as we noted in the
previous chapter. When Paul then talks about his didactic
and pastoral methods, and even his way of supporting
himself financially, the clearest analogies available to us

---

[79] Diogenes Laertius 6.51.

[80] Dio 6.31.

[81] Ps.-Crates 11; ps.-Diogenes 34; Diogenes Laertius 6.104; Dio 6.31;
ps.-Lucian, *The Cynic* 12. The 'friends of the Gods' motif is, of course,
closely akin to this strand. Cf. also ps.-Diogenes 7; 26; 36.6 (here,
Herakles); Dio 4.31–32.

turn out to be from Cynic or Cynic-influenced sources (Dio in particular). Like the Cynics in rejecting any easy surrender to popular whim, Paul is nonetheless willing with the kindlier Cynics to accommodate his manner of presentation to meet people as they are; and where tough and tender Cynics diverge, Paul seems to deploy some of the specific motifs of those gentler ones who accepted Odysseus as their model. Claiming as he did a divine origin for his message and ministry, rather than arguing from what popular opinion might judge 'reasonable', Paul would again sound like many of the Cynics.

This is not at all to suggest that Paul set out to incorporate as much of Cynicism as he could, for its own sake. But it is to suggest (*b* and *c*) that of the models and motifs available it was clear to Paul that these Cynic-derived ones were the most appropriate both for the content of what he was drawn to share and for the enabling of the sharing. That is still not to imply a picture of Paul going through a list of doxographies, and then on reflection selecting mostly Cynic matter. Much of what we have found is much more likely by the time of his encounter with the risen Christ to have been already well assimilated as part of his practical, emotional intellectual and spiritual store. As A. J. Malherbe has recently insisted, 'The philosophic traditions are for him not merely a pile of topoi or slogans from which he can draw in order to lay a pseudo-philosophical veneer over a wooden argument.' Malherbe then goes on to add, 'Neither does he, conversely, use these traditions in a manner that shows him to be captive to any one school of thought.'[82]

Though I would accept the 'neither . . . captive', I have argued for still more consistently Cynic strands in

---

[82] A. J. Malherbe (1995), 255.

Paul than Malherbe himself finds. The implicit (and sometimes explicit) criteria for the adoption of these Cynic-derived models and motifs probably come mostly from Paul's inherited Judaism and his recently acquired (and elaborating) Christian sources. But Cynicism in fact affords a remarkably well-adapted language of ideas and life-styles, and just this must also have provided some of the stimulus, some of the prompting.[83]

As we have argued, Paul could hardly have been initially unaware or at any rate remained for any length of time unaware of the Cynic resonances of his deeds and words as he talked with visitors to his workshop or with those drawn into the new Christian communities; or when he encountered travelling Christians arriving from other communities, likely to be sensitive to fresh innovations. Though Paul at Corinth was drawn to oppose on some issues a more radical Cynic interpretation of Christian ethics than his own, at no point do we find him having to defend the Cynic-derived motifs we have discerned being positively deployed as in others' eyes in any way a foreign importation into the new life and faith. The Christian and Cynic strands may well, then, belong together in some

---

[83] Scholars have at times also thought significant for Cynic influence on Paul the appearance in his letters and in Epictetus in particular of such terms as ἄγγελος, ἀπόστολος–ἀποστέλλω, διάκονος–διακονία, κῆρυξ–κηρύσσω, (especially in Epictetus 3.22: 3.22.3; 23; 38; 46; 69–70). Their use by Paul is of interest, of course, and further shows how at ease he is with the language. If anything, of course, their use would point to Stoic rather than to Cynic echoes in Paul (and these we shall consider further in chapter 9, below); but they are probably not distinctive enough in themselves for us to base much on them. Considerably more important is the ethos of Paul's message. Early in Paul's ministry its character must have looked and sounded distinctly Cynic, in his own Jewish–Christian style. Later it does seem to have become more Stoic in mood, as will be argued, in brief, below.

manner, from the outset. It could well be the case (*e*) that some of this 'readiness' for a Cynic expression was already there in Christianity's origins in the ministry of Jesus.

Appendix - Epicurean psychogogy

Clarence E. Glad has recently argued carefully and at length that Cynic discussions of 'the teacher' are much less apposite for our understanding of Paul than are Epicurean approaches to 'psychogogy', especially as these are set out in Philodemus' *Peri Parrhêsia, On Frank Criticism*.[84] Glad is certainly able to show that the 'Odyssean' style preferred by gentler Cynics is not the only model of kindly counselling available in Paul's world; it and Epicurean concern for sensitivity in advice and correction have much in common. It is also clear from the many passages adduced by Glad that this Epicurean 'psychotherapeutic' ethos was well known outside Epicurean circles. And Glad also notes that, as Paul did, so did Epicureans welcome people into their communities without any lengthy novitiate, without any prior social or moral 'screening'.[85]

There is, however, no sign that 'mutual psychogogy' was itself a major concern of the Pauline communities. In crises Paul was clear that a sensitivity which we may well find akin to that urged by Philodemus was called for, from him as from other Christians among themselves: 'My brothers and sisters, if any one of you is caught up in some transgression, those of you who are spiritual[ly mature] are to restore him or her very gently' (Gal 6.1). But there is no indication that such psychogogy as such

---

[84] C. E. Glad (1995), 4–12, 89–98.
[85] C. E. Glad (1995), 162; *idem* (1996), 53.

was a constant preoccupation for his converts. As Glad himself notes, Paul does not deploy the medical 'therapy' metaphor.[86] Only three passages in Paul seem at all open to the interpretation Glad proposes: 1 Thessalonians 5.14, Galatians 6.1 (just quoted) and Romans 15.14; and none of them demand it. If Paul had really been welcoming people into a mutually therapeutic community at all analogous to an Epicurean one, we would have expected much more discussion of method, on something of the scale and of the kind we do find in Philodemus. (It is also the case that Epicureans expected newcomers to learn and accept to the letter and in elaborate detail the metaphysical doctrines of the master,[87] and for this there is no analogy in Paul.)

Paul and other early Christians certainly do seem to have welcomed people into their communities without prior screening or novitiate; but entry was by way of a massive social break with civic conventions, as we have emphasised, and here Epicureans (as we have documented above) differ, leaving Paul's way with only a Cynic parallel.[88] Epicureans provide an interesting but largely irrelevant aside.

---

[86] C. E. Glad (1995), 66.

[87] Diogenes Laertius 10.

[88] G. Tomlin (1997), apparently independently of Glad (1995) or (1996), suggests 'the theology of a group of well-off Corinthian Christians was influenced by the kind of ideas and behaviour most prevalent in Epicurean circles (72).' Epicurean public social conformity in fact indicates rather more of a contrast on most of the topics Tomlin considers (death and resurrection, sexual morality, idol worship, self-sufficiency, group-formation, and wisdom, culture and rhetoric). Overall the Cynic resonances seem more pervasive, coherent and fundamental.

7

ONE GOD, ONE LORD[1]

(i) Imitating the divine

'The gods are not models for ethical behaviour . . . and seldom provide the warrants for ethical conduct.' So Neil Richardson concludes with regard to pagan religions in the sketches of 'God-language' in Jewish and then in Graeco-Roman paraenesis which introduce his very thorough analytical survey of 'Paul's language about God'. Much more clearly with Paul, avers Richardson, do we find 'a marked continuity with the Old Testament and Jewish tradition in the deployment of God-language in a warranting function'.[2] In fact, Richardson finds little in his Jewish sources, either, to suggest that God's character be taken as a model to be imitated.[3]

We have, however, in the previous chapter, already noted something of the themes of obedience to and imitation of God, Gods or demi-Gods in some of our Cynic

---

[1] The title of the very useful book by L. Hurtado (1988), though it is concerned only with 'Early Christian Devotion and Ancient Jewish Monotheism.'

[2] N. Richardson (1994), 235, 237.

[3] N. Richardson (1994), 219–27. Lev 19.2 etc. affords no precise example ('you shall be distinct as I am'); more specific imitation of God tends to be implicit (e.g., Exod 20.11; Deut 5.15). Richardson's Graeco-Roman sources are Epictetus, Plutarch and Seneca.

sources. When Paul adduces divine backing for his moral advice or prescriptions, and in particular when he urges the imitation of the 'divine' Christ-figure, to Hellenised pagans he would sound most like many of the Cynics (even where the sources of Paul's paraenesis may appear to us clearly Jewish or specifically Christian). There would be proportionately more '*imitatio dei*' talk in Paul; but the next most frequent users of such language in the wider (non-Jewish) Graeco-Roman world of the day were the Cynics. However distinctive on closer acquaintance Paul's God-talk turned out to be, the initial impression would be that here was yet another variant of a Cynic claiming divine sanction for his disruptive life-style; and that would remain the continuing closest comparison.

Thus, if Cynics talk of God or Gods, it is as beings relevant to and even concerned with the way humans live. As we already seen, it is not simply the call to philosophy that Dio ascribes to 'the God' or 'the Gods', but the actual advice, the paraenesis itself is God-given: 'The Gods provide, not just good and willing counsellors, but also the appropriate and helpful words themselves . . . if we hear wise advice, we must accept that it comes from God.'[4] So, too, we earlier marked pseudo-Diogenes, 'living in a style that is not determined by public opinion but according to nature, free under Zeus, *crediting the good to him* and not to my neighbour'.[5] Pseudo-Socrates has God as his counsellor and guardian in the admonitory task to which God appointed him; it is the Gods who provide the Cynic

---

[4] Dio 32.12, 14; cf. 34.4–5 and 13.9 and following and 1.58.

[5] Ps.-Diogenes 7.1–2. Richardson rightly notes that 'according to nature' as an indication of the divine purpose is infrequent in Paul (Rom 2.26–27; 1 Cor 11.14); I draw attention here to 'crediting the good' prescription for life to Zeus.

with his 'weapons', his accoutrement and life-style.[6] It is in this sense that the Cynic is the messenger of the Gods.[7] It is, of course, very hard to tell what this 'really means', and it may well have been formal or figurative. But the language remains on the surface at least (and maybe deeper) as 'theological', as 'religious' in our kind of use of those terms,[8] as what we find in Paul.

And so, as we noted briefly in passing at the end of the previous chapter, in a wide range of Cynic sources God or the Gods themselves also provide a model for Cynic behaviour. Dio claimed that Diogenes 'imitated the life of the Gods' in minimising his needs; by emulating the Gods who have no needs, the Cynic becomes like them.[9] Pseudo-Heraclitus claims to imitate God; and on this basis good (that is, Cynic-approved) humans are images of the Gods.[10] 'By and large only humankind among living creatures is an image of God . . . high-minded, beneficent and humane (that's how we conceive God to be), so we must think of human beings in his image, so long as they live according to [their divinely given] nature', explains Musonius.[11]

Although Paul himself in fact never explicitly urges that his hearers 'imitate God', it is clear that more generally, 'God' as well as Christ provides 'a paradigm' for

---

[6] Ps.-Crates 16; *Socratic Epistle* 1.7, 12.

[7] I note again the list in J. H. Moles (1993), 270, and notes: Strabo 15.1, 63–64; Plutarch, *Life of Alexander* 65.2; Diogenes Laertius 6.102; Dio as above; Epictetus 2.22.2; 2.23.53, 69 (I have omitted some).

[8] See especially the discussion in M.-O. Goulet-Cazé (1990), 2785–88.

[9] Dio 6.31; cf. 4.21–22, 31, 40–41; ps.-Crates 11; ps.-Diogenes 34; Diogenes Laertius 6.104.

[10] Ps.-Heraclitus 4.2–3; 5.1; Diogenes Laertius 6.51; ps.-Lucian, *The Cynic*, 12; see, again, J. H. Moles (1993), 270.

[11] Musonius 17 (C. Lutz (1947), 108); O. Hense (1905), 88–93.

Christian behaviour, as Richardson argues. He cites in particular Romans 14.3 – we are to welcome any who are weak in faith, because God has welcomed them.[12] We might compare in 1 Corinthians, 1.26–29, God choosing to shame the 'wise' (and we should share his attitude in this); 12.24, God's design of the human body indicates how congregations should live; 14.33, God is a God of peace (so Christian meetings should be orderly!); in 2 Corinthians 1.18 Paul's consistency mirrors God's faithfulness; at 9.6–15, God's generosity should inform as well as enable the Corinthians; and the Galatians should not value the observance of (some of) the Jewish law more than God, who ignored such observance in giving them the Spirit (Gal 3.1–5). Further, as Richardson also argues, if Christ is the image of God and is to be imitated, then implicitly we are being enjoined to imitate God.[13] (The motif appears still more explicitly in other early Christian writings: Luke 6.36 [Matt 5.48], Eph 4.32.)

(ii) Herakles and Odysseus, once more

However, the imitation of Christ as a being who is divine (though never unqualifiedly designated 'God') is an explicit strand in Paul which would have harmonised even more readily with the other Cynic-seeming motifs that his earliest hearers are likely to have discerned. We have already noted in the last two chapters a number of passages where hearers are likely to have picked up echoes of commonplace paradigmatic portrayals of Odysseus and of

---

[12] N. Richardson (1994), 135 and 189.
[13] N. Richardson (1994), 135, again.

Herakles in particular.[14] The most obvious passage in Paul would be Philippians 2.5–11. Half a century ago now, and apparently independently, both Wilfred Knox and Arnold Ehrhardt suggested we should note in the Pauline passage some very clear resonances with (in particular) Plutarch's character-sketch of Alexander as a Herakles figure.[15] On his civilising mission (as Plutarch presents it) Alexander 'did not overrun Asia on a looting expedition . . . nor its territories as things to be seized (ἅρπαγμα; cf. ἅρπαγμον in Phil 2.6) . . . He sought [sc. by his own obedient compliance] to show that earthly things are obedient (ὑπήκοα . . . just as Jesus is obedient, ὑπήκοος) to one rationality and one πολιτεία and all humankind, one people, and to this conformed himself (ἐσχημάτιζεν; cf. σχήματι, in Phil 2.7). And if the divine being who sent Alexander's soul to earth had not so soon recalled him, one law would have illumined all humanity . . . .' [16] In brief, the descent of a semi-divine agent of deity, his 'shaping' for 'ungrasping' service and his re-ascent, has world-wide implications.

Neither Knox nor Ehrhardt suggested any direct influence of Plutarch's source(s) on Paul, and it is clear that there are more echoes still from Paul's Jewish tradition (Adam in Genesis, the servant figure in 2 Isaiah) and maybe others besides.[17] But the structure of the thought and some of the language about Herakles, here and else-

---

[14] See further the discussion in A. J. Malherbe (1988) and D. E. Aune (1990); neither refer to Phil 2; nor does D. Georgi (1991), 65–71.

[15] A. A. Ehrhardt [1945] (1964); W. L. Knox (1948).

[16] Plutarch, *De Alexandri Magni fortuna* 1.8, 330D, using mostly Ehrhardt's rendering. Alexander 'was himself obedient' in 'conforming' himself to the universal Logos.

[17] See the survey in G. F. Hawthorne (1983), 71–96; and D. Seeley (1994b), who underlines the challenge to the divine emperors.

where on the one hand, and the parallels in Philippians
2.5–11 and other descent–exaltation passages in Paul on
the other, indicate at least a narrative pattern that Paul's
hearers would very likely recognise, and so most likely a
mode of expression ready for Paul's quite deliberate use.[18]
Ehrhardt notes that Plutarch plays down the theme of
divine origin in applying this complex motif to Alexander;
but Herakles as such is of course ἴσα θεοῖς, just as Paul's
Christ Jesus is ἴσα θεῷ. It is difficult to suppose that Paul
could cite this hymn without being made aware that ἴσα
θεῷ was a generic term.[19] Herakles performed menial
tasks at another's bidding; Jesus assumed the form of a
slave.[20] Dio's Diogenes, presenting Herakles as someone
to be emulated, notes that after his troublesome life people
'honour Herakles above all others and consider him a
God'. Paul, though quoting a sacred Jewish text, expresses
a similar conclusion: 'at the name of Jesus, every knee
shall bow'. Paul began by urging the Philippians to 'have
in themselves the mind that is in Christ Jesus', τοῦτο
φρονεῖτε ἐν ὑμῖν ὃ καὶ ἐν Χριστῷ Ἰησοῦ. If he adopted
Herakles' life-style, writes pseudo-Diogenes to 'Crates',
the mind of Herakles would come alive in him, οὕτω γὰρ
ἂν Ἡράκλειον διαναστείη σοι φρόνημα.[21]

---

[18] W. L. Knox (1948), 239; A. A. Ehrhardt (1964), 38.

[19] Ehrhardt (1964), 39, cites in particular ps.-Plato, *Axiochus* 364A
and the *Bibliotheke* of Diodorus, 1.2.3; but also its use for the Roman
emperors. Lucian mocks the idea of Herakles as a god very like a
human or a human very like a God in *Dialogues of the Dead* 11 (16)
and *Parliament of the Gods* 6.

[20] Dio 8.28; Epictetus 3.26.32; compare also Odysseus, of course, as
king appearing like a slave, Dio 9.9; Lucian, *Parliament of the Gods* 7.

[21] Ps.-Diogenes 26. In the light of all the evidence it is hard to
understand its dismissal by R. P. Martin (1967), 79. On Jesus' exalted
judicial function, see further below. On secondary divine figures in
Judaism, A. Segal (1977); L. Hurtado (1988).

In chapter 5 we noted, with Martin Ebner, how Paul's summary of his troubles at 1 Corinthians 4.11–12a in particular would echo the world mission of Herakles, facing hunger and thirst, homeless, labouring with his own hands.[22] Giving one's body to be burned (1 Cor 13.3) would recall Herakles, of course, as well as the legendary practice of some Hindu 'naked philosophers' admired by some Cynics.[23] Later Paul drops in an aside which could hardly have been otherwise heard than as a reference to Herakles as a model, as Abraham Malherbe has shown: 'If for this life only we have had our hopes centred in Christ . . . Why am I in peril every hour? . . . what do I gain, if – to use the commonplace expression – "I fought with wild beasts" in Ephesus? If the dead are not going to be raised, "let's eat and drink, for tomorrow we die"' (1 Cor 15.30, 32). Paul can hardly have meant a literal fight in the arena, which he would have been very unlikely to have survived (and, if Luke is right on Paul's Roman citizenship, he would have been very unlikely to have faced in the first place). The context as Paul himself states it is his choice between hardships and hedonism, the dangers of his mission or the enticements of the table (Isaiah 22.13): that's where the fight took place, like the struggle of Dio's Herakles, who 'fought with wild beasts' the passions that lure to pleasure and the easy life; and Dio's Diogenes fought the same battle, as does Lucian's auctioned Cynic.

---

[22] M. Ebner (1991), 170–72.

[23] Cf. Lucian, *Peregrinus* 23–35; other self-immolating figures are also alluded to earlier still, in the narrative, but in the main account Herakles is the focus; and cf. C. Muckensturn (1993) and R. Stoneman (1994), 505–506 and (1995).

(Pleasure's victims, Epicureans in particular, could also be stigmatised as 'wild beasts'.)[24]

Though Odysseus is not a deified figure, he, too, is a heroic model admired, as we have seen, by some (milder) Cynics. Here the motif of slavery is even more prominent than in the portraits of Herakles that we have noted. When Paul talked of not pleasing himself but making himself a slave to all, to save as many as he could, it would have been easy to pick up the resonances with the ideals of these gentler Cynics. But when Paul was refusing to please himself he also saw himself as imitating Christ, the Christ who did not please himself (1 Cor 11.1; Rom 15.3). Paul's Christ is himself an Odysseus-like figure, accepting tribulation (1 Thess 1.6) and poverty (2.Cor 8.9), adopting the role of a slave, serving others (Phil 2.7; Rom 15.8) as Paul in turn strove to do. The Paul who urged his hearers to emulate a human and more than human model *of just this character* would be markedly reminiscent of those Cynics who took Odysseus for their ideal.

Perhaps again it is worth emphasising, we are attempting to discern (*a*) how Paul would have been likely to have been 'heard' by pagan partners in conversation, and (*b*) Paul's likely awareness of his reception. The influence of servant motifs in distinctively Jewish tradition is not here at issue; it is certainly not being precluded.

---

[24] A. J. Malherbe [1968] (1989), referring here to 79–80 and 82–87 in particular; Malherbe cites among other sources Lucian, *Lexiphanes* 19, for 'thêriomachos'; Dio 5.21–23; 8.20–28; Lucian, *Philosophies for Sale* 8.

(iii) One God

Looking for contrasts between Pauline language about God
and what is found in much other (non-Jewish) Graeco-
Roman writing of the day Richardson notes in the latter
'the way that the singular θεός and the plural θεοί are
interchangeable',[25] and we may register Diogenes' catch-
phrase about 'the friends of the Gods' (plural), even if all is
filled with a (single) divine presence.[26] Without argument,
Paul's 'God is one' (Rom 3.30; 1 Cor 8.4, 6; Gal 3.20;
1 Thess 1.9) stands firmly in the Jewish tradition. Nonetheless, as has already been explained, among 'pagans' it was
some of the Cynics who were most likely to be seen as
monotheistic, and Antisthenes (now clearly identified as
the founder of Cynicism) specifically. Cicero (disagreeing
with the argument) tells us, 'Antisthenes, in his book
entitled *The Natural Philosopher*, says that while there are
many Gods in popular belief, there is by nature just one.'
Cicero's testimony is supported by Philodemus and
Clement of Alexandria, and by Minucius Felix and
Lactantius.[27] Paul's 'although there may be so-called Gods
in heaven or on earth - as indeed there are many "Gods"

---

[25] N. Richardson (1994), 231.

[26] Diogenes Laertius 6.72, but compared with 6.37.

[27] Cicero, *De natura deorum* 1.13, 32; Philodemus, *De pietate* 7;
Giannantoni (1990) V A 179. Minucius Felix, 19.7 and Lactantius,
Institutes 1.5.18–19 and *de ira* 11.14 are, however, almost certainly
dependent on Cicero. We may also note Dio 31.11, accepting Dio's
openness to Antisthenes. Cf. also Diogenes Laertius 6.51 and
ps.-Heraclitus 4. 'That Cynics were strict monotheists who scorned
popular religion is certain' – A. J. Malherbe (1978), 47, in agreement
with Th. Gomperz on Antisthenes, 48; cf. also H. W. Attridge (1976),
who cites in addition Oenomaus' criticism of cult objects, in Eusebius,
Praep. ev. 5.36; and M.-O. Goulet-Cazé (1996), 68–69.

and "Lords" - yet for us there is one God' (1 Cor 8.5–6)
would sound very similar. (On the other hand, Paul's
'prepositional metaphysics', 1 Cor 8.6 and Rom 11.36,
would probably suggest a popular Stoicism.)[28]

(iv) No traditional cults or cult objects

The congruence (initial, at least) between Paul's disturbing
message and that of many Cynics is reinforced by the still
stronger tradition of Antisthenes as one who rejected idols:
'God resembles no one, so no one can learn anything of
God through images.'[29] 'We know', agrees Paul in the
same context, 'that an idol represents nothing real.' 'A God
is not made of stone,' insists pseudo-Heraclitus; 'don't you
know that God is not made with hands? from the beginning
he's had no pedestal.'[30] Paul's opposition to idols obviously stems primarily from his Jewish tradition; but as clearly
it is here presented with no reference to any Jewish
supporting or explanatory context. Then it may well be
significant by way of contrast that both Philo and Josephus
maintain that Jews refrain from any public criticisms of
others' deities.[31] Paul's uncompromising language here

---

[28] H. Conzelmann [1969] (1975), 144, n. 44, referring to Seneca and
Marcus Aurelius, but also Philo.

[29] Clement of Alexandria, *Protreptikos* 6.71.1; 7.75.3; *Stromateis*
5.14.108; Eusebius, *Praep. ev.* 13.13.35; Theodoret, *Graec. affect. cur.*
1.75, Giannantoni (1990), V A 181.

[30] Ps.-Heraclitus 4.2; cf. 4.5; cf. Origen, *Contra Celsum* 7.62. At
ps.-Heraclitus 4.5 there is also the claim to 'know God' which, too,
occurs in the Pauline sequence, 8.1–7. Compare, further, Oenomaus,
The Charlatans, in Eusebius, *Praep ev.* 5.34.14; 36.1–4.

[31] Josephus, *Apion* 2.237; *Antiquities* 4.207; Philo, *Moses* 2.205; *De
spec. leg.* 1.53.

and at Galatians 4.8 could have sounded natural in a Cynic, while (perhaps) unusual in a Jew among non-Jews in public.

Criticisms of popular piety and its practices are to be found in Seneca and in Plutarch, as well as in non-Cynic writings of Dio and elsewhere.[32] Stoics, Platonists, Aristotelians and Epicureans all have their own objections to the Homeric and popular mythologies. But they mostly follow conventional practice, either for a quiet life (Epicureans) or to maintain social cohesion (and their own place in things).[33] A trenchant and consistent public critique combined with a refusal to conform in public practice was characteristically and for the most part distinctively Cynic. Mysteries, rituals, offerings and temples are all mockingly disparaged in the Diogenes tradition,[34] as they were later by Menippus in Lucian's re-writing[35] and also by Lucian's Demonax, who very publicly refuses to conform. Accused of never having offered sacrifice and of refusing initiation, he told the assembly that Athena had no need of any offerings from him; and as for the mysteries, he could never keep the secret: if they turned out to be deleterious, he'd have to warn against initiation, and if good, his Cynic philanthropy

---

[32] Seneca, *Epistulae morales* 95.47; Dio 31.15; H. W. Attridge (1976), 16–23.

[33] For instance, all three protagonists in Cicero's *De natura deorum* explicitly maintain traditional religious practice: Velleius the Epicurean (1.45, 123), Balbus the Stoic (2.2, etc.) and Cotta the Academic (3.5–6); on Epicureans cf. Epictetus 2.20.27; Diogenes Laertius 10.123; M.-O. Goulet-Cazé (1996), 66–67.

[34] Diogenes Laertius 6.24, 39 (mysteries); 37, 64 (holy places); 42 (purificatory ritual); 59, 63 (votive offerings).

[35] Cf., e.g., Lucian, *Zeus Catechised*; *Zeus Rants*; *Parliament of the Gods*.

would oblige him to tell the world.[36] We have already noted the dismissal of images and temples in Heraclitus and of images by Antisthenes (who also rejects initiation).[37]

So when some Galatians turned away from 'those who by nature are no Gods' (Gal 4.8–9), and when some Thessalonians agreed to 'turn from idols to serve a living and true God' (1 Thess 1.9), and some people in Corinth were no longer 'led astray to dumb idols' (1 Cor 12.2), they had accepted an invitation and a challenge that would have seemed Cynic at least on first hearing to those who accepted as well as to those who refused. In conversation in and out of synagogues friendly Jews might well have been found urging people to change from their own established ethnic cultic practice to the ancient practice and community of Judaism. But Paul had invited people to a total break from their own time-honoured traditions without drawing them into any other ancient national cult or convention. They are to be bound by the laws and customs of no recognised and ancestrally rooted group. Such a rupture in communal belonging and structures of meaning was otherwise only urged by Cynics (as we argued in chapter 1), and abhorred by others. Converts 'are the worst kind of people', fumed Tacitus; these Christians 'have transgressed totally by denying the Greek Gods', fumes Lucian.[38] Instead were people in Galatia, Macedonia, Achaea to accept a way of life modelled on an ascetic

---

[36] Lucian, *Demonax* 11 (sacrifice) and 11 and 34 (mysteries); 27 (holy places).

[37] See above, and Diogenes Laertius 6.4.

[38] Tacitus, *History* 5.5.1; Lucian, *Peregrinus* 13; see above, ch. 1 and notes 40, 41.

teacher, Paul, in a fellowship where there was neither Jew nor Greek, bond nor free, no male and female (Gal 3.28).

(v) Friends of God

As has been remarked previously, with no temple, images, altar, votive or expiatory offerings or any recognisable sacrificial system, but with its ascetic ethic, its own understanding of deity and of the future of the cosmos, Paul's message would look much more like a philosophy than the lore of a cult, proposing a philosophy rather than a 'religion' in our contemporary sense; and, of course, as is being argued, a Cynic sort of philosophy at that. Lacking temple, images, altar, votive or expiatory offerings and any recognisable sacrificial system, early Christianity was of course also free from the cultic items most liable to Cynic criticism.[39]

However, it would still not be entirely surprising for Paul's as yet uncommitted hearers to find that along with this thorough-going and Cynic-seeming rejection of traditional cults and their myths there was still, at the level of verbal expression if no more, the positive 'theology' noted already from time to time, including John Moles' list of positive references to God or Gods even in the *chreia* traditions ascribed to Diogenes. Difficult though we agree it is to discern what these 'really mean', this Diogenes is

---

[39] For images, see above; temples, below; votive and other offerings, Diogenes Laertius 6.43, 45, 59, 64, 73; Lucian, *Demonax* 11, 27. For early Christianity's resemblance to a 'philosophical school', see e.g., E. A. Judge (1960) and (1972); L. Alexander (1993) and (1995). R. Jewett (1986) ignores this distinction and so severely weakens his attempt to place the Thessalonian correspondence against the background of the cult of the Cabiri.

said to be a friend of the Gods, their messenger, affording
people an image of them, calling attention to the pervasive
divine presence.[40] A very Cynic Stoic such as Musonius
could display 'a warm religious strain'. Pseudo-Lucian's
Cynic sees the world's resources as God-given.[41] Dio and
Peregrinus suggest that both 'gentle' and 'austere' Cynics
could work with or at least express quite a vivid sense of
divine reality. Certainly, as we have had a number of
occasions to remark, Dio seems to have experienced no
unease in publicly ascribing his wandering Cynic mission
to a specific divine guidance and enabling. And Peregrinus
not only seems (according to Lucian) to have integrated his
Christian episode with his later more explicit Cynicism, but
also to have articulated his Cynic self-immolation in 'theological' terms.[42]

References, then, to turning from idols to the one
living God, to obey him, in emulation of his leading ascetic
emissaries, would have seemed quite in tune with other
Cynic resonances in Paul's life-style, presentation and
message, even if the extent of the references to God and
the divine figure of Jesus Christ might still have seemed
somewhat idiosyncratic. (But Cynics tended to individualism, did they not?)

It must be emphasised, there is no suggestion here
that Cynicism provided a significant articulation for Paul's
Christian piety, let alone a primary stimulus. Such may
have been the contribution of Cynicism at other points, but
not here. Here we are simply arguing that Paul's piety

---

[40] J. H. Moles (1993), 270, again.
[41] 'The Gods have given the earth for all to enjoy,' ps.-Lucian, *The
Cynic* 7.
[42] M.-O. Goulet-Cazé (1990), 2786; Lucian, *Peregrinus* 11–13, 16,
20–29.

could well have seemed quite at home with much else that would seem distinctively Cynic at first sight, and even on closer acquaintance, a piety that would in no way importantly disturb that Cynic impression.

Even the less obviously 'pious' Cynics, as we have noted more than once, claimed to be 'friends of the Gods', and to share with them the common possession of 'all things'.[43] So, as we saw earlier, Paul similarly agrees with the Corinthians, 'all things are yours' (1 Cor 3.21, 22), although he disputes the corollary, that 'all things are lawful' (1 Cor 6.12).[44] The major premise remains unstated, Paul nowhere explicitly asserting that it is as God's 'friends' that all things are theirs. 'Slave' is Paul's most frequent term for himself, with occasional variants such as 'attendant' and 'steward';[45] while on other occasions Christians are grown children impelled by God's Spirit to address God as 'Abba' (Gal 4.6; Rom 8.15–16). This juxtaposition would not, however, itself be particularly surprising, certainly not in the context we have been exploring. Odysseus and Herakles both accept the role of slave, while (implicitly both) were convinced of God's fatherly care for all, and called him father (according to Epictetus).[46]

Perhaps more significant still, over all, are other conventional *topoi* from contemporary discussions of 'friendship' deployed by Paul in passing in his elaboration of the relationship with God into which he and his fellow Christians have been brought and are being drawn further. We Christians, insists Paul, are privy through the Spirit God gives to God's most secret plans, we know 'the mind

---

[43] E.g., Diogenes Laertius 6.37, 72; ps.-Crates 26, 27, again.

[44] M. Plunkett (1988), 179.

[45] On which, again, D. B. Martin (1990).

[46] Epictetus 3.24.13–16; cf. 26.30–33.

of the Lord', 'we have the mind of Christ' (1 Cor 2.6–16);
one may compare John's commonplace aside, 'a slave does
not know what his master is doing'; only with friends are
such thoughts shared (John 15.15). To be 'of one mind'
with another is to be a friend, 'unus quasi animus . . . ex
pluribus'.[47] Mutual love is then possible.[48] And so (unlike
John the evangelist) Paul can also talk of Christians loving
God as well as being loved by God (1 Cor 2.9 – quoting
Isaiah – and 1 Cor 8.3; Rom. 8.39 and 2 Cor 13.13). The
'face-to-face' encounter that Moses enjoyed as 'friend of
God' is already there in part for all Christians already, and
it will be complete (1 Cor 13.12; 2 Cor 3.18); indeed
Christians can enjoy a relationship much closer than that of
Moses with his (reinterpreted) veiling of his face. Whatever various Cynics actually meant by their claim to be
'friends of the Gods', Paul's assured offer of such intimacy
with God would further strengthen the impression of a bold
– even brash – Cynic contention (as perhaps his *parrhêsia*
at 2 Corinthians 3.12 signifies), even if his reluctance to
talk of 'knowing God' (1 Cor 8.3; 13.12; Gal 4.9) makes
pseudo-Heraclitus, with his 'I who alone know God' seem
bolder still.[49]

 For some in the Cynic tradition, as has been
intimated in the foregoing, it is very unlikely that such
claimed 'friendship' involved imagined 'conversation'
with, prayer to God or the Gods. Pseudo-Crates 19 seems
specifically to exclude any such possibility; yet clearly the
Cynics who admired the figure of Odysseus *were* 'doing

---

[47] Cicero, *De amicitia* 92; cf.15, 20, 61; Dio 4.42; and Plutarch, *De amicorum multitudine*, *Moralia* 96EF

[48] Cicero, *De amicitia* 26–27; Dio 3.89 (ἀγαπάω); and Plutarch, *De amicorum multitudine*, *Moralia* 96D.

[49] Ps.-Heraclitus 4.5.

everything with God'.[50] The Diogenes of the *chreia* tradition criticises most people for the content of their prayers, and we may presume it is their desires as such that are really in focus; yet they are not rebuked for the praying itself.[51] So Demonax mocks an invitation to walk to the Asklepieion to pray ('You must think Asklepius very deaf, if he can't hear our prayers from here'), but does not in fact chide the intention to pray.[52] So pseudo-Heraclitus insists the whole world is God's sanctuary, which must in context be taken to mean, where God may be approached.[53] None of this is as firm and positive - or as frequent - as the allusions to prayer which we find in Paul; but neither would Paul's prayerfulness at all obviously have seemed incompatible with the more widely shared Cynic traits we have been identifying in his letters.

(vi) The gifts of the Spirit

The initial reception of the Spirit among Pauline Christians entailed at least potentially 'knowing the mind of the Lord', 'having the mind of Christ'. But behaviourally it involved rather more, it involved speaking with tongues, prophesying and healing. Paul makes this explicit only in 1 Corinthians 12–14, but we should probably assume that the same range and extent of phenomena are indicated by Galatians 3.1–5, and 1 Thessalonians 1.5 and 5.19–20, and

---

[50] So, too, Epictetus' Herakles, 3.24.16 (where he is linked with Odysseus); Epictetus' ideal Cynic does of course pray, 3.22.56.

[51] Diogenes Laertius 6.42; cf. 28 and 63.

[52] Lucian, *Demonax* 27; cf. again Diogenes Laertius 6.38, 'all things are full of the divine presence'.

[53] Ps.-Heraclitus 4.2.

then by Romans 15.19. And whereas the many leading elements of Paul's life-style and expressed ideas reviewed so far would, we have seen, have looked and sounded significantly similar to popular Cynic actions and teaching, and may often have been advisedly so; yet when it comes to the very important issue of glossolalia in particular, but also those of healing and of prophecy, it has to be accepted, there are no longer close Cynic parallels. If the evidence so far deployed and the interpretation suggested have been at all persuasive so far, then our next conclusion must simply be that neither Paul nor his more receptive hearers themselves found any decisive incompatibility between an invitation initially couched mostly in terms of Cynic-seeming praxis and often in Cynic-sounding utterances, and then some occasional very striking 'ecstatic', or mantic or thaumaturgic behaviour.

It is, however, worth tentatively exploring the issues a little further to see whether even here there may be at least underlying points of contact with strands of Cynic tradition. 'Prophecy' is the easiest, at least so far as the term itself is concerned (though what constituted 'prophecy' in Paul's communities is by no means clear in detail).[54] The topic has of course already in effect been discussed in the treatment above of divine guidance and inspiration; and the word προφήτης itself is used in self-reference by pseudo-Diogenes, and by Lucian of his

---

[54] Despite D. Hill's assurance, 'we can learn a good deal about prophecy from 1 Corinthians 14' (1979), 122, παράκλησις and παραμυθία (1 Cor 14.3) do not tell us much, but encouragement to appropriate behaviour seems most likely; cf. also D. E. Aune (1983), 189–231. The 'oracular utterances' in Paul picked out by Aune (247–62) refer mostly to the knowledge of God's future, the 'knowledge of God's mind' discussed just above.

auctioned Cynic.[55] On its own, a tacit or overt claim to issue a divinely inspired invitation to a divinely ordered life-style, and even to insight into the divine mind would not have been unprecedented among Cynics.

Extravagant and disturbing behaviour, of the sort that outsiders would be likely to categorise generally as 'mad' (1 Cor 14.23) would also be expected from Cynics – even though we have no evidence from Cynic sources for glossolalia in particular.[56] All you need to be a Cynic is to be willing to be 'loud-mouthed and annoying' and behave outrageously, explains Lucian.[57] Whereas Dio insists that his kind of prophecy is calm and rational (like Paul's, in effect), Lucian pictures Peregrinus' Cynic follower, Theagenes, as very disturbed (if only for effect), 'with copious perspiration, shedding a ridiculous quantity of tears, tearing at his hair'.[58]

So far as 'gifts of healing' (1 Cor 12.9) are concerned, we have plenty of evidence for Cynic interest in physical well-being, for its maintenance and restoration. Health is a characteristic concern of Cynics; their fine physical state shows that they are 'living according to nature'. [59] For any expectation of 'miraculous' activity

---

55 Ps.-Diogenes 22; Lucian, *Philosophies for Sale* 9; cf. also his *Peregrinus* 11 (and 28).

56 On Cynic 'madness', Diogenes Laertius 6.54, 82; *Socratic Epistle* 6.1.

57 Lucian, *Philosophies for Sale* 12, 10; cf. *Peregrinus* 3; *Runaways* 15. 'You abuse all and sundry', says Lucian, *Sale* 10. Does Paul actually mean that speaking with tongues could include a shout of ἀνάθεμα Ἰησοῦς?

58 Lucian, *Peregrinus* 6; cf. Dio 1.56.

59 Ps.-Lucian, *The Cynic*, passim; Diogenes Laertius 2.27, 32; 6.28, 30, 70; Lucian, *Demonax* 63, 65; *The Cock* 22–23; *Peregrinus* 28; ps.-Crates 13, 33; Epictetus of Diogenes, 1.24.7; Dio 32.14. L.Vaage

(1 Cor 12.10 – if that is what ἐνεργήματα δυνάμεων means), or of the 'signs and wonders' (τερατῶν, Rom 15.19; cf. 2 Cor 12.12, Gal 3.5) for the restoration of health or any other end, among Cynics, we have very little that is at all significant. There is the apparently figurative use of similar language in Diogenes Laertius' account of Menedemus, who 'went so far in creating marvellous effects (or, astonishing behaviour, εἰς τοσοῦτον τερατείας ἤλασεν) as to go round dressed as a Fury, saying he'd come from Hades'.[60] And there is Lucian in the second century CE expecting Peregrinus' followers to claim to have been healed by him.[61] Yet, if it is not easy to integrate these asides in Paul with the Cynic colours we have otherwise been highlighting, we must also note that Paul himself achieves very little integration of such 'wonders' with the rest of his message and life-style. Neither 'tongues' nor 'wonders' are characterised in any way that allows supportive inferences from them for any of the issues Paul writes about in the surviving letters. Their appearance affords some support for his claim to be an apostle, but no insight into the kind of apostolic mission Paul is sure is his; their appearance marked the Galatians' initiation, but offered no clear indications of how that discipleship was to be practised. Tongues are an embarrassment, wonders are incidental. Paul himself, in the letters at least, places much

---

(1987), 334–41, has argued for a much more closely analogous Cynic 'royal power to heal', but the evidence is far from clear; cf. *idem* (1994a), 33–36, leaving the kind of 'healing' more open; and my own (1987a), 446 and G. Anderson (1994), 35 (the 'physician' topos).

[60] Diogenes Laertius 6.102, cited also by L. Vaage (1994a), 34; Vaage also cites Lucian's Peregrinus promising 'messengers from the dead', *Peregrinus*, 41.

[61] Lucian, *Peregrinus* 28. On baptism and mysteries, A. J. M. Wedderburn (1987).

more emphasis on those issues which in our investigation so far we have found do in fact afford many striking and positive echoes of Cynic concerns and Cynic language and imagery. Paul's ascetic and Cynic-seeming life-style and wealth of Cynic-sounding utterances are much more significant *to Paul himself*, judged by the attention he pays them in his letters, than are any other 'signs of an apostle'.

(vii) Symbols and sacraments

Even allowing for the importance among the members of Paul's Christian communities of prayer, prophecy, tongues and wonders, the movement still lacked much of the apparatus of a religious cult. However, in baptism it had an initiatory rite, one that could (among other things) be seen as a kind of washing (1 Cor 6.11). Diogenes is said to have mocked such purifications, and he, Antisthenes and Demonax all ridiculed initiation into mysteries, as we recalled recently above.[62] It is nonetheless clear that for many the adoption of some or all of the varied symbols of Cynicism – staff perhaps, satchel for some, long hair and beard for males, doubled cloak or some equivalent – was itself also a sort of initiation. So pseudo-Diogenes tells of his 'conversion' by 'the companion of Socrates' (Antisthenes), and explains, 'When I had chosen this (short, steep) road, he took off my mantle and tunic, put a double, coarse cloak around me, and hung a wallet from my shoulder . . .'.[63] Similarly, 'Crates' (or some such figure) is converted by 'Diogenes', who says of his pupil, 'He distributed his property among his family, then from

---

[62] Diogenes Laertius 6.4, 24, 39; Demonax 11.
[63] Ps.-Diogenes 30.3; cf. Diogenes Laertius 6.13 and 21–23.

the next day took up the satchel, doubled his coarse cloak, and followed me (ἐμοὶ εἴπετο).'[64] Lucian's Cynic on sale promises, 'When I take you on, first I'll strip you of your luxury, bind you to want and put a scanty cloak on you.'[65] This was the decisive move, once the would-be Cynic had learned the slogans, notes Lucian, unimpressed.[66]

The immediate point is the indication this affords that Cynics, too, accepted some kind of initiation, albeit informal. But there may be a closer parallel, as least for some, in one aspect of early Christian baptism. It is often assumed that behind the metaphor of 'putting on Christ' (Gal 3.28) lies a Christian baptismal ceremony in which initiates donned fresh clothing.[67] For Paul and his fellow apostles if not for others, their Christian commitment meant their then going around in clothing scanty enough to count as naked, γυμνός (1 Cor 4.11; 2 Cor 11.27); and we noted in chapter 5 that simply appearing in public thus deliberately 'ill-clad', 'near-naked', was a distinguishing mark of Cynic allegiance in the eyes of many. Thus the fully initiated Christian leaders could have looked very like Cynics of some kind (even if the rest of the membership still normally dressed more respectably).

It is also perhaps worth noting that even though Cynics mocked initiation into the mysteries (for the advantages said to be quite amorally gained), some at least were as content as Paul seems to be in 1 Corinthians 2 to

---

[64] Ps.-Diogenes 38.5. For the importance of the equipment as such, see M.-O. Goulet-Cazé, (1990) 'L'accoutrement', 2738–46.

[65] Lucian, *Philosophies for Sale*, 9.

[66] Lucian, *Runaways* 13–14.

[67] R. N. Longenecker (1990), 156; J. D. G. Dunn (1993), 204.

use the language metaphorically.[68] But the most important point to emphasise is the one made in the first chapter: to initiate people from all quarters with a minimal preparation into a 'school' which disrupted social allegiance and conformity, claiming that for its members there was in practice neither Jew nor Greek, bond nor free, no male and female, would inevitably appear Cynic, and give even a quite distinctive initiation procedure a clear Cynic colouring.

I have elsewhere argued a similar conclusion for the Christian Eucharist, 'the Supper of the Lord'.[69] Certainly in the next centuries we find Christian 'brothers and sisters' who ate and drank the body and the blood of their Lord having to respond to charges that they were engaged in a Cynic-sounding cannibalism and incest. Diogenes in his *politeia* was held to have justified such Thyestian and Oedipean practices, as eminently in accord with nature.[70] It is often argued that rumours of this sort were regularly levelled at cults, especially foreign ones; but in fact there seems to be no evidence for this combined charge being made against cultic groups. It is an extreme Cynic 'philosophical' naturalism that underlies the theory (there are no stories of any such practice). We noted earlier

---

[68] Ps.-Crates 2; ps.-Diogenes 25; Dio 4.31–32; cf. also Epictetus 3.21.13–19, of Socrates, Diogenes and Zeno; on the lack of evidence for any direct dependence on contemporary mystery cults, see A. J. M Wedderburn (1987).

[69] F. G. Downing (1993a).

[70] The main evidence is provided by Philodemus, *On the Stoics* (W. Cronert [1906] (1965)), and Diogenes Laertius 6.72–73; that Diogenes wrote both an *Oedipus* and a *Thyestes* is noted at 6.80; cf. Dio 10.30–33; and see especially R. G. Andria (1980) and T. Dorandi (1982). Philodemus is attempting to tar the Stoics with the Cynic brush, but the later Stoics dropped this part of their tradition, leaving it to the Cynics.

that Corinthian Christians had supposed a form of incest tolerable. There is no hint of any unease among them at talk of 'sharing the body', 'sharing the blood of Christ', language that later Greeks and Romans (and not just Jews) claimed to find so shocking and abhorrent. Only Cynics were known publicly not just to countenance but to propose anything of the kind.

Both initiation and community meal would confirm rather than weaken the impression that here was some sort of Cynic fellowship.

(viii) Saving grace

The more robust and radical Cynics were determined to offend popular 'unnatural' conventions, displaying their bold independence of society around them; and were as determinedly independent of any divine power. God or Gods had no active part to play in their lives. If Gods were acknowledged at all, at most they provided an image of self-sufficiency to be emulated and by *askêsis* shared, a realm to be attained by one's own self-discipline. Those who claimed the Cynic name, but, like Odysseus, 'did nothing without God', were to be spurned and despised, we have seen, as unworthy of Diogenes.

Some of Paul's converts in Corinth may possibly have seen their discipleship in such terms, as a challenging and stimulating but self-reliant ascetic discipline. The issue is not raised overtly. We do, however, find Paul insisting that his own much more painful and rigorous, Cynic-style progress is achieved quite specifically in reliance on God: 'not I, but the grace of God which is with me' (1 Cor 15.10); his Lord says, 'My grace is sufficient for you, my power is made perfect in weakness' (2 Cor 12.9). Paul's

God reconciles, cleanses, sets people right with himself, saves, hallows, makes new, enables. But that still means it is like the softer Cynics' Odysseus that Paul, too, 'does nothing without God'. It is of course quite clear that Paul has a much richer and much more pervasive vocabulary for God's beneficent (and punitive) activity than we find in any of our Cynic sources. But some of the same or similar terms are to be found, and at times at least they are used in similar ways. 'God is faithful, and will not allow you to be tempted beyond your strength, and with the temptation will provide a way through, so you may be able to cope with it' (1 Cor 10.13). 'A divine power (δαιμόνιον) lightens the burden according to the importance of the affair, and then to suit the strength and mental character of the person involved', muses Dio as he reflects on his exile and Cynic wanderings.[71]

'We live in total peace, freed from every evil by Diogenes of Sinope', asserts psseudo-Crates (ἡμεῖς δὲ εἰρήνην ἄγομεν τὴν πᾶσαν, παντὸς κακοῦ ἐλεύθεροι γενόμενοι ὑπὸ . . .).[72] We may compare, 'We have (or let us have) peace with God through our Lord Jesus Christ' (Rom 5.1),[73] 'set free from sin' (Rom 6.22).[74] In another letter, addressed to 'Diogenes' 'Crates' acknowledges 'the freedom for which your word has released us';[75] and we

---

[71] Dio 13.3.

[72] Ps.-Crates 7.

[73] Perhaps note besides in particular Romans 2.10, 'peace for those who do good (rather than evil)'. As well as his epistolary greetings, Paul often writes of 'peace' as one or the main gift of God somehow achieved by or through Jesus and/or the Spirit: Rom 8.6; 14.17; 15.33; 1 Cor 7.15; Gal 5.22; 2 Thess 3.16; etc.

[74] See the very similar phrase, Rom 6.18; also 8.2.

[75] Ps.-Crates 8.

may compare Paul's 'For freedom has Christ set us free' (Gal 5.1).

Even the self-reliant Cynic of pseudo-Crates 19 celebrates 'Diogenes, who delivered (τὸν ἐξελόμενον) many from evil to virtue, both in his lifetime and then after his death by the teaching he left us.'[76] So Paul can talk of being in the grip of sin, and ask who will rescue (ῥύσεται) him (Rom. 7.21, 24).

When Paul proclaims salvation, σωτηρία, he clearly means more than a Cynic this-worldly fulfilment, contentment, happiness. We are (being) saved in hope, saved from the wrath to come (1 Thess 1.10), saved for resurrection life (1 Cor 15.2). But phrases like 'for the salvation of everyone who believes' (Rom 1.16), 'repentance that leads to salvation' (2 Cor 7.10) would initially at least not sound much different from 'Socrates' talking of 'being saved for virtue', or pseudo-Diogenes' claim that 'we (Cynics) work for the salvation (σωτηρία) of humankind', 'for the salvation of all', or the promise to the tyrant Dionysius, that were he to accept Cynic discipline, he would be saved.[77] Christian initiation was meant to 'cleanse' from much the same sorts of vices as Herakles and Diogenes made it their business to eradicate.[78] The Corinthians were reminded that in this initiation they were 'set right' (ἐδικαιώθητε; one of the rare appearances of this particular motif in the earlier letters). 'Setting errors right' (ἐπανορθοῦν) was the 'divine or at least Godlike' (θεοῦ ἢ ἰσαθέου) aim of Demonax.[79]

---

[76] Ps.-Crates 19.

[77] *Socratic Epistle* 6.6; ps.-Diogenes 6.2; 10.1; 29.2, 4; cf. 37.5.

[78] Compare 1 Cor 6.9–11 with Dio 5.22–23 and 8.8; and Lucian, *Philosophies for Sale* 8.

[79] 1 Cor 6.11, again; Lucian, *Demonax* 7.

With this commonplace, flexible and widely shared vocabulary Paul and the Cynics here cited embrace a range of paraenetic options very similar to those deployed by other contemporary moral teachers, as Troels Engberg-Pedersen is able amply to illustrate. Paul's practice of exhortation and his explicit references to possibilities of progress and regress, and much more of his hortatory discourse, show that no more for him than for other contemporary moral philosophers does the help of God or any other superhuman power overwhelm the individual. Divine and other aid is very likely available, but it demands mental, volitional and physical effort from any who would avail themselves of it. For the Paul of the earlier letters, as for the Cynics, the distinctive focus, as we have seen, is on meeting the physical trials, while cognitive elements, growth in understanding, are nonetheless also involved.[80]

More generally, it is important in this context to bear in mind the evidence and the arguments assembled by David Seeley in his *The Noble Death*. In the cultural context of Paul and his hearers, talk of benefiting from the death of some heroic figure most obviously means being taught, inspired, enabled by the example given.[81] The centrality of the death of Jesus in Paul's message, includ-

---

[80] T. Engberg-Pedersen (1995d), 'Paul on Spiritual and Moral Progression and Regression: Where and how does Paul differ from the Moral Philosophers?' – paper given at the SBL convention, Philadelphia, 1995. Pedersen draws his illustration mainly from among Stoics, and so stresses the notes of cognitive growth in Paul, which I shall argue predominate in the later letters, while certainly present earlier as well. Engberg-Pedersen is arguing in particular against D. B. Martin (1995a), that there is in Paul, as in the moral philosophers, a real 'self' for whom progress is a matter for oneself, if not solely up to oneself.

[81] D. Seeley (1990).

ing the occasional language of sacrifice, would reinforce rather than disturb the impression that the invitation was to a demanding and apparently Cynic-style discipline. (We considered the place of the imitation of Christ in Paul's teaching, above, § (*i*).)

Paul's 'soteriological' language, the ways he talks about God's saving purposes focused through Jesus' death and resurrection, would on their own, then, probably have appeared fairly commonplace; many philosophical ethicists deploy a similar vocabulary of ideas and even of words, as Seeley illustrates. On its own, this material would not suggest any particular Cynic allegiance. However, as we have just seen, some Cynics at least could as readily as any other moralists deploy these motifs, and their appearance in Paul is entirely compatible with (though not especially supportive of) the Cynic character we have discerned in much else of his early writing.

(ix) The beginning of the end

Much less at home in a Cynic milieu, at least at first sight, is Paul's eschatology. The Thessalonians did not simply turn (as Cynics might desire) 'to God from idols', but turned in the same move 'to wait for his Son from heaven, whom he raised from the dead, Jesus who delivers us from the wrath to come' (1 Thess 1.9–10). The Corinthians were 'waiting for the revealing of our Lord Jesus Christ' (1 Cor 1.7). Cynics ridiculed soothsaying, deriding any attempts to foretell the future on any scale. When Diogenes saw interpreters of dreams or diviners, he thought no living

thing stupider than humans, Laertius tells us.[82] The theme
is taken up in one of the longer of the pseudo-Diogenes
Letters, and again by Dio in his Diogenes narratives, and
by Demonax.[83] The most elaborate rebuttal that survives is
Oenomaus of Gadara's *The Charlatans*, in the extracts
included by Eusebius in his *Praeparatio euangelii* 5 and 6.
In addition, no more for us than for Paul's contemporaries
was the future of the cosmos simply a question for
soothsayers. It was a theme in 'natural philosophy' – in our
terms, a scientific problem. And Cynics also despised
philosophical speculations about natural phenomena quite
as much as they derided the dreamers and seers. 'How long
did it take you to get back to earth?' Diogenes asks
someone spouting his astronomical theories.[84]

On the basis of much of the discussion of early
Christianity and its Jewish context it would be very easy to
conclude, of course, that 'apocalyptic', and especially
'eschatology' were a Judaeo-Christian preserve: foreign
not only to Cynics, but to the rest of the Graeco-Roman
world as well, 'a depiction of salvation far removed from
the main currents of Graeco-Roman thought'(J. M. G.
Barclay).[85] Apocalyptic is linear, Greek thought is cyclical

---

[82] Diogenes Laertius 6.24, 43.

[83] Ps.-Diogenes 38. ' "Am I going to hit you with my staff?" "Er, no",
replies the soothsayer, hopefully. Diogenes thwacks him. "You're a
rotten soothsayer!" ' Cf. Dio 8.9; but especially 10.17–29 on the
pointlessness of consulting oracles; Lucian, *Demonax* 37.

[84] Diogenes Laertius 6.39; cf. 28, on the mathematicians, and
Laertius' summary, 6.103; Lucian, *Demonax* 22 ; cf. Diogenes in
Stobaeus, *Florilegium* (W.H. 2.1.23, Giannantoni (1990), V.B. 372);
and Demonax in Stobaeus, *Florilegium*, W. H. 2.1.11, L. Paquet
(1988), 237 § 61; Bion, in Stobaeus, *Florilegium* W. H. 2.1.20
(L. Paquet (1988) 132 § 58).

[85] J. M. G. Barclay (1996), 390.

- or so it is said.[86] A Paul who announced an 'End' which is 'closer than when we first believed' (Rom. 13.11) would, on this view, presumably sound bizarre to most and quite weird to any who thought they had detected sympathies with Cynicism.

As it turns out, however, there is a great deal of generally 'apocalyptic' pagan writing preserved for us (concerned with 'the beyond');[87] and ideas of an imminent end (our specific concern here) were also, it would seem, commonplace. We may start with Pliny the Younger describing the eruption of Vesuvius in which his uncle died: 'Many besought the aid of the Gods, but still more imagined there were no Gods left and that the universe was plunged into eternal darkness for evermore.' Pliny himself is more sceptical, and claims, 'I derived some consolation in my deadly peril from the belief that the whole world was dying and I with it.'[88] Earlier than this we find the idea of a world in terminal old age in his uncle's *Historia naturalis:* 'You can almost see that the stature of the whole human race is decreasing daily, with few men taller than their fathers, as the crucial conflagration which our age is approaching exhausts the fertility of human semen.'[89]

But the idea of a world in the throes of senile decay also occurs, and prominently, in near contemporary (late first or early-second century CE) Jewish apocalyptic. So 4 Ezra tells us, 'You and your contemporaries are smaller

---

[86] The classic statement, O. Cullmann (1946), 44; cf. M. Werner [1941] (1957), vii, 52–53, 292–94; more recently, such as E. Käsemann, E. Ferguson, W. A. Meeks.

[87] See especially D. Hellholm (1983). For the following see F. G. Downing (1995a) and (1995b).

[88] Pliny the Younger., *Letters and Panegyricus*, 6.20.17, LCL.

[89] Pliny the Elder., *Natural History*, 7.16.73, LCL.

in stature than those who were born before you, and those who come after will be smaller than you, as if born of a creation which is also ageing and passing the strength of its youth.'[90] And with this we may compare 2 Baruch, 'The youth of this world has passed away, and the power of creation is already exhausted, and the coming of the time is very near, indeed has passed by. And the pitcher is near to the well and the ship to harbour and the journey to the city and life to its end.'[91]

The idea of a final conflagration can be traced to Stoicism (out of Empedocles); the idea of a decaying world as an aged mother producing undersized offspring is as clearly Epicurean, occuring most explicitly in Lucretius, *De rerum natura*: 'Even now the power of life is broken, and the exhausted earth scarce produces tiny creatures, she who once produced all kinds and gave birth to the huge bodies of wild beasts.'[92] When Paul writes of 'the creation' about to be 'freed from the bondage of decay', adding 'we know that the whole creation has been groaning in travail until now' (Rom 8.21–22) it is within this context that he would have been understood, and the 'we know' suggests he is aware that he is repeating a commonplace his Roman readers would recognise.[93] Unlike the synoptic evangelists, Revelation and 2 Peter, Paul does not in our letters describe the end of the universe as such, 'the sun darkened, the

---

[90] 4 Ezra 5.51, as in M. E. Stone (1990), 142. There is more in similar vein; e.g., 4.26; 14.10.

[91] *2 Baruch* 85.10, in A. F. J. Klijn (1983).

[92] Lucretius, *De rerum natura* 2.1150–53; there is much more in similar vein in Lucretius. That it is in origin an Epicurean theme is argued in detail in F. G. Downing (1995c).

[93] Argued in more detail in F. G. Downing (1995b), noting that the often suggested reference back to the 'curse on the ground' in Gen 3.17–19 is strained indeed.

moon giving no light, the powers of the heavens shaken'
(Mark 13.24); though here, too, there are similar sketches
of the final scene in pagan as well as Jewish sources.[94] The
expectation of a near and final cosmic catastrophe is
widespread in the first century. The only question we are
left to consider is whether Paul's variants on these common
themes seriously disturb the Cynic impression made by
much else in his earlier letters, or not.

First we need to recall the wider ramifications of
first-century Graeco-Roman and Jewish eschatology. Interest in 'the last things' usually if not universally involves
thoughts not only about the present, but also about the past.
The end is the restoration of the beginning. Certainly many
Cynics imagined an original 'Golden Age', 'the kingdom
of Kronos', when life was lived simply, without
possessions, luxury, technology, rivalry.[95] Jewish writers
could include similar motifs (for instance, Philo's *De
praemiis et poenis* and the *Sibylline Oracles 3*). Although
there are no accounts of such a stage of world history in
Paul, clearly he, too, presupposes something better before
'sin came into the world' (Rom 5.12). 'New creation'
(2 Cor 5.17; Gal 6.15) refers us back to God's original
work 'before' any need for renewal.

A conviction that our present state is one of
deterioration – and increasing deterioration – is in fact the
main thrust of the Golden Age myth. Things now are so
much worse than they were at first. In a recent study
Stanley Stowers very appositely compares both Seneca's

---

[94] E.g., Seneca, *Hercules Oetaeus* 1102–17; *Thyestes* 835–84; and
more in F. G. Downing (1995c).

[95] A. O. Lovejoy and G. Boas (1935), for the generalisation; on
Cynics, 117–54; and compare Seneca, *Epistulae morales* 90; some
further supporting evidence follows, below.

Cynic-based *Epistula moralis* 90 and the Cynic pseudo-Anacharsis *Letter* 9, with the sketch of human corruption in Romans 1.[96] This is part of Stower's own summary of ps.Anacharsis: 'The earth was once the common possession of both the gods and humans. Humans, however, transgressed (*parênomêsan*) the law by dividing the earth among themselves and the gods.' In return 'the gods gave back fitting gifts: strife, pleasure and meanness of spirit', and other 'unnatural' activities follow (tilling the soil, waging war). As Stowers rightly points out, for Paul the decline stems from idolatry, for pseudo-Anacharsis, from possessive greed, and the 'fitting' punishment in each is different. As it happens, however, the (homosexual) practices whose 'unnatural' adoption Paul finds 'dishonouring' are also widely (and distinctively) condemned (also as 'unnatural') among Cynics.[97] A Paul who proclaimed human decline, and even a decline marked by precisely this departure from 'nature', would at least not be weakening the Cynic impression made by many of the other strands

---

[96] S. K. Stowers (1994), 97–100. We might add Dio 30.26–27 and 28–49, which has seemed to many to include Cynic elements (J. W. Cohoon (1939), 395–98); and ps.-Lucian, *The Cynic*, 6.

[97] See ch. 4, above. Ps.-Diogenes 35.2 may indicate a more tolerant acceptance of homoerotic arousal as 'natural', though Diogenes' response is to masturbate, nothing other; and the dominant response, certainly to any male 'effeminate' behaviour, is strongly antagonistic: Diogenes Laertius 6.46, 53, 65, 67, 85 (on 6.85, see further, below); Epictetus 1.16.9–14; 3.1.24–25 (citing the Diogenes tradition), and 3.22.10; Lucian, *Demonax* 15, 16, 18, 50; ps.-Lucian, *The Cynic* 15–17; etc. An important article by D. B. Martin (1995b) confirms Stower's analysis of parallel accounts of ongoing decline in the two passages. In the light of other contemporary texts Paul is to be taken as seeing anyone's assuming an 'extra' mode of sexual intercourse and 'inordinate' gratification as a fit punitive consequence of polytheism, 'extra' deities (my summary). Cf. also R. B. Ward (1997).

we have surveyed so far, and might even be further confirming such an inter-pretation among his hearers.

We have in the foregoing concentrated on Romans, where otherwise the Cynic-seeming strands are less frequent and less strong. But a conviction of human and wider 'fallenness' seems clearly indicated in the earlier letters, too: we may note 1 Thessalonians 1.9–10; 5.4–5; 2 Thessalonians 2.7; 1 Corinthians 2.6; 15. 25–26, 56; Galatians 3.19; 4.3.

(x) A return to the good beginning, away from today's corruption

In contrast with the corruption of civic society around them, as Cynics saw it, they themselves claimed to be able to live here and now the simplicity and purity of the Golden Age. In their austere but easy life-style, the kingdom of Kronos had reappeared. Lucian, of course, mocked the claim: it was the ease they were after, not the austerity.[98] In Corinth, as we saw earlier (chapter 4), Paul had to deal with Christians who were sure they were 'already reigning'. Paul seemed to drop a very heavy hint that their claim was a little premature. But this would certainly suggest that Paul himself had left them open to that sort of conclusion. To what extent, then, if at all, does Paul enact, and announce, an 'inaugurated' eschatology with features that would have any recognisable Cynic cast to them?

---

[98] Lucian, *Runaways* 17 makes it explicit; cf. Epictetus 3.22.79 and 4.8.34; ps.-Diogenes 32.3; ps.-Anacharsis 9, again: at the end it is clear that the 'Scythians' (Cynics) live now the unpossessive mutuality and harmony of the age when Kronos reigned.

'If anyone is in Christ Jesus, he is a new creation; the old has passed away, the new has come' (2 Cor 5.17; cf. Gal 6.15, again). A fresh age has certainly dawned. Where there is 'no male and female' (with its echo of Genesis 1.27), and where there is also neither Jew nor Greek, bond nor free, all are one (Gal 3.28), we seem thought able to live already to a discerned original divine intention, without the social divisions Cynics, too, saw as part of a decline from original unity and harmony. For Cynics that original harmony included the divine realm, and could be reasserted as they enjoyed life as friends of the Gods; we have seen earlier how Paul deploys friendship *topoi* in explaining the new relationship with God which God has enabled by reconciling us to himself through Christ. Original humanity is Godlike in the Cynic tradition we have surveyed, and, as we have noted, for Cynics that Godlikeness can again and already be seen; just so, it would seem, for Paul, the image of God is being restored among Christians (2 Cor 3.18; cf. Rom 8.29).[99] ('The kingdom of God' as such is at times in Paul a future state that the wicked – and the untransformed – will not inherit, at other times it seems to be a present reality of whose character, however, Christians need to be reminded.)[100]

In all likelihood still more significant than any of these common ideological motifs would be Paul's praxis, his daily enactment of a life-style that could only look Cynic to observers, the austerity we examined in some detail in the previous two chapters. It was precisely in

---

[99] For a fuller exposition see, for instance, J. C. Beker, (1980), ch. 14, 'The Church as the Dawning of the New Age.'

[100] 'Inherit', 1 Cor 6.9,10; 15.50; Gal 5.21; cf. 2 Thess 1.5; present, Rom 14.17; 1 Cor 4.20; 15.24; unsure, 1 Thess 2.12.

living 'in hunger and thirst, naked, buffeted, homeless, labouring' (1 Cor 4.11–12), 'in toil and hardship, through many a sleepless night, in hunger and thirst, in cold and exposure' (2 Cor 11.27) that the more radical and consistent Cynics showed how the austerities of the kingdom of Kronos could again be happily endured. Paul and his fellow apostles live the way Cynics said the new age was to be lived, here and now; and Paul's converts are invited to imitate him, just as they are also to 'remember the Lord Jesus Christ, who though rich, for their sakes became poor . . .'.

Paul clearly intended his chosen laborious gainful employ as part of his ascetic discipleship, and as a model for others. Some of those he had won over in Thessalonica seem to have responded instead as Lucian later surmises all plebeian converts to Cynicism will, in re-enacting the reign of Kronos now: to live in the present the simplicity of the Golden Age they will immediately down tools and sponge on others.[101]

(xi) Vice and virtue

We have acceped that Paul (like the gentler Cynics) nonetheless did not demand of his converts quite the severe austere poverty he and his immediate colleagues themselves practised. But expectations there were. 'Do not be deceived,' warns Paul, 'neither the immoral, nor idolaters, nor the effeminate, nor homosexuals (earlier, more briefly, no πόρνος), nor thieves, nor the greedy, nor drunkards, nor revilers, nor robbers will inherit the kingdom of God'

---

[101] 1 Thess 2.9; 4.11–12; together with 2 Thess 3.7–12; Lucian, *Runaways* 17; *Icaromenippus* 31; cf. A. J. Malherbe (1987), 99–101.

(1 Cor 6.9–10); such are not to be part of the Christian community in Corinth at all (1 Cor 5.11). Similarly, Crates, as we saw earlier, allowed into his 'City of Pera' from the 'vinous futility' around it, 'no fool, parasite, glutton, sexual deviant (πόρνης . . .)'. There was nothing there for men to fight for, 'no money, no fame'.[102] The rules for exclusion from these respective new age communities are very similar.

Lists of vices to be avoided are compiled by many, but by Stoics and by Cynics in particular. The Stoic lists tend characteristically to emphasise interiority, control of the emotions, passions to be avoided, and Paul's list at Galatians 5.19–21 does contain some elements of that sort, in addition to behavioural items of the kind stressed in writing to Corinth. The Cynic lists are much more clearly and specifically about overt behaviour, as Paul's were for the Corinthians, in the catalogue just quoted which he says he had earlier still urged them to take very seriously.[103] So

---

[102] Diogenes Laertius 6.85; Paul specified πόρνος in the earlier list, 1 Cor 5.11, ἀρσενοκοῖται in the later list; πόρνης ... πυγῇσιν in Crates' poem seems to mean 'sodomite'; see chapter 4, above, n.35. H. Conzelmann [1969] (1975) may be right in suggesting that πόρνος indicates a central Jewish concern; but whatever its source for Paul, Crates' poem shows that a similar concern expressed in a non-Jewish context could also readily appear as Cynic.

[103] For typical Stoic lists, see Diogenes Laertius 7.110–18; Cicero, *Tusculan Disputations* 4.5–38; Epictetus 2.16.45, and next note. Cynic lists appear in ps.-Lucian, *The Cynic* 8–11; Dio 8.8, and 66.1 (from his exile), and, much elaborated, 4.91–138; ps.-Diogenes 36.6; Musonius 3 and 7 (C. Lutz (1947), 40, ll. 17–20 and 56, l. 25–58, l. 4: Musonius in Cynic vein, stressing 'toil and hardship', respectively; Lucian, *Dialogues of the Dead* 20 (10), Lampichos, Craton, the Philosopher; *Icaromenippus* 15, 29 (here and elsewhere Lucian adopts the Cynic behaviourist stance from his Menippean models: cf. H. D. Betz (1961), 185–94). Unfortunately the distinction does not seem to be noted by the commentators or their secondary sources: e.g., H.

the virtuous behaviour Paul inculcates by example and by teaching, and the vicious behaviour he specifically precludes both leave the 'new creation' which Paul celebrates looking very like a Cynic anticipation of a renewed Golden Age. Whatever the mix of sources for Paul's way of life and proclamation, this is how they would most likely have appeared in the 'pagan' cities of the east Mediterranean.

Taking a rather different line on chapter 5 of Galatians, Troels Engberg-Pedersen has argued that in verses 16–25 Paul's concerns are significantly akin to those of the Stoics: the problem Paul outlines is the distinctively Stoic *topos* of the divided self whose harmony can be restored only when virtue has become the sole aim; Paul's equivalent solution to the conflict beteween flesh and Spirit which the law cannot help resolve is for the Spirit to be allowed complete control, and the 'harvest of the Spirit' sketches the character that results. The suggestion is interesting, and would be in line with other hints we have discerned already of occasional Stoic motifs in Paul's earlier letters. But the content of Paul's vice list (Gal 5.20–21) is very different from the Stoic lists we have. Paul's initial emphasis is still on the overt 'works', ἔργα, engaged in, rather than on inner perturbations and their avoidance. The problem for Paul is primarily discrepant and stultified actions (Gal 5.17) rather than the discordant desires they may betoken. Stoic vice lists do touch on actions, but place far greater emphasis on interiority, on dispositions, intentions and emotions. Cynic vice lists, like Paul's, emphasise what is actually done.[104]

Conzelmann [1969] (1975), on 1 Cor 5 and 6; H. D. Betz (1979), 281–83.

[104] T. Engberg-Pedersen (1995b) (as yet unpublished paper given at SNTS, Prague, 1995). among Stoic lists, see, e.g., Diogenes Laertius

The 'harvest of the Spirit', Galatians 5.22, on the other hand, might at first sight more readily be taken as an inner, dispositional list for a virtuous person; yet even here there is little in common with catalogues of Stoic virtues (χαρά, ἐγκράτεια, yes; εἰρήνη, possibly), and the outcome for Paul is not inner harmony and imperturbability, but 'bearing one another's burdens', 'doing good for all'. A Stoic sage, too, would choose to identify his own interests with the interests of the wider community (even though such a course does not constitute virtue as such), as Engberg-Pedersen explains.[105] For Paul, however, such loving, joyful, peaceable . . . action 'towards all, and especially the household of faith' is itself to be the primary and unifying result of the Spirit's dominance in the lives of Galatian Christians.

(xii) The exalted sufferer

The centre of Paul's conviction is, of course, the once crucified, now risen Christ. We have already discussed briefly how such a Herakles-like figure, one who accepted

---

7.87–98 ('virtue is the state of mind which tends to make the whole of life harmonious', 7.89; 'vices are forms of ignorance', 7.93; wicked actions are vicious only in a derived sense, 7.95); 7.110–18, one paragraph on actions, seven on intentions and dispositions; Cicero, *Tusculan Disputations* 3.12–23 (it is perturbation, distress, that is to be avoided; wrong actions (17) seem only important as symptoms of inner disharmony); 4.5–38 (mostly long lists of dispositional and emotional terms); *De finibus* 3.32 (intention is primary; so too, *Paradoxa Stoicorum* 24-25); Epictetus 2.16.45. Paul's Jewish tradition tends to emphasise overt action over against intention and interiority, without ignoring the latter: Philo, *De mutatione* 241–43; Mishnah, *Makk* 3.15.

[105] T. Engberg-Pedersen (1995c), 12-14; and for a fuller account of the Stoic theory of *oikeôisis*, *idem* (1990).

slavery, but is now exalted, might appear to people who at other points also discerned major Cynic strands in Paul's life and conversation. Such an apotheosis of a hero figure is one thing; for it to have involved for Jesus a return to life in a manner that entailed the transformation of his corpse would seem much harder to fit into any known Cynic scheme; and for all Jesus' followers to be promised a share in just such a transformation after their deaths or while still alive, very difficult if not impossible to present as part of a Cynic Christian message. Most Cynic tradition is very sceptical about any life after death, and certainly, nothing important is going to happen to corpses. They can be left for wild animals or for fishes; or the stink will get them buried.[106] Of course, Cynics were not the only people around with no hope for any life after death; scepticism on this issue seems to have been widespread;[107] but it is Cynic scepticism that concerns us here, and that is certainly compatible with the insistence Paul has met in Corinth, that 'there is no resurrection of the dead'.

However, it is hard to puzzle out in quite what sense anyone at all who was firmly convinced that there is no life after death, and, *a fortiori*, that 'there is no resurrection of the dead', could then have believed Paul when he proclaimed Christ dead, buried and raised on the third day (1 Cor 15.3); and later have gone in for 'baptism for the dead' (1 Cor 15.29 – supposing Paul was not misled on that). Obviously there has been little agreement among the

---

[106] Lucian, *Demonax* 35, 66; Diogenes Laertius 6.52, 79; ps.-Diogenes 22; 25.1; Teles 30H, 31H; and M. Plunkett (1988), 223–28.

[107] R. MacMullen (1981), 51–57.

commentators, so at least the suggestion that follows is not competing with an established scholarly consensus.[108]

It is quite clear (general scepticism about life after death apart) that some Cynics could entertain the possibility – if only as a 'myth' – of a Cynic leader being exalted to the Gods, to a position of authority, judicial or more general.[109] Pseudo-Heraclitus is made to say that this is the role he expects to fulfil: 'My soul will not sink. As a deathless possession it will fly high to the heavens. The ethereal dwellings will receive me, and I shall prosecute the Ephesians. I shall be a citizen among the Gods, not among humans.' Similar claims are made for Diogenes and for Socrates in the *Letters*, and for both Diogenes and Heraclitus by Epictetus.[110] However literally or figuratively these suggestions were intended, the fact is that Cynics could talk in a way not so far removed from Paul's talk of 'the judgment seat of Christ' (2 Cor 5.10). And once we have the idea of deathless life for some entertained, the possibility is open for its extension to more.

There could also be talk among some Cynics of messengers coming from the place of the dead. According to Diogenes Laertius, Menedemus 'went so far in wonderworking (εἰς τοσοῦτον τερατείας, perhaps just

---

[108] H. Conzelmann [1969] (1975), 261–63, 275–77, and references there.

[109] For this kind of 'myth', understood as a serious but made-up story, see, for instance, Dio 36.42, 61; and the various (partly Cynic-inspired?) stories told in Dio 30 (which also talks of good people being taken up to heaven: 30.44). J. W. Cohoon, *Dio Chrysostom* II, LCL (1939), 395–98, surveys earlier discussions of possible Cynic strands in Dio 30. Some or all Christians will share this judicial function: 1 Cor 6.2–3; cf. Lk 22.30/Mt 19.28.

[110] Ps.-Heraclitus 5.2, cf. 9.3; ps.-Diogenes 39.3 (if this heavily Platonised piece is Cynic; cf. A. J. Malherbe (1977), 15); Epictetus, *Encheiridion* 15; *Socratic Letter* 25.1.

'astonishing behaviour') as to go round dressed as a Fury, saying he'd come up from Hades to investigate people's sins and then descend again to report back to the divine authorities there.'[111] Lucian tells us that before his death Peregrinus sent 'testamentary letters' to major Greek cities by the hand of chosen 'ambassadors' to whom he gave the titles of 'messengers from the dead', 'couriers from below' (νεκραγγέλοι, νερτεροδρόμοι). This has Peregrinus apparently confident that such language could make sense in a Cynic context. Not only so, but according to Lucian Peregrinus also foretold that he would himself live again 'as daimon of the night'.[112] In the years that followed rumour spread among Peregrinus' Cynic followers that he lived, that he had ascended, and also had been seen alive after his self-immolation (though Lucian claims it was he himself who got the rumour going).[113]

In Menippean mood Lucian also relates many tales of life among the dead; and in *The Dead Come to Life*, for instance, again Diogenes appears as prosecutor. Other dialogues have Menippus or some other Cynic ascending to the Gods.[114] These Menippean dialogues underline the need to allow that maybe in actuality all the other talk of a Cynic leader alive after death may indeed have been meant and taken as 'myth', as figurative, by some or all who articulated it. But the fact remains that this sort of talk (even if it is no more than that) appears in many Cynic

---

[111] Diogenes Laertius 6.102.

[112] Lucian, *Peregrinus* 41 and also 27–28; see A. M. Harmon's note, *Lucian* V, LCL (1936), 47.

[113] Lucian, *Peregrinus* 39–40.

[114] Lucian, *The Downward Journey*; *Zeus Catechised*; *The Cock*; *Icaromenippus*; *Menippus* (or, *Descent into Hades*); *The Parliament of the Gods*; *Dialogues of the Dead*.

contexts. It is at the very least plausible that some
Corinthians, perceiving Paul as an engaging and persuasive
Cynic teacher, might have taken for granted that his talk of
Jesus raised from the dead was a variant of conventional
Cynic picture language, might have accepted it as such –
and then been astonished to find that Paul meant it
'literally'.[115] Figuratively or literally understood, talk of
Jesus raised to a judicial role in heaven would initially at
least have fitted without undue strain within the Cynic
impression made by Paul's life-style and much of his
spoken message.

It is appropriate at this juncture to recall our earlier
discussion, stimulated by Mark Plunkett. Whereas it is
often supposed that in opposing sexual promiscuity, and
again in stressing bodily (albeit transformed bodily)
resurrection, Paul was addressing 'gnostic' or other
'dualists', for whom bodies were irrelevant, we concluded
that Paul was almost certainly contending with physical
monists, monistic (but to Paul) unacceptably hedonistic
Cynics. He is not engaging with people for whom souls fly
free of bodies (and for whom 'resurrection' is therefore
irrelevant or absurd), but those for whom 'in this life only'
is Christ relevant (1 Cor 15. 19) – in fact addressing Cynic-
minded Christians for whom the charge of Epicurean
pleasure-seeking (1 Cor 15.32) should be a particularly
stinging rebuke.[116]

Judgment, and Christ as judge, we have touched on.
That seems still to leave us with 'the whole creation

---

[115] Dio has to accept just such conflict between poetic myth-making
and a stubborn literalism, 36.42.

[116] Ch. 4, above, § 6; M. Plunkett (1988), 167–68; on the Epicurean
sound of Paul's rebuke, A. J. Malherbe [1968] (1989), 84–86. That it is
a rebuke Paul can take for granted, he does not have to argue the point
against 'Epicurean' Christians (contra G. Tomlin (1997)).

labouring in travail' (Rom 8.22; 1 Cor 7.29–31); the 'wrath of God' (e.g., Rom 2.5, 5.9; 1 Thess 1.10), with the drama announced by the trumpet blast (1 Thess 4.15; 1 Cor 15.52), involving the resurrection-and-transformation of all who belong to Christ (1 Cor 15.53–55; 1 Thess 4.16–17), the conquest of death which is Christ's final victory (1 Cor 15.25); and then 'the end', Christ's surrender of his rule (1 Cor 15.24) 'so God may be all in all' (or 'everything to everyone', πάντα ἐν πᾶσιν, 1 Cor 15.29).

There seem to be no specifically Cynic anti-cipations for any of these strands. Although pseudo-Anacharsis 9, as we have seen, presents current human society as subject to divine punishment in a way that affords some parallels with Romans 1.18–32, there is no suggestion there of a final 'wrathful' condemnation. Some of Lucian's Menippaean pieces imagine encounters with those who have died: but there is nothing like a general resurrection to 'be with the Lord in the air'. (Dio's *Discourse* 36.54–57 conjures up a vision of divine unity before the rebirth of the universe, but this is Stoicism with a touch of Magian mysticism.)

What we can say, repeating what was argued above, is that these strands in Paul could well have seemed to constitute interesting variant 'barbarian' myths express-ing in their own ways the widespread conviction that the world was in terminal moral and physical decay, heading for some final deserved catstrophe;[117] although Cynics doubted others' confident forecasts of the future, they had no investment in any Platonic or Aristotelian dogma of the eternity of this universe. The world was in decline from its Golden Age, even if it was not a decline to a final punish-ment and cleansing. That Paul's 'barbarian' version of this

---

[117] F. G. Downing (1995b) and (1995c), again.

common conviction included some distinctive details, even a resurrection to deathless life for many, would not be enough to undermine the much stronger impression forged by much else of what he did and said, that here was a new and perhaps revitalised Cynicism.

(xiii) In conclusion: the five theses, again.

Some of the Pauline material discussed in this chapter has significant Cynic analogies which would readily have been perceived (*a*). The imitation of God (*i*) whom one treats as a friend (*v*); the unity of God (*iii*), and the refusal to participate in the cultic activity of the community (*iv*), would seem to have been quite distinctive Cynic themes, as were admiration (among milder Cynics) for a divine hero who accepted servitude (*ii*). Combined with Paul's life-style, his sparse clothing displaying his shameful scars from beatings, his total self-presentation as a teacher, these would certainly confirm the impression that here was some sort of Cynic. Other items which we have surveyed would not have been likely on their own to have suggested this Cynic interpretation, but would readily have seemed compatible with such a view of Paul, including his approach to vice and virtue, his realised eschatology, and even his expectation of an exalted human figure as judge. Some, but very little, of Paul's 'barbarian wisdom' might have seemed somewhat surprising to a hearer, a partner in conversation who had taken him to be just another idiosyncratic Cynic.

Paul's message is clearly not bound by any conventional variety of Cynicism. He can enunciate and live themes that no pagan Cynic would have been at all likely to propose, themes drawn from the native Hellenistic

Jewish context of his earlier years, together with his new (and evolving) Christian faith. With such resources Paul presumably could have articulated much of what he tried initially to share with people in Galatia, Macedonia and Achaea in terms significantly less open to any Cynic reading, had he so wanted. The authors of the Fourth Gospel, of the Pastoral Epistles, of 1 Peter and of Hebrews all manage with little if any matter that invites a Cynic reading. But Paul does not. There is no sign of him using his other important (Christian and Jewish) resources to distance himself from Cynicism, or to make the Cynic-sounding strands look less Cynic. This Paul who could (we may supppose) have put things very differently had he so wished was quite content (*b*) to let the Cynic-seeming motifs emerge without any sign of embarrassment, and to qualify them very often in terms of inner-Cynic debate, as we have seen; even though we have again noted in passing signs of others around him taking Paul's Christian Cynicism to conclusions he could not accept (*d*) (on realised eschatology in Thessalonica, and disbelief in resurrection in Corinth). Still more significantly, Paul's Cynic strands are, as we have observed in some detail in this present chapter, quite integral to his 'theology' proper (*c*).

In the remaining chapters we shall try to indicate something of how Paul's Cynicism relates to his Jewish origins, to other pagan Hellenistic currents (mainly Stoicism), and, lastly, (*e*) to his emergent Christian context.

8

PAUL, AN 'ANOMALOUS' JEW[1]

Among elements in Paul's Christian way of life and teaching, and in the responses of some of his converts, we have been considering some that seem closely akin to specific strands in popular Cynicism. On the basis of their life-style and of some of the things they said, Paul and his associates (and their followers, too) might well have been taken for Cynics of a sort. In no way does this amount to claiming that Paul 'was' a Cynic, or would ever have thought of himself as such, either before or after his encounter with the risen Christ.[2] Nor does this study allow us to decide whether any of Paul's converts had lived as 'pagan' Cynics before they joined one of the early Christian communities, though that is, of course, not impossible. All that we may hope to have shown is that at various very significant points Paul behaved and expressed himself in ways that both could and would have been perceived as Cynic, ways that could and would have been comprehensible and *communicable* because they had been prepared for in Cynicism.

Some of these strands, I have argued (*a and b*), would have appeared as characteristically and even distinctively Cynic: these would have been the ascetic life-

---

[1] Borrowing the designation from J. M. G. Barclay (1996).

[2] Cf. D. Seeley (1996) and (1997).

style and its articulation together with the closely linked self-presentation as an adaptable but unflattering teacher, the negative appraisals of enacted and customary 'law' over against a new 'freedom', and the insistence on a unity unrestricted by race, status or gender. Responses, in Corinth most obviously, on issues of freedom in matters of sexual relations and of food and of traditional cults, indicate (*d*) that this was in fact how Paul was understood by some at least. Much else in Paul, it has been suggested, would at least have seemed compatible with such a Cynic (Christian–Cynic) interpretation of his practice and important elements in his message. And all this would have been so clear that it would of necessity have been brought home to Paul. Even if these Cynic elements had initially been adopted by him unawares their resonances would have become so clear to him that he must have maintained them deliberately and (for a while at least) without qualms. In the Thessalonian and Corinthian letters and still in Galatians, they are (*c*) integral to his theology (even if later again, as will be argued, Paul appears less happy with such links).

But Paul was a Christian Jew, not a Cynic. Even at his own most Cynic-seeming, the Cynicism that he had apparently absorbed from his popular oral Hellenistic culture, the variegated Cynicism that was there to hand in Paul's mental world ('naturally', and not for studied 'translation'), the Cynicism that was there in the world of his 'pagan' contacts, will have provided elements of the phrasing and the style – promptings, even – but not the main impetus for what he did and said. The predominant underlying impulse derives from Paul's Christian and Jewish convictions and his Jewish heritage.

That is certainly the conclusion urged on us by the canonical letters we rely on. Obviously Paul never cites a recognisable Cynic oral *chreia*, let alone any known Cynic literary source,[3] even though we have seen him cite in their Cynic sense catchphrases used by Cynics and Stoics alike. Only in discussions of his own authority does the persuasive force of a Cynic-seeming ascetic life-style appear to be expected to stand on its own without further backing from Scripture or 'word of the Lord'.[4] Beyond dispute, this persuasive force he expects his ascetic practice to exert must be of considerable importance for our understanding of Paul. Yet when he is later openly challenged on other issues (including matters of law and freedom, whose Cynic resonances we have displayed) he now mostly falls back on either his Jewish or his new Christian–Jewish resources. This conclusion does not need to be argued or illustrated at any great length. Recent and older discussions of Paul as Jew and Christian are entirely adequate for present purposes, even allowing for continuing disagreements on important details among the specialists.

Paul can, of course, attempt to clarify an issue without falling back on any authority other than his own. But if some piece of teaching is in dispute Paul mostly and quite specifically cites either common Christian tradition (as he understands it) or he cites Jewish Scripture; or both. If it is Scripture, it is cited with an unquestioning assumption of its authority (however tendentious his 'reading' may seem to us).[5] Most accept that this practice evinces a

---

[3] The nearest we ever get to a Cynic saying is the pseudo-Pauline 1 Tim 6.9, apparently citing a variant of the saying of Diogenes, 'the love of money is mother-city of all evils', Diogenes Laertius 6.50.

[4] Rom 8.35–36 is the one example of a tribulation list given a (slight) scriptural warrant.

[5] C. D. Stanley (1994), 53, finds 74 clear 'citations' of Paul (as distinct from possible 'allusions'); he notes that his most respected predecessor (D.-A. Koch (1986)) allows for 93.

very real and basic Jewishness in Paul's thought. Even those who find it hard to believe that Paul had shared in 'normative' or even 'formative' Judaism would mostly accept that Paul's Jewishness before as well as after his encounter with the risen Christ was from his side genuine and important, albeit from some critics' stance, perverse and distorted. Hyam Maccoby is the least persuaded among recent commentators. He allows that his Paul has 'a tenacious attachment to Jewish tradition and milieu', but is sure that his actual use of Jewish Scripture betrays the hand of an 'uneasy convert to Judaism', and is not what would be expected from the self-styled erstwhile zealous Pharisee of Philippians 3.5-6.[6] Maccoby's Paul 'garbles' his Scriptural quotations; and Maccoby insists, 'A rabbi might depart far from the plain meaning of a biblical text in his interpretation. He might even resort to an outrageous pun on a word in a text, in order to extract a meaning that is not there. But what he would never do is to misquote the text deliberately in the first place.'[7]

---

[6] H. Maccoby (1991), 183.

[7] H. Maccoby (1991), 151; Maccoby is arguing with another Jewish scholar of a previous generation, J. Klausner (1943/44), who was convinced that Paul was a genuine, but 'Hellenistic' (as opposed to Palestinian and Talmudic) Jew, 450–53; 'authentic Judaism with a non-Jewish coloring', 466, including Paul's use of Scripture (454, 502). Mid-way might be the still earlier essay by C. G. Montefiore (1914), where aspects of Paul are 'essentially Jewish', 217, but his pre-Christian Judaism had been very unlike that of the rabbis (101–29). All these writers find traces or more of pagan mystery cults in Paul. S. Sandmel (1958), 45, says Paul's 'Judaism is explicit in his every paragraph'; 'Paul is a Jew . . . in his own way loyal to the Jewish Bible' (59). For a still more nuanced view, both of Judaism in Paul's day, and of Paul, see A. Segal (1990); and, from a gentile scholar, E. P. Sanders (1977) and (1983), though urging a readier use of later rabbinic writings as evidence for Paul's day than does Segal. See now,

However, this latter point seems to have been effectively answered by Christopher D. Stanley's *Paul and the Language of Scripture*. Stanley shows in much greater detail the extent to which Paul adapts his citations not just to his syntax and rhetoric but also to the purpose in hand; yet then also shows that this represents the common practice of Paul's day, a practice equally shared by other Jewish writers.[8] Stanley also notes among features of Paul's use of Scripture the frequency with which he includes γράφειν in citation formulae, and concludes from this and other factors, 'there is no questioning the fact that Paul regarded the words of scripture as having absolute authority for his predominantly Gentile congregations'.[9]

The conclusion is well warranted, but does still need to be clarified along the lines of what was argued in the first chapter of this study. Paul shows no sign of having supposed that any such authority would have been accorded the Jewish Scriptures by his pagan contacts when first he attempted to share his good news with them. Even in the established congregation at Thessalonica no such appeal to Jewish Scripture is made (and little Scriptural allusion, even, has been detected in the letter). The recipients of Galatians were by the time of its writing quite clearly

also, J. Murphy-O'Connor (1996); but especially J. M. G. Barclay (1996), on Paul as an 'anomalous Jew'.

[8] C. D. Stanley (1994), again, e.g., 348, 'Paul was simply following the normal literary conventions of his day.' Of contemporary Jewish writers Stanley concludes, 'it can be affirmed with confidence that the methods followed by the authors examined here differs little from those documented already for Greco-Roman writers working outside the Jewish sphere.' Stanley also makes the significant point, from Sh. Talmon, that only with the later fixing of the Masoretic text does this comparative freedom seem to disappear (357), citing Sh. Talmon (1975), page reference not given.

[9] C. D. Stanley (1994), 253, 338–39; quoted from 338.

beginning to take Jewish traditions very seriously; but when Paul refers to their initial conviction (Gal 3.1–5) there is no reference to the passing on of Scriptural texts, to the fulfilment of prophecy, nor to anything else of the kind. Only now when the Galatians have become acculturated to Scripture can Paul use it, but now with full conviction, to support his understanding of the good news, and to oppose new ideas that appear to be being urged on his hearers.

In Corinth Paul had proclaimed 'Christ crucified'; yet there is no sign of his supporting his use of 'Christos' from Scriptural texts, and it appears mostly just as a name. The conviction that Christ's death for our sins and his resurrection from the dead were both 'according to the Scriptures' is part of the Christian tradition Paul passed on (1 Cor 15.3–4), but whatever Scriptural passages might have been intended, in the rest of the discussion he at no point suggests he is using texts initially alluded to. Some such very general reference to ancient Jewish writings might have been well enough in keeping with a first approach deploying Cynic motifs, for Cynics often claimed to respect 'barbarian wisdom' as potentially closer to nature than their own corrupt Hellenic urban culture.[10] But by the time we meet the Corinthian Christians they are longer established, and Paul can now happily deploy passages from the Scriptures he fundamentally relies on. He nonetheless still does not on every occasion have recourse to Scripture; we noted above that when he castigates the incestuous relationship that has been brought to his attention he makes no reference to Leviticus 18.7-8, but only to the consensus 'among the nations' (1 Cor 5.1–8): 'barbarian wisdom', perhaps. For the rest, though, he

---

[10] D. R. Dudley (1937), 152; C. Muckensturn (1993); C. P. Jones (1993).

seems in most contexts to have at least one text with which he can now buttress or even clinch most of the conclusions he intends (as we shall illustrate in a little more detail, below).

Yet even when Paul feels he can usefully cite Scripture, he still does not teach as many suppose Jewish teachers already did. He produces no comprehensive *halakah*, he writes no 'manual of discipline'.[11] Compared with other Hellenised Jews from his time of whom we know, Paul is, as J. M. G. Barclay argues, 'anomalous'.[12] And his portrayal of his own role and ethos remains, as we have recalled, pervasively informed by Cynic models.

Until questions of Jewish Torah spirituality are raised Paul uses words from the δικαιοῦν group only rarely and in passing, and nowhere as coinage for elaborating the relationship he trusts that God makes possible through faith in (or the faith of) Jesus Christ (with no more reference to Jewish than to pagan cultural conventions). Rainer Riesner among others is probably right to argue that the same positive convictions nonetheless underlie what Paul writes using other key words in 1 Thessalonians.[13] But it is only briefly, in 2 Corinthians (3.9, 5.21 and 11.15), that we find Paul using this terminology, before it comes to full flower in Galatians and Romans, where it then becomes clear that for Paul it constitutes a vital expression of his own faith and Christian existence. It was not, however, a terminology that would have made much sense to pagans without some considerable exposure to some current Jewish ways of thinking. Lucian's Demonax does say 'It's human to err, but it's the

---

[11] E. P. Sanders (1983), 95.

[12] J. M. G. Barclay (1996), 381–95, again.

[13] R. Riesner (1994), 349–58.

work of a God or a godlike man to set right (ἐπανορθοῦν) what has gone wrong', yet nothing else even as close as that from among our Cynic sources comes to mind.[14] 'Setting right' (or 'justifying') is very much a theme from Paul's Jewish heritage, as its prominence in the Dead Sea Scroll *hodayot* suggests. Alan F. Segal (following Nils Dahl) quotes,

> For to God belongs my justification [*mishpati*]
> And the perfection of my way is in his hand, with the
>   uprightness of my heart.
>   And by his righteousness [*sidkato*]
>   is my sin blotted out.
> And from the fount of his righteousness [*sidkato*] comes
>   my justification [*mishpati*].[15]

But the terminology is already there in the canonical Psalter; Psalm 105.30-32 (Septuagint) could have been particularly significant for Paul the zealot: the retribution exacted by the proto-zealot Phineas 'was reckoned to him for righteousness' (ἐλογίσθη αὐτῷ εἰς δικαιοσύνη). But, whatever the specific textual sources for Paul's concern, it was obviously his continuing *Torah* spirituality that made the issue of how 'righteousness' was to be 'reckoned' so intensely important for him (Gal 3.6; Rom 4).

Paul the Jew nonetheless came to announce some very negative judgments on 'law' and 'the law'. As we noted in chapter 3, the only available preparation for such an onslaught would have been found among Cynic critics of codes and conventions. There is nothing like this to be found among Jews who still considered themselves Jewish, as Paul clearly did of himself. Attention is often drawn, as

---

[14] Lucian, *Demonax* 7.

[15] A. F. Segal (1990), 175–76, citing 1QS 11.2 and 5, following N. A. Dahl (1977), 98.

we recalled above, to some 'ultra liberal' Jews noted briefly by Philo. These claimed to value highly the philosophical, theological and ethical ideas they discerned in the laws for the Sabbath, festivals and circumcision, yet quite without qualms abandoned the practices themselves.[16] There are superficial similarities with the conflict in Galatia, where it appears that circumcision was the main issue, together with food laws, and very likely sabbaths and festivals (Gal 6.12, 2.12, and 4.10, respectively). These were 'the works of the law' that people were aware of, as 'markers' of Jewish identity.[17] But Paul does not propose a programme of allegorising appraisal of the practices.[18] Rather does he insist that if the way into a positive relationship with God is to be through 'the law' at all, then the whole law must be kept (Gal 3.10; 5.3.). The option of allegorising but otherwise abandoning only the ritual markers just does not arise for Paul. It is the most readily 'internalisable' commandment (not to covet) whose weakness Paul chooses to criticise in Romans 7. And yet still the law remains holy, and the commandment remains 'holy and just and good' (Rom 7.12; cf. Gal 3.21).

And so, when Paul has completed his critical (not allegorising) appraisal of the law, he celebrates his Jewish heritage and explodes into praise to God for it, 'the sonship, the divine glory, the covenants, the gift of the law, the pattern of worship, the promises, the ancestors, and the human descent of the Messiah. May God who remains over all be blessed for all ages. Amen' (Rom 9.4–5). We may

---

[16] Philo, *De migratione* 89–93; cf., e.g., J. M. G. Barclay (1996), 177.

[17] On which see J. D. G. Dunn (1990), (1992) and (1993); E. P. Sanders (1983); and chapter 3, above.

[18] Rom 2.29 simply takes up Deuteronomic teaching: Deut 10.16; 30.6; Jer 4.4.

compare Paul's earlier insistence that he remains a Hebrew, an Israelite (2 Cor 11.22), and note that he has submitted five times to synagogue beatings. Of course Paul is convinced that his fellow Jews are wrong to refuse the new relationship with himself that God offers 'in' and through Jesus, the relationship that brings gentiles in on equal terms with Israelites, a relationship whose enjoyment is neither initiated, enabled nor even structured by the observance of some or all of the law. His fellow Jews are wrong to hold to their old understanding of what God intended in the giving of the law; they should accept the interpretation that Paul has reached.

Quite how Paul came to the conclusions he sketches in Galatians (and which, it has been suggested, already underlay his initial 'law-free' presentation of the good news in Galatia and Thessalonica and elsewhere) continues to be debated, and this is not the place to rehearse the arguments in any detail. Perhaps Paul both had what he understood as an encounter with the crucified Jesus and was told or at once realised the implications for a 'lawless' salvation for gentiles, or perhaps, as Alan Segal concludes, 'Although his initial insight may have come at conversion, Paul implies that the legal consequences of his conversion were worked out over time, as he began to understand what being in Christ meant for gentiles.'[19] We note that Paul and Luke (though Luke rather differently) both insist that the encounter entailed a call to evangelise the gentiles.

Segal makes a strong case for continuing to use the word 'conversion' for what happened in Paul's life, even though others have rejected it (rejected it on the grounds

---

[19] A Segal (1990), 142.

that Paul shows no sign of the prior tension and guilt that
form an integral part of some accounts of 'conversion'.[20]
Paul's understanding of what God was up to was beyond
dispute changed. He came to quite a new mind on the
matter. His own past enjoyment of the law was now seen to
have been based on a misunderstanding; that period now
looked so much shit, by comparison with his present
experience, says Paul with Cynic crudeness (Phil 3.4–10).
The encounter with the risen Christ had brought Paul a
relationship with God that had never been his as a Pharisee
delighting in God's law, and this was now a relationship he
was to share with others. The *Torah* had no positive part
for Paul or anyone else in bringing them into or maintaining them in this (for Christian Paul) sole worthwhile
relationship with God. Any attempt to engage with the law
as a way into this uniquely right relationship with God
would be a fatal mistake. And so, as we argued earlier, and
recalled just above, Paul could readily make use of the
critical accounts of law and custom elaborated among
Cynic contemporaries.

Yet for Paul Jewish law and custom (and gentile
law and custom, but to a much lesser extent) still in
practice had much to contribute. Paul makes various
attempts to find some positive but non-salvific divine
purpose in the law. These are much discussed, but it is not
they that display its continuing importance for him. We
may instance the speculation in Galatians that the law
might have been intended to stimulate sin, τῶν παραβάσεων χάριν (Gal 3.19), but this is not repeated in

---

[20] A Segal (1990), the whole essay; debating with, among others,
K. Stendahl (1976).

Romans; nor is the idea of the law as a stern but necessary παιδαγωγός (Gal 3.24).[21] In Romans Paul decides rather that the law allows sin to become overt and chargeable (Rom 5.13), and also provides the opportunity or stimulus for hypostatised 'sin' to get to work (Rom 7.7–8). All of these ideas are of interest. But the law's real and very positive continuing hold on Paul is shown by his continuing (implicit or explicit) reliance on it as traditionally interpreted and understood, for his Christian ethical decision-making and advice.

Paul's ethics are clearly eclectic and 'situational'.[22] In his own case he can refuse to obey a clear 'command of the Lord' (that those who proclaim the gospel should get their living from it, 1 Cor 9.14), even though Paul has himself already argued for this as a right from a text of 'the law' (1 Cor 9.8–9). Where we might have expected Paul to quote Leviticus on incest, he prefers (as we have already noted) to cite supposed common custom, although the upshot is the same (1 Cor 5.1–2). More characteristically, however, the command of the Lord against divorce stands for any married partners among his followers (1 Cor 7.10–11), but where a separation is initiated by an unbelieving partner, the Christian is not bound (1 Cor 7.15). In this, as in most of 1 Corinthians 7, as earlier in 1 Thessalonians 4.1–8 (against adultery), Paul relies on instincts inbred by Jewish tradition. His objection to coitus with a prostitute (though that is not forbidden to men in the law) is supported by reference to Genesis 2.24 (1 Cor 6.16). The Jewish (and wider) gender–markers that Paul grew up with are reaffirmed on the basis of Genesis 2 (1 Cor 11.8).

---

[21] On this interpretation of Gal 3.19, 'for the sake of transgressions', see ch. 3, above, § 5; and H. Räisänen [1983] (1986), 140–44.

[22] Cf. J. I. Porter (1996) on Aristo of Chios' (Cynic) 'situational' ethics.

Paul's preference for private arbitration (1 Cor 6.5) probably mirrors Hellenistic Jewish practice. The obligation to avoid contamination by idolatry and the demons involved in it is simply taken for granted, once it has been categorised in these commonplace Jewish terms, and is supported only by cases in the law of divine punishment for lawbreakers (1 Cor 10.1–14); and so on. The behaviour Paul expects from new Christians is (so E. P. Sanders) 'largely in accord with the law and Jewish traditions. As Heikki Räisänen puts it, "Paul obliged his Gentile converts to lead a decent life according to normal Jewish standards".'[23] And so the law is still meant to be 'fulfilled' (Gal 5.14; 6.2; Rom 8.4; 12.8). The law is fulfilled in love of neighbour, which refers us, of course, to Leviticus 19.18.

Yet, we have to emphasise yet again, in the light of our earlier chapters, this is *not*, obviously still is not the whole story. Paul lived an austere, risky, penurious life for which, as we have seen, there are (outside the Christian records) no close Jewish but many clear Cynic precedents. And Paul urged others to imitate him, to engage in and allow a continuous process of transformation along the same lines.[24] While the minimum Paul could accept was the very high standard Jewish communities inculcated, that was to be the base on from which further change, growth, transformation was expected; and if that further transformation happened it would result in individuals and groups who would appear Cynic rather than Jewish. A gentler Cynicism would have provided the most obvious compar-

---

[23] E. P. Sanders (1983), 94–95, himself quoting H. Räisänen (1980), 312; a conclusion accepted by A. Segal (1990), 169.

[24] On the importance and significance of 'transformation' language in Paul (initial and ongoing), A. Segal (1990), especially ch. 5, 'Paul's New Conversion Community among Gentiles', 150–83.

ison, the most likely apparent model. I shall indeed argue again briefly below that this would have been a Christian Cynicism with its roots in the Jewish Cynicism of Jesus of Nazareth. However, I shall also resume my argument that Paul himself appears quite soon to have abandoned this difficult goal of a Christian Cynicism after his frustrating experience with the Corinthian Christians, and settled for a less disruptive interior *askêsis*, more in tune with the ethos of popular Stoicism (as it appears in Philippians and Romans, with adumbrations already in 1 and 2 Corinthians).

For now we remain with the earlier Paul of the very young communities. He had found and was sharing a new freedom (even while he was concerned that some were abusing it, risking their own and others' liberty). Words like 'freedom' and 'liberty' are notoriously slippery. One person's freedom to live by a code of practice is another's captivity; many of the paradoxes were widely recognised in Paul's day, and Paul is himself aware of at least some of them (e.g., Rom 6.15–19).[25] It remains true that in an important and meaningful sense, Paul quite objectively gained some wider freedoms when he allowed his mind to be changed by his encounter with the risen Christ. He was, as we have been noting, 'free' to pick and choose his ethical decisions (even if he still often instinctively picked what the law said or was taken to say). He was free to conform to Jewish expectations only when it seemed appropriate to him. We do not seem in a position to tell whether when he was thrashed in synagogues (2 Cor 11.24) it was for his reputation, or for what he contributed to the

---

[25] Commonplaces on 'freedom': Philo, *Quod omnis probus liber sit*; Dio, *Discourses* 14 and 15.

studious discussion of *Torah*,[26] but he tells us clearly that
he exercised the freedom to appear as Jew or as gentile at
will (1 Cor 9.19–21), a Cynic freedom in the face of
others' settled expectations. To be as 'adaptable' as this
(on principle; others, of course, would say 'fickle and
false') was, as we have seen, to emulate a Cynic Odysseus
(or even appear as 'Protean' as the Cynic Peregrinus in the
next century) – especially as all the while Paul, it would
seem, maintained his half-naked and austere Cynic life-
style. Though what is chosen is so often clearly Jewish, the
freedom to choose would be manifestly Cynic.

Paul's 'theology', his 'God-talk' (employing our
kind of distinction) we also found to be fundamentally
Jewish, while its emphases would still have left Paul
sounding *among pagans* closer to Cynicism than to other
contemporary philosophies (or, for pagan visitors to
synagogues, closer to Cynics than to Paul's fellow Jews).
Paul's God may well be (is) fundamentally the God of the
Jewish *Torah*, yet this God has stopped demanding *Torah*
observance, even of a Jew such as Paul, while still (as
Cynics publicly and Jews perhaps only privately taught)
rejecting idols and their temples and the sacrifices offered.
Paul himself would look very much a Cynic worker–
philosopher (not a rabbi, if the term is appropriate for the
date; still less a mystagogue). One of Paul's Christian
congregations meeting in people's homes would look more
like a philosophic school symposium (singing included).
Chaotic babble might bewilder (as Paul fears), shocking
talk of consuming someone's 'body and blood' might well
reinforce the Cynic impression. And a penetrating analysis
of any chance visitor's moral condition (1 Cor 14) could

---

[26] Cf. A. E. Harvey (1985), especially 83–84.

well convince that here were people who (as we noted some Cynics also claimed) spoke for God, as 'prophets'.

The figure of a human or semi-divine hero now endowed with celestial authority analogous to the Christ Paul proclaimed was also, we found, not without precedent in Cynic thought. Herakles in particular comes to mind, with Philippians 2.5–11 including some common motifs. Cynic tradition can accord Socrates, Diogenes and Heraclitus heavenly judicial authority after death. This is how Paul's proclamation would most likely have appeared, even while the most significant *formative* influence remained contemporary Judaism, with its hypostatisations of divine attributes, its discussions of 'two powers in heaven', and its speculations concerning figures such as Enoch and Moses.[27]

Although we have argued that elements in Paul's offering of well-being, 'salvation', now and to come, included many of the elements of moral transformation promised by Cynics (and others, of course), Paul's eschatology, we had to accept, stemmed in the main from his Jewish inheritance, and the futurist strands would seem quite foreign to any 'pagan' Cynic we are aware of. We noted Stanley K. Stowers' apposite comparison of the sketch of human decline in Romans 1 with *Letter* 9 of pseudo-Anacharsis, but of course there is much more in common still between Romans 1 and Wisdom of Solomon.

Much more significant for pagan observers, however, we have argued, would be Paul and his closer colleagues (and maybe others) living the austerity that for Cynics showed the age of Kronos could be re-enacted in the present, in a community sharing many features with Crates' 'City of Pera': an 'inaugurated eschatology', even

---

[27] See A. F. Segal (1978); L. Hurtado (1988).

though when Paul talks of the new life now available it is in terms drawn from Genesis 1–2, such as 'new creation', 'no male and female', 'a second Adam'.

Much of the impetus, then, that we have so far briefly surveyed is Jewish; and much of the rest, we shall argue, briefly, is Jewish–Christian. Paul was a Jewish Christian; but one who was nonetheless content – better, determined – for the most part to appear in a very well-fitting, and entirely appropriate Cynic guise. 'Underneath' and in the background is Paul's Judaism and developing Christian conviction. But for 'pagan' citizens of the Hellenised towns Paul's habitual ascetic practice, and some major elements of what he shared in words, will have looked and sounded Cynic – so much and so clearly, this could not have been unawares, even though it may well also have been quite natural.

9

STOIC AND EPICUREAN STRANDS

(i) The Porch

'Stoics' and 'Stoicism' crop up much more often in scholarly discussions of Paul than do 'Cynics' and 'Cynicism'. Luke's Paul in Acts 17 addresses Stoic and Epicurean, but not Cynic or any other philosophers, and he quotes a Stoic poet, Aratus, or Cleanthes before him. Cicero's and Epictetus' socially conservative Stoicism had a continuing influence on western Christianity, and perhaps for that reason traces of Stoicism are more readily discerned in the Pauline canon.

We have already discussed in passing passages in Galatians and the Corinthian letters where others have sometimes discerned Stoic (but not Cynic) ideas, and have mostly but not always argued to the contrary, both for Paul and for those whose ideas he gives the impression of addressing. Thus we urged (chapter 1) that Galatians 3.28, 'Neither Jew nor Greek, neither bond nor free, no male and female' taken as a programme for action, would have sounded quite clearly Cynic, not Stoic, as would Paul's disparagement of 'the law' (chapter 3). It must certainly be agreed that for Stoics as well as for Cynics, only the wise man is rich, is king, and so forth (1 Cor 4.8); but it is also clear that the 'already' is a claim a Cynic could make seriously, whereas for Stoics this was an 'impossible possibility'. And the kinds of freedom Paul believes some

in Corinth are claiming are maintained at this date by
Cynics; in Stoicism such anarchic ideals have long been
abandoned.

Faced with such radical assaults on convention
(chapter 4) we found Paul drawing back, and in effect
himself taking a more Stoic (and 'conservative') line: οὐ
πάντα συμφέρει (1 Cor 6.12). Only what is helpful is to
be done, otherwise you lose your inner freedom to effect
what you know is right. Though then along these lines we
disputed Malherbe's claim that the 'strong' in Corinth
were accusing others of an intellectual and moral weakness
as discerned by Stoics, it would seem that Paul himself by
contrast was indeed making just that kind of distinction:
for him it was a weakness in awareness (συνείδησις) that
was at issue. Again, when he asserts his own 'willingness'
in the face of (divinely imposed) necessity (1 Cor 9.16–
17), Paul sounds Stoic, as he does when he encourages
people to maintain their civil status (1 Cor 7.27–28); and
as he does when he dismissed the thought that God might
care for animals (1 Cor 9.9–10); and on the issue of head-
dress, when he insists that conventional gender–markers be
retained (1 Cor 11.13–14); and so too, when to a (Cynic-
like) dismissal of Gods and idols he adds a brief sequence
of Stoic-sounding prepositional theology (1 Cor 8.6).
These traces of Stoic-aligned expressions and attitudes
indicate something of the breadth of popular culture available to Paul and absorbed by him; but at the same time,
something of an important alternative and much more
conformist stance to which he could be drawn – and
which, we shall argue shortly, in due course he did in fact
adopt. (Stoicism, after all, was Cynicism's acknowledged
offspring and constant sparring partner.)

However, Paul's own life-style in the early fifties,
especially appearing 'half-naked' and displaying his

shameful scars, the way he articulates that life-style, and the stress he places on it in his correspondence with Corinthian Christians, would together have created a much more distinctively Cynic impression overall than would these occasional traces of a Stoic ethos (chapter 5). Overt behaviour affords a much more significant 'social marker' than do the niceties of religious or popular philosophical discourse. And even given attention to his words, precisely Paul's emphatic (though not exclusive) articulation for overt behaviour, the scant attention accorded to intentions, attitudes, dispositions at this stage, would have seemed to anyone attuned to contemporary debate Cynic rather than Stoic. And we also noted, largely on the basis of others' work, that Paul's self-image as a teacher seems to pick up further readily recognisable (gentle) Cynic themes and motifs (chapter 6).

This is the Paul of the early 'independent' missionary work, the approach later recalled in Galatians, and as unsystematically echoed much closer to the events in the Thessalonian and Corinthian letters.[1] This is a Paul, then, who has deployed and enacted some very significant and often distinctive Cynic themes and motifs with every indication of being at home with them; albeit to articulate and communicate his understanding of the Christian good news in terms already in his hearers' vocabulary of ideas. Cynic-seeming appearance and behaviour, Cynic-sounding strands in his talk, drawn from the variegated popular culture he had absorbed, have helped Paul to make effective contact with some.

---

[1] Thus taking Galatians as written later than the others listed, though obviously often referring back to Paul's first contacts with people there.

But even at this early stage he has shown (as we have just been recalling) very clear signs of disquiet at the way some are taking the Cynic strands further than he is ready to: those giving up gainful employ, in Thessalonica; and, in Corinth, the women extending their equal rights, and still worse, those people who are insisting on an unrestricted freedom in matters of sex and food (as we saw above, chapters 4 and 7). Implicit Cynicism had afforded a quite appropriate and apparently effective articulation of important elements of what Paul felt called to and very much wanted to live and to share. But now it seems to have been borne in on him that a Cynic approach was risky, too open to what Paul could only see as misunderstanding. If Paul was going to speak the language of popular philosophy at all, popular Stoicism would be much safer, at least in terms of its social implications.

And in fact, when we reach Philippians and Romans there are only traces of the earlier Cynic Paul remaining. There is the crude language of Philippians 3.2 (κατατομή) and 3.8 (σκύβαλα), and the echoes of the Herakles myth at 2.5–11; and perhaps the assessment of homosexuality at Romans 1.26–27. There are no fresh Cynic themes, and many that we have met fail to reappear or are actually heavily qualified or even contradicted; while on the other hand much more with a strong Stoic resonance appears.

The presence of some Stoic strands in Philippians has been cogently argued by Troels Engberg-Pedersen, from whom I derive much but not all of what now follows.[2] Engberg-Pedersen finds in Philippians not just some terms used in Stoic social ethics, but a significantly

---

[2] T. Engberg-Pedersen (1995b). (Most of the Stoic terms adduced by M. Pohlenz (1949) in his study of Paul are from Romans or Acts 17.)

similar use, as Paul attempts to further his aim of realising proclaimed high ideals recognisably in this actual community: Philippians 1.27 taken with 3.20, life together reflecting the life of the heavenly city, just as Chrysippus is to be taken as having sketched an ideal πολιτεία 'of Gods and men' which could 'then be put to use in actual social and political practice in a number of ways. This is the *telos* or *skopos* for which one strives (διώκειν).' 'And so we are already in the middle of Philippians 3 (vv. 12–14).' In determining the 'end' of action it is essential to discern what matters and what does not (δοκιμάζειν τὰ διαφέρ-οντα, Phil 1.10). For the individual as for the community, the end is 'excellence' (virtue, ἀρετή, Phil 4.8), which means to be complete, perfect (Phil 3.12, 15).

Stoic intellectualism means that this excellence is fundamentally a state of mind that accords with how things are; so Paul emphasises the importance of 'knowing' Christ (Phil 3.8, 10), and of the Philippian Christians' mind-set (Phil 2.5). The example of Christ Jesus, hymned in Philippians 2.5–11, is agreed by most to be older than the letter, most likely composed by someone else; its echoes of a Cynic Herakles I have sketched above. Paul's τοῦτο φρονεῖτε . . . ὃ καὶ ἐν Χριστῷ 'Ιησοῦ now, I suggest, would seem to focus attention on intellection and interiority, rather than the overt action emphasised in the hymn itself. Then at Philippians 3.17 Paul risks offering himself as a model (a Cynic trait which we noted was usually avoided in the Stoic tradition). However, here it is Paul's attitudes (ἥγημαι, ἡγοῦμαι, Phil 3.7–8) and his knowledge that are to be imitated; there is no repetition of the lists of physical tribulations we meet in the Corinthian letters. It will also be recalled that in contrast with the Cynic short-cut which we argued Paul's life-style display-ed, Stoics insisted on slow, steady (but still arduous) progress (προκοπή) to an (impossible) perfection; and so Paul means to enable the progress (προκοπή) of his Philippian community (Phil 1.25), following the example of his own struggle to a far from attained goal (Phil 3.12–14).[3] And the emphasis in the letter on χαρά may even reflect the Stoic insistence that this must be the sage's constant response to all he discerns.[4]

Later, and also both interestingly and cogently, it is argued that there is a tension between hierarchical subordination and non-hierarchical *koinônia* in the letter; while the latter predominates in Paul's account of his own response to God and to the Lord Jesus (and which the Philippian Christians are to make their own), the former comes to the fore in Paul's own relationship with the Philippians themselves. Yet the former is shown to be most in accord with Stoic accounts of being grasped by an ideal and freely responding.[5]

Paul's understanding of the life that he hopes and endeavours to gain on his death is quite other than a Stoic such as Epictetus would expect. Samuel Vollenweider has shown that Paul's reflections on life and death (Phil 1.21–26) deploy a well-known *topos*; but Paul's actual option for life for the sake of others (rather than the death that is

---

[3] We may usefully contrast again 1 Cor 9.24–27, where Paul is maintaining his fitness, rather than, as here, emphasising the as yet unattained goal and the arduous progress towards it.

[4] Mostly from T. Engberg-Pedersen (1995), 268–74, condensed and slightly reordered and rephrased by me.

[5] T. Engberg-Pedersen (1995b), 282–89. I have to ask whether the hierarchical model is a further relic of one strand in Cynicism – the call to 'rule' fellow humans. Not all of the Cynic ethos persuades the present author! (If Phil 3.2–21 were not so clearly directed against 'Judaisers', then τοὺς κύνας of v. 2, and ὧν ὁ θεὸς ἡ κοιλία καὶ ἡ δόξα ἐν τῇ αἰσχύνῃ αὐτῶν, οἱ τὰ ἐπίγεια φρονοῦντες of v. 19 would have afforded a still clearer sign of a break with Cynics!).

preferred) seems paralleled among near contemporaries only in Stoic sources. Epictetus insists that a good man will play his social role right and only leave when it is clear that 'God' intends it (by showing that authentic existence is no longer possible).[6] Musonius judged that 'One who by living is of use to many has not the right to choose to die, unless by dying he may be of use to more.' (Epictetus, however, mocks the man who snatches at this excuse when death really is the better option).[7]

I would wish to enter one small disagreement in detail with Engberg-Pedersen. Early on he notes that *autarkeia* (Phil 4.11) 'is originally philosophic and specifically Cynic and Stoic; but by Paul's time it need not have any philosophical overtones at all'. However, later on Engberg-Pedersen also seems to take *autarkeia* to indicate here the Stoic *telos*, the perfection where the sage 'will have no need of anything else'.[8] In fact Paul's insistence that he is αὐτάρκης 'in plenty and in hunger, in abundance and in want' is very specifically Stoic in ethos. It is for Stoics that wealth is a matter of indifference, so indifferent it may even be 'preferred', so long as it creates no inner attachment or disturbance; as opposed to Cynics, for whom wealth is an evil to be disposed of, a tyrant to be destroyed. Martin Ebner appositely cities Seneca, 'Thus the sage will pursue excellence with wealth if he is able to, in poverty if he is not', 'sic sapiens virtutem si licebit in divitiis explicabit, si minus in paupertate.'[9] Paul is here

---

[6] S. Vollenweider (1994); Epictetus 3.24.95–102; cf. 4.1.86–90.

[7] Musonius, frag. 29; Epictetus 4.1.167–68.

[8] T. Engberg-Pedersen (1995b), 263 and 270.

[9] M. Ebner (1991), 341, citing Seneca, *Epistulae morales* 85.40; see the whole discussion, 338–45, including Epicurean and other sources.

entirely Stoic in ethos (whether aware of it or not, as Engberg-Pedersen allows of his own analysis), unlike the very Cynic-seeming earlier Paul opting for poverty (1 Cor 4.11–12; 2 Cor 6.10; 11.27). [10]

Engberg-Pedersen summarises what he designates 'the story' of Philippians, and then offers this interim conclusion:

> it is noteworthy that the story also reflects very precisely the basic ideas that went into Stoic moral and political philosophy: the directedness towards an end, the concept-ualization of the end as an ideal community, the strategy of using the notion of the end to inform people's under-standing and behaviour here and now, the exact way in which this application is thought to occur (it creates a certain mind-set with a distinct content). All of this is both centrally Stoic and also sufficiently specific to make it highly unlikely that it is anything *but* Stoic. [11]

Paul's letter to Christians in Rome also has seemed to many to contain significant direct or indirect traces of Stoicism. We earlier discounted one supposed trace, 'the Stoic–Cynic diatribe', even in S. K. Stower's modified

---

The trust in a divine enabling (albeit distinctive) means the Stoic analogy is closest.

[10] So it certainly appeared to Ambrose, *De officiis* 2.17. A. J. Malherbe has recently urged the analogy of Bion in Teles (fragments II and IVB, 11H and 15H) commending adaptation to whatever circumstances, poverty most likely, but εὐπορία possibly. However, this seems to be Bion in Cyrenaic mood (cf. Diogenes Laertius 4.51–52 and 2.66); there are no clearly Cynic texts urging such indiscriminate adaptability. (Epictetus 1.1.27, cited by Malherbe, is obviously Stoic; Dio 30.33 is precisely criticising those who take more than they need of what is to hand, as does ps.-Lucian in *The Cynic* 6–7; cf. Diogenes in Philo, *Quod omnis probus liber sit* 122, sharing his surplus): A. J. Malherbe (1996), especially 132–34; and compare K. L. Berry (1996); also M.-O. Goulet-Cazé (1996), 78-79.

[11] T. Engberg-Pedersen (1995b), 279.

version: there is no sign of any such recognised *genre* either of public address or of small group teaching with the cluster of common stylistic devices and range of common topics that has been posited. [12]

The 'natural theology' expressed at Romans 1.19–20 has firm roots in earlier Jewish tradition (e.g., Ps 19.1), and even as a polemical argument had been a part of some Jewish tradition for a century and a half (cf. Wis 13.1–9). Some of the key abstract terms Paul uses (τὰ ἀόρατα . . . ἀΐδιος δύναμις . . . θειότης) echo popular philosophical theology, even though here used to argue an exclusive rather than an inclusive conclusion. But as a philosophical argument, when heard by non-Jews in the ancient Mediterranean world, it would sound like commonplace Stoicism (which may well itself have earlier influenced Wisdom): we may compare Cicero, *De natura deorum* 2.16–17, 87–88. [13] Cynics tended to eschew such speculative abstractions. The larger, polemical argument in which this snatch of natural theology figures has been discussed briefly earlier, along with the Cynic resonances both of a myth of decline and of a refusal of any truck with idolatry. [14] For Paul here the cardinal sin is the idolatrous refusal to acknowledge the one God, and an 'unnatural' (excessive) sexuality is the initial punishment (Rom 1.24–26). We have also noted Cynic objections to (male) homo-

---

[12] S. K. Stowers (1981); P. P. Fuentes González (1990); F. G. Downing (1992a), 44–45; and above, ch. 2, 27–28.

[13] O. Michel (1963), 63, n.3, and C. E. B. Cranfield (1975), 114–15, referring us in particular to Cicero, *De natura deorum* 1.(18) 44, but 1.(17) 45 seems to be the passage intended; however, see all of 1.(16) 43–(18) 49 (here discussing Epicurus); cf. Epictetus 1.6.7–8; Dio 12.27–28, 40.35.

[14] Ch. 7, above, 235-37, referring to ps.-Anacharsis 9 and Dio 30.26–27; and § 4, referring to Antisthenes.

sexuality, at least in so far as it involved 'effeminacy'; though Stoics (like Paul) also emphasised the natural fittingness of heterosexual (marital) union.[15] The further list of vices, headed by the Stoic-sounding τὰ μὴ καθ-ήκοντα (Rom 1.28–32)[16] is as mixed as that at Galatians 5.19–21, but both contain (as we noted above) a preponderance of overt and active terms, rather than the heavy stress on disposition which we find among Stoics; and Paul, of course, emphasises the doing, τὰ γὰρ αὐτὰ πράσσεις (Rom 2.1; cf. 2.6–13).

More distinctively Stoic, and much more significant for Paul's changed approach, are many of the ways he now discusses 'the law', when compared and contrasted with the very negative material from Galatians which we considered in chapter 3: 'When gentiles who do not have the law do by nature what the law requires, they are a law unto themselves; they show that what the law requires is written on their hearts, as their conscience [self-awareness] testifies . . .' (Rom 2.14–15). Even if such language and such ideas had come to Paul from Jewish sources, we must again realise that to non-Jews this could only sound Stoic, and Paul is very unlikely to have been unaware of such resonances or, indeed (in general terms), the source. So Cicero, for instance, talks of 'nature's laws' that anyone can 'listen to', and 'Law is the highest reason, planted in nature, which commands those things that are to be done

---

[15] On homosexuality, above, ch. 4, § 4; on heterosexuality, Epictetus 1.6.7–8 again and Musonius 12 and 14. S. K. Stowers (1994), 94, insists that it is the male passivity (effeminacy) that it is at issue, rather than 'same-sex' relationships as such; D. B. Martin (1995) argues that the issue in contemporary context is primarily one of sexual excess.

[16] Cf. Diogenes Laertius 7.88, 108–109; and J. I. Porter (1996), 161.

and prohibits their opposites.'[17] But, whereas the earlier Stoics had maintained something of the radicalism of their Cynic origins, and were critical of positive and customary law, later Stoics, as we saw above, took custom and positive law very seriously, especially where common strands could be discerned: these 'must' reflect 'the law of nature'. The once Cynically-inclined Paul who told his Galatian Christians 'the law was for the sake of transgressions' and made slaves of those who followed it (Gal 3.19; 5.1) now insists 'the law is holy and just and good' (Rom 7.12).

As compared with the debate in Galatians, the discussion of 'law', 'faith' and 'righting' and 'Israel' in Romans 1–11 is primarily concerned with interiority, despite the odd expections just noted. In Galatians Paul was concerned for the most part with the external 'markers', with circumcision, food laws, and (if only in passing) Sabbath observance.[18]

In Romans, however, issues of interior disposition and conviction – faith – lead the argument (1–11). There is

---

[17] Cicero, *De officiis* 3.24 and.*De legibus* 1.(6) 18; cited by C. K. Barrett (1957), 52; but also Diogenes Laertius 7.88–89. 'Conscience', συνείδησις, in Paul may well not be as technically Stoic as is *conscientia* in Cicero's Latin; but cf. *idem, De officiis* 3.44; *De natura deorum* 3.85 (and cf. C. H. Dodd (1932), 36; U. Wilckens (1978), 133–34). C. E. B. Cranfield (1975), 155–62, argues for a different interpretation (and translation) of these verses. It seems very unlikely that Paul would have left himself so open to the more obvious 'Stoic' sense of his words had he intended something as different as Cranfield suggests. S. K. Stowers in a careful discussion (1994), 109–13, argues that this would be too inconsistent for Paul to have intended it; on which see, however, H. Räisänen [1983] (1986), 101–109.

[18] Arguing against T. Engberg-Pedersen (1995c); cf. ch. 7, § xi, above.

no discussion of getting circumcised,[19] and having been circumcised has little or no relevance; it is only inner disposition that really matters (Rom 2.28–29). The importance of attitude (or intention) as well as action is emphasised in the canonical Jewish source (Deut 10.16 etc.); but for the conviction that attitude (or intention) on its own is what matters, whatever the accompanying action, it is very hard to find any Jewish antecedent, even in such as Philo, as we noted in chapter 3. If it rang any bells among those erstwhile pagans who heard it read, Romans 2.28–29 could only have sounded Stoic.

There are similar contrasts on other issues that were important in Galatians. Now people are to be allowed to retain food laws and special days, 'as long as they are convinced in their own minds' (Rom 14.5–6, 14, 23), whereas in Galatians there was no suggestion of compromise on food, and observing days and seasons amounted to a return to slavery (Gal 2.11–12; 4.9–11).[20]

As in Stoicism, so now in Paul, once the convictions and inner dispositions have been sorted out (Rom 14.1–11), the right actions follow (Rom 14.12–15). And the actions Paul commends often evince an ethos perceptibly closer to Stoicism than does the behaviour urged in the earlier letters (and, even more clearly, are mostly a long way from Cynicism). First we may note that the very Cynic-sounding baptismal slogan 'Neither Jew nor Greek, neither bond nor free, no male and female' (Gal 3.28) has

---

[19] If Romans 2.25 includes a Christian accepting circumcision, then the contrast with Gal 5.2 is even stronger – and stranger.

[20] It is probably a rhetorical coincidence that Paul refers in passing to God as 'Another' (Rom 14.4); but we may perhaps compare Epictetus 1.30.1, 'Another looks from above, and he it is that you must please'; cf. 3.1.43; 3.13.13; *Encheiridion* 17, where it is 'Another' who decides what role each is to play.

no place, no positive echoes, even. So, for instance, Stanley Stowers tellingly points out that implicit in the conviction that heterosexual coitus is 'natural' (Rom 1.26–27) is the assumption that it also expresses the integrally linked and equally 'natural' control by males and subordination of females.[21] 'Neither bond nor free' finds no practical elaboration in Galatians, only passing and ambiguous allusion in the Corinthian letters, but no reference at all in Romans. And rather than 'neither Jew nor Greek' we have now, as we remarked just above, *both* Jewish Christians and gentile Christians, each following their own practice (circumcised and keeping the law, observing purity laws, keeping festivals; or not), so long as they have the appropriate inner attitude (just as Epictetus can allow for pig-meat being held holy or unholy where it is the underlying conviction that constitutes the holiness).[22] (Each of these 'revised' positions indicated in Romans is characteristic of Stoicism, though none is distinctive.)

So Paul prefaces his practical injunctions with an exhortation 'to present your bodies as a living sacrifice', at once explained as λογικὴν λατρείαν, and that as 'the renewal of your minds' (Rom 12.1–2). Again the nearest parallels are in Stoic or Stoic-influenced sources. We may compare Cicero: 'The best and also the purest, holiest and most pious way of worshipping the Gods is always to venerate them with purity, sincerity and innocence both of thought and speech.'[23] In similar vein Epictetus says, 'I would have you know that the most important element in worship of the Gods is to have the right opinions of them as existing and administering the universe well and justly;

---

[21] S. K. Stowers (1994), 94.
[22] Epictetus 1.22.3–4.
[23] Cicero, *De natura deorum* 2.71.

and to have set yourself to obey them and to submit to everything that happens, and to follow voluntarily.'[24]

The remainder of Romans 12 can be readily paralleled from Jewish, other early Christian and varied pagan sources. The final passage where Paul's now clearly Stoic-coloured leanings are displayed is Romans 13.1–7. It is justly pointed out that many Jewish writers agree that rulers are set in power by God.[25] What seems to be missed is that those Jewish authors do not say that therefore rulers must simply be obeyed, nor that they are doing their job well, nor even that people should pay their taxes; a number of them in fact promise the imminent removal of the ruler in question. The optimism and the compliance are Stoic.[26] 'Kings derive their power and stewardship from Zeus', claims Dio, in one of his Stoic pieces, though they must still endeavour to exercise their power in accord with the laws and ordinances of Zeus (sc., of nature).[27] Epictetus can be very critical of individual emperors, but insists, 'I must always obey the state law in every particular'; 'a fine

---

[24] Epictetus, *Encheiridion* 31.1; cf. *idem*, 1.16.15-21: as himself λογικός he celebrates the divine gift of comprehension. Philo, *De spec. leg.* 1.271–72, has worshippers offer themselves as the best of sacrifices: having noble lives to offer, they do so in an interior dialogue. The primacy of the inner mental transformation here in Paul is still closest to this Stoic piety; cf. O. Michel (1955), 292; C. K. Barrett (1957), 231; C. E. B. Cranfield (1979), 602–603.

[25] C. K. Barrett (1957), 245, cites Wisdom 6.3 and Josephus, *War* 2.140; and behind that we may note Dan 4.25, Isa 45.1 and, earlier, 10.5; cf. C. E. B. Cranfield (1979), 663–64; P. Stuhlmacher [1989] (1994), 201–202.

[26] The discrepancy between Paul here and his Jewish tradition known to us has been pointed out by others; cf. J. C. O'Neill (1975), 207–14. O'Neill refers to Stoicism without citing any passage, only Seneca's obedience to Nero's order to commit suicide; cf. also E. Barnikol (1961), 73–74, to whom O'Neill refers.

[27] Dio 1.45; cf. 3.8.

and good man subordinates (ὑποτέταχεν, cf. Paul's ὑπο-
τάσσασθαι) his will to him who administers the universe,
precisely as good citizens [subordinate themselves] to civic
law'.[28] This is a much more Stoic-sounding Paul than the
one who told the Corinthians to stay away from the civic
legal system (1 Cor 6.1–8). But for those who caught the
resonances, they would harmonise well with the firm trust
in divine providential ordering expressed in Romans 8.28–
30, and chapters 9–11.

In his recent *The Tapestry of Early Christian
Discourse*, Vernon Robbins argues against such as Edwin
Judge that the earlier Paul of the Corinthian correspondence had already a 'contra-cultural' as opposed to a
'counter-cultural' stance. For Robbins Paul implicitly
promotes rather than rejects the dominant Mediterranean
culture of his day.[29] Robbins can make this case for the
earlier Paul only by misreading 1 Corinthians 9 simply in
terms of the very idealised and Stoic 'Cyncism' of
Epictetus 3.22. Stoicism is avowedly 'contra-cultural',
Cynicism resolutely 'counter-cultural'.[30] The earlier Paul
had been much closer to Cynicism, much more socially
disturbing. But Robbins' categorisation remains apt for the
later Paul, when much that is potentially disturbing is
internalised, and public conventions are much more widely
maintained. Perhaps strands of popular Stoicism afforded
an altogether safer and more sensible and digestible ethos

---

[28] Epictetus 3.24.108; 1.12.7; cf. 4.7.33; cf. also Cicero's enlisting
religion to support the state and good order, *De natura deorum* 1.3–4,
118; Musonius 15.
[29] V. K. Robbins (1996), 182–89, referring to (among others) E. A.
Judge (1984).
[30] Cf. F. G. Downing (1996c), 210–11.

for vulnerable little communities in Nero's reign than did even the mildest colouring of Cynic radicalism.

It would be very easy from a position of comfort to criticise Paul for a loss of nerve. And some, if they admit at all the movement sketched here from earlier to later Paul, may by contrast see Philippians and Romans as indicative of Paul's growing maturity, discarding all but the last vestiges of an ill-considered flirtation with Cynic radicalism. After all, it was a 'Stoicised', quietist Christian ethos that became dominant, at least in the western church, and that has the continuing allegiance of many Christians. But there may also be involved a loss of some of the heart of Jesus' radicalism, too.

(ii) The Garden

We have noted from time to time suggestions that Epicurean practice and thought may also have provided models for Paul and the early Christians, whether overtly or less directly, through elements of Epicureanism absorbed into popular thought and practice. Wayne Meeks has suggested, 'There is much in the life of these communities that remind us of the Pauline congregations . . . they strove to produce the intimacy of a family among the members, who included male and female, slave and free, bound together by love (philia) . . . there was no rigid hierarchy of office, but some functional differentiation, based on one's advancement in the school's thought . . . Epicurus undertook to maintain that unity among groups of his followers, by writing letters.'[31] Abraham Malherbe had earlier noted

---

[31] W. A. Meeks (1983), 83–84, citing P. H. de Lacy (1948) and N. de Witt (1967) and A. J. Malherbe (1977); cf. also G. Tomlin (1997), and the brief discussion, above, p. 203 and note.

a possible similarity of ethos between the quiet withdrawal of Epicurean groups and the 'quiet life' Paul commended to the Thessalonians; and he then spelled this out in a little more detail later.[32] We have in particular addressed Clarence Glad's argument that the Epicureans provide a much more worthwhile set of analogies for the 'psychogogy' allegedly exercised by Paul in and with his communities than do the Cynic sources on which Malherbe (and I even more) have concentrated.[33]

Malherbe in fact argues that Paul

consciously sought to distinguish Christians from Epicureans [as well as from the Cynics . . . (see above)] . . . he does not speak of friends or friendship, but of brotherly love . . . When Paul says that the Thessalonians were taught by God (*theodidaktoi*) to love one another (1 Thess 4.9), he further distinguishes them from the Epicureans . . . Epicurus had claimed to be self-taught (*auto-didaktos*) . . . The most obvious difference . . . lies in their respective attitudes toward society. Epicureans shunned society . . . Paul's entire discussion [sc., in 1 Thess], on the other hand, is aimed at earning the respect of society by promoting self-sufficiency . . . not an Epicurean withdrawal from society, but the quiet pursuit of the Christians' ordinary lives [earning their livelihoods in ways that such as Philodemus would have despised].[34]

We have also seen that Malherbe has argued that at 1 Corinthians 15.32 Paul is echoing popular polemic against Epicureans as those who pandered to their passions, the 'wild beasts' within.[35]

---

[32] A. J. Malherbe (1977), 25–26 and (1987), 40–43, 84–87, 101–106.
[33] C. E. Glad (1995), 4–12 and 89–98.
[34] A. J. Malherbe (1987), 104–106.
[35] A. J. Malherbe [1968] (1989).

In earlier chapters of this book I have myself allowed that Epicureans as well as Cynics did as Pauline Christians did, they accepted newcomers with no social or moral 'screening' nor any novitiate prior to joining; but I argued that the break from conventional public civic behaviour demanded of Christians would clearly distinguish them from Epicureans and align them much more with Cynics (refusing public cultic rituals and social markers (chapter 1); having at least their leader, Paul, appearing half-naked, displaying the scars of shameful beatings, risking public disturbance, courting further ill-use (chapter 5). And, further, once 'in' one of Paul's communities, members would not in fact find themselves drawn into a mutual 'psychogogy' as a major preoccupation: only in an occasional crisis might they be expected implicitly to exercise the kind of sensitive care for one another that Epicureans sought constantly to practise (chapter 6, *Appendix*). I have myself argued elsewhere that Paul's passing reference to the decay of a creation in travail as 'common knowledge' (Rom 8.19–22) may well echo a popular acceptance of specifically Epicurean cosmology; cf. also 1 Cor 7.31.[36] But among Pauline and other Christians there is no sign of anything like the stress on assimilating a detailed physics (and metaphysics, in effect) that was also an integral part of Epicurean formation (Diogenes Laertius 10.35–36). The *telos* of each group would very obviously have been seen to be quite different.

It is abundantly clear that Epicurean tradition was 'hedonist' only in the most austere and intellectualist way (Diogenes Laertius 10.11). Nonetheless, the movement's

---

[36] F. G. Downing (1995b) and (1995c).

reputation was quite other (as Diogenes Laertius indignant-ly acknowledges, 10.3-9). We have just above recalled Malherbe's discussion of 1 Corinthians 15.32, where he finds Paul seeming to assume that 'Let us eat and drink, for tomorrow we die' (Isa 22.13) represents an unquestionably unacceptable Epicureanism.[37]

Epicureans acknowledged the reality of the Gods of common belief – but not the popular understanding of their powers.[38] Paul's congregations, on the other hand, 'knew' that the beings represented by idols had no divine reality – while Paul himself insisted they were powerfully danger-ous. Epicureans rejected any notion of divine providence (as did many Cynics, too, of course); Paul's congregations were expected to be convinced of God's effective care (as were some Cynics, we have also noted). Epicureans continued to join in the popular cult, as homage to the ideal beings represented.[39] Even if some Pauline Christians felt free to eat sacrificial meat, and that in temple dining rooms, they had turned from idols, and took no part in either local or any other traditional, ancestral cults. When they had to appear in public Epicureans were conformist (whatever their mental reservations). Christians, very like (though not identical with) Cynics, mostly refused to conform.

Such occasional analogies as do appear between early Christian and elements of Epicurean theory and practice that have become part of common culture (as may well be the case with 'frank criticism' in psychogogy) are

---

[37] For the Jewish tradition, *Mishnah Sanhedrin* 10.1; *Aboth* 2.14.

[38] Diogenes Laertius 10.123; Cicero, *De natura deorum* 1.43-51.

[39] Epictetus 2.20-27; Cicero, *De natura deorum* 1.45, 123.

obviously worth our attention. But the Epicurean communities are too different at most points of ethos, practice and aim for them to have been adopted as an overt model by Paul or other early Christians, or to have had any extensive indirect influence. *Pace* Clarence Glad, it seems clear that the Cynic analogies remain much more apposite – and significant.

10

PAUL AND OTHER EARLY CHRISTIANS,
AND THEIR TRADITIONS OF JESUS;
AND JESUS

(i) Early Christian Cynicism

Paul's surviving letters show him in dispute with many and perhaps quite varied fellow-Christians. When we compare his thought with the rest of early Christian writing it is often significantly different. Even if an at all persuasive case has been made out for Paul having assimilated important strands of Cynicism in practice and verbal expression, that might merely indicate just one more Pauline idiosyncrasy. On the other hand, if Paul can be seen perceiving something of the Cynic configuration a number of critics including the present author have discerned in the synoptic tradition in particular, Paul himself seems less arbitrary, he is not wilfully imposing a Cynic reading on a quite alien tradition; and, furthermore, a Cynic reading of the synoptic tradition itself gains something in plausibility.

As a zealot for his people and their sacred traditions, Paul persecuted some early Christian communities (Gal 1.13–14; Phil 3.6). Presumably he saw their life-style and their announced views as a threat to the security and integrity of both nation and inheritance. The insistence of these followers of Jesus that a man whom God had allowed to suffer crucifixion was nonetheless God's anointed leader, God's Messiah, on its own might well have disturbed Paul ('a stumbling-block', 1 Cor 1.23); but much more significant would have been the life-style these 'Messianic Jews' had adopted. As we are often reminded of Judaism over the ages, it is 'orthopraxis' that is central; ideas are secondary, important only if they threaten or actually disturb the faithful observance of the *Torah* as interpreted.[1]

Yet Paul became convinced that he had been encountered by (and himself enlisted by) the Christians' crucified leader, now totally vindicated by God, glorified Messiah and Lord (as his disciples had been claiming). So what Jesus' followers had apparently been *doing* wrong would now be seen by Paul as pre-eminently right. The life-style Paul had tried to eradicate he would now himself adopt and propagate. The Christian-Cynic way of life we have seen Paul enacting and articulating must, then, be presumed to have been his version (even if not a precise imitation) of what he had up to then seen and detested. He now propagated the πίστις, the faithful response to God, that he had tried to destroy (Gal 1.23). At least in broad terms the conclusion seems irresistible; otherwise one would be imagining a Paul become convinced that what his erstwhile opponents had been doing was right, yet himself then doing something other again.

Certainly we must acknowledge that once Paul found himself bound to propagate the faith he had tried to destroy and had reflected on it (over whatever period), the evidence we have shows that the enactment he chose as most appropriate, and large strands of its articulation were

---

[1] G. F. Moore (1927), 110–11; though in our period there was clearly less uniformity of practice than Moore supposed before the Qumran library had been discovered; cf., e.g., J. Neusner (1987), ix–xiii.

patently Cynic in appearance. To live a life that matched his new convictions in a way that would also create the appropriate impression in the Greek towns where he was at home, he would seem to have had to adopt many facets of a fairly gentle but still rigorously self-disciplined Cynicism. If he were to live out and display his new convictions in action, this was (at the time) the most apposite manner. His praxis obviously must be presumed to have mirrored quite closely, if not precisely, that of those he had been opposing, but with whom he now had allied himself.

We need now to consider whether and to what extent we have evidence to support the *a priori* argument just sketched. Does any of the early Christian life-style and discourse witnessed to in our other sources look Cynic; and does Paul show any specific awareness of such Christian–Cynic traits evidenced elsewhere?

A full response to the first question lies in my *Cynics and Christian Origins* and *Christ and the Cynics*.[2] Whether or not Jesus himself had been ´influenced by Cynicism (perhaps spreading into Galilee from one of its historic centres in Gadara), individuals and groups who lived and repeated in the Greek cities of the first-century east Mediterranean much of the material ascribed to Jesus in our synoptic gospels would inevitably have appeared at first sight and still at closer acquaintance to be some kind of Cynic. Cynics provide not just the best and most extensive available analogy (which critics hostile to the further conclusions themselves admit), they provided at many points very close analogies to material in 'Q' (the common material used by Luke and Matthew), in Mark, and in much of the matter peculiar to Matthew. That this is not only the most obvious general comparison, but also the

---

2 F. G. Downing (1992a) and (1988c).

one most apposite in many particulars is clear from discussions among Christian and pagan writers in the following centuries, who make it explicit.[3]

Most significant is the 'mission charge' material in 'Q', in Matthew's and Luke's respective versions, and in Mark. People who followed these varied injunctions, or others at all close, would have seemed to be kinds of Cynic. Cynics varied in their shabby dress, itinerancy, and ways of obtaining food. They did not adopt a uniform practice from which those following the gospel injunctions would be distinguished (though that convenient misinterpretation continues to be parroted by many, with scant or no reference to the varied evidence).[4] It would be enough for some shabbily dressed wanderers, with or without sandals, with or without staff, with or without begging-bag, deliberately to attract attention and invite a following by public address and/or other activity, for them to be discerned as Cynic. Some Cynics begged, some relied on spontaneous contributions, some on patrons; some worked for their living. All made a show of their poverty, rather than maintaining a proper shamefaced reticence. So, as we have seen, Paul parading himself 'hungry and thirsty, [half-]naked and homeless' is displaying an image and deploying slogans from Cynic stock; but he does all this precisely because it is the appropriate working out of the new life he has been drawn into. It provides the appropriate 'spectacle', it is to imitate Christ so others may too, it is to

---

[3] F. G. Downing (1992a), 19–23 (Lucian, Aristides, Galen, Celsus, Justin Martyr); and chapters 7–10, 169–301 ('fathers' of the church); on which see also G. Dorival (1992) and (1993), 419-43; S. Matton (1996); D. Kinney (1996).

[4] F. G. Downing (1992a), 8–12, 26–34; and *JBL*, forthcoming (1998).

allow Christ's power (his kind of power) to be effective.[5] It may well be that it is by living so that Paul is 'crucified with Christ' and thus able to portray him publicly (Gal 2.20; 3.1); certainly it is by accepting tribulations in a Christian–Cynic way, he tells us, that he 'carries round in his body the death of Jesus' (2 Cor 4.8–11).[6]

Paul clearly knows that aspects of this arduous life-style are inculcated in the mission charge in the Jesus tradition and enacted by other wandering 'apostles and the brothers of the Lord, and Kephas' (1 Cor 9.14; 9.4–5). Much of the vocabulary of the various versions of the mission charge is deployed in other parts of Paul's argument in 1 Corinthians 9: the words 'worker', 'hire', 'command', 'eating and drinking', 'authority', 'preaching'. (For details of the case for Paul's awareness of the wider context, the reader is referred to other studies, especially David Wenham's recent survey.)[7] Paul himself, of course, maintains a Cynic freedom to adopt a variant method of obtaining a livelihood; but it is still 'in poverty' that he makes others rich (2 Cor 6.10; as in his own way his Lord has done, 2 Cor 8.9). Though quite obviously it is the match between his life-style and his understanding of Jesus Christ his Lord that is most important to Paul, he is fully aware that this Cynic-seeming way of living is rooted in a part of the wider church's Jesus tradition.

Some other closely related items in the synoptic gospels, however, find no clear echo in Paul's surviving writings. We have noted already that Paul does not warn against wealth, and does not directly insist that others

---

[5] 1 Cor 4.9, 16; 9.1; 1 Thess 1.6; 2 Cor 4.11; 6.4; 12.9–10.

[6] Of course, discipleship involves a cross in the Q tradition, Lk 14.27; D. Wenham (1995), 154–55; D. Seeley (1992).

[7] D. Wenham (1995), 190-200; cf. D. Dungan (1971), 1–80.

adopt the poverty he accepts. There is no encouragement to
emulate the *insouciance* of grass and birds (Luke 12.22–
31). Of course, it is possible that those in Thessalonica who
had given up work had been influenced by these words of
the Lord; but they could as easily have been guided by
common Cynic practice, as we suggested previously
(1 Thess 2.9; 4.11–12; 5.14; cf. 2 Thess 3.6–13).

That much of Paul's own teaching could, however,
readily be interpreted by others along radically Cynic lines
we have argued in connection with the breaches of dietary
and sexual tabus in Corinth. Other passages in Paul's
letters where echoes of early Christian gospel tradition
have often been discerned are mostly compatible at least
with the gentler strands of Cynicism, if not as distinctively
Cynic; Romans 12 is a prime instance.[8]

The way into a Pauline Christian community is
through baptism, in which the identification with the
crucified Christ begins, and the life-style is adopted in
which the identification is continuously to be enacted. Paul
can assume that this will make sense to the Christians in
Rome (Rom 6.1–11). Earlier he had reminded his Galatian
hearers of the 'baptismal formula' which assured those
who had put on Christ that there is now 'no Jew nor Greek,
no bond nor free, no male and female, but all are one in
Christ Jesus' (Gal 3.28). This 'formula', as most take it to
be, most also (as we saw in chapter 1) take as having
belonged to the wider Christian community into which
Paul had been accepted, and not just to the Christian
communities Paul himself founded.

We showed above how distinctively Cynic this
formula would sound; but even more, how 'Cynically'

---

[8] D. Wenham (1995), 287 (and see index); for Cynic analogies, see
F. G. Downing (1988c), 21–28, etc.

disruptive in practice it would have been. It would have needed at least such a practical threat to the Mosaic *Torah* as this would have posed, to have aroused Paul's zealous hostility in the first place: something like this must represent the position of the disruptive Christian groups Paul first encountered, and whose baptism and consequent life-style he was drawn to accept. They must have presented a threat of a seriousness akin to that of Zimri [Zambrias] to have aroused Paul's Phineas-like persecutory zeal in defence of the law (see above, chapter 3). The baptismal formula itself, however, has no clear roots in the Jesus tradition as such. Even if some current scholarship overemphasises indications in the surviving traditions of Jesus' observance of traditional law, there is certainly no sign there of a wholesale repudiation of it. More importantly for the present discussion, while some discern adumbrations of this early Christian practice in stories of Jesus disrupting the patriarchal family, mixing with people of whatever status, and ignoring purity and Sabbath regulations, there is no sign in the earlier letters of any awareness of these specific traditions, either, on Paul's part. (Later on Paul does write, 'I know, and am persuaded in the Lord Jesus that nothing is unclean in itself; but is unclean for anyone who thinks it unclean', Romans 14.14; and this seems to echo Mark 7.15, ascribed to Jesus. But Paul says nothing of the sort in the earlier discussion in 1 Corinthians 8 and 10.)[9]

What we should conclude is that on these fundamental programmatic issues Paul is at one with some at least of the wider Christian communities, and has for now adopted their programmatic Christian–Cynic baptismal

---

[9] D. Wenham (1995), 92–94. That this may be a community or Markan comment is not itself relevant at this juncture.

slogan, whose enactment not long before had aroused his principled and zealous hostility. We have seen in particular how clearly Cynic would have sounded Paul's own consequent very critical discussion of 'law' in Galatians, how Cynic his life-style would have appeared, as well as what he had to say about it in general, and also his self-presentation as a teacher. Whether the Christian churches' origins were genuinely Cynic or not (whether or not they stemmed, as I argue, from a Jewish–Cynic Jesus), 'interpreting' them from out of his own Jewish Hellenistic context Paul has discerned much of their practice and ethos as Cynic, most naturally to be interpreted by him to others in practice that could only look Cynic and best put into words and phrases that could only sound Cynic.[10]

Obviously these findings (if in fact found persuasive) are important for our understanding of Paul; but they are also highly significant for our understanding of the churches prior to his 'conversion–conscription'. Paul tells us that 'after fourteen years' he checked out the message he'd been sharing with leading Christians in Jerusalem 'lest somehow I should be running or had been running in vain' (Gal 2.2).[11] It was apparently agreed that in essentials he was on the right lines. The implications for legal matters (circumcision, diet and Sabbath, in particular) of the 'neither Jew nor Greek' in the baptismal formula did

---

[10] It is probably worth noting that Paul's later emphasis on 'interiority' (which we have agreed, suggests a more Stoicising ethos) also has some antecedent in the gospel tradition. We have noted Mark 7.14–23 already; but also relevant are Lk 11.37–41 (Q), and Mt 5.28; see the parallels from Epictetus listed in F. G. Downing (1988c), 64 and 93.

[11] As is well known, the period covered by Paul's 'three' and 'fourteen' years could be as little as twelve, as much as sixteen; cf. R. Jewett (1979), 95–100; G. Lüdemann [1980] (1984), 59–64; J. Murphy-O'Connor (1996) 7–8.

become controversial. On no other point where Paul
appears Cynic in his behaviour and his articulation of it
does he have to defend himself: in fact, quite the opposite.
His Cynic-seeming practice and Cynic-sounding accounts
of it are deployed as having considerable apologetic value
in controversy, and especially in 2 Corinthians, in response
to those who (even if not original apostles) represent a rival
'conservative' strand among the early communities. Paul
can match their claims both to Jewish inheritance and to
Cynic life-style: 'Hebrews . . . Israelites . . . descendents of
Abraham . . . ministers of Christ... in laborious hard work,
going without sleep, hungry, thirsty, fasting, cold,
[half-]naked' (2 Cor 11.22, 27). For his response to have
seemed to Paul himself to have had worthwhile force, he
must have seen the Cynic presentation of these central
strands in his practice as affording quite uncontrovertibly
important and agreed common ground.

Already before Paul joined them around 33CE,
within a year or within at most three of the crucifixion of
Jesus, the early Christian communites in many significant
ways looked and sounded Cynic, to others like Paul, and to
themselves; and then went on doing so.

(ii) Jesus as a Cynic for a Cynic church and a Cynic Paul

From Paul, then, it would seem there is no evidence for a
church that ever looked or sounded other than recognisably
Cynic in many important respects. Acts, written perhaps
half a century later, certainly presents a rather different
impression: but that is very much in line with Luke's
deliberate decision to divide the radical Jesus of the
Galilaean spring from the summer of the early community
(and the fruitful autumn of Paul's mission). Luke 22.35–38

explicitly restricts the Cynic-seeming mission of Jesus to the time before his death. The other gospels make no such division; and, as we have seen, Paul presupposes the continuing relevance of the mission charge which Luke decades later thus relegates to the closed period of Jesus' time in Galilee.

This conclusion would then seem to afford strong support for the conviction that the Jesus movement had been wide open to such a Cynic 'reading' from its very inception, in Jesus' own deeds and words. And the sheer quantity of Cynic resonances in the oldest Jesus traditions would point to a popular culture in which such life-styles and such ideas were already current, available for Jesus to develop in social interplay among people used to such talk and such behaviour.

The evidence is presented in some detail in my *Christ and the Cynics* and my *Cynics and Christian Origins* already referred to.[12] As I have allowed there and in other studies, the data I adduce is open to other [re-]constructions; I have argued that these rival interpretations should simply prove less persuasive.

The most thorough way to rebut my case is to take those accounts of utterances and other actions in the gospels that most closely resemble available Cynic materials, and provide the gospel matter with contexts that would indicate something distinctively other than Cynic is intended, and that this distinctive intention would have been readily discerned in the setting in life of Jesus and/or the early Christians. I responded to one such essay (that of C. M. Tuckett) in my *Cynics and Christian Origins*, and do

---

[12] F. G. Downing (1988c) and (1992a).

not intend to repeat that here.[13] The most recent at all detailed attempt along such lines that has come my way is that of Ben Witherington III in his *Jesus the Sage – The Pilgrimage of Wisdom*[14] (which unfortunately does not refer to the more developed arguments of my *Cynics and Christian Origins*, where further attention is given to possible Jewish prophetic and Wisdom sources).

Witherington discusses a small selection of the evidence for Cynic dress, overemphasising (as do many) its supposed uniformity so as to distinguish Cynics from Christian emissaries; but in fact provides no evidence from Jewish or other sources for non-Cynic wandering preachers making this or any other kind of overt poverty the focus of their approach to people at large. (Josephus' account of Essenes travelling light to visit other known or unknown members of their dispersed community affords no close analogy at all.)[15]

Keeping for the moment to the central theme of poverty, Witherington notes that Proverbs is as ready to suggest lessons from 'nature' as any Cynic, and argues that so it affords a more plausible context in Jewish Wisdom for Jesus' lesson from flowers and birds. But the fact is that none of the Jewish material anyone has so far adduced

---

[13] F. G. Downing (1992a), 1–18 and 115–68, responding to C. M. Tuckett (1989), in his rather hasty and over-generalised criticism of F. G. Downing (1988a)); see also F. G. Downing (1994a), and more recently L. Vaage (1994a) and (1995b). For a more general critique of various 'Cynic Jesus' hypotheses, see H. D. Betz (1994), and P. R. Eddy (1996); with response from D. Seeley (1996) and (1997); and F. G. Downing *JBL* (1998) (forthcoming).

[14] B. Witherington (1994), 123–45 (responding to other work beside my own). I note also N. T. Wright' very courteous discussion (1997), 66-73, but find there no fresh arguments against the Cynic reading of the Jesus traditions which I have been proposing.

[15] Witherington (1994), 126, citing Josephus, *War* 2.125–27.

commends such *insouciant* simplicity as Jesus does at Luke 12.22–31; whereas the Cynic tradition provides numerous examples. Witherington, however, is sure that the motivation is different – for Cynics, *autarkeia*; for Jesus, dependence on God. In fact some of the Cynic instances also include an explicit reference to the underlying divine care being relied on, and no Jewish sources are cited proposing that dependence on God takes this form.[16]

The Jesus of the gospel tradition opposes wealth absolutely, as do the Cynics. Witherington only touches on this in passing, discussing a passage I cited from Epictetus to illustrate Mark's snapshot of Jesus approached as a moral philosopher. One might well find material in Jewish sources as critical of wealth, as aware of its dangers as Epictetus in Cynic mood. But certainly for the most part Wisdom writers see wealth as a relative good; for the prophetic tradition, wealth is a sign of divine favour. Essene initiates shared with their new community any wealth they brought, they did not give it away. For a total rejection of wealth no wider Jewish context seems to be forthcoming.[17]

Other issues touched on by Witherington may be dealt with more briefly. The dating of the available Cynic material is no more crucial than that of some of the Wisdom or other Jewish evidence adduced by him or others; especially when many classical scholars discern a high degree of continuity in (varied) Cynic practice and teaching.[18] It is enough that we have some of the sorts of

---

[16] Witherington (1994), 133–34, citing Proverbs 6.6, which says the exact opposite: 'Go to the ant, you sluggard!'; cf. F. G. Downing (1988c), 68–71, for numerous Cynic or Cynic-influenced examples.

[17] B. Witherington (1994), 137–38; Mk 10.17–26, and other passages.

[18] For references, F. G. Downing (1992a), 78, n. 85; but see especially J. H. Moles (1983a), 103 and notes 3 and 7: 'The continuity of Cynic ideas over the centuries is indeed striking.'

things done and said by acknowledged Cynics around the first century CE. (The 'early Jewish parables' instanced by Witherington are, of course, recorded much later than the main Cynic or Cynic–Stoic analogies cited by me.) That the Jesus tradition lacks the 'Cynic–Stoic diatribe' invented by nineteenth-century philologists is irrelevant.[19] That it lacks the sexual 'shamelessness' of some strands of Cynic tradition is not particularly significant; other 'shameless' traits – including a deliberate display of shabbiness – were as important and more common (as is argued above, chapter 2). For theistic Cynics 'living according to nature' was living as God or Gods intended, and so has that at least in common with Jesus' Jewish theism. Some Cynics travelled widely, others (like Jesus) did not.

More often Witherington admits this or that similarity between the two traditions, but insists it represents a 'non-Cynic specific' feature. That I have in no way denied. It was enough for my case to display compatibility with Cynicism in a great many instances (even that some Cynics could talk of 'daimones' is not irrelevant). It is only in a limited but central range of features (especially those summarised above) that I have argued for distinctively Cynic characteristics shared by the Jesus tradition. However, when the whole pattern, both of distinctive traits *and* of the complex in each of characteristic though individually not distinctive traits is assembled, then the marked similarities between the two movements emerge (still allowing for differences *within* both and *between* both).[20]

---

[19] P. P. Fuentes González (1990), again.

[20] Witherington's discussion then of work by B. Mack (1988) and J. D. Crossan (1991) I shall leave on one side. But any arbitrary exclusion from consideration of healing stories and eschatological hopes in the

The overlap between the whole (varied) complex of tradition ascribed to Jesus and the whole (also varied) complex of Cynic tradition is not total (and for my own part I have refused the temptation to prune the Jesus tradition to fit (which others have done by excising the Christology, eschatology, healing and exorcisms). Only in a range of instances, especially on the impoverished life-style, as just rehearsed, is the overlap both close and distinctive. But it is the extent of the total that is remarkable. As I have pointed out before, there is a greater degree of overlap between the synoptic traditions of Jesus and Cynic tradition than, for instance, between such Christian documents as the Johannine epistles and James, respectively. The Jesus traditions and Paul are themselves, in turn, not only close to different strands of Cynicism, but mostly closer *verbally* to those than to each other. It is no effective rejoinder to insist strenuously that the apparent Christian–Cynic parallels are 'only apparent', and that in context each is (or is likely to be shown to be) rather or quite different in intent.[21] There are so many 'apparent' Cynic parallels in the gospel material that they create their own context of meaning – and it is very like that of some of the Cynics. (This point will be elaborated a little further, below.)

On occasion Witherington allows that a substantial similarity in attitude and praxis appears in both of the traditions, gospel and Cynic, but suggests coincidence, as others have, too.[22] The most reflective statement of this approach that I have met comes from Leif Vaage,

---

Jesus tradition, I would agree (as Witherington notes), is to be deprecated.

[21] E. g., H. D. Betz (1994), 474, § 5.

[22] E.g., M. Goodman (1990).

especially in his *Galilean Upstarts - Jesus' First Followers According to Q*.[23] Vaage characterises previous work of mine as 'genealogical', too concerned with origins. It is far better to deploy comparison so as to achieve a more effective social description. And in line with this Vaage concludes,

> Recognising that the specific diction of Q cannot simply be equated with the speech of other Cynic documents, Q nonetheless shares with Cynicism the same basic socio-historical strategy. Both the formative stratum of Q and the Cynics pursued in word and deed a posture of committed marginality, programmatically suspicious of local society's promises to provide through conformity to its norms and codes a measure of happiness. Both the persons whom Q represents and the Cynics opted instead for a different way, some of whose more notable peculiarities have been noted in the preceding pages. If the first followers of Jesus in Galilee were not 'just' Cynics, they were at least very much like them.[24]

I remain unconvinced that the issue may reasonably be left as this last sentence puts it. Vaage himself has argued, as I have, that there is significantly less in common between Q and other suggested cultural contexts provided by Judaism (Jewish Wisdom writings, or the prophets). So in what socio-cultural context could the Q material plausibly come to life? Surely it must be one in which something of this way of living, these attitudes and ways of articulating them, was already in some measure available.

---

[23] L. Vaage (1994a); cf. also his review of F. G. Downing (1992a), L. Vaage (1994b), and more recently (but perhaps written earlier), *idem* (1995b).

[24] L. Vaage (1995b), 228–29. (With the discrimination of 'strata' in Q, and a preference for one stratum in particular I am much less happy: see F. G. Downing (1996).)

The variegated original Cynicism our accepted sources display did not spring fully fledged from the bearded head or bare shoulders of Diogenes; it clearly had its origins in the Socratic circle and its antecedents; and what we see had developed over the centuries since then.[25] So it seems to me extremely unlikely (though perhaps not utterly impossible) that the Q material (coming from Jesus or Jesus and some early followers) should have been shared as an effective praxis and *lived* language-game without major significant antecedents. To rephrase the point, it is hard to imagine Jesus (or even Jesus and a few friends) inventing a 'private language' of actions and utterances as characteristically and often as distinctively Cynic-seeming as Vaage and others (including myself) have shown the Q material to be; inventing such a social praxis *e nihilo*, and still encountering others who found it comprehensible enough to share it.[26]

If we mean to elaborate an hypothesis which places the Q material (from Jesus or Jesus and friends) in the Galilee of the second quarter of the first century CE, then we seem to have to suppose Cynic ways and Cynic talk were already in some measure in circulation there. There are yet other hypotheses, as I have noted.[27] We might, at the least implausible, suggest that the most distinctively Cynic-seeming strands had been added later, when Jesus' followers moved into the Greek cities, though no one has

---

[25] M.-O. Goulet-Cazé (1986).

[26] Vaage cites J. Z. Smith (1990) in support of his preference for interpretative comparison over against any 'genetic' interest. Smith's main concern, on my reading, is with the acceptance or rejection of 'genealogy' for 'apologetic' reasons, and he presents no arguments against an unprejudiced concern for origins as part of a full attempt to describe and understand.

[27] F. G. Downing (1992a), 150–53.

yet offered a convincing reconstruction of how this could have happened. And now that we have found Paul 'reading' Christianity in Cynic terms in the early thirties CE, it seems even less likely. We would have to suppose a very swift and very smooth adaptation for this to be the one agreed Christian life-style which Paul found in Damascus within three years at most of the death of Jesus, and which was reaffirmed in his later meetings with the leaders in Jerusalem. Certainly it cannot have been Paul's own particular Cynic reading of Christian discipleship that had subsequently found its way into the gospel tradition, for there the verbal parallels are so slender, as we have already had cause to recall.

(This is a necessary refinement of my earlier brief discussions of the implications for our understanding of the Jesus tradition of Paul's links with Cynicism, whose extent I previously failed to appreciate.)[28]

Yet what warrant have we, what evidence at all, for a Galilaean culture where some leading strands of Cynicism were at home, for Jesus to select, elaborate, develop? Apart from the very tenuous evidence of Josephus' willingness to designate Judas of Galilee's ideas, the 'fourth' Jewish philosophy, in apparently Cynic terms,[29] it is clear that we have no independent testimony for any Cynicism in Galilee whatsoever. But the important fact to recall (the fact that my critics and others seem conveniently to overlook) is that *we have no considerable independent evidence of any kind from any source for the general*

---

[28] F. G. Downing (1992a), 150–53, again.

[29] Josephus, *Antiquities* 18.3–25: 'freedom', refusal of any human master, acceptance of *ponos*, disparagement of the temple; F. G. Downing (1992a), 153–54. This more positive account than Josephus' usual disparagement offers, as I have said, 'some small support' to my thesis. Perhaps it is a genuine recollection.

culture of Galilee in the twenties and thirties CE.[30] The only at all extensive documentary evidence we have that even purports to relate to Galilee in these decades is that of the Christian gospels. And the three synoptic gospels, generally taken as the closest to Galilee, clearly indicate that Cynic-seeming practices and ideas for which few if any more traditional Jewish antecedents are to be found could be readily understood and adopted, in a mix with other items whose traditional Jewish context is as obvious. If we agree that the synoptic gospels take us back to Galilee at all, it is to a Galilee where something that functions like a kind of Cynicism (Vaage) and that looks very like a kind of Cynic Judaism, makes good sense to the indigenous population.

I insist, yet again, this is a hypothetical recon-struction on the basis of the gospels. Other hypotheses may be advanced. They are no less hypothetical, though often less plausible. We might want to imagine a Galilee whose culture can be illuminated by the roughly contemporary collection of scrolls from around Qumran. If we may designate the scrolls' collectors as Essenes (at least, Essenes of some kind), we still have to admit that we have no independent evidence for Essene influence on the culture of Galilee. For what the point is worth, Josephus never refers to Essenes in the north. But, more importantly, the synoptic gospels overlap very little with matter emanating from around Qumran, and clearly very much less than with our Cynic texts.[31] The same has to be said

---

[30] Cf. S. Freyne (1980), (1988a), (1988b) and (1992); R. A. Horsley (1987), (1989), (1985 with J. Hanson), (1995); H. C. Kee (1992); F. G. Downing (1992a), 146.

[31] G. Vermes (1977), 210–21; J. C. VanderKam (1994); contrast C. A. Evans (1995), 47 and 153–54; and *pace* B. Thiering (1996), 216, n. 4.

for any use of later Rabbinic materials to illustrate the culture of first-century Galilee; even drawing from as generous a chronological and ideological range as for instance S. T. Lachs has done produces far less for close comparison than do our Cynic sources.[32]

The initial plausibility of the hypothesis of a Galilaean culture already in some measure influenced by strands of Cynicism depends on a number of arguments I have previously repeated from others, or advanced myself, and which I do not intend to defend again here. First, that Judaism was part of the Hellenised east Mediterranean world, and had been for centuries. Second, that Cynicism was widespread in that east Mediterranean world. Third, that there are indications which others have tended to overlook, of Cynics taking to the villages and the countryside; and clearly they would not restrict themselves to towns and deliberately avoid villages en route in their travels on foot.[33] Fourth (as has been recently pointed out to me) if anyone in Galilee learned to read and write Greek, they would meet Diogenes and Crates and their Cynic traditions in the *progymnasmata*, the basic school texts. Fifth, Gadara, in the Palestinian Decapolis, seems to have sustained a Cynic tradition (and was of course much closer to Galilee than were Qumran or Jerusalem).[34]

---

[32] S. T. Lachs (1987); made full use of in F. G. Downing (1988c).

[33] F. G. Downing (1992a), 57–112; and 145–49.

[34] Allowing this (but not the influence on Galilee), H. D. Betz (1994), 471, and n.112, citing the Cynics Menippus, Meleager and Oenomaus; I have also noted the relevance of the Gadarene Epicurean writer Philodemus' interest in Cynicism. Quite how B. Mack (1993), 58, managed to co-opt Philodemus as himself a Cynic I cannot, however, tell. A. E. Harvey's insistence (1993) that this still leaves us with no evidence for Cynics in Palestine is simply perverse. (Even if one were to choose arbitrarily and unilaterally to redefine 'Palestine' as com-

To repeat, Paul encountered a Jesus movement which he readily interpreted in Cynic terms. Some aspects of that interpretation (circumcision, diet, sabbath) did become controversial. But not only did Paul find no need to defend his Cynic interpretation as a whole against his predecessors, he could continue for some years to deploy very significant aspects of it in defence and attack, as we have seen. It seems extremely unlikely (but of course, not impossible) that the Jesus movement could have taken so strong a Cynic cast overnight, as it were; much more likely that it had been Cynic in many respects from the start, in Jesus' practice and his articulation of it, in a Galilaean context where this was already a plausible option. The Jesus tradition and the Christian communities that followed seem to have had their own clear and specific Cynic colouring(s) from the very start.

---

prising only land west of the Jordan, the proximity of Gadara to Galilee, and their interdependence would still remain as relevant. Josephus, as our main source, treats the Decapolis as part of a single area of Palestine, and indicates Gadara's links with Galilee.) B. Witherington III (1994), 127, 142, while himself preferring the inner-Jewish context for Jesus, accepts on the basis of Gadarene Cynicism and some of the parallels I have adduced that one must not too quickly dismiss the possibility of Cynic influence on Jesus; cf. also H. Chadwick (1994), 209–10. (Intriguingly, Robert Graves' recalled T. E. Lawrence in 1920 discussing with the current Regius Professor of Divinity in the University of Oxford 'the importance of the University of Gadara' for early Chrstianity: R. Graves (1960), 243.)

11

CONCLUSIONS

So, what may we suppose we have shown?

It may with fair confidence be claimed (*a*) that we have shown that it is very likely that Paul would have been seen and heard by Hellenistic gentiles as some sort of Cynic. If such people were to 'place' Paul at all, this was their only ready category. This is not a particularly novel deduction in itself; it has often been suggested in more general terms, without the benefit of a detailed examination of the evidence such as has been offered here. The visual impression is foremost: Paul, hungry and thirsty, half-naked, displaying his shameful scars, homeless, sweating his guts out to earn a crust – and making a virtue of it, as he articulates it in Cynic terms, as the necessary (not Stoic-incidental) expression of his mission, his self-presentation as a teacher. He invites to membership of a group which is neither Jew nor Greek, where (in those early days, for sure) there is no distinction of slave or free, and 'no male and female'. He draws people away from their own sacred traditions, without substituting any ancient equivalent, rather, disparaging 'law', offering many prized conventions no respect.

Hellenised gentiles used to attending synagogue might well have discerned much Jewish (including the new Christian–Jewish) impetus in what Paul meant, but even they could not have missed the pervasive Cynic strands in what Paul said as well as in what he did. And there do not seem in the event to have been many such gentile synagogue regulars, acculturated to Judaism, among those drawn in by Paul initially – few if any in Galatia or Macedonia.

The Cynic strands in Paul's ascetic praxis and in his verbal articulation of it are so strong and so pervasive that it seems very unlikely that Paul could have been left unaware that it was in this light that people were seeing and hearing him. This second conclusion (*b*) seems to be entailed by the first.

From that it seems to follow (*c*) that it was deliberate. Even if Paul had hit on these Cynic-seeming strategies initially unawares, his persistence with them must have been deliberate; it would have been so easy, had he so wished, to change the impression, to smarten the appearance, to adapt some other of the many intellectual language-games available - even to use the ready-made Hellenistic Jewish materials that John Barclay has shown Paul so largely and so surprisingly refuses. But could Paul have drifted into this life-style, this Cynic field of discourse unawares? It seems scarcely probable. As Abraham Malherbe has argued (and as often cited above), Paul shows clear signs of knowing his way round this material, of being able to work with the details of the inner-Cynic debate. Once (*a*) and (*b*) are accepted, it seems we must also accept that for Paul this Cynic-looking praxis and these Cynic-sounding ways of saying things, there at a popular level in his shared Hellenistic culture, must have seemed at the start best suited to evince and articulate and to communicate what he intended. A 'Jewish–Christian Cynicism' was in the early years integral to Paul's emerging sense of mission, to his evolving self-understanding, to his developing response to God, Christ, Spirit.

Because we only have Paul's side of the 'conversation' even when he seems to be quoting those he addresses, we only have indirect evidence of (*d*), the ways in which converts responded to the clearly Cynic ethos of much of what Paul did and said, and our conclusions must therefore be that much more tentative (given that all historical reconstructions are provisional, even if some are more tentative than others). First-century east Mediterranean Cynicism came in many varieties; once the resonances were perceived it would have been only too easy to make different choices than Paul saw fit, from the rich menu of associated ideas and practices. So people in Thessalonica may well have given up work as the appropriate response to the new age, people in Corinth seem still more clearly to have decided to indulge their newly acquired royal prerogative. Whether driven by such unwelcome readings of his message or not, Paul himself then appears to move away from his earlier radicalism to the more Stoic-seeming – and more seemly – stance evinced in Philippians and Romans.

If conclusions (*a*), (*b*) and (*c*) seem well warranted, then we may have a more coherent picture of Paul's place in the Jesus movement (a more coherent picture than was offered in my *Cynics and Christian Origins*). Could a language of Cynic performance and ideas have seemed best suited to Paul because the Jesus movement he had persecuted but now attached himself to had itself looked to him significantly Cynic in ethos? and could Paul then have been right, the Jesus movement was in some effective measure (and not just coincidentally) Cynic as well as Jewish in origin? Among competing reconstructions it may seem that this (*e*) is at least no less plausible than the best of the rest. It would make good sense. But, of course, history does not have to.

This study has been primarily concerned with (*a*), with evidence for the likely reception of Paul by those he approached, as some sort of Cynic; from which (*b*) and (*c*) would seem to follow (with (*d*) and (*e*) as plausible corollaries). We have not discussed at length how this may affect our overall understanding of Paul, nor our interpretation of themes in Paul only touched on or passed over here, although (*b*) and even more (*c*) are obviously relevant. Suffice it to sketch some possibilities.

The theologians' Paul tends to be cerebral, or perhaps cerebral and emotional. The Lutheran Paul of 'justification by faith'[1] must not rely on 'doing'; and even the post-Lutheran Paul of E. P. Sanders and of J. D. G. Dunn and others eschews social markers.[2] All the distinctive things he says he does must be read in a Stoic sense as events that happen to him, and in which his faith and God's grace sustain him. A Cynic Jewish–Christian Paul, on the other hand, does very distinctive and socially disruptive things and presents the doing as integral to his enacted response to what God has effected in the life, death and resurrection of Jesus. To put it bluntly, in first-century context, Paul's ascetic practice is part and parcel of his gospel (just as Jesus' ascetic practice was part and

---

[1] 'My' Paul for a long while (for what the note is worth), and still a Paul to whom I remain attached, as part of the picture.

[2] J. T. Sanders (1997) has recently argued that Paul nonetheless insitutes his own 'social markers'. What I have tried to show is that any such would have appeared Cynic, as the closest (and often very close) analogy available.

ABBREVIATIONS

In the names of publishing houses words such as 'press' and 'Verlag' have been omitted; so, too, the word 'university' where a press is known by a university's locality.

AB	Anchor Bible.
AC	*L'Antiquité Classique*
ANRW	*Aufstieg und Niedergang der römischen Welt* (ed. W. Hasse & H. Temporini).
BETL	Bibliotheca ephemeridum theologicarum Lovaniensum.
BHT	Beitrage zur historischen Theologie.
Bib.	*Biblica.*
Bib.Int.	*Biblical Interpretation.*
BIS	Biblical Interpetation Series.
BNTC	Black's New Testament Commentary.
BR	*Biblical Research.*
BSP	Bochumer Studien zur Philosophie.
CBQ	*Catholic Biblical Quarterly.*
CCWJC	Cambridge Commentaries on Writings of the Jewish and Christian World 200 BC to AD 200.
CNT	Commentaire du Nouveau Testament.
CQ	*Classical Quarterly.*
CS	Classical Studies.
CUP	Cambridge University Press.
DLT	Darton, Longman & Todd.
EKKNT	Evangelisch-katholischer Kommentar zum Neuen Testament.
ET	English translation.
FRLANT	Forschungen zur Religion und Literatur des Alten und Neuen Testaments.
FzB	Forschung zur Bibel.
GR	*Greece and Rome.*
GRR	Graeco-Roman Religion.
GTA	Göttingen theologische Arbeiten.
HCS	Hellenistic Culture and Society.
HTR	*Harvard Theological Review.*
HTS	Harvard Theological Studies.
IBS	*Irish Biblical Studies.*
ICC	International Critical Commentary.

IDB	*Interpreter's Dictionary of the Bible .* (ed. G. A. Buttrick).
IVP	Inter-Varsity Press.
JAC	*Jahrbuch für Antike und Christentum.*
JAP	*Journal of Applied Philosophy.*
JBL	*Journal of Biblical Literature.*
JEH	*Journal of Ecclesiastical History.*
JfSJ	*Journal for the Study of Judaism.*
JHC	*Journal of Higher Criticism.*
JHS	*Journal of Hellenic Studies.*
JJS	*Journal of Jewish Studies.*
JQR	*Jewish Quarterly Review.*
JR	*Journal of Religion.*
JRS	*Journal of Roman Studies.*
JSNT	*Journal for the Study of the New Testament.*
JSNTSS	*Journal for the Study of the New Testament* *Supplement Series.*
JSOT	*Journal for the Study of the Old Testament.*
JTS (NS)	*Journal of Theological Studies (New Series).*
LCL	*Loeb Classical Library.*
LCM	*Liverpool Classical Monthly.*
Nov.T.	*Novum Testamentum.*
NTS	*New Testament Studies.*
NTD	Das Neue Testament Deutsch.
PA	Philosophia Antiqua.
RAC	*Reallexikon für Antike und Christentum.*
RQ	*Restoration Quarterly.*
RTP	*Revue de théologie et philosophie.*
SAC	Sheffield Academic Press.
SBB	Stuttgarter biblische Beiträge.
SBLDS	Society of Biblical Literature Dissertation Series.
SBLSBS	Society of Biblical Literature Sources for Biblical Study.
SBLTT	Society of Biblical Literature Texts and Translations.
SBS	Sources for Biblical Studies.
SBT	Studies in Biblical Theology.
SCM	Student Christian Movement Press.
SHTC	*Studies in the History of Christian Thought.*
SNTS	Society for New Testament Study/ Studiorum Novi Testamenti Societas.
SNTSMS	Society of Biblical Studies Monograph Series.
SPCK	Society for the Promotion of Christian Knowledge.
SWR	Studies in Women and Religion.
TAPA	Transactions of the American Philological Association.
TDNT	Theological Dictionary of the New Testament.

TJT	*Toronto Journal of Theology.*
TPI	Trinity Press International.
TU	*Texte und Untersuchungen.*
TZ	*Theologische Zeitschrift.*
V & R	Vandenhoeck & Ruprecht.
WBC	Word Biblical Commentary.
WUNT	Wissenschaftliche Untersuchungen zum Neuen Testament.
YCS	Yale Classical Studies.
ZNW	*Zeitschrift für die neutestamentliche Wissenschaft.*
ZTK	*Zeitschrift für Theologie und Kirche.*

BIBLIOGRAPHY

There is a fuller Bibliography for Cynicism as such, including Cynicism as it relates to Christian writings of the second to the fifth centuries, in F. Gerald Downing, *Cynics and Christian Origins* (Edinburgh: T & T Clark, 1992), to which this volume is now the sequel.

Not all the books and articles listed here are referred to in the preceding text, but they have been used in thinking through the contents.

J.-N. Aletti, 1990, 'La présence d'un modèle rhétorique en Romains: Son rôle et son importance,' *Biblica* 71.1, 1–24.

J.-N. Aletti, 1992, 'La *dispositio* rhétorique dans les épîtres pauliniens: Proposition de méthode,' *NTS* 38.4, 385–401.

L. Alexander, 1993, 'Acts and Ancient Intellectual Biography,' in Winter and Clarke (eds), 31–64.

L. Alexander, 1995, 'Paul and the Hellenistic Schools: The Evidence of Galen,' in *Paul in his Hellenistic Context* (ed. Engberg-Pedersen), 60–83.

G. Anderson, 1994, *Sage, Saint and Sophist. Holy Men and their Associates in the Early Roman Empire* (London: Routledge).

S. B. Andrews, 1995, 'Too Weak not to Lead: The Form and Function of 2 Cor 11.23b–33,' *NTS* 41.2, 263–76.

R. G. Andria, 1980, 'Diogene Cinico nei Papiri Ercolanesi,' *Cronache Ercolanesi*, 10. 129–51.

W. F. Arndt and F. W. Gingrich (eds), 1979, *A Greek-English Lexicon to the New Testament* (ET of W. Bauer; Chicago: U. P.).

H. von Arnim, 1903, *Stoicorum Veterum Fragmenta* (Leipzig: Teubner).

H. W. Attridge, 1976, *First Century Cynicism in the Epistles of Heraclitus* (HTS XXIX; Missoula: Scholars).

D. E. Aune, 1983, *Prophecy in Early Christianity and the Ancient Mediterranean World* (Grand Rapids: Eerdmans).

D. E. Aune, 1990, 'Herakles and Christ: Herakles Imagery in the Christology of early Christianity,' in *Greeks, Romans* (ed. D. Balch *et al.*), 3–19.

F. C. Babbitt, 1927 (ed. & tr.), Plutarch, *Moralia* (LCL; Cambridge, Mass: Harvard; London, Heinemann).

D. Balch, 1983, '1 Cor 7:32–35 and Stoic Debates about Marriage, Anxiety and Distraction,' *JBL* 102.4, 429–39.

D. Balch, E. Ferguson, & W. A. Meeks (eds), 1990, *Greeks, Romans and Christians: Essays in Honor of A. J. Malherbe* (Minneapolis: Fortress).

H. C. Baldry, 1965, *The Unity of Mankind in Greek Thought* (Cambridge: U.P.).

J. M. G. Barclay, 1988, *Obeying the Truth. A Study of Paul's Ethics in Galatians* (Edinburgh: T & T Clark).

J. M. G. Barclay, 1996, *Jews in the Mediterranean Diaspora from Alexander to Trajan (323 BCE–117 CE)* (Edinburgh: T & T Clark).

E. Barnikol, 1961, 'Römer 13,' in *Studien zum neuen Testament und zur Patristik. Erich Klostermann zum 90 Geburtstag* (TU 77; Berlin: Akademie).

C. K. Barrett, 1957, *The Epistle to the Romans* (BNTC; London: A & C Black).

S. S. Bartchy, 1973, ΜΑΛΛΟΝ ΧΡΗΣΑΙ: *First Century Slavery and 1 Corinthians 7:21* (SBLDS 11; Atlanta: Scholars).

J. R. Bartlett, 1985, *Jews in the Hellenistic World. Josephus, Aristeas, the Sibylline Oracles, Eupolemus* (CCWJC 1i; Cambridge: Cambridge University Press).

S. C. Barton, 1986, 'Paul's Sense of Place: An anthropological Approach to Community Formation in Corinth,' *NTS* 32.2, 225–246.

S. C. Barton, 1989, review of F. G. Downing (1987b), *Theology* XCII 745, 50–52.

J. M. Bassler (ed.), 1991, *Pauline Theology I: Thessalonians, Philippians, Galatians, Philemon* (Minneapolis: Fortress).

J. M. Bassler, 1993, 'Paul's Theology: Whence and Whither?,' in *Paul's Theology II* (ed. D. M. Hay), 3–17.

R. A. Batey, 1984, 'Jesus and the Theatre,' *NTS* 30.4, 563–73.

R. Bauckham, 1991, 'The Rich Man and Lazarus: The Parable and the Parallels,' *NTS* 37.2, 353–68.

F. W. Beare, 1959, *The Epistle to the Philippians* (BNTC; London: A & C Black).

J. Becker, 1993, *Paul, Apostle to the Gentiles* (ET, Louisville: Westminster/John Knox).

J. C. Beker, 1980, *Paul the Apostle. The Triumph of God in Life and Thought* (Philadelphia: Fortress; Edinburgh: T & T Clark).

S. Benko & J. J. O'Rourke (eds), 1971, *Early Church History* (London: Oliphants).

S. Benko, 1984, *Pagan Rome and the Early Christians* (Bloomington, Indiana: U. P.).

K. Berger, 1984a,'Hellenistische Gattungen im Neuen Testament,' ANRW II 25.2 (Berlin and New York: de Gruyter), 1031–1432, 1831–85.

K. Berger, 1984b, *Formgeschichte des Neuen Testaments* (Heidelberg: Quelle & Meyer).

K. L. Berry, 1996, 'Friendship Language in Philippians 4:10–20,' in *Friendship, Flattery and Frankness of Speech* (ed. Fitzgerald) 111–24.

E. Best, 1988, *Paul and his Converts* (Edinburgh: T & T Clark).

H. D. Betz, 1961, *Lukian von Samosata und das Neue Testament*, TU 76 (Berlin: Akademie).

H. D. Betz, 1972, *Der Apostel Paul und die sokratische Tradition* (BHT 45; Tübingen: Mohr).

H. D. Betz, 1975, 'The Literary Composition and Function of Paul's Letter to the Galatians,' *NTS* 21.3, 353–79.

H. D. Betz, 1979, *Galatians: A Commentary on Paul's Letter to the Churches in Galatia* (Hermeneia; Philadelphia: Fortress).

H. D. Betz, 1994, 'Jesus and the Cynics: Survey and Analysis of a Hypothesis,' *JR* 74.4, 453–75.

M. Billerbeck, 1978, *Epiktet. Vom Kynismus* (PA 34; Leiden: Brill).

M. Billerbeck, 1979, *Der Kyniker Demetrius* (PA 36; Leiden: Brill).

M. Billerbeck, 1982, 'La reception du cynisme à Rome,' *AC* 51, 151–73.

M. Billerbeck, 1991, *Die Kyniker in der modernen Forschung* (BSP 15; Amsterdam: Grüner).

M. Billerbeck, 1993, 'Le cynisme idéalisé d'Epictète à Julien,' in *Les Cyniques* (M.-O. Goulet-Cazé and R. Goulet, eds) 319–38.

P. Bonnard, 1950, *L'Épitre de Saint Paul aux Philippiens* (CNT X; Neuchatel: Delachaux et Niestlé).

P. Borgen, 1995, '"Yes," "No," "How Far?"': The Participation of Jews and Christians in Pagan Cults,' in *Paul in his Hellenistic Context* (ed. Engberg-Pedersen).

G. Bornkamm, 1975, *Paul* (ET of 1969; London: Hodder & Stoughton).

F. Bovon, 1982, 'Pratiques missionaires et communication de l'évangile dans le christianisme primitif,' *RTP* 114, 369–81.

P. Bowers, 'Paul and Religious Propaganda in the First Century,' *Nov.T.* XXII.4, 316–23.

R. B. Branham, 1993, 'Diogenes' Rhetoric and the Invention of Cynicism,' in *Les Cyniques* (M.-O. Goulet-Cazé and R. Goulet, eds), 445–74.

R. B. Branham, 1994, 'Authorizing Humor: Lucian's *Demonax* and Cynic Rhetoric,' in *The Rhetoric of Pronouncement* (ed. Robbins).

R. B. Branham and M.-O. Goulet-Cazé (eds), 1996a, *Introduction* in *The Cynics* (ed. Branham & Goulet-Cazé), 1–27.

R. B. Branham & M.-O. Goulet-Cazé (eds), 1996b, *The Cynics* (HCS XXIII; Berkeley: California U. P.).

E. Bréhier, 1950, *Les Idées philosophiques et religieuses de Philon d'Alexandrie* (Paris: Vrin).

G. J. Brooke (ed.), 1992, *Women in the Biblical Tradition* (Studies in Women & Religion 31; Lewiston/Queenston/Lampeter: Mellen).

R. Bultmann, 1910, *Der Stil der paulinischen Predigt und die kynisch-stoische Diatribe* (FRLANT 13; Göttingen: V & R).

R. Bultmann, 1951, *Theology of the New Testament* I (ET; New York: Scribners).

R. A. Burridge, 1992, *What are the Gospels? A Comparison with Graeco-Roman Biography* (SNTSMS 70; Cambridge: U. P.).

E. de Witt Burton, 1921, *A Critical and Exegetical Commentary on the Epistle to the Galatians* (ICC; Edinburgh: T & T Clark).

C. Bussmann, 1971, *Themen der paulinischen Missionspredigt auf dem Hintergrund der spätjüdisch-hellenistischen Missionliteratur* (Europaïsche Hochschulschriften, Reihe XXII; Theologie Bd. 3; Bern: Lang).

A. Cameron, 1980, 'Neither Male nor Female,' *Greece and Rome* 27, 60–68.

R. Cameron (ed.), 1990, *The Apocryphal Jesus and Christian Origins* (*Semeia* 49; Atlanta, Georgia: Scholars).

M. Carrez, 1986, *La deuxième épître de Saint Paul aux Corinthiens* (CNT 2nd series VIII; Geneva: Labor et Fides).

M. Casey, 1991, *From Jewish Prophet to Gentile God. The Origins and Development of New Testament Christology* (Cambridge: James Clark; Louisville: Westminster/John Knox).

E. A. Castelli & H. Taussig (eds), 1996, *Re-imagining Christian Origins* (Valley Forge: TPI).

H. Chadwick, 1994, review of F. G. Downing (1992a), *JTS* (NS) 45.1, 209–210.

J. H. Charlesworth, 1983, *The Old Testament Pseudepigrapha*. I: *Apocalyptic Literature and Testaments* (London: DLT).

G. F. Chesnutt, 1978, 'The Ruler and the Logos in Neopythagorean, Middle Platonic and Stoic Political Philosophy,' *ANRW* II.16.2 (Berlin/New York: de Gruyter).

R. F. Church & T. George (eds), 1979, *Continuity and Discontinuity in Church History* (for G. H. Williams; Studies in the History of Christian Thought XIX; Leiden: Brill).

A. D. Clarke, 1993, *Secular and Christian Leadership in Corinth. A Socio-historical and Exegetical Survey of 1 Corinthians 1–6* (Leiden: Brill).

D. Clay, 1996, 'Picturing Diogenes,' in The Cynics (ed. Branham & Goulet-Cazé), 366–87.

J. W. Cohoon & H. L. Crosby (eds & trs), 1932, *Dio Chrysostom* (LCL; Cambridge, Mass.: Harvard U. P.).

R. F. Collins (ed.), 1984, *Studies in the First Letter to the Thessalonians* (BETL LXVI; Leuven: Peeters).

R. F. Collins (ed), 1990, The Thessalonian Correspondence (BETL LXXXVII; Leuven: Peeters).

F. H. Colson (ed. & tr.), 1929, *Philo* (LCL; Cambridge, MA: Harvard).

H. Conzelmann, 1975, *1 Corinthians* (ET of 1969; Hermeneia; Philadelphia: Fortress).

C. E. B. Cranfield, 1975, *Romans* vol I., I–VIII (ICC; Edinburgh: T & T Clark)

C. E. B. Cranfield, 1979, *Romans* vol. II, IX–XVI (ICC; Edinburgh: T & T Clark).

C. E. B. Cranfield, 1991, '"The Works of the Law" in the Epistle to the Romans,' *JSNT* 43, 89-101.

W. Cronert, 1906, *Kolotes und Menedemus* (TU; Leipzig: J. C. Heinrich).

J. D. Crossan, 1991, *The Historical Jesus. The Life of a Mediterranean Jewish Peasant* (San Francisco: HarperCollins).

O. Cullmann, 1946, *Christus und die Zeit* (Zürich: Zollikon).

D. Davidson, 1980, *Essays on Actions and Events* (Oxford: Clarendon)

P. H. de Lacy, 1948, 'Lucretius and the History of Epicureanism,' *TAPA* 79, 12–23.

W. Deming, 1995, *Paul on Marriage and Celibacy. The Hellenistic Background of 1 Corinthians 7* (SNTSMS 83; Cambridge: U.P.).

D. A. deSilva, 1996, '"Worthy of the Kingdom": Honor Discourse and Social Engineering in 1 Thessalonians,' *JSNT* 64, 49–79.

N. de Witt, 1954, *Epicurus and his Philosophy* (repr. 1967; Cleveland: Meridian).

M. Dibelius, 1953, *Paul* (ed.W. G. Kümmel; ET of 1947; London: Longmans, Green).

S. Dill, 1905, Roman Society from Nero to Marcus Aurelius (London: Macmillan).

C. H. Dodd, 1932, *The Epistle of Paul to the Romans* (London: Hodder & Stoughton).

K. P. Donfried, 1990, 'The Early Paul,' in *The Thessalonian Correspondence* (ed. Collins), 1-17.

G. Dorival, 1992, 'Cyniques et Chrétiens aux temps des Pères grecs,' in a ms. generously shared, to appear in forthcoming Festschrift.

G. Dorival, 1993, 'L'image des Cyniques chez les Pères grecs,' in *Les Cyniques* (M.-O. Goulet-Cazé & R. Goulet, eds), 419–44.

T. Dorandi, 1982, 'Filodemo. Gli Stoici,' *Cronache Ercolanesi* 12, 91–133.

D. J. Doughty, 1994, 'Pauline Parallels and Pauline Authenticity,' *JHC* 1, 95–128.

F. G. Downing, 1968, *The Church and Jesus* (SBT 2.10; London: SCM).

F. G. Downing, 1972, 'Games, Families, the Public and Religion,' *Philosophy* XVII, 38-54.

F. G. Downing, 1981, 'Ethical Pagan Theism and the Speeches in Acts,' *NTS* 27.4, 544–63.

F. G. Downing, 1982, 'Common Ground with Paganism in Luke and in Josephus,' *NTS* 28.4, 546–59.

F. G. Downing, 1985, *Strangely Familiar. An Introductory Reader to the First Century* (Manchester: Downing).

F. G. Downing, 1987a, 'The Social Contexts of Jesus the Teacher: Construction or Reconstruction,' *NTS* 33.3, 439–51.

F. G. Downing, 1987b, *Jesus and the Threat of Freedom* (London: SCM).

F. G. Downing, 1988a, 'À bas les aristos: The Relevance of Higher Literature for the Understanding of the Earliest Christian Writings,' *Nov.T.* XXX.3, 212–30.

F. G. Downing, 1988b, 'Law and Custom: Luke–Acts and Late Hellenism,' in *Law and Religion* (B. Lindars, ed.; Cambridge: J. Clarke), 148–58.

F. G. Downing, 1988c, *Christ and the Cynics* (JSOT Manuals 4; Sheffield: JSOT).

F. G. Downing, 1992a, *Cynics and Christian Origins* (Edinburgh, T & T Clark).

F. G. Downing, 1992b, 'The Syro-Phoenician Woman and her Doggedness,' in *Women in the Biblical Tradition* (ed. G. J. Brooke).

F. G. Downing, 1993a, 'Cynics and Christians, Oedipus and Thyestes,' *JEH* 44.1, 1–10.

F. G. Downing, 1993b, 'Cynics and early Christianity,' in *Les Cyniques* (M.-O. Goulet-Cazé & R. Goulet, eds), 281–304.

F. G. Downing, 1994a, 'A Genre for Q and a Socio-cultural Context for Q: Comparing Sets of Similarities with Sets of Differences,' *JSNT* 55, 3–26.

F. G. Downing, 1994b, 'Cynicism, Idealism, Green Theology – and the Stoics,' *Theology in Green* 4.3, 19–25.

F. G. Downing, 1995a, 'Words as Deeds and Deeds as Words,' *Bib.Int.* 3.2, 129–43.

F. G. Downing, 1995b, 'Common Strands in Pagan, Jewish and Christian Eschatologies in the First Century,' *TZ* 51.3, 197–211.

F. G. Downing, 1995c, 'Cosmic Eschatology in the First Century: «Pagan», Jewish and Christian, *AC* LXIV, 99–109.

F. G. Downing, 1995d, 'Theophilus' First Reading of Luke–Acts,' in *Luke's Literary Achievement* (ed. Tuckett), 91-109.

F. G. Downing, 1996a, 'A Cynic Preparation for Paul's Gospel for Jew and Greek, Slave and Free, Male and Female,' *NTS* 42.4, 454–62.

F. G. Downing, 1996b, 'Word Processing in the Ancient World: The Social Production and Performance of Q,' *JSNT* 64, 29–48.

F. G. Downing, 1996c, 'On Applying Applied Philosophy,' *JAP* 13.2, 209–14.

F. G. Downing, 1998a, '"Honor" among Exegetes,' *CBQ*.

F. G. Downing, 1998b, 'Deeper Reflections on the Jewish Cynic Jesus,' *JBL*.

F. G. Downing, 1998c review of B. W. Winter, *Philo and Paul*, *JTS*.

J. W. Drane, 1975, *Paul: Libertine or Legalist?* (London: SPCK).

D. B. Dudley, 1937, *A History of Cynicism* (London: Methuen; repr. 1967, Hildesheim: Olms).

D. Dungan, 1971, *The Sayings of Jesus in the Churches of Paul* (Oxford: Blackwell).

J. D. G. Dunn, 1990, *Jesus, Paul and the Law* (London:SPCK).

J. D. G. Dunn, 1991, *The Partings of the Ways between Christianity and Judaism and their Signficance for the Character of Christianity* (London: SCM; Philadelphia: TPI).

J. D. G. Dunn, 1992, 'Yet Once More - "The Works of the Law": A Response,' *JSNT* 46, 99–117.

J. D. G. Dunn, 1993, *The Epistle to the Galatians* (BNTC; London: A & C Black; Peabody: Hendrickson).

J. D. G. Dunn, 1994, 'Jesus Tradition in Paul,' in *Studying the Historical Jesus* (ed. Evans and Chilton), 155–78.

J. Dupont, 1949, *Gnosis - la Connaissance Religieuse dans les Épîtres de Saint Paul* (Paris: Gabalda).

M. Ebner, 1991, *Leidenlisten und Apostelbrief. Untersuchungen zu Form, Motivik und Funktion der Peristasenkataloge bei Paulus* (FzB 66; Würzburg: Echter).

P. R. Eddy, 1996, 'Jesus as Diogenes? Reflections on the Cynic Jesus Thesis,' *JBL* 115.3, 449-69.

A. A. Ehrhardt, 1945, 'Jesus Christ and Alexander the Great,' *JTS* XLVI, 45-51.

J. H. Elliott (ed.), 1986, *Social-Scientific Criticism of the New Testament* (*Semeia* 35; Decatur: Scholars).

J. H. Elliott, 1993, *Social Scientific Criticism of the New Testament. An In Introduction* (Minneapolis: Augsburg/Fortress).

T. Engberg-Pedersen, 1990, *The Stoic Theory of Oikeiosis: Moral Development and Social Interaction in Early Stoic Philosophy* (Aarhus: U. P.)

T. Engberg-Pedersen (ed.), 1995a, *Paul in his Hellenistic Context* (Minneapolis: Fortress).

T. Engberg-Pedersen, 1995b, 'Stoicism in Philippians,' in *Paul in his Hellenistic Context* (ed. Engberg-Pedersen), 256–90.

T. Engberg-Pedersen, 1995c, 'Stoicism in Galatians,' unpub. paper, SNTS meeting, Prague.

T. Engberg-Pedersen, 1995d, 'Paul on Spiritual and Moral Progression and Regression: Where and how does Paul differ from the moral Philosophers?' unpub. paper, SBL, Philadelphia.

P. F. Esler, 1994, *The First Christians in their Social World. Social -scientific approaches to New Testament Interpretation* (London & NY: Routledge).

P. F. Esler (ed.), 1995, *Modelling early Christianity. Social-scientific studies of the New Testament in its context* (London & NY: Routledge).

C. A. Evans & B. Chilton (eds), 1994, *Studying the Historical Jesus* (Leiden: Brill).

C. A. Evans, 1995, *Jesus and his Contemporaries. Comparative Studies* (Leiden: Brill).

E. Ferguson (ed.), 1981, *Christian Teaching: Studies in Honor of Lemoine G. Lewis* (Abilene: University Bookstore).

E. Ferguson, 1987, *Backgrounds of Early Christianity* (Grand Rapids: Eerdmans).

J. Ferguson, 1975, *Philosophy under the Empire* (Milton Keynes: Open U. P.).

J. Ferguson, 1990, 'Epicureans under the Roman Empire,' *ANRW* II 36.4 (Berlin and New York: de Gruyter), 2257–2327.

M. S. Ferrari, 1991, *Die Sprache des Leids in den paulinischen Peristasenkatalogen* (SBB 23; Stuttgart: Katholisches Bibelwerk).

E. S. Fiorenza, 1983, *In Memory of Her* (Philadelphia: Fortress).

H. A. Fischel, 1968, 'Studies in Cynicism in the Ancient Near East: the Transformation of a Chria,' in *Religion in Antiquity* (J. Neusner, ed.; Leiden: Brill), 372-411.

H. A. Fischel, 1977, *Essays in Greco-Roman and related Talmudic Studies* (New York: Ktav).

J. T. Fitzgerald & L. M. White (eds & trs), 1983, *The Tabula of Cebes* (SBLTT 11, GRR 3; Chico: Scholars).

J. T. Fitzgerald, 1988, *Cracks in an Earthen Vessel. An Examination of Hardships in the Corinthian Correspondence* (SBLDS 99; Atlanta: Scholars).

J. T. Fitzgerald, 1996, *Friendship, Flattery and Frankness of Speech. Studies on Friendship in the New Testament Period* (Nov.T. Supp LXXXII; Leiden: Brill).

R. L. Fox, 1986, *Pagans and Christians in the Mediterranean World from the second century AD to the conversion of Constantine* (London: Viking).

D. E. Fredrickson, 1996, 'ΠΑΡΡΗΣΙΑ in the Pauline Epistles,' in *Friendship, Flattery and Frankness of Speech* (ed. Fitzgerald), 163–83.

W. H. C. Frend, 1984, *The Rise of Christianity* (London: DLT).

S. Freyne, 1980, *Galilee from Alexander the Great to Hadrian, 323 B.C.E–135 C.E.* (Wilmington: Glazier; Notre Dame: U. P.).

S. Freyne, 1988a, *Galilee, Jesus and the Gospels* (Dublin: Gill & Macmillan).

S. Freyne, 1988b, 'Bandits in Galilee: A Contribution to the Study of Social Conditions in First -Century Palestine,' in *The Social World of Formative Christianity and Judaism* (J. Neusner et al., eds), 50–69.

S. Freyne, 1992, 'Urban–Rural Relations in First-Century Galilee,' in *The Galilee in Late Antiquity* (ed. Levine), 75–91.
P. P. Fuentes González, 1990, 'Historia critica del Concepto "Diatriba",' ch.1 in *idem, Las Diatribas de Teles: Estudio introductario y Comentario de los Textas conservandos* (Granada: unpublished doctoral thesis, forthcoming, Paris: Vrin (?)).
H. Funke, 1970, 'Antisthenes bei Paulus,' *Hermes* 98, 459–71.
V. P. Furnish, 1984, *II Corinthians* (AB 32a; New York: Doubleday).
V. P. Furnish, 1993, *Jesus according to Paul* (Cambridge: U. P.).

R. Garrison, 1997, *The Graeco-Roman Context of Early Christian Literature* (JSNTSS 137; Sheffield: JSOT).
D. Georgi, 1964, The Opponents of Paul in Second Corinthians (ET, 1987; Edinburgh: T & T Clark).
D. Georgi, 1991, *Theocracy in Paul's Praxis and Theology* (Minneapolis: Augsburg/Fortress).
F. Gerke, 1940, *Die christlichen Sarkophagen der vorconstantinischen Zeit* (Berlin: de Gruyter).
G. Giannantoni, 1990, *Socratis et Socraticorum Reliquiae* I-IV (Elenchos XVIII; Naples: Bibliopolis).
C. E. Glad, 1995, *Paul and Philodemus: Adaptability in Epicurean and early Christian Psychogogy* (Nov.T. Supp LXXXI; Leiden: Brill).
C. E. Glad, 1996, 'Frank Speech, Flattery and Friendship in Philodemus,' in *Friendship, Flattery and Frankness of Speech* (ed. Fitzgerald), 21–60.
Th. Gomperz, 1902, *Greek Thinkers* II (London: John Murray).
E. R. Goodenough, 1928, *The Political Philosophy of Hellenistic Kingship* (CS 1; New Haven: Yale U. P.)
M. Goodman, 1989, 'Proselytising in Rabbinic Judaism,' *JTS* (NS) 40, 175-85.
M. Goodman, 1990, review of F. G. Downing (1988c), *JJS* 12.1, 127.
M. Goodman, 1994, *Mission and Conversion: Proselytising in the Religious History of the Roman Empire* (Oxford: U. P.).
H. B. Gottschalk, 1982, 'Diatribe again,' *LCM* VII 91–93.
H. B. Gottschalk, 1983, 'More on Diatribe,' *LCM* VIII 91–93.
M. Goulder, 1994, *A Tale of Two Missions* (London: SCM).
M.-O. Goulet-Cazé, 1982, 'Un syllogisme stöicien sur la loi dans la doxographie de Diogène le Cynique. A propos de Diogène Laërce VI 72,' *Rheinisches Museum* N.F. 125, 214–40.
M.-O. Goulet-Cazé, 1986, *L'ascèse cynique* (Histoire des doctrines de l'antiquité classique; Paris: Vrin).
M.-O. Goulet-Cazé, 1990, 'Le cynisme à l'époque impériale,' *ANRW* II 36.4 (Berlin and New York: de Gruyter), 2720–2823.
M.-O. Goulet-Cazé, 1992, 'Le livre VI de Diogène Laërce,' *ANRW* II 36.6 (Berlin and New York: de Gruyter), 3880–4048.

M.-O. Goulet-Cazé & R. Goulet (eds), 1993, *Le cynisme ancien et ses
— prolongements* (Paris: Presses Universitaires de France).
M.-O. Goulet-Cazé, 1993, 'Les premiers cyniques et la religion,' in *Le
cynisme ancien* (Goulet-Cazé & Goulet, eds), 117–58; repr. (ET)
1996, in *The Cynics* (Branham & Goulet-Cazé, eds), 47–80.
A. Grabar, 1967, *The Beginnings of Christian Art* (ET, London:
Thames & Hudson).
A. Grabar, 1968, *Christian Iconography: A Study of its Origins*
(Princeton, N J: U. P.).
R. M. Grant, 1951, 'The Wisdom of the Corinthians,' in *The Joy of
Study* (ed. S. E. Johnson), 51–61.
R. M. Grant, 1992, 'Neither Male nor Female,' *Biblical Research* 37,
5–14.
R. Graves, [1929](1960), *Goodbye to all that*, Harmondsworth:
Penguin
M. Griffin, 1996, 'Cynicism and the Romans: Attraction and
Repulsion,' in *The Cynics* (ed. Branham & Goulet-Cazé), 190–
204.
R. H. Gummere, J. W. Basore, *et al.*, 1917, (eds and trs.),
Seneca,Epistulae Morales and *Moral Essays* (LCL; Cambridge,
Mass.: Harvard U. P.)
R. Gundry, 1976, *ΣΩΜΑ in Biblical Theology with Emphasis on
Pauline Anthropology* (SNTSMS 29; Cambridge: U. P.).

M. Hadas, 1931, 'Gadarenes in Pagan Literature,' *Classical Weekly*
XXV.4, no.667, 25–30.
W. R. Halliday, *The Pagan Background of early Christianity* (London:
Hodder & Stoughton).
J. Hammerstaedt, 1990, 'Der Kyniker Oenomaus von Gadara,' *ANRW*
II 36.4 (Berlin and New York: de Gruyter), 2834–2865.
J. Hammerstaedt, 1992, 'Le courant littéraire du cynisme à l'époque
impériale,' in *Le cynisme ancien* (ed. Goulet-Cazé & Goulet),
399–418.
J. A. Hanson & R. A. Horsely, 1985, *Bandits, Prophets and Messiahs:
Popular Movements at the Time of Jesus* (Minneapolis: Winston).
A. M. Harmon, 1932, *Lucian of Samosata* (LCL; Cambridge, Mass.;
Harvard U.P.).
J. A. Harrill, 1995, *The Manumission of Slaves in Early Christianity*
(Tübingen: Mohr).
A. E. Harvey (ed.), 1985, *Alternative Approaches to New Testament
Studies* (London: SPCK).
A. E. Harvey, 1985, 'Forty Strokes Save One: Social Aspects of
Judaizing and Apostasy,' in *Alternative Approaches* (ed. Harvey),
79–96.
A. E. Harvey, 1989, review of F. G. Downing (1987b) and (1988c),
JTS (NS) 40.1, 550–53.

A. E. Harvey, 1993, review of F. G. Downing (1992a), *Church Times*, 11th March, 15.

A. E. Harvey, 1996, *Renewal through Suffering* (Edinburgh: T & T Clark).

G. F. Hawthorne, 1983, *Philippians* (WBC 43; Dallas: Word Inc.)

D. M. Hays (ed.), 1993, *Paul's Theology* II. *I & II Corinthians* (Minneapolis: Fortress).

C. W. Hedrick & R. Hodgson (eds), 1986, *Nag Hammadi, Gnosticism and Early Christianity* (Peabody: Hendrickson).

D. Hellholm (ed.), 1983, *Apocalyptic in the Mediterranean World and the Near East* (Tübingen: Mohr).

M. Hengel, 1974, *Judaism and Hellenism* (ET, London: SCM).

M. Hengel, 1980, *Jews, Greeks and Barbarians* (ET, London: SCM).

M. Hengel, 1983, *Between Jesus and Paul* (ET, London: SCM).

M. Hengel, 1989, *The 'Hellenization' of Judaea in the First Century after Christ* (ET, London: SCM).

M. Hengel, 1991, *The Pre-Christian Paul* (ET, London: SCM; Philadelphia: TPI).

O. Hense (ed.), 1905, *C. Musonius Rufus Reliquiae* (Leipzig: Teubner).

J. Hershbell, 1987, 'The Stoicism of Epictetus,' *ANRW* II 36.1 (Berlin and New York: de Gruyter), 2148–2163.

R. D. Hicks (ed. & tr.), 1925, *Diogenes Laertius, Lives of Eminent Philosophers* (LCL; Cambridge, Mass.: Harvard U. P.).

D. Hill, 1979, *New Testament Prophecy* (London: Marshall, Morgan & Scott).

R. F. Hock, 1980, *The Social Contexts of Paul's Ministry* (Philadelphia: Fortress).

R. F. Hock & E. N. O'Neill, 1986, *The Chreia in Ancient Rhetoric*. I: *The Progymnasmata* (Texts & Translations 27, GRR 9; Atlanta: Scholars).

R. F. Hock, 1987, 'Lazarus and Micyllus: Greco-Roman Backgrounds to Luke 16: 19-31,' *JBL* 106.3, 447–63.

R. Hodgson, 1983, 'Paul the Apostle and First Century Tribulation Lists,' *ZNW* 74, 59–80.

R. Hoïstad, 1948, *Cynic Hero and Cynic King* (Uppsala: Lundeqvist).

H. W. Hollander & J. Holleman, 1993, 'The Relationship of Death, Sin and Law in 1 Cor 15:56,' *Nov.T.* XXXV.3, 270–291.

B. Holmberg, 1990, *Sociology and the New Testament* (Minneapolis: Augsburg/Fortress).

T. Holtz, 1986, *Der erste Brief an die Thessaloniker* (EKKNT 13; Zürich: Benziger).

R. A. Horsley, 1977, 'Wisdom of Word and Words of Wisdom in Corinth,' *CBQ* 39, 224–39.

R. A. Horsley, 1978, 'The Background of the Confessional Formula in 1 Kor 8 6,' *ZNW* 69, 130–35.

R. A. Horsley, 1987, *Jesus and the Spiral of Violence* (San Francisco: HarperCollins).

R. A. Horsley, 1989, *Sociology and the Jesus Movement* (New York: Crossroad).

P. W. van der Horst, 1974, 'Musonius and the New Testament,' *Nov.T.* XVI, 306–15.

P. W. van der Horst, 1994, *Hellenism–Judaism–Christianity. Essays on their Interaction* (Kampen: Kok Pharos).

J. L. Houlden, 1970, *Paul's Letters from Prison* (Harmondsworth: Penguin).

H. Hübner, 1984, *Law in Paul's Thought* (Edinburgh: T & T Clark).

F. W. Hughes, 1989, Early Christian Rhetoric and 2 Thessalonians (JSNTSS 30; Sheffield: JSOT).

L. W. Hurtado, 1988, *One God, One Lord. Early Christian Devotion and Ancient Jewish Monotheism* (London: SCM).

I. Hutter, 1971, *Early Christian and Byzantine Art* (London: Weidenfeld & Nicholson).

A. Jagu, 'La morale d'Epictète et le Christianisme,' *ANRW* II 36.1 (Berlin and New York: de Gruyter), 2165–2199.

J. L. Jaquette, 1995, *Discerning what Counts. The Function of the Adiaphora Topos in Paul's Letters* (SBLDS 146; Atlanta: Scholars).

R. Jewett, 1979, *Dating Paul's Life* (= *A Chronology of Paul's Life*) (London: SCM).

R. Jewett, 1986, *The Thessalonian Correspondence - Pauline Rhetoric and Millenarian Piety* (Philadelphia: Fortress).

L. T. Johnson, 1989, 'The New Testament's anti-Jewish Slander and the Conventions of Ancient Polemic,' *JBL* 108.3, 419–41.

S. E. Johnson (ed.), 1951, *The Joy of Study* (New York: Macmillan).

C. P. Jones, 1992, 'Cynisme et sagesse étrangère: le cas de Pérégrinus Proteus,' in *Le cynisme ancien* (ed. Goulet-Cazé & Goulet), 305–318.

F. S. Jones, 1981,»*Freiheit*« *in den Briefen des Apostels Paulus. Eine historische, exegetische und religionsgeschichtliche Studie* (GTA 34; Göttingen: V & R).

H. Jones, 1989, *The Epicurean Tradition* (London: Routledge).

J. W. Jones, 1956, *Law and Legal Theory of the Greeks* (Oxford: Clarendon).

E. A. Judge, 1960, *The Social Pattern of Christian Groups in the First Century* (London: IVP).

E. A. Judge, 1972, 'St Paul and Classical Society,' *JAC* XV 19–36.

E. A. Judge, 1984, 'Cultural Conformity and Innovation in Paul: Some Clues from Contemporary Documents,' *Tyndale Bulletin* 35.

J. Jüthner, 1923, *Hellenen und Barbaren aus der Geschichte des Nationalbewusstseins* (Das Erbe der Alten NF 8, Leipzig: Dieterich)

G. A. Kennedy, 1984, *New Testament Interpretation through Rhetorical Criticism* (Chapel Hill: N. Carolina U. P.).

H. C. Kee, 1980, *Christian Origins in Sociological Perspective* (Philadelphia: Fortress).

H. C. Kee, 1989, *Knowing the Truth: A Sociological Approach to New Testament Interpretation* (Minneapolis: Fortress).

H. C. Kee, 1992, 'Early Christianity in the Galilee: Reassessing the Evidence from the Gospels,' in *The Galilee in Late Antiquity* (ed. Levine), 53–73.

G. A. Kennedy, 1984, *The New Testament through Rhetorical Criticism* (Chapel Hill: N. Carolina U. P.).

S. Kim, *The Origin of Paul's Gospel* (WUNT 2.4; Tübingen: Mohr).

J. F. Kindstrand, 1976, *Bion of Borysthenes* (Studia Graeca XI; Uppsala: U. P.).

J. F. Kindstrand, 1986, 'Diogenes Laertius and the Chreia Tradition,' *Elenchos* 7.219–43.

D. Kinney, 1996, 'Heirs of the Dog: Cynic Selfhood in Mediaeval and Renaissance Culture,' in *The Cynics* (ed. Branham & Goulet-Cazé), 294-328.

M. Kitchen, 1994, *Ephesians* (London: Routledge).

W. Klassen, 1996,' ΠΑΡΡΗΣΙΑ in the Johannine Corpus,' in *Friendship, Flattery and Frankness of Speech* (ed. Fitzgerald), 228–33.

J. Klausner, 1943/44, *From Jesus to Paul* (ET New York 1943; London 1944: Allen & Unwin).

A. F. J. Klijn, 1983, '2 (Syriac Apocalypse of) Baruch,' in *The Old Testament Pseudepigrapha* I (ed. Charlesworth).

J. S. Kloppenborg (ed.), 1995, *Conflict and Invention: Literary, Rhetorical and Social Studies on the Sayings Gospel Q* (Valley Forge, PA: TPI).

J. S. Kloppenborg, 1996, 'Egalitarianism in the Myth and Rhetoric of the Pauline Churches,' in *Re-imagining Christian Origins* (ed. Castelli and Taussig), 247–63.

J. Knox, 1950, *Chapters in a Life of Paul* (New York: Abingdon).

D.-A. Koch, 1986, *Die Schrift als Zeuge des Evangeliums* (Tübingen: Mohr).

G. Koch, 1995, *Early Christian Art and Architecture. An Introduction* (ET, London: SCM).

H. Koester, 1979, 'I Thessalonians – An Experiment in Christian Writing,' in *Continuity and Discontinuity in Church History* (ed. Church & George), 33–44.

D. Krueger, 1996, 'The Bawdy and Society: The Shamelessness of Diogenes in Roman Imperial Culture,' in *The Cynics* (ed. Branham & Goulet-Cazé), 222-39.

D. C. G. Kühn (ed), 1823, *Medicorum Graecorum Opera quae extant*, V, *Claudii Galieni* (Leipzig: Car. Cuoblochii).

S. T. Lachs, 1987, *A Rabbinic Commentary on the New Testament* (Hoboken, N. J.: Ktav).

Lacy, de - see de Lacy.

F. Lang, 1986, *Die Briefe an die Korinther* (NTD 7; Göttingen: V & R).

R. Laurenti, 1987, 'Musonio, Maestro di Epiteto,' *ANRW* II 36.1 (Berlin and New York: de Gruyter), 2105-46.

L. I. Levine (ed.), 1992, *The Galilee in Late Antiquity* (for the Jewish Theological Seminary of America; Cambridge, Mass.: Harvard U. P.).

S. Liebermann, 1974, *Hellenism in Jewish Palestine* (New York: Ktav).

B. Lindars, SSF (ed.), 1988, *Law and Religion. Essays on the Place of the Law in Israel and Early Christianity* (Cambridge: James Clark).

D. Litfin, 1994, *St. Paul's Theology of Proclamation* (SNTSMS 79; Cambridge: CUP).)

A. H. B. Logan & A. J. M. Wedderburn (eds), 1983, *The New Testament and Gnosticism: Essays in Honour of R. McL. Wilson* (Edinburgh: T & T Clark).

A. H. B. Logan, 1996, *Gnostic Truth and Christian Heresy* (Edinburgh: T & T Clark).

A. A. Long, 1996, 'The Socratic Tradition: Diogenes, Crates and Hellenistic Ethics, ' in *The Cynics* (ed. Branham and Goulet-Cazé), 28–46.

R. N. Longenecker & M. C. Tenney (eds), 1974, *New Dimensions in New Testament Study* (Grand Rapids: Zondervaan).

R. N. Longenecker, 1974, 'Ancient Amanuenses and the Pauline Letters,' in *New Dimensions in New Testament Studies* (ed. Longenecker & Tenney), 281–97.

R. N. Longenecker, 1990, *Galatians* (WBC 41; Dallas: Word Inc.)

A. O. Lovejoy & G. Boas, 1935, *Primitivism and related Ideas in Antiquity* (Princeton: U. P.; repr. 1965, Baltimore: Octagon).

G. Lüdemann, 1984, *Paul, Apostle to the Gentiles* (ET, Philadelphia: Fortress).

G. Lüdemann, 1989, *Early Christianity according to the Traditions in Acts* (ET, Philadelphia: Fortress).

G. Lüdemann, 1996, *Heretics: The Other Side of Early Christianity* (ET, London: SCM).

D. Lührmann, 1992, *Galatians* (ET of 1978; Minneapolis: Fortress).

D. J. Lull, 1986, '"The Law was our Pedagogue": A Study of Galatians 3:19-25,' *JBL* 105.3, 481-98.

C. Lutz (ed. & tr.), 1947, *Musonius Rufus: "The Roman Socrates"* (YCS 10; New Haven: Yale U.P).

M. Luz, 1987, 'Abnimos, Nimos and Oenomaus: A Note,' *JQR* LXVII 2-3, 191–95.

M. Luz, 1988, 'Salam, Meleager!' *Studi Italiani di Filologia Classica* 3.6, 222–31.

M. Luz, 1989, 'A Description of the Greek Cynic in the Jerusalem Talmud,' *JSJ* XX.1, 49–60.

M. Luz, 1991, 'Oenomaus and Talmudic Anecdote,' *JSJ* XXIII.1, 42–80.

G. Lyons, 1985, *Pauline Autobiography* (SBLDS 73; Atlanta: Scholars).

H. Maccoby, 1991, *Paul and Hellenism* (London: SCM; Philadelphia: TPI).

M. Y. McDonald, 1988, *The Pauline Churches: A Socio-historical Study of Institutionalisation in the Pauline Churches and deutero-Pauline Churches* (SNTSMS 60; Cambridge: U.P.).

B. L. Mack, 1988, *A Myth of Innocence: Mark and Christian Origins* (Philadelphia: Fortress).

B. L. Mack, 1990, *Rhetoric and the New Testament* (Minneapolis: Fortress).

B. L. Mack, 1993, *The Lost Gospel. The Book of Q and Christian Origins* (Shaftesbury, Dorset & Rockport, MA: Element).

B. H. McLean, 1996, *The Cursed Christ. Mediterranean Expulsion Rituals* (JSNTSS 126; Sheffield: SAC).

R. MacMullen, 1966, *Enemies of the Roman Order* (Cambridge, Mass: Harvard U. P.).

R. MacMullen, 1974, *Roman Social Relations* (New Haven: Yale U. P.).

R. MacMullen, 1981, *Paganism in the Roman Empire* (New Haven: Yale U. P.).

R. MacMullen, 1984, *Christianising the Roman Empire* (New Haven: Yale U. P.).

A. J. Malherbe, 1968, 'The Beasts at Ephesus,' *JBL* 87.1, 71-80; (repr. in *idem* 1989).

A. J. Malherbe, 1970, '"Gentle as a Nurse": the Cynic Background to 1 Thessalonians 2,' *Nov.T.* XII, 203–17, (repr. in *idem* 1989).

A. J. Malherbe, 1976, 'Cynics,' in *IDB* Supp., (Nashville: Abingdon), 201–203.

A. J. Malherbe (ed.), 1977, *The Cynic Epistles. A Study Edition* (SBL SBS 12; Missoula: Scholars).

A. J. Malherbe, 1978, 'Pseudo-Heraclitus Epistle 4: The Divinization of the Wise Man,' *JAC* 21, 42–64 (repr. in *idem* 1989).

A. J. Malherbe, 1982, 'Self-definition among Epicureans and Cynics,' in *Jewish and Christian Self-definition* 3 (ed. Meyer and Sanders), 46–59 (repr. in *idem* 1989).

A. J. Malherbe, 1983a, 'Antisthenes, Odysseus, and Paul at War,' *HTR* 76.2, 143–73 (repr. in *idem* 1989).

A. J. Malherbe, 1983b, 'Exhortation in I Thessalonians,' *Nov.T.* XXV 238–56 (repr. in *idem* 1989).

A. J. Malherbe, 1986a, *Moral Exhortation* (Philadelphia: Westminster Press).

A. J. Malherbe, 1986b, 'Paul - Hellenistic Philosopher or Christian Pastor?' *ATR* 3.3 (repr. in *idem* 1989, 67-77, as cited here).

A. J. Malherbe, 1987, *Paul and the Thessalonians* (Philadelphia: Fortress).

A. J. Malherbe, 1988, 'Herakles,' *RAC* 14, 560–83.

A. J. Malherbe, 1989, *Paul and the Popular Philosophers* (collected essays including many listed above; Philadelphia: Fortress).

A. J. Malherbe, 1992, 'Hellenistic Moralists and the New Testament,' *ANRW* II 26.1 (Berlin and New York: de Gruyter), 267–333.

A. J. Malherbe, 1994, '*PAULUS SENEX*,' *RQ* 36, 197–207.

A. J. Malherbe, 1995, 'Determinism and Free Will in Paul: The Argument of 1 Corinthians 8 and 9,' in *Paul in his Hellenistic Context* (ed. Engberg-Pedersen), 231–55.

A. J. Malherbe, 1996, 'Paul's Self-sufficiency (Philippians 4:11),' in *Friendship, Flattery and Frankness of Speech* (ed. Fitzgerald), 125–39.

B. Malina, 1981, *The New Testament World: Insights from Cultural Anthropology* (Atlanta: John Knox).

I. H. Marshall, 1966, 'Salvation, Grace and Works in the Later Writings of the Pauline Corpus,' *NTS* 42.3, 339-58.

P. Marshall, 1987, *Enmity in Corinth: Social Conventions in Paul's Relations with the Corinthians* (Tübingen: Mohr).

D. B. Martin, 1990, *Slavery as Salvation. The Metaphor of Slavery in Pauline Christianity* (New Haven: Yale U. P.).

D. B. Martin, 1995a, *The Corinthian Body* (New Haven: Yale U. P.).

D. B. Martin, 1995b, 'Heterosexism and the Interpretation of Romans 1:18-32,' *Bib. Int.* 3.3, 332–55.

R. P. Martin, 1967, *Carmen Christi: Philippians 2.5–11 in Recent Interpretation and in the Setting of Early Christian Worship* (Cambridge: U. P.).

R. P. Martin, 1991, *2 Corinthians* (WBC; Dallas: Word Inc.).

T. W. Martin, 1995, 'The Scythian Perspective in Col. 3.11,' *Nov.T.* XXXVII.3, 249–61.

T. W. Martin, 1996, *By Philosophy and Empty Deceit. Colossians as a Response to a Cynic Critique* (JSNTSS 118; Sheffield: JSOT).

V. Martin, 1959, 'Un recueil de diatribes cyniques. Pap. Genev. inv. 271,' *Museum Helveticum* 16.2, 77–115.

T. F. Matthews, 1993, *The Clash of Gods. A Reinterpetation of Early Christian Art* (Princeton, NJ: U. P.).

S. Matton, 1996, 'Cynicism and Christianity from the Middle Ages to the Renaissance,' in *The Cynics* (ed. Branham & Goulet-Cazé).

W. A. Meeks, 1973/4, 'The Image of the Androgyne: Some Uses of a Symbol in earliest Christianity,' *HR* 13, 165–208.

W. A. Meeks, 1983, *The First Urban Christians* (New Haven: Yale).

W. A. Meeks, 1986, *The Moral World of the First Christians* (Philadelphia: Westminster Press).

W. A. Meeks, 1993, *The Origins of Christian Morality. The First Two Centuries* (New Haven: Yale U. P.).

F. van der Meer & C. Mohrmann (eds), 1959, *Atlas of the Early Christian World* (London: Nelson).

B. F. Meyer & E. P. Sanders (eds), 1982, *Jewish and Christian Self-definition* 3: *Self-definition in the Graeco-Roman World* (London: SCM).

O. Michel, 1963, *Der Brief an die Römer*³ (KEK; Göttingen: V & R).

M. M. Mitchell, 1992, *Paul and the Rhetoric of Reconciliation. An Exegetical Investigation of the Language and Composition of 1 Corinthians* (Tübingen: Mohr; Louisville: Westminster/John Knox).

J. H. Moles, 1983a, '"Honestius quam ambitiosus"? An Exploration of the Cynic's Attitude to Corruption in his Fellow Men,' *JHS* CIII 103–23.

J. H. Moles, 1983b, 'The Fourth Kingship Oration of Dio Chrysostom,' *Classical Antiquity* 2.2, 251–78.

J. H. Moles, 1993, 'Le cosmopolitanisme cynique,' in *Le cynisme ancien* (ed. Goulet-Cazé & Goulet), 259–80; repr. (ET) in *The Cynics* (ed. Branham & Goulet-Cazé), 105–20.

C. G. Montefiore, 1914, *Judaism and St. Paul. Two Essays* (London: Max Goschen).

G. F. Moore, 1927, *Judaism in the First Centuries of the Christian Era. The Age of the Tannaim.* I (Cambridge, MA: Harvard U. P.).

H. Moxnes, 1995, 'The Quest for Honor and the Unity of the Community in Romans 12 and in the Orations of Dio Chrysostom,' in *Paul in his Hellenistic Context* (ed. Engberg-Pedersen).

C. Muckensturm, 1993, 'Les gymnosophistes, étaient-ils des Cyniques modèles?' in *Le Cynisme ancien et ses prolongements* (ed. Goulet-Cazé & Goulet).

J. Munck, 1959, *Paul and the Salvation of Mankind* (ET of 1954, London: SCM).

J. Munck, 1962-63, 'I Thess. I. 9–10 and the Missionary Preaching of Paul,' *NTS* 9, 95–110.

J. Murphy-O'Connor, 1993, *Paul the Letter Writer. His World, His Options, His Skills* (Collegeville: Glazier/Liturgical Press).

J. Murphy-O'Connor, 1996, *Paul - A Critical Life* (Oxford: Clarendon).

G. Mussies, 1972, *Dio Chrysostom and the New Testament* (Leiden: Brill).

J. Neusner (ed.), 1968, *Religions in Antiquity* (Leiden: Brill).

J. Neusner *et al.* (eds), 1987, Judaisms and their Messiahs at the Turn of the Christian Era (Cambridge: U. P.).

J. Neusner *et al.* (eds.), 1988, *The Social World of Formative Christianity and Judaism* - in tribute to H. C. Kee (Philadelphia: Fortress).

J. H. Neyrey (ed.),1991, *The Social World of Luke-Acts. Models for Interpretation* (Peabody: Hendrickson).

G. W. E. Nickelsburg, 1981, *Jewish Literature between the Bible and the Mishnah* (Philadelphia: Fortress).

A. D. Nock, 1972, Essays on Religion and the Ancient World (ed. Z. Stewart; Cambridge, MA: Harvard U. P.).

W. A. Oldfather, 1925, *Epictetus. The Discourses as reported by Arrian, The Manual, and Fragments* (LCL; Cambridge, MA: Harvard).

A. Oltramare, 1925, *Les origines de la diatribe romaine* (Geneva & Lausanne: Payot).

E. N. O'Neill (ed. & tr.), 1977, *Teles, The Cynic Teacher* (SBL GRR 3; Missoula: Scholars).

J. C. O'Neill, 1975, *Paul's Letter to the Romans* (Harmondsworth: Penguin).

J. C. Paget, 1996, 'Jewish Proselytism at the Time of Christian Origins: Chimera or Reality?' *JSNT* 62, 65-103.

A. Papathomas, 1997, 'Das agonistische Motiv 1 Kor 9.24ff im Spiegel zeitgenössischer dokumentarischer Quellen,' *NTS* 43.2, 223-41.

L. Paquet, 1988, *Les Cyniques grecs*[2] (Ottowa: U. P.).

B. Pearson, 1973, *The Pneumatikos–Psychikos Terminology in I Corinthians* (SBLDS 12; Missoula: Scholars).

P. Perkins, 1993, *Gnosticism and the New Tesatament* (Minneapolis: Fortress).

S. Pétrement, 1990, *A Separate God* (ET of 1984; London: DLT).

V. P. Pfitzner, 1967, *Paul and the Agon Motif* (Nov.T. Supp 16; Leiden: Brill).

P. Photiadès, 1959, 'Les diatribes cyniques du papyrus de Genève 271, leurs traduction et élaborations successives,' *Museum Helveticum* 16.2, 116–30.

J. J. Pilch & B. Malina (eds), 1993, *Biblical Social Values and their Meanings. A Handbook* (Peabody: Hendrickson).

R. A. Piper (ed.), 1995, *The Gospel behind the Gospels. Current Studies on Q* (Leiden: Brill).

M. A. Plunkett, 1988, *Sexual Ethics and the Christian Life: A Study of 1 Corinthians 6:12–7:7* (unpub. dissertation, Princeton, NJ: Princeton Theological Seminary).

S. M. Pogoloff, 1992, *Logos and Sophia. The Rhetorical Situation of 1 Corinthians* (SBLDS 134; Atlanta: Scholars).

M. Pohlenz, 1949, 'Paulus und die Stoa,' ZNW 42, 69–104.

M. Pohlenz, 1959, *Die Stoa: Geschichte einer geistigen Bewegung* (Göttingen: V & R).

M. Pohlenz, 1966, *Freedom in Greek Life and Thought* (Dordrecht: Reidel).

S. B. Pomeroy, 1975, *Goddesses, Whores, Wives and Slaves* (New York: Schocken).

J. I. Porter, 1996, 'The Philosophy of Ariston of Chios,' in *The Cynics* (ed. Branham &   Goulet-Cazé).

B. Radice (ed. & tr.), 1969, Pliny *Letters and Panegyricus* (LCL; Cambridge, MA: Harvard).

H. Räisänen, 1986, *Paul and the Law* (ET, Philadelphia: Fortress).

N. Richardson, 1994, *Paul's Language about God* (JSNTSS 99; Sheffield: JSOT).

R. Riesner, 1994, *Die Frühzeit des Apostels Paulus* (Tübingen: Mohr).

V. K. Robbins (ed.), 1994, *The Rhetoric of Pronouncement* (*Semeia* 64; Atlanta: Scholars).

V. K. Robbins, 1996, *The Tapestry of Early Christian Discourse* (London: Routledge).

C. Roetzel, 1991, *The Letters of Paul - Conversations in Context*[3] (Louisville:Westminster/John Knox).

G. H. Sabine, 1952, *A History of Political Theory*[3] (London: Harrap).

J. P. Sampley, 1991, 'Moving from Text to Thought World: General Considerations,' in *Pauline Theology* I (ed. Bassler), 5–22.

E. P. Sanders, 1977, *Paul and Palestinian Judaism* (London: SCM).

E. P. Sanders, 1983, *Paul, the Law and the Jewish People* (Philadelphia: Fortress).

J. T. Sanders, 1997, 'Paul between Jews and Gentiles in Corinth,' *JSNT* 65, 67-83.

S. Sandmel, 1958, *The Genius of Paul. A Study in History* (Philadelphia: Fortress).

S. Sandmel, 1962, 'Parallelomania,' *JBL* 81.1, 1–13.

S. Sandmel, 1969, *The First Christian Century in Judaism and Christianity. Certainties and Uncertainties* (London & New York: OUP).

S. Sandmel, 1978, *Judaism and Christian Beginnings* (New York: OUP).

S. L. Satlow, 1997, 'Jewish Construction of Nakedness in Late Antiquity,' *JBL* 116.3, 429-54.

A. A. Schiller, 1978, *Roman Law* (The Hague, New York: Mouton).

C. J. Schlueter, 1994, *Filling up the Measure: Polemical Hyperbole in I Thessalonians 2.4-6* (JSNTSS 98; Sheffield: JSOT).

W. Schmithals, 1971, *Gnosticism in Corinth* (ET, Nashville & New York: Abingdon).

F. Schulz, 1946, *A History of Roman Legal Science* (Oxford: Clarendon).

J. R. Searle, 1983, *Intentionality* (Cambridge: U.P.).

D. Seeley, 1990, *The Noble Death: Graeco-Roman Martyrology and Paul's Concept of Salvation* (JSNTS 28; Sheffield: JSOT).

D. Seeley, 1992, 'Jesus' Death in Q,' *NTS* 38.2, 222-34.

D. Seeley, 1994a, *Deconstructing the New Testament* (BIS 4; Leiden: Brill).

D. Seeley, 1994b, 'The Background of the Philippians Hymn (2:6–11),' *JHC* 1, 49–72.

D. Seeley, 1996, 'Jesus and the Cynics: A Response to Hans Dieter Betz,' *JHC* 3.2, 284–90.

D. Seeley, 1997, 'Jesus and the Cynics Revisited,' JBL 116.4, 704-12.

A. F. Segal, 1977, *Two Powers in Heaven* (Leiden: Brill).

A. F. Segal, 1990, Paul the Convert. The Apostolate and Apostasy of Saul the Pharisee (New Haven: Yale U. P.).

C. Senft, 1979, *La première épître de saint Paul aux Corinthiens* (CNT 2nd series VII; Lausanne: Labor et Fides).

J. Sievers, 1994, review of L. Feldman, *Jew and Gentile in the Ancient World* (Princeton: U. P), in *Bib.* 76/2, 277-81.

Silva, de - see deSilva.

M. Simon, 1955, *Hercule et le Christianisme* (Paris: Belles Lettres).

J. Z. Smith, 1990, *Drudgery Divine. On the Comparison of Early Christianities and the Religions of Late Antiquity* (Jordan Lectures XIV; London: School of Oriental and African Studies).

T. Söding, 1994, 'Starke und Schwache. Der Götzenopferstreit in I Kor 8–10 as Paradigma paulinischer Ethik,' *ZNW* 85, 69–92.

J. Stambaugh & D. Balch, 1986, *The Social World of the First Christians* (London: SPCK) = *The New Testament in its Social Environment* (Philadelphia: Westminster Press).

C. D. Stanley, 1992, *Paul and the Language of Scripture* (SNTSMS 74; Cambridge: U. P.).

M. E. Stone, 1990, *Fourth Ezra* (Hermeneia; Philadelphia: Fortress).

R. Stoneman, 1994, 'Who are the Brahmans? Indian Lore and Cynic Doctrine in Palladius' *De Brahmanibus* and its Models,' *CQ* 44.ii, 500–510.

R. Stoneman, 1995, 'Naked Philosophers: the Brahmans in the Alexander Romance and the Alexander Historians,' *JHS* 115, 99–114.

S. K. Stowers, 1981, 'A "Debate" over Freedom: 1 Corinthians 6:12-20,' in *Christian Teaching* (ed. Ferguson), 59-71.

S. K. Stowers, 1984a, *The Diatribe and Paul's Letter to the Romans* (SBLDS 57; Chico: Scholars).

S. K. Stowers, 1984b, 'Social Status, Public Speaking and Private Teaching: The Circumstances of Paul's Preaching Activity,' *Nov.T.* 26.1, 59–82.

S. K. Stowers, 1994, *A Re-Reading of Romans. Justice Jews and Gentiles* (New Haven: Yale U. P.).

P. Stuhlmacher, 1989, Der Brief an die Römer (NTD 6; Göttingen: V & R).

J. L. Sumney, 1991, *Identifying Paul's Opponents. The Question of Method in 2 Corinthians* (JSNTSS 40; Sheffield: JSOT).

C. H. Talbert, 1975, 'The Concept of Immortals in Mediterranean Antiquity,' *JBL* 94.4, 414–41.

P. Testini, 1966, *Le Catacombe e gli Antichi Cimiteri Cristiani in Roma* (Bolgna: Cappelli).

H. St.J. Thackeray *et al.* (eds & trs), 1926, Josephus, *Life, Jewish War, Antiquities*, etc. (LCL; Cambridge, MA: Harvard U. P.).

G. Theissen, 1973, 'Wanderradikalismus. Literatursoziologische Aspekte der Überlieferung von Wörten Jesu im Urchristentum,' *ZTK* 70.3, 245–71.

G. Theissen, 1975, 'Legitimation und Lebensunterhalt: Ein Beitrag zur Sociologie urchristlicher Missionare,' *NTS* 21, 192-221.

G. Theissen, 1978, *The First Followers of Jesus* (ET; London: SCM).

G. Theissen, 1982, *The Social Setting of Pauline Christianity* (ET, London: SCM).

B. Thiering, 1996, 'Jesus and the Dead Sea Scrolls: The Question of Method,' *JHC* 3.2, 215–36.

G. Tomlin, 1997, 'Christians and Epicureans in 1 Corinthians,' *JSNT* 68, 51-72.

C. M. Tuckett, 1989, 'A Cynic Q?' *Biblica* 70.2, 349–76.

C. M. Tuckett (ed.), 1995, *Luke's Literary Achievement* (JSNTSS 116; Sheffield: SAC).

C. M. Tuckett, 1996, *Q and the History of Early Christianity* (Edinburgh: T & T Clark).

L. E. Vaage, 1987, 'Q: The Ethos and Ethics of an Itinerant Intelligence,' (dissertation, Claremont).

L. E. Vaage, 1992a, 'Like Dogs Barking: Cynic *parresia* and Shameless Asceticism' , *Semeia* 57, 25–39.

L. E. Vaage, 1992b, 'Monarchy, Community, Anarchy: The Kingdom of God in Paul and Q,' *TJT* 8.1, 52–69.

L. E. Vaage, 1994a, *Galilean Upstarts. Jesus' First Followers According to Q* (Valley Forge, PA: TPI).

L. E. Vaage, 1994b, review of F. G. Downing (1992a), *CBQ* 56, 587-89.

L. E. Vaage, 1995a, 'Composite Texts and Oral Mythology: The Case of the "Sermon" on Q,' in *Conflict and Invention* (Kloppenborg, ed.), 75–97.

L. E. Vaage, 1995b, 'Q and Cynicism: On Comparison and Social Identity,' in *Studies in Q* (Piper, ed), 199-229.

J. C. VanderKam, 1994, *The Dead Sea Scrolls Today* (Grand Rapids: Eerdmans).

G. Vermes, 1977, *The Dead Sea Scrolls. Qumran in Perspective* (London: Collins).

S. Vollenweider, 1989, *Freiheit als neue Schöpfung. Eine Untersuchung zur Eleutheria bei Paulus und in seiner Umwelt* (FRLANT 147; Göttingen: V & R).

S. Vollenweider, 1994, 'Die Waagschalen von Leben und Tod. Zum antiken Hintergrund von Phil. 1,21–26,' *ZNW* 85, 93–115.

R. Walzer, 1949, *Galen on Jews and Christians* (London: OUP).

C. A. Wanamaker, 1990, *Commentary on 1 & 2 Thessalonians* (NIGTC; Grand Rapids: Eerdmans; Exeter: Paternoster).

A. J. M. Wedderburn, 1981, 'The Problem of the Denial of the Resurrection in I Corinthians XV,' *Nov.T.* XXIII.3, 231–41.

A. J. M. Wedderburn, 1987, *Baptism and Resurrection. Studies in Pauline Theology against its Graeco-Roman Background* (Tübingen: Mohr).

A. J. M. Wedderburn, 1988, *The Reasons for Romans* (Edinburgh, T & T Clark).

A. J. M. Wedderburn (ed.), 1989, *Paul and Jesus. Collected Essays* (JSNTSS 37; Sheffield: JSOT).

L. L. Welborn, 1987, 'On the Discord in Corinth: I Corinthians 1-4 and ancient Politics,' *JBL* 106.1, 85–111.

D. Wenham, 1995, *Paul - Follower of Jesus or Founder of Christianity?* (Grand Rapids and Cambridge: Eerdmans).

M. Werner, 1957, *The Formation of Christian Dogma* (ET of 1941; London: A. & C. Black).

C. Wessely, 1902, 'Neues über Diogenes den Kyniker,' in *Festschrift Theodor Gomperz* (Vienna: Hölder; repr. Aalen, 1979), 67–74.

M. Whittaker, 1984, *Jews and Christians: Graeco-Roman Views* (Cambridge Commentaries on Writings of the Jewish & Christian World 200 BC to AD 200; Cambridge: U. P.).

U. Wilckens, 1978, *Der Brief an die Römer* (EKK VI, I) (Zürich: Benziger).

B. Wildhaber, *Paganisme populaire et prédication apostolique* (Geneva: Labor et Fides).

F. Williams, 1994, review of F. G. Downing (1992a), *Irish Biblical Studies*, 138–44.

W. L. Willis, *Idol Meat in Corinth* (SBLDS 68; Chico: Scholars).

V. L. Wimbush, 1987, *Paul, the Worldly Ascetic* (Macon, GA: Mercer U. P.).

V. L. Wimbush (ed.), 1990, *Ascetic Behavior in Greco-Roman Antiquity - A Source Book* (Minneapolis: Fortress).

B. W. Winter, 1991, 'Civil Litigation in Secular Corinth,' *NTS* 37.4, 559–72.

B. W. Winter & A. D. Clarke (eds), 1993, *The Book of Acts in its First Century Setting*. I. *The Book of Acts in its Ancient Literary Setting* (Grand Rapids: Eerdmans).

B. W. Winter, 1994, *Seek the Welfare of the City. Christians as Benefactors and Citizens* (Grand Rapids: Eerdmans; Carlisle: Paternoster).

B. Winter, 1997, Philo and Paul among the Sophists (SNTSMS 96; Cambridge U. P.).

A. C. Wire, 1990, *The Corinthian Women Prophets* (Minneapolis: Fortress).

F. Wisse, 1975, 'Die Sextus-Sprüche und das Problem der gnostischen Ethik,' in Zum Hellenismus (ed. Wisse & Böhlig), 55-86.

F. Wisse & E. Böhlig (eds) 1975, *Zum Hellenismus in den Schriften von Nag Hammadi* (Wiesbaden: Harrassowitz).

Witt, de, see de Witt.

B. Witherington III, 1981, 'Rite and Rights for Women – Galatians 3.28,' *NTS* 27.4, 593–604.

B. Witherington III, 1994, *Jesus the Sage – The Pilgrimage of Wisdom* (Louisville: Augsburg/Fortress; Edinburgh: T & T Clark).

L. Wittgenstein, *Philosophische Untersuchungen/Philosophical Investigations*[2], (Oxford: Blackwell).

N. T. Wright, 1992, *Christian Origins and the Question of God* I: *The New Testament and the People of God* (London: SPCK; Minneapolis: Fortress).

N. T. Wright, 1996, *Christian Origins and the Question of God* II: *Jesus and the Victory of God* (London: SPCK; Minneapolis: Fortress).

E. Yamauchi, 1973, *Pre-Christian Gnosticism* (London: IVP).

O. L. Yarbrough, 1985, *Not Like the Gentiles: Marriage Rules in the Letters of Paul* (SBLDS 80; Atlanta: Scholars).

N. H. Young, 1987, 'Paidagogos: The Social Setting of a Pauline Metaphor,' *Nov.T.* XXIX.2, 150–76.

ANCIENT AUTHOR INDEX

In this and the following Indices a page number on its own indicates a reference in the main text. A lower case 'n' indicates a simple reference in a footnote, while an upper case 'N' indicates an expanded footnote. A page number may also be followed by '& n' or by '& N', etc., indicating plural references.

MODERN AUTHOR INDEX

'N' indicates an extended discussion; 'n', a simple reference.

J. I. Porter, 1996 – 261n; 276n

H. Räisänen, 1986 – 57nn; 71n;
  261n; 277n
N. Richardson, 1994 –
  204 & nN; 205n; 207 & nn;
  212&n
R. Riesner, 1994 – 256n
V. K. Robbins (ed.), 1996 –
  36n; 106n; 185n; 194n;
  281 & n
C. Roetzel, 1991 – 4n; 33n

G. H. Sabine, 1952 – 62n
J. P. Sampley, 1991 – 3n; 14n
E. P. Sanders, 1977 – 53n; 55n;
  253n
E. P. Sanders, 1983 – 53n; 56n;
  57n; 253n; 256n; 258n;
  262 & n
J. T. Sanders, 1997 – 72n; 94n;
  95n; 310n
S. Sandmel, 1958 – 253n
S. Sandmel, 1962 – 9 & n
A. A. Schiller, 1978 – 62n
C. J. Schlueter, 1994 – 105n
F. Schulz, 1946 – 62n
J. R. Searle, 1983 – 98n
D. Seeley, 1990 – 230–31 & N
D. Seeley, 1994a – 5n
D. Seeley, 1994b – 208n
D. Seeley, 1996 – 250n; 297n
D. Seeley, 1997 – 240n; 297n
A. F. Segal, 1977 – 209n; 265n
A. F. Segal, 1990 – 5n; 53n;
  58n; 75n; 253n; 257 &n; 259
& n; 260; 262nn
C. Senft, 1979 – 6n
J. Sievers, 1994 5n
Silva, D. A. de-, see deSilva
J. Z. Smith, 1990 – 302N
T. Söding, 1994 – 87N
J. Stambaugh & D. Balch, 1986
  – 83N
C. D. Stanley, 1992 – 252N;
  254&NN
M. E. Stone, 1990 – 234N

R. Stoneman, 1994 – 114N;
  210N
R. Stoneman, 1995 – 210N
S. K. Stowers, 1981 – 100N
S. K. Stowers, 1984 –
  27–28 & N
S. K. Stowers, 1994 –
  235–36 & N; 265; 275N;
  276N
P. Stuhlmacher, 1989 – 280N

G. Theissen, 1973 –34N
G. Theissen, 1975 – 33N; 36n;
  169n
G. Theissen, 1982 – 30n; 87n;
  118n
G. Tomlin , 1997 – 203N;
  246n; 282n
C. M. Tuckett, 1989 – 34n;
  297n

L. E. Vaage, 1987 – 222–23n
L. E. Vaage, 1994a – 34n;
  233nn; 301–303 & n
L. E. Vaage, 1994b – 35n; 48n;
  297n; 301n
L. E. Vaage, 1995b – 34n;
  41nn; 297n
J. C. VanderKam, 1994 – 304n
G. Vermes, 1977 – 304n
S. Vollenweider, 1989 – 17n;
  30n; 67n; 82n; 124n
S. Vollenweider, 1994 –
  273 & n

C. A. Wanamaker, 1990 – 4n;
  5n; 6n; 33n
A. J. M. Wedderburn, 1987 –
  7n; 223n; 226n
D. Wenham, 1995 – 194n;
  291 & nn; 292n; 293n;
M. Werner, 1957 – 233n
C. Wessely, 1902 – 51n
M. Whittaker, 1984 – 16nn
U. Wilckens, 1978 – 277n
F. Williams, 1994 – 38n
W. L. Willis – 30n; 118n

SUBJECT INDEX

Individuals in the ancient world mentioned in the text figure here; but see also the Ancient Author Index, and the Modern Author Index for more recent persons. Again 'N' indicates discussion in the notes, 'n', a simple reference.

Acceptance [of others as they are] – 11; 95–6; 160–62; 202–03; 228–31; 256; 282–83
action [deeds vs. words/abstract ideas] – 43–4; 45-6; 118–23; ch. 5, 128–73; 194–99; 230; 239; 240–42; 269–70
adaptable [see Odysseus] – 184–89
agôn, ἀγών [see toil] – 28; 128–37
allegorisers [see Philo] – 57n; 62 & n
'all things' [shared] – 98–103; 114–16 & n; 125; 166; 218
'already' [as a Cynic claim] – 88–90
ἀναίδεια [see shamelessness, under Cynics]
Anacharsis – 117n; 133
animals [see nature; but also wild beasts] – 42; 47; 114; 115; 120n; 197
Antisthenes – 14; 17; 20; 47; 67; 91n; 96 & n; 108; 116n; 117 & n; 119–20; 132 & n; 137–40; 143N; 151; 157 & n; 189 & n; 197; 212–13 & nn; 224
ἀπάθεια [see indifference]
ἀπόστολος, ἀποστέλλω – 201N
aretê, ἀρετή [virtue, excellence] – 129; 139; 271
Aristotle – 20; 61
askêsis, ἄσκησις [training; see athletes, hardship] – 35; 44 & n; 46; 78–80; 90; 102; 114; 123; 125; ch. 5, 128–73
ἀταραξία [unpertubedness; see interiority] – 113; 167N; 197
athletes [despised by Cynics – 197], athletic imagery [see *askêsis*, hardship] – 28 & n; 29n; 128; 132–37; 171
αὐτάρκεια [(self-)sufficiency – 35; 130; 272–73
αὐτεξούσιος [see ἐξουσία]

Barbarians – [see Greek, Jew] 13-19; wisdom of – 94&n
body [see dualism] – 104–06

Cannibalism [see incest] – 91-92; 114; 126n
Christians, early Christian beliefs before Paul [see formulae] – 3–4; 10; 24; ch. 10, 287–306
    communities – passim
    Christian diversity [see socio-cultural context]
    Christian cult – 213-16; Baptism – 11–12; 22; 224–26; 292
        Lord's Supper [Eucharist] – 87; 118; 125; 226–27
Cicero – 16; 166; 212; 267
circumcision [see Jewish tradition] – 100 & n; 111; 277–78
city [see town]